The Journal Of Experimental Pedagogy V5, 1919-1920: And Training College Record

John Alfred Green

The Journal of

Experimental Pedagogy

AND

Training College Record.

EDITED, ON BEHALF OF

THE TRAINING COLLEGE ASSOCIATION,

BY

PROFESSOR J. A. GREEN.

Vol. V, 1919-20.

LONGMANS, GREEN & Co., Paternoster Row, London;
New York, Bombay, Calcutta, and Madras.

SHEFFIELD:
J. W. NORTHEND LTD., PRINTERS, WEST STREET.

CONTENTS OF VOLUME V.

LIST OF AUTHORS.

Vol. 5, No. 1. .   *Mar. 5th, 1919.*

PRESIDENT'S ADDRESS TO TRAINING COLLEGE ASSOCIATION.

THIS has been a momentous year. As we look back to January 8th, 1918, the date of our last Annual Meeting, we penetrate to a time very different from that in which we now meet. On that day we were looking forward to a period then dim and remote to us, but now a reality, the period After the War. Now the heroic sacrifice of our countrymen and their brothers in arms have brought us peace, and to-day we remember, with deep gratitude and thankfulness, those of our Colleagues who have given their lives that this day of peace and reconciliation might dawn. May they find their memorial in a more enlightened and devoted profession, ready to sacrifice, as they have sacrificed, even life itself in their endeavour to serve the best interests of their country.

This has been a year momentous also in the history of Education. Never before, I believe, in our time at least, has an ex-professor been received in royal state in this country or recognized as a leader in the Councils of the world. President Wilson's fame is already established, and the recent election of Professor Masaryk to the Presidency of the new Czecho-Slovak government is of happy augury for the future of the Professor-President.

In England, the passing of the Education Act of 1918 and of the Teachers' Superannuation Act register, not only the skill and devotion of the first Minister that the profession has supplied, but also a rising tide of national interest and belief in Education.

The springs of any movement are difficult to penetrate, the deeper the movement, the more remote are its springs. Undoubtedly the present interest in education derives its strength from a wide spread desire, vague it may be, but genuine enough, to reconstruct on the ruins of the old world a better England in the future. But it cannot be due to chance alone that 1918 has given us not only an Education Act but a great Franchise Act as well. The extension of effective citizenship, and of universal education have proceeded side by side for the last century, each deriving its force from that larger view of human life and individual worth, with which Rousseau and his followers first inspired Europe.

Let me remind you of a few dates. In 1832 the Great Reform Bill was passed. In 1833 the first grant of public money was made to elementary education. In 1867 the second Franchise Act was passed, and in 1870 came the great Education Act; in 1887 the third Franchise Act, and in 1888 and 1891 Education was made free and compulsory. Now again in 1918 we have passed a double landmark— a Franchise Act and an Education Act, challenging in importance any of those which have preceded them. The interdependence of Democracy and Education in their development is so intimate, so essential to the nature of each that without apparently conscious forethought, they have kept pace with each other in their advance.

Your Executive, having regard to the wishes expressed at the last general meeting decided to ask a representative of the Labour Movement to speak to us this afternoon. I cannot imagine a wiser use to make of our Annual Conference this year than to listen to and to discuss the views of the Labour Movement on Education. Not only is it important in view of the extension of the suffrage, and also of the share taken by representatives of labour in moulding the Education Act, but the relation of education to labour is now at an important and critical stage.

Our elementary schools grew up in the clatter of the industrial revolution, and in 1870 education presented itself rather as an alternative method of employing children under 13, or as a way of escape from mill or factory. The new industrialism called for hands in the mass, brains only in the few. The schools could not then educate the future worker, for craftmanship was perishing, and unskilled labour daily increasing. The cutting off of all educational influences at 12 or 13 and the subsequent life of monotonous uneducative toil chilled the efforts and outlook of the schools. Education failed to see what it could do for the mass of unskilled workers as such, to whom even leisure was denied, and a breach between school and industry was then made which has been a source of weakness ever since.

But now the outlook for mutual understanding and co-operation is much brighter. May I remind you of three movements in industry, each of them of great interest to teachers ?

(1) There is the shortening of hours. It has been well established that in many cases mechanical labour does not of itself necessarily debase the mind of the worker. It is the long hours which destroy freshness and initiative. Reasonable working hours would give opportunity for that joy in creation which the nature of many a man's work denies him. Best of all it is to have joy in daily paid work, but under modern conditions that is not possible for all, but leisure *is* possible and must be secured, or the dehumanizing of the race will result.

(2) Secondly, there is the Welfare Movement in whatever form it may take in the future. " The recognition of individuality and individual responsibility" is defined as "the keystone of the arch in Welfare Work" in the best known book on the subject, and the Prime Minister, when he was Minister of Munitions, stated the object of Welfare Work as the " humanizing of Industry." But what is education, widely interpreted but the recognition of individuality and individual purpose, and is it not also the greatest humanizing force we know? Thus, we teachers may hear echoed back from the very heart of industrialism words with which we would choose to describe our own work and aspirations.

(3) The third Movement, perhaps of the greatest interest, is the growing demand on the part of the workers for further control over the conditions of their work. This demand of labour for participation in the government of industry is undoubtedly at bottom psychological. It is part of the movement towards freedom and individual responsibility, reaching industry. But education, too, has been borne along on the same current. We talk of the " new teaching," " the new education," and find that everywhere it

emphasizes the need for the freedom of the individual, and the development of his sense of responsibility. But where do self-government, education for liberty, self-direction, our modern Shibboleths lead us ? Surely only to revolution if the conditions of modern industry remain unchanged.

If we leave the broad field of Education as a whole, and glance at our special corner of it, Training Colleges, we find that again 1918 has been an important year. But just as now in this January of 1919 the effect of the two great Acts of 1918 is yet unknown, so, in the Training Colleges, important movements have been on foot but they are not yet come to fruition. For the moment we drift uncertain of the exact goals towards which we are tending.

The unification of the regulations for training for Elementary and for Secondary Schools is an accomplished fact, but many of the results of this important step are yet to be seen ; and we have to establish courses for teachers in Continuation Schools and Nursery Schools and to secure their recognition on the same footing as the other two types of training. The question of the recognition of these different kinds of training is still in abeyance. It is an important question as it affects the free circulation of teachers through different types of schools, and this is essential to the health of the profession. Then, should this recognition be given by one General Certificate, or by a selected panel of certificates all of equal validity, though issued by different bodies ? In any case it would appear that appointing committees should bear the responsibility of deciding whether the special gratifications and particular training of the candidate fit him or not for the post they offer.

The special bias in the training of a student towards one type of teaching should not be taken as unfitting him for all other kinds of schools. The essentials of good teaching are fundamentally the same. At present the Government Certificate competes with diplomas and certificates granted by the Universities or by other bodies, and up till now it has given admission to one particular type of school. This has had the effect of stereotyping over much both the course of training which it has recognized and the teacher who has held it. The old barriers will begin to break down under the revised regulations, for a student may now receive government grants for secondary training as for elementary.

If the control of the Board of Education is thus about to strengthen over the training of teachers, the nature of that control is one of the important questions before us in this time of transition. At present we all greatly appreciate the kindness and consideration of the Board of Education, and during the last year we have had signal proof of their desire for co-operation in the important Conferences both in London and York on the professional and academic subjects offered in the Two Year Colleges. But intermittent conferences, advisory and not executive, leading to decisions over which we have no real control, and the results of which are long in reaching us, are not a permanently satisfactory organization, if indeed they can be called an organization at all. Manifestly, they are a transition from the old regime, now long past, under which the Board dictated and the Colleges obeyed, and a new, under which the Training Colleges must have a larger degree of corporate initiative and responsibility in the decision of questions of policy large and small. An interesting step forward has been taken this morning in the adoption of the motions sent up by the Goldsmiths' College. The provision of a representative Standing Committee in each subject included in the Training College Curriculum provides us—as far as curriculum is concerned—with the nucleus of an organization that should be capable of useful development and further extension in the future.

The affiliation of Training Colleges to Universities, so often quoted, but less frequently defined or discussed, owes not a little of its attraction to the contribution that it is felt such a connexion might make to this complicated question of control.

It is often difficult to know exactly what kind of connexion is advocated, and the terms in which it is described are frequently intentionally vague. We should all like to see a larger number of intending teachers reading for Degrees ; then of course they should be University students for, at any rate, the three years of a Degree Course. But there are large numbers of students who would not profit by a Degree Course and for these I do not believe, myself, that the University would successfully provide. They do not want the kind of lectures appropriate to the Intermediate stage of a Degree Course ; whatever they have must lead forward to a final stage appropriate to themselves. To bring such students into the Universities to read for Diplomas or special certificates would be a dangerous policy. It would flood the Universities with boys and girls below the academic level of the Degree student, and, owing to their shorter sojourn, difficult to discipline and absorb. It would over-concentrate our efforts without deepening them, and obscure real educational problems which are demanding solution.

The Training Colleges must provide a higher education for such students which is neither school work nor University. The nature of this course, the number of subjects to be included, their relation to each other and their right treatment, we are now, it seems to me, engaged in discovering. It is thus extremely important that under the new regulations there should be a very large liberty for the Colleges, so that there may be as much experiment and discovery as possible.

But a closer connexion between the Colleges and the Universities would help the Colleges enormously and could be achieved in various ways. Diploma Courses which could be taken in one year by well-qualified students, such as the Geography Diploma at Cambridge University, would be of the greatest assistance in helping the Colleges to develop useful Third Year Courses for those who wish to teach in the higher Standards or Central Schools. Again the final examination for the Certificate could be reformed and revised out of knowledge by University help. Surely the College of the future will run its own courses in the various subjects it professes, courses adapted to its own genius and its own resources, and authorized by the Controlling authority ; but external examiners in each subject would be necessary, and the University with which the College was connected could provide as an essential part of that connexion an Examiner who could also be the expert adviser in that subject for the time being.

Exactly how a University and a College can best co-operate will have to be determined gradually and by the circumstances of each College. Obviously one under the shadow of a University would make very different use of such a connexion from one at a considerable distance. We do not desire, I am sure, to see too great a concentration and unification of our higher educational life. It will be in any case many years before every Training College could be in really close proximity to a University, and when that day does come, we may hope that the number of Universities will be largely increased.

One inestimable benefit the University connexion—and even the desire for it—has to confer upon the Colleges. In an interesting appreciation of Mr. P. A. Barnett, H.M.I., in the last number of our "Journal," the writer notes how the curriculum, discipline and spirit of an Elementary Training College in 1889, when Mr. Barnet went to the Boro' Road, were moulded on the model of the existing elementary schools. The curriculum, he writes, would hardly have inspired a good fourth form in a County Grammar School. Now at any rate, we have ceased to subordinate our students' development thus closely to the standards of the schools. They have as much need for a liberal education such as will set "free the human spirit," and lead to a worthy maturity as any other students in the country. Old ideas die hard, but unless a young teacher has a worthy vision of his work, and has gained, through the study of even one subject only, some idea of the value of knowledge, and the joy of imparting it, it is but waste labour to prepare him assiduously to reach all the subjects ordinarily taught in an Elementary School. The machine may have been provided with material, but the power that should make it productive has never been generated.

We are all agreed that we must have three years, though we are not all agreed, and it is to be hoped that we never shall all agree, how those three years must be spent. In any case another year of education, however planned, would give us finally a more mature student. Not only could a higher standard of academic work be reached, but it should then be possible to make the professional training primarily the acquisition of new experience rather than of knowledge. The professional certificate could then be awarded on an examination mainly of the student's own records of his experience rather than on answers to questions which test his reading and lectures, but do not test his power of applying his knowledge in the classroom, or the ideas by which he is himself inspired.

Though the University has much to give us we must not be overpowered by the University model as our predecessors were by the school. We have much to learn from the University, but not everything. We must not forget the school. Elementary schools are becoming more and more the centres of an increasing number of social activities. The Training College of the future may widen and regenerate its work, not only by affiliation with a University, but by becoming a school of social service for all those who in various ways desire to work for the welfare of childhood and youth.

There is never any alternative between advance and decadence, between development and atrophy. Let us then advance, drawing our inspiration on the one hand from the Universities and on the other from the Schools, remembering that neither learning alone, nor the spirit of social service alone can make a teacher, but a union of the two—a union which it is the unique duty of the Training Colleges to make as their special contribution to the education of the nation.

Yet at this hour who dare talk of the future ? The end of the war has not yet brought us 'peace. The future has become since November full of hope, but full also of anxiety and uncertainty. The tides of time rush swiftly, and the rapids and shallows in front of us are dangerous. Still as in war

" Faiths and Empires gleam like wrecks of a dissolving dream."

Yet in this hour of danger the country turns to Education as never before to save society from dissolution and to inspire men with good-will and with wisdom in the solution of the great problems before us.

The hour has struck foi Cinderella. Her turn has come at last. Long neglected and overlooked she has been busy tidying and mending and cleaning the nation for many years past. But now her proud sisters—Wealth and Force and Power and Privilege—are for the moment waved aside, and the Prince sends for Cinderella. How will she develop in her day of prosperity ? So long misunderstood by her sisters, so young in many ways, and undeveloped, will she know her real duty ? Will she be loyal to the best interests of her Prince ?

For there are many claimants in his court for his interest. The spirit of Nationality, strongest always after War, has before now subjugated Education to its too exclusive service, and we have realized of late how efficiently the conscious moulding of a nation by the state for state ends may be accomplished and to what it may lead. We are not likely to desire to follow Germany's example. But peoples and individuals have been known ere now to grow into the semblance of that against which they have fought. Industry also has great claims on Education, but here again Education must create and transform and not merely serve. The Industrialism of the last 100 years based on a substratum of labour little removed from slavery, with its extreme inequalities of wealth and poverty, and its attendant squalor must go. Cinderella herself must overthrow it.

And we, who have ever been the devotees of Cinderella, and would believe in her even if no one else did, let us never forget her fairy origin, her mysterious nature, her disconcerting power of transformation. We know little of her after all. " There is more in Education and a child," Pestalozzi reminded us, " than we have ever fathomed." We may see efficient organization, and we may see impressive results, but let us seek that faith, which finds in each child the image of God, that power, which can inspire him to make this image clear.

WINIFRED MERCIER.

WHAT IS SUGGESTION?

By Professor R. L. ARCHER.

THE columns of the *Journal of Experimental Pedagogy* have happily always been open to those who have no new experimental investigations to disclose, but are occupied in teaching the results of others' investigations to students. A teacher's views may be right or wrong ; he may choose one of two opposing views or he may state the arguments on both sides and leave the matter open ; as long as the views are clear, we cannot, in a subject where views are in a rapid state of flux, legitimately complain. But a student is entitled to claim clearness in the views presented to him ; and a teacher becomes conscious, as soon as he sets about preparing a lecture with a view to a clear presentation of a difficult subject, whether he is dealing with clear views or not. The writer of this article ventured a few years ago to write in this Journal on the difficulties which surround an exposition of Attention to a class of training-college students owing to the lack of any precise significance attaching to the word, and he now ventures to raise a similar protest with regard to the use of the word Suggestion.

Whatever differences exist among writers on this topic, they are all agreed that Suggestion is one of the most powerful instruments in the hands of the educator, and that he ought to know something of its use. We cannot ignore the subject unless we are going to regard the functions of the educator as limited to an appeal to the reason. Even were we to impose such a limitation, which no educator of the twentieth century would dream of doing, we should be confronted by the fact that suggestibility is held up to us as one of the main factors which often render appeals to the reason fruitless. We are bound to deal with Suggestion ; but, as this article will attempt to show, we do not know what it is with which we are dealing.

It is not always easy to know what is being generally taught in training colleges. The chief sources from which we can infer what is the prevailing custom are examination questions and text-books. It is probably safe to assume that no great change has taken place during the War and that the orthodox training college account of Suggestion may be obtained from two text-books published in the year 1913, which aimed at gathering together the contributions of the leading psychologists on the topics treated in the various chapters, namely, Sandiford's " Mental and Physical Life of School Children " and Rusk's " Introduction to Experimental Education." Examination questions mainly centre round Keatinge's " Suggestion in Education," and at the back of all is of course Binet.

At first sight all seems to be plain sailing. There is no hint of a doubt as to what Suggestion means. Investigators research and writers expound as if they were all investigation and researching on the same thing. Definitions appear to be exact and compatible. Sandiford, who has a curious facility for adhering to the exact noun of educational orthodoxy, quotes a definition by Shrenk-Nötzing, " Suggestion is the narrowing of the association-activity to definite contents of consciousness, solely through the employment of memory and imagination in such a way that the influence of combinations of contrariant ideas is weakened or removed, as a result of which the intensity of the suggested contents of consciousness rises above the normal." This is certainly the meaning from which Keatinge sets out to write.

But, as soon as we look at the investigations and examples, we are startled to find how little they keep to their definition. Let us mention a few phenomena which are treated by one writer or another as instances of Suggestion. The Müller-Lyer and Poggendorf illusions, the contagious excitement of crowds, the effect of a sermon, confidence or lack of confidence in one's own ability to do a thing, the effect of expectancy, the effect produced by the form of a question in creating an impression that the questioner is giving away information or holds a particular view, the acceptance of belief on authority, the adoption of standards of value from our associates, sympathetic adjustment to the standpoint of others, the effect of iteration, unwillingness to contradict arising from whatever cause it arises, unwillingness to be peculiar ;—all these are lumped together as Suggestion. Any " contrariant ideas " which the reader may possess as the result of past experience, in which he has commonly found the same word to be applied only to objects more or less alike, are laid to rest by the division of Suggestion into " direct " and " indirect " Suggestion and " auto-suggestion." The " suggestible " person is generally impressed by the use of technical language.

It would be contrary to all human experience to expect that none of the alleged examples would conform to the definition given. The definition covers the effect of a sermon quite satisfactorily, with the exception of the word " ideas," since it is rather contrariant emotions than contrariant beliefs which are weakened or removed. But apply it to the Müller-Lyer illusion, and it becomes grotesquely inapplicable. " Definite contents of consciousness " do not enter at all ; the whole process by which the sensation leads to the illusion is sub-conscious ; neither imagination nor memory is used ; there are no contrariant ideas till for some reason or other you take a ruler. It is the same in the case of many of the other examples. The results are due to a whole gamut of different causes—to the influence of one's own mental outfit and to the influence of externals, to the influence of persons and to the influence of things, and in the case of persons to influence exercised intentionally and to influence exercised unintentionally. The appeal may affect belief, or emotion, or the sense of values. *Prima-facie* there is, therefore, something wrong with the definition ; let us analyse it, phrase by phrase, to see what it is.

This is the first clause :—" Suggestion is the narrowing of the association-activity to definite contents of consciousness." The definition is in perfect logical form ; the first clause states the genus, the remainder the differentia. Our criticism is this. Every conscious process, whether its outcome be belief, feeling, or action, obviously proceeds by " narrowing " consciousness to " definite contents " ; we are finite creatures and can only be conscious of a certain amount at a time. The essential words are therefore the " association-activity." Suggestion is made to consist in the fact that, for reasons stated in the later part of the definition, A does not bring into consciousness B, which, in the absence of those reasons, it would have done. So far the definition escapes any danger to which it might be exposed by the use of the word " ideas." If A is the sight of

Smith's face and B a feeling of dislike, it is as much an instance of association-activity as if B were a belief capable of being expressed in the form of a proposition. We are therefore left with a clear issue : x is alleged to produce y by excluding z. In a sense of course, this must always happen. In the case of the apple which is alleged to have suggested to Newton the theory of gravitation, the theory would not have come into his mind if the thought of the apple as a possible ingredient in a dumpling had come in. Had he been hungry, this thought might have taken the place of the other ; therefore, in a sense, internal feelings of a satisfied stomach, by excluding one possible exercise of the association-activity, rendered more likely the exercise of another ; and, in this negative sense, it was not the apple but the satisfaction of a good breakfast which suggested the theory. One thing only actually is " suggested " ; the number which might have been suggested under slightly different circumstances is indefinite. Lest we should be thought to be trifling, we will at once state the point to which we are leading up. Are we to lay the stress on the possible associations which do not take place or on that one which does ? We think, on the latter. Newton was a perfectly open-minded searcher after truth ; there were in his mind no " contrariant ideas " in the sense that they would prevent his accepting the law of gravitation if once he were to conceive it. He was in fact waiting for some association to work which would bring the required theory into his mind. Of the hundred allied ideas, ninety-nine were stored in his mind. An external cricumstance supplied the hundredth. This hundredth idea in consciousness, combining with the ninety-nine in sub-consciousness, " suggested " the theory. Any possible other ideas were not " contrariant " in the sense that they would tend to prevent his accepting the theory, only in the sense that they would have so occupied his mind as to prevent him conceiving it. They were not excluded by the hundredth idea, but by the ninety-nine. The definition will not suit the case.—Are we then to say that popular language is at fault ? that this is no case of Suggestion in the scientific sense ? We must be careful before we do so ; for, by so doing, we exclude the quality which is on the intellectual side, as Keatinge admits, the mark of the very best teaching, " suggestiveness." That supreme stimulus by which the original mind contrives to arouse the learner to start on a track which ultimately leades him to conclusions or discoveries of which the teacher had never thought is no longer to be spoken of as Suggestion. If so, Suggestion has been sailing under false colours ; it has been enjoying the éclat due to something called by the same name which is not the same thing ; it loses its intellectual prestige, and must depend for its credit on what it can do in the moral sphere. But does it not lose its importance in that sphere too ? It is true that a great stimulus to high endeavour will incidentally stamp out much of a lower kind which would otherwise have had a greater chance. Barnardo's life work was " suggested " by a chance meeting with a single waif. You may say that this meeting overpowered " contrariant " inclinations to a life of ease. My point is that, even if Barnardo has been an ideally perfect being, the incident was necessary to turn his philanthropy in that particular direction. The snowing under of other conceivable possibilities is incidental. Let us go a step further ; imagine Barnardo constituted exactly as he was ; had a friend purposely directed his activities by narrating a case of a waif, would that not have been suggestion ? Yet there was no more need in the one case than the other, Barnardo being what he was, first to exclude other possibilities and then to introduce the idea. In the home, where contrariant factors have not had time to form, is not nine-tenths of parental influence of this positive character ? and quite free from the necessity of swamping contrariant tendencies ? The positive effect, not the negative, seems to us the essential factor. So of all contagion of emotion. Excitement over a football match is conveyed positively ; whether there are contrariant tendencies to be overcome or not, such as the fear of catching cold on a wet day, is a matter of accident, which does not alter the essential character of the influence.

To proceed with the analysis—" solely through the employment of memory and imagination in such a way . . ." Even if the intention in choosing the words " memory and imagination " was primarily to exclude reasoning processes, yet the actual effect is two-fold. First it lays down that *cognitive* processes are the essential part of Suggestion, whereas in many of the examples what appears to take place is an infection of one person with the *emotional* attitude of another towards some particular object or idea. Secondly, it assumes that the effect is brought about by what goes on in the level of full consciousness, whereas we may be sure that sub-consciousness plays a very large part in the result.

Next " that the influence of combinations of contrariant ideas is weakened or removed." We have already shown that, if there are contrariant ideas, they must inevitably be weakened or removed in the process of strengthening that to which they are contrariant, but that in many so-called cases of Suggestion there are no ideas which in any true sense are contrariant at all.

Finally—" as a result of which the intensity of the suggested contents of consciousness arises above the normal." This would not appear to be consistent with Keatinge's " indirect suggestion " where the new " content of consciousness " slinks in upon the fringe and bides its time for growing and displacing the old ideas.

The examples of Keatinge, of Binet, and of the writers of the various articles quoted in Sandiford do not then fit in with the conception of Suggestion from which we believe that all set out. How then are we to find out what they really mean by Suggestion ? for clearly the idea has *some* content to them. Only one way seems open ; to take the instances and see what they have in common, and then to reach a definition by a procees of induction.

Binet's instances will, we believe, all conform to one definition, which, however, neither he nor anyone else has put forward, viz., that Suggestion is the misleading operation of any experience which, operating otherwise than through conscious reasoning, results in the formation of a wrong judgment. We said that neither Binet nor anyone else had put forward such a definition ; nor are they likely to do so, for it brings out the fact that in many cases the wrong judgment is brought about by precisely the same mental processes as normally produce a right judgment. Most illusions would come under it. A man who " perceives " a ghost where all which is there is his shirt hanging up reaches the belief in the ghost by precisely the same process as that by which we recognize a friend when we only see his back. Take the case of the ascending series of longer lines which is suddenly broken. In ninety-nine cases out of a hundred the expectation that the series would continue would be right. Hence the error is due to our normal methods of thinking, and it is unfair to condemn normal methods of thinking because they do not prepare children to deal with psychological camouflage experts. Again, children's experience leads them to believe the truth of their teachers' statement on matters which are plainly within the teacher's experience. They are accustomed to being made April Fools of by other children, but all experience is against teachers indulging in such practical jokes. When, therefore, Binet condescends to tell direct lies to children for the purpose of seeing how many will believe him, he cannot complain, if they do believe him, that they are using processes which normally result in error. Again, when he set the children to draw from memory something which in reality was not among the objects shown, surely the legitimate conclusion was that they had overlooked it, and the action of drawing something which might by good luck resemble the object overlooked would, as examinations are usually conducted, be sound policy. Binet's own experiments, as distinguished from those of others to which he refers at the beginning of his book, are all either of this character, that is, he ingeniously uses processes which normally lead us right to lead us wrong, or else are cases where he compels a child to pretend a belief through fear, respect, or politeness. True, the child, in order to avoid acknowledging to himself either fear or untruthfulness, struggles to believe that which it is his interest to believe ; but who would speak of suggestion where Cranmer temporarily managed to convince himself that he believed in transubstantiation or where we contrive to convince ourselves of a friend's innocence in spite of strong evidence of his guilt ?

Indeed, the writer himself is in exactly the same position at the present moment. Binet's reputation, his other work, his ingenuity in this matter in inventing tests, the importance of the chapter in which he shows the bearing of his experiments into mistakes of memory and the effect of " forcing the memory " on French legal procedure, make it seem presumptuous to express one's real opinion of the book. That opinion is that, valuable as the book is on very many points, yet as an analysis of a supposed single mental process called Suggestion it is dealing with a fictitious entity, an entity so fictitious that we never get a clear grip of its elusive form from beginning to end. Almost anything except formal errors of reasoning which leads us astray is dubbed Suggestion, and most of the things so-called are things which normally guide us aright. Binet's "Suggestion" is not a mental process at all ; it is an accident which may happen to any mental process.

Keatinge is far more precise. He presents us with two clear ideas " direct suggestion " and " indirect suggestion," though he seems to recognize a more confusing notion, namely " auto-suggestion." Here, however, he is following the French, whereas the clearness of the first two ideas is his own. Our doubt is not as to the clearness of the two ideas taken separately, but as to the nature of the similarity which entitles them to be treated as two species of the same genus, and whether that similarity corresponds, as he clearly thinks that it corresponds, with the usual senses of the word Suggestion, as for instance, in the case of hypnotic suggestion, suggestive teaching, or the suggestion by innuendo which takes away a man's character.

Direct Suggestion is illustrated by the effect of Thomas Arnold's sermons. It consists in attaching an affective accompaniment to certain ideas about conduct which will result in the pursuance of the desired line of conduct. It is limited to cases where there are contrariant ideas, or, we should prefer to say, contrariant feelings attaching to ideas, which have to be overcome. It acts through respect for the preacher and, we presume, by anything which works through the instincts (using the term in MacDougall's sense) and not through argument. It is here that Keatinge's analysis appears to us to be defective. At the one end we have the preacher clearly depicted expressing his approbation and disapprobation, pleading for the one line of conduct and against the other, showing himself a man of intense conviction ; at the other end we have the hearer profoundly moved and henceforth more or less successfully and consistently pursuing the path marked out for him. What we are not told, it may be because it is too obvious, is that the effect is produced by attaching the universal instincts of disgust, admiration, " elation," " depression " (to use MacDougall's terms, though they hardly would express the intended meaning to anyone not acquainted with his book), anger in the form of righteous indignation, or love (including gratitude), to certain lines of conduct or to certain persons. The point is an important one, because it means that, ordinarily at any rate, there is no immediate transfer of conation but of feeling, which ultimately leads to action. This distinguishes the effect of a sermon from hypnotic suggestion, as, for instance, where the subject after recovering from the trance performs an action suggested to him during its continuance without knowing why.

Indirect suggestion is illustrated by a teacher's use of literature to produce a similar effect on the feelings without the pupil knowing that he is being influenced. The teacher sets the boy down to what is apparently a purely intellectual task such as " comparing and contrasting " two poets' ideas on duty. He hopes that some of their sentiments will evoke a like response in the pupil. Here the prefix sub- in suggestion has one of its two original meanings, that of something furtive, and possibly also the other, that of something on a small scale, as Keatinge insists that such teaching is best given " in marginal doses." In Direct Suggestion neither of these two meanings can be found. On the other hand, Keatinge tells us that the conditions on which the energy of ordinary non-suggestive ideas depends are necessary also for suggestive ideas and that these are massiveness, a certain opposition to other ideas such as in cases of contrast, unusual occurrences and first impressions, expectancy or desire, meaning, and a pleasant or painful character. These conditions are clearly found in cases of Direct Suggestion, but seem inconsistent with the character of Indirect Suggestion. How can an idea be at once massive and introduced in " marginal doses." ? How can it stand out clearly and create a shock and at the same time enter without being recognized? Or how can it fail to be recognized if it is expected and has a meaning ? Nor can its pleasurable or painful character be very marked when it makes so slight an impression. We cannot avoid suspicion that Keatinge took his two uses of the word, the first from a supposed (but we believe erroneous) resemblance to hypnotic suggestion, and the second from the two etymological meanings of the prefix sub-.

Keatinge's alleged essential similarity between Direct and Indirect Suggestion, which we have seen differ in all the other properties which he would have 'us believe to be common to both, is the presence of contrariant ideas and their ultimate suppression. The means taken to suppress them are different, but any way which accomplishes the task is to be called Suggestion. But, whereas the method of Indirect Suggestion is, we are given to understand, resorted to precisely to meet the difficulty of dealing with contrariant ideas, it is difficult to see any reason why a method exactly similar to that of Direct Suggestion should not be adopted where there are no contrariant ideas. We admit that a little ingenuity could always invent such ideas and that there is no course of conduct conceivable for which something could not be alleged as impelling us to an alternative. The point is that the contrariant ideas, or, we should prefer to call them by some such names as impulses, are negligible. The view of the Kaiser entertained by very many Englishmen is such that nothing in their mental outfit is contrariant to hanging him. Nevertheless, many of them required to be stirred up by politicians who advocated such a course before they would take any action in that direction. The truth is that an idea may never have occurred at all, that even if it does it has to face the force of inertia, which can surely not be called a " contrariant idea," and that even enthusiasm may be roused to greater enthusiasm. Keatinge indeed makes one attempt to prove that there must be contrariant feelings—on this occasion he speaks of them as " feelings " and not as " ideas "—and that is by alleging that feelings readily pass over into their opposites through fatigue of the nervous centres. It certainly happens occasionally ; but, as a rule, the same feelings remain attached to the same objects. The essence of the process described as Direct Suggestion is therefore the creation of driving power, not the overcoming of friction.

But, if Direct and Indirect Suggestion do not resemble in any of the points on which Keatinge lays stress, they at least resemble one another in that both are means of attaching emotion to particular ideas or objects. What we cannot see, however, in the case of Indirect Suggestion is that the actual process in the mind of the " subject" is different from what it would have been had the " idea " met him accidentally in that particular environment and not by design. Suppose the master *had* set the comparison of Wordsworth's idea of duty with that of Tennyson purely as an intellectual question without any ulterior design, would not the result have been precisely the same ? To what then was it due ? To the mental outfit of the " subject " himself. His emotional constitution is such that Wordsworth and Tennyson, carefully compared, would produce that particular result upon it. In that sense he is not as mistaken as Keatinge supposes in believing the idea to be his own. Should the spark say to the gunpowder, " the credit for the explosion is mine; for without me you would not have exploded," the gunpowder might well reply, " And if I were not an explosive, a hundred such sparks might have flown about me in vain."

The fundamental parts of Keatinge's book would remain equally valuable were it so re-worded that the term Suggestion never appeared, and some such phrase as " direct and indirect moral appeal " substituted. The first three chapters, which are merely summaries of French views, would have to disappear, but the essential argument maintained through the remaining chapters would stand. The argument for the greater general efficacy of the indirect moral appeal would be equally effective, the practical applications would be unaltered, the original views on "Education as Creative" would be no less "suggestive." In fact we would have preferred Keatinge without the alloy of Binet.

Space forbids a discussion of the meaning attached to the word Suggestion by the numerous experimenters into suggestibility. Obviously the investigations are into something real in each case. But, when all kinds of correlation between various kinds of susceptibility to error have been worked out, between the effect of expectation in estimating weights and its effect in estimating lengths, between either of these and liability to be made an April fool, it will probably.be found that not one but several factors enter and the term "suggestibility" will have to be limited to one of them or dropped.

The use of a misleading term tends to hinder the framing of a clear explanation of the facts involved. In the matters covered by the term Suggestion some of the forces at work are readily explained, others involve more difficulty.

To our mind the main principle is that among the general tendencies common to mankind and intended to facilitate adaptation to environment are tendencies to feel, think and act as those around us feel, think and act or as we think that they feel, think and act. The tendency to act, as they act has a name, Imitation : the other two have not. But writers on social psychology none the less give them their due importance. The tendency to think as others think in regard to matters of pure objective truth where no question of values arises, though it is a very necessary tendency in view of the fact that each single individual cannot investigate everything from first principles for himself, was most apparent when it happened to make against the acceptance of new truths. It is a tendency which is so strong as to need no encouragement, whereas in a civilized and scientific environment it needs to be counteracted in many spheres. Hence, especially since the time of Locke, it has been treated as a misleading tendency and the chief foe against which education on its intellectual side is arrayed. The tendency to feel as others feel was not emphasized so early, because psychology was for a long time the handmaiden of logic. Thought was the province of logic, action of ethics ; feeling was only considered in so far as it affected one or the other. But the tendency to feel as others feel is less restricted in its scope by external checks than are the other two tendencies. If you act as others act, and their action is foolish, you may be brought to account by the results. The whole of your society may keep its windows closed but loss of health will in the long run compel it to change its course of action. False beliefs taken on authority have to face argument. There is no such objective restraint on feeling, till feeling results in belief or action. Neither consequences nor argument have anything to do with it. Hence it is mainly derived from others by a process which we may describe as infection.

Morality is not the exclusive property of any one of the three. There is the intuitive moral judgment, telling us that the good of every man is of equal .worth. There is reason working out the consequences of particular lines of conduct. There is will, differing ·

as a person's resolves of to-day persist or disappear to-morrow. There are the emotions which constitute the great driving power. But though morality is concerned with all, moral education is primarily concerned with the emotions. The great axiom of the moral judgment stands immovable, but διάνοια οὐδὲν κινεῖ. Children rarely need to think out the remoter consequences. Will-power is, like memory, a brute force given at birth ; and what is called a training of the will is really a training of three instincts, " elation " into self-respect, " depression " into shame, and the fighting instinct into perseverance. The real moral training is of the instincts, to attach disgust, admiration and love to the right objects and to carry our purposes into act through the three instincts mentioned in the previous sentence. Hence alone does the moral judgment get driving power. And the education of these instincts mainly comes from direct infection. A good home is all-powerful in this respect.

" Direct Suggestion " is merely a case of a deliberate attempt to set into action this tendency to feel as others feel. " Indirect Suggestion " needs a little more explanation. We defined the tendencies crudely as a tendency to think, feel or act as others think, feel or act. More strictly, the tendency is that we tend to believe, feel or do anything which is presented to our minds as being or having been believed, felt or done. · Direct contact with the other person greatly intensifies the tendency, but the image has some of the same power. " Indirect Suggestion " is this less personal use of the tendency. A direct attempt by one person to infect us with his feelings undoubtedly often calls into play a counter-tendency. Why ? We believe that the real source of the " contrariant ideas " of Keatinge is precisely the same in origin as the power which he is himself seeking to use : it is in short the tendency to feel as others, not being the person there and then trying to influence us, feel. We have already imbibed their feelings ; they are part of our mental outfit. A series of marginal doses creates the same general impression that people in general, and not one person, feel in a particular way, as do a series of posters all turned out from a single printing-press.

This original tendency to feel as others feel is then quite a simple principle, but it covers most of the facts dealt with under Suggestion. But feeling is mixed up with both belief and action ; hence account has to be taken of the other two tendencies. The part played by the tendency to believe as others believe is subordinate to that played by the tendency to feel as they feel, but it is responsible for Keatinge's use of the word " idea," which tends to complicate what is in reality a simple matter. For instance he distinguishes between " ideas about morality " and " moral ideas." The former really are ideas, and it is for them that the tendency to believe as others believe is responsible. The latter are mainly feeling-attitudes, sentiments. Of course, I must have a cognition of Jones or of patriotism to admire either, but the relevant matter is the admiration.

But there is one far more difficult matter of enquiry, the nature of the hypnotic process, which has undoubtedly affected our ideas about " Suggestion." Most writers are at pains to prove that the hypnotic process is nothing more than the working of the normal tendency to believe as others believe (or as we think they believe), exercised free from all the counteracting tendencies which neutralize it in ordinary life. If this be really so, we fail to see what good is

obtained by introducing hypnotism into the discussion at all,
especially by starting the enquiry from that point. If hypnotism is
really only a very difficult example of a very simple principle, its
introduction does not seek to explain *obscurum per obscurius* but
clarissimum per obscurissimum. We suspect that this stress on
hypnotism is due to a suspicion that there is something more in it
than this normal tendency and that this " something more " may be
operative in ordinary life. Why does Binet tell us that different
persons possess different powers of " Suggestion " and that it is
found at its highest in those who can look another straight in the
eyes ? The issue seems to be this. The limitations of " normal "
influence on another's beliefs, feelings or acts are that the " subject "
judges of the other's beliefs, feelings or acts by ordinary external
indications, and is influenced by them according as he loves, respects
or fears the person in question. In that case the power of " looking
a person straight in the eyes " is, like certain tones of voice, etc., one
of the indications by which we judge of the sincerity and strength of
feeling, belief or will, and one of the reasons which make us fear,
respect or love him. (The way we look may lead to love and confidence as well as to fear and awe). But it is possible that there is
something which exceeds these limitations. If " direct " thought
transference, without any of the ordinary means of communication,
is possible, it has been pointed out frequently that " direct " transference of feeling or resolve may be possible. But no writer dares to
go further. But the suspicion that this is so gives a touch of mystifi-
cation to what is written on the very simple tendencies which have
been previously considered.

Personally we are inclined to believe in this further power. It
is difficult to see, in cases where a person carries out an action, dictated
to him in the hypnotic trance, after it is over, how this can be the
result of a belief that he would do so, which arose out of an impression
that the operator believed he would do so ; for this is what the
" normal " explanation really amounts to. The objection is that the
person does not, in his waking condition, believe he will do so till he
does it ; in fact, he knows nothing about it. Sub-consciousness is a
vitally important thing, but a " sub-conscious belief " is no explanation of what occurs here. A sub-conscious belief is a belief which
could become conscious and this hypothetical belief, in the waking
state, could not. Surely it is a simpler explanation to say that,
just as when a person makes up his mind to get up at eight next
morning and does so, so in this case it is purpose and not belief which
has been fixed in the hypnotic state. The conation is clearly in
consciousness when the moment comes ; why not assume that it
was the conation what was originally fixed there ? But it is difficult
to see how the conation got fixed there by any normal means ; for
purpose normally arises out of desire. With the analogy of thought-
transference the popular idea seems probable, that A wills that B
shall form a certain purpose and he forms it. Of course, the possibility
of this is limited by the opposition met from the normal workings
of desire and emotion and, if the same thing is possible in waking
consciousness, will be helped by the co-operation of the " normal "
factors.

If such a factor be at work, then it is in " Direct Suggestion "
only that it co-operates. In this case its presence is some counter-

poise against Keatinge's arguments—sound as far a they go—in favour of " Indirect Suggestion." How large a counterpose depends on the extent and distribution of the power. The matter is, however, concerned with the explanation of influence, not with its detection. The extent of a teacher's influence and disciplinary power is known by results ; governing bodies and head masters, in making appointments, do not need to trouble as to its source. And, as to the extent to which each teacher uses the direct or indirect moral appeal, experience alone will guide him. The theoretic consideration of the matter only becomes important when bodies like the Moral Education League try to compel teachers to use the direct rather than indirect appeal. Here disastrous consequences may result from attempting to make a person try to use a power which he does not possess or possesses only in a small degree.

The purpose of this article is to plead that for the time being the word Suggestion should be abandoned. The effect of this will be :—

(1) That in the psychological explanation we shall lay stress on what is going on in the *pupil's* mind, not in the *teacher's*. This is what we do in training college work in explanations of intellectual processes, why not in the case of moral processes ? We shall, moreover, trace back what goes on to elements in the original outfit of the pupil ; we shall lay stress on the direction of innate tendencies and not create the idea that we are operating *ab extra*. (Even if " direct " transference is true, it is a comparatively rare addition ; the other internal factors should be understood first). We shall therefore begin with the very simple principle that we tend to think, feel and act as we think others do.

(2) When we turn to the teacher's work in directing these primitive tendencies, we shall bring the matter down to a level where the student will feel on firm ground on which he can use his own experience, common-sense and tact. " Should the *moral appeal* be direct or indirect ? " is a question on which he will think for himself. But the introduction of pseudo-technical language like " Direct or Indirect *Suggestion* " makes him think the matter to be beyond him and to take on authority statements which he does not know how to apply.

(3) The question whether there is or is not such a thing as immediate transmission of purpose or feeling can be then discussed as a separate problem. It will stand out more clearly itself ; just as the other factors became quite clear when disentangled from this.

Our objections to the word " Suggestion " may be summed up thus :—(a) it confuses at least two distinct questions ; (b) it suggests certain answers to questions before they are discussed ; (c) it introduces an atmosphere of the mysterious and occult ; (d) it prevents students using their own thought on the questions involved.

THE CASE FOR STANDARDIZATION OF THE CURRICULUM IN ELEMENTARY AND OTHER SCHOOLS.

By BENJAMIN DUMVILLE, M.A.

THE Code of Regulations for Elementary Schools of thirty years ago, issued by the Board of Education—or, as it was then called, the Education Department—together with the system of examination and payment by results which accompanied it, was a fabrication on which educationists of to-day may well look with disapproval.

Of the evils attendant upon those regulations it is unnecessary to speak. All those who have grown grey in the service of elementary education are only too painfully aware of them.

But there was one desirable feature in the old system which we seem to have largely lost. With all its faults, the Code conferred a definiteness of aim which induced a thoroughness of application such as cannot be found in these days of elasticity. If a boy had passed the Fourth Standard, the work of the Fifth Standard was expected of him in the succeeding year. And in spite of all the imperfections of the examination, it could be tolerably well determined at what stage of progress any individual had arrived.

At the present time, however, there is no such certainty. A boy may come from a school in which he has passed what is called the Fourth Standard, and be unfit even for the work of the Third Standard in the new school. And even if the total intellectual outfit of a " Fifth-Standard " boy coming from one school is approximately equal to that of the average boy of the same standard in the new school, the details of his knowledge and skill may be so different in range and kind that it is not satisfactory to put him to work in any standard of the new school. It is impossible, indeed, to know exactly what a " new " boy has done, and what he is consequently fit for proceeding to do, without reference to the syllabuses of the school he has left, and without some knowledge as to how far and how thoroughly those syllabuses are covered by the instruction given.

Now, when it is realized that the number of boys who shift from school to school during the period of elementary education forms a very large proportion of the whole, the variation of syllabuses becomes a matter of great regret on this account alone. But there is the further consideration that the present indefiniteness of aim has produced a serious falling-off in the character of the work. Accuracy and thoroughness are far to seek. Though the recent severe criticisms of business men and other employers are probably exaggerated, there is little doubt that a basis of truth underlies many of their allegations. And if it is possible, without going back to the pernicious system of compulsory examination and payment by results, to set up a modernized form of the old standardized curriculum, one may well ask whether we should not be acting for the advantage of elementary education by striving in this direction.

· But there is a still more serious consideration. We are now selecting the best pupils of our elementary schools for more advanced work in central or secondary schools. And further selections are made later on for still higher education. Under the present system of varying curricula, the pupils coming from a number of different schools, although they may be of approximately equal general intelligence, are often very unequal with respect to their knowledge of certain subjects.

Take, for instance, English grammar. Some elementary schools still attempt to give their upper scholars a thorough grasp of the subject. Others neglect it almost entirely. There are, of course, differences of opinion among educationists as to how much is necessary for the children of elementary schools, and as to when a beginning should be made. But there is no doubt of the necessity of grammar when the study of foreign languages is begun. And the task of the language teacher in a central or secondary school is often needlessly complicated by the vast differences which exist in the grammatical knowledge of pupils of the same class or form. The limitations of the time-table and the other requirements of the curriculum of the higher school often render it impossible to devote sufficient time to the laying of a complete grammatical foundation. And even when this is possible, there is the unsatisfactory circumstance that those children who have already been taught the elements are largely marking time. Would it not, then, be much more conducive to efficiency if, in spite of differing views on the subject, an attempt were made to settle what parts of grammar should be taught in the elementary school, and the stages of the elementary course at which those parts should be dealt with ?

As a further example, we may cite the case of history in still higher institutions. In a recent report on the teaching of this subject in London, Dr. Boas states that at one training college he interviewed twenty students who came from thirteen different secondary schools, and that he found " considerable differences in the range of their school work." Dr. Boas suggests that " steps should be taken, when the students enter college, to find out the exact extent of their course of historical study in the secondary schools and to build, as far as possible, upon that." Dr. Boas does not indicate how it is possible to build the same superstructures on a number of foundations in which there are " considerable differences." The only way would be to give, especially during the early stages of the higher course, a large amount of separate tuition to each different individual. It needs no great pedagogical insight to realize the disadvantages of such procedure. And if we come to close grips with the problem, keeping always in view the object of securing the fullest possible result from the educational courses of all the schools through which the pupil passes, we shall be led to the conclusion that the proper solution of the difficulty is rather to be found in securing the establishment of similar foundations for all the pupils. In other words, the ideal of high educational efficiency demands that for each type of school a standard curriculum should be framed, prescribing at any rate a certain minimum of definite knowledge for all the scholars of that type.

The objection of the teacher that such a proceeding would limit his freedom is both rash and injudicious. It is rash because the freedom in question carries with it a weight of responsibility which no single person, and not even a small group of persons, *with full knowledge of the extent of the task*, would be prepared to bear. It is injudicious because it presupposes that the teacher has the right to decide what is to be taught, whereas it is the community which, by some means or other, must always have the ultimate decision. The freedom which the teacher should claim, *and which he has hitherto neglected to strive for*, is that which is concerned with the conditions,

methods, and organization of school work. Too long has he submitted to regulations framed without any advice from himself by
those who do not understand his work and its difficulties. It is of
the highest importance that he should send to every education
committee trusted representatives who can be relied upon to state
the point of view of the practical teacher with no uncertain voice.
Lastly, the acceptance of a curriculum framed with due authority by
the educational representatives of the community would give the
teacher freedom in another sense of the term. Freed from anxiety
with respect to this matter, and relieved of the burden of long reflection upon it, he would be able to devote himself whole-heartedly
to the question of devising the best methods of carrying on the
prescribed work.

It is not clearly known why the Board of Education, after giving
up its practice of examination and payment by results, also gave up
its claim to standardize the curriculum. The chief reason alleged is
that elementary schools have varying educational needs, depending
on the social character of the boys attending them and the industrial
conditions of the districts in which they are severally placed. Further,
it has been pointed out that teachers differ in their interests and
attainments, and that what can be profitably taught by one teacher
or group of teachers cannot always be successfully attacked by
others.

Taking the last reason first, we may remark that the things to
be taught to a boy should not depend upon what his teacher happens
to like, but upon what is best for him as a future member of the
community. If a school does not possess a teacher able and willing
to instruct the boys in the things considered most profitable, the
sooner a change is made in the composition of the staff, the better.
Let us by all means consult the interests of the members of the staff
in allocating the work to be attacked. But let this be done in due
subordination to the principle that there are certain things which
the boys must be taught.

The argument for adapting the curriculum of a school to local
conditions seems to have been grossly over-stated. We must,
however, first be quite clear as to what is meant by this adaptation.
If it merely means that illustrations and concrete material for observation and reflection are to be drawn from the surrounding neighbourhood, no true educationist can do other than agree with it. The
great principle in all teaching, and especially in that of elementary
schools, is that we should start from the " here and now " of the
scholars. And this will influence the choice of the material dealt
with by way of illustration in almost every subject. If the problems
set in arithmetic, for instance, are to be " real " ones, so that they
interest the pupils, they must deal very largely with the circumstances'
of the daily life of the district in question. The sums set, therefore,
in a colliery district will be different in concrete characteristics from
those set in a cotton town, and still more from those of an agricultural
neighbourhood. *But the rules taught may still be largely the same.*
To take one further example, history ; we may all agree that considerable attention should be given to relics of historical interest
which are to be found in the vicinity of the school and to a study of
the past events connected with those relics. But this course is
pursued not because we desire to teach a different part of history,

but rather in order to obtain an intensely realistic basis for that general body of historical truth which should be taught in all schools. It is unnecessary to cite examples from the teaching of other subjects. In general, however, it may be said that with that adaptation of the curriculum to local circumstances which confines itself chiefly to *method* rather than to *principles* we can · all be in whole-hearted agreement.

We may also agree that some adaptation is necessary according to the intelligence and capacity for work of the boys in a given district. It is obvious that in a good neighbourhood, in which the majority of the boys come from respectable homes and are not only well fed and clothed, but able to do some amount of home work and private reading, more progress should be expected than in a poor district. The difference in achievement, however, need not be so much in kind, but rather in rapidity. In other words, the boys in the better districts would, in a large number of cases, reach the higher standards earlier than those of the poorer neighbourhoods. Here, once again, then, there need be no real difference in the curriculum as such.

It may well be that in the schools of the poorer neighbourhoods there will be · more handwork and " practical " occupations. But here also the difference is rather in *method* than in *matter*. The teacher of dull children must always proceed more slowly, giving more concrete examples than he finds necessary with bright pupils. And this, not only because his pupils are slower in comprehension, but also because in many cases their opportunities for observation and general enlightenment outside of school have been more limited.

But the adaptation of curriculum suggested by many educational thinkers is one which involves different systems of general truth as well as different concrete examples and different rates of progress. Thus some would advocate a much simpler scheme in arithmetic for a country school than for a school in a commercial centre, and would even go so far as to suggest variations for different parts of the same town.

Now this assumes that the majority of the boys living in a district will remain in that district and will take up the work carried on in it. But in these days of rapid· and cheap transit, such an assumption is very far from the truth. How many of the boys attending a school in a given suburb of London find work on leaving in the neighbourhood of the school ?

And even were it possible, it is by no means desirable to fix the employment of a boy according to the district in which his parents happen to live during the period of his school life. Choice of employment is more and more being made according to the capacity of the youth. And the influence of After-Care Committees will, it is hoped, do still more in the future to increase this tendency. There are some boys born in agricultural districts who are most fitted for commercial life, and there are some born in towns who will do best in the country.

With regard to the social status of the boys, similar remarks may be made. Because a boy comes from a good home, it does not necessarily follow that he should enter a higher sphere of work than that of a boy from a poor home. The *capacity* of the youth should be the chief consideration.

Now it is quite true that a larger proportion of children coming from good homes than of those from poor homes will enter the more intellectual occupations. But this does not necessitate the alteration of the elementary school curriculum. That curriculum should consist of all the items of knowledge and skill which every normal child must acquire before going further in life. The bright child may skip through it more rapidly than the average child. But the point is that *he should go through it*. By all means let the work be arranged in such a way that the clever child can cover the ground more quickly than the dull one. The arrangement of the syllabus so that the second half of each year's course is largely an extension and amplification of the work of the first half-year will go far to allow of that rapid promotion of bright pupils which permits the latter to pass on to secondary education at the earliest possible time. There still remains, however, the fact that an irreducible minimum of knowledge and skill should be required of all normal children. As to what this irreducible minimum is, and how it should be apportioned throughout the elementary school course, there is likely to be much dispute. It is conceivable that the Board of Education in giving up the claim to definite prescription was not unmoved by apprehension of the criticism which educational awakening is bound to bring in its train. But the mere fact that there is so much difference of opinion is evidence that the problem is an exceptionally difficult one. And how is it at present solved ? A task which professors of education, inspectors, and other high officials would shrink from attacking as a whole is lightly thrown over to the head master of each individual school.

Now the head master of an elementary school is usually, before all else, a practical teacher. Let us hope that he has had his time of study and reflection on the ends of education. But he can scarcely be expected to bring to bear on this most difficult task that breadth of view and that comprehensive knowledge of all the subjects which are necessary for a satisfactory solution of the problem. *No single person can be expected to do this.*

What the head master actually does is to patch up a curriculum which is usually a mosaic formed of much that is current in the schools around him, of a few things introduced on account of his own and his staff's personal predilections, and of a good deal that he imagines the inspectors will look for. It would be interesting to get a body of head masters to confess how they have severally attacked this gigantic task. Some have faced it manfully. Some have shelved the difficulty by blindly copying the work of those considered to be " sound " or " advanced." Others have gone on from year to year making slight alterations in a curriculum which has come down from the times of the old " code." Not a few have avoided the work by calling on their assistants to do the chief part. In one school, for instance, each class teacher has been asked to make up the syllabus of work for the year, bearing in mind what the teachers in the classes next above and below were doing. What organic unity can be expected in a curriculum framed in this haphazard way ? Yet probably it is sounder than that of many a head teacher who has been more courageous.

Is it not high time to introduce order into the present chaos of curricula ? But how can it best be done ? Certainly not by leaving the matter to a few inspectors at Whitehall. What is wanted is a conference of experts of all types—experts in the subjects, experts in the teaching of them, experts in the general conduct of education, experts in psychology, and, above all, experts in life, *i.e.*, men and women of high intelligence who are engaged in handling the youths and maidens leaving our schools and who realize in what they are most lacking.

In such a conference, there would have to be a large amount of give and take, and on some crucial matters definite decisions would probably be reached only by falling back on votes. But such decisions, if they were made binding, would be far preferable to the more or less irresponsible variations which at present exist. And even if some of them were wrong, they could be revised in the light of further experience.

Changes in the curriculum, however, should not be very frequent. If, for instance, the curriculum were changed each year, there would be no continuity about it for the individual child. Probably it would be best to have a thorough revision every three years. And in such revisions account would have to be taken of what has already been done in the previous three years. Thus, any changes made with respect to the work of the last three years of the elementary school curriculum would require to be such that the new curriculum for the three years in question could be dovetailed not only into the new curriculum for the first three years but also into the old curriculum for the same period. If this could not be satisfactorily done, it would be necessary, either to allow the old curriculum for the last three years to remain in force for the scholars who have already completed the first three years or to effect a temporary compromise between the old and the new curricula for the last three years, which would enable the scholars in question to proceed smoothly with their work and to obtain as much profit as possible from the improved curriculum.

The advantages of such a standardized curriculum are many and great. Reference has already been made to the more satisfactory conditions under which the numerous transfers of scholars could be effected. But there are further benefits of a much more important kind.

In the first place, with a standardized curriculum everybody concerned in the work of elementary schools would be able to become familiar with the complete course of instruction. And practically the whole of the energies of teachers and supervisors would be free to strive for the most effective working out of the syllabus. Under present circumstances, an inspector having half a day to give to a school, and being anxious to do justice to it, would require to spend a considerable portion of his time in studying the curriculum of it. In many cases, too, the teachers of a school are ignorant of all but what concerns their own classes. True, there are some head masters who undertake the formidable task of making sufficient copies of the complete syllabus of the school to enable each teacher to have one. But this practice is comparatively rare. And even where it exists, there can never be such definite knowledge of the whole as would exist with a curriculum definitely standardized for all schools during a period of several years.

A curriculum framed in the way which has been suggested would be invested with far greater authority than can be expected under existing conditions. The average head teacher is usually considered as only *primus inter pares*. And where his opinion differs from that of some of his subordinates, especially where certain of those subordinates have strong views of their own, the work prescribed cannot be undertaken with the same application as would be the case with an official syllabus.

No educationist of any worth would agree that teachers should blindly accept a syllabus thrust on them from without. It is of the utmost importance to ensure that the man or woman who teaches a subject should fully appreciate the educational aims involved. But from requiring individual teachers to attack the whole question of a curriculum to giving them some voice in the selection of the work to be prescribed is a very far cry. By all means let the teachers take a keen interest in, and have great influence upon, the prescription of work. The suggested conference on the curriculum should most certainly contain a strong body of representatives of the teachers. But, as we have already noted, the elementary teacher is so engrossed in the practical side of the work that he cannot be expected to have the breadth of view, the time, and the energy, to work out the whole scheme for himself. If we are beginning to realize that no single teacher can do justice to all the subjects of the elementary school curriculum, ought we not also to admit that no individual and no small group of individuals can elaborate the most satisfactory scheme for a whole school ?

And the difficulties of the present system become all the greater in those schools in which the teachers, head and assistant, are growing old. In such cases, the tendency is to continue with the old syllabuses indefinitely. No one can summon sufficient energy and courage to make a complete revision. A few changes may be introduced on account of inspectorial and other pressure. But the net result is often more unsatisfactory than continuance under the old regime would have been. It is not infrequent to find syllabuses which, after having been tampered with by disconnected attempts at revision in various parts, contain serious gaps and omissions which nobody could justify. This is all the more common because it is impossible for inspectors to make a thorough examination of the syllabuses of all the schools under their jurisdiction.

A further advantage which would accrue with a standardized curriculum would be that much more assistance could be given to teachers in the elaboration of methods of teaching. In France, where such a standardized curriculum exists, there are to be found a large number of periodicals whose chief function is to aid the teacher with hints and suggestions on the methods of instruction in the various subjects. Similar periodicals are not unknown in England. But they would be much more stimulating and comprehensive if the work to be done were fixed and generally known. In France, where the work in each subject is definitely prescribed month by month throughout the year, the teacher can find assistance in almost every branch of instruction just at the time when he requires it.

There are some educationists who are strongly opposed to the use of these aids to teaching. The only cure for this prejudice would be to require such individuals to teach all the subjects of the curriculum throughout the year, giving due time after school to their families, to society, and to some of the usual recreative occupations of leisure. Nobody who has had to switch his attention from Arithmetic to Nature Study, from Physical Exercises to History, from English to Hygiene, and from Singing to Drawing, can have any doubt as to the value of hints from a person who has specialized on the teaching of the particular subject in question. While some amount of specialization in teaching can certainly be undertaken in many elementary schools, especially in the larger ones, anything approaching the complete specialization which obtains in many secondary schools will always be impossible in elementary schools, even if it were desirable. And the harassed teacher who has to dive into so many subjects has every right to take advantage of the work of the various specialists in the teaching of those subjects.

And much improvement could also be obtained with a standardized curriculum in the books published for the use of elementary schools. Not a few of the modern books are very good. But they cannot be dove-tailed into the curriculum of every individual school, and hence their circulation is comparatively restricted. Some head masters, not altogether unwisely, choose their books first and frame their syllabuses accordingly. Where, however, a head master first draws up what he considers to be the best course in a given subject, and then looks round for books to be used in connexion with the teaching prescribed, he usually finds it impossible to light upon any series of books corresponding satisfactorily to his schemes.

In this connexion it should be noted that there would be a greater incentive for publishers to spare no pains in the production of the common school books. For a really good book would appeal not merely to a comparatively small number of schools taking work on special lines as is the case at present, but to all the schools of the country. In the old days of a standardized curriculum, a certain geographical reader ran into over a million copies. And with a change, not indeed to the old curriculum but to a modern counterpart of it, similar, and even greater, successes would be possible. Each publisher would be conscious that if he could produce a book which was clearly the best of its kind, a very large proportion of the schools would adopt it.

Again, with the establishment of a conference to determine the main outlines of the curriculum of elementary schools, a vast amount of thought and endeavour which is now scattered and largely ineffective would be focussed in such a way as to achieve definite progress. Conferences of teachers on various aspects of the curriculum have been very frequent of late years. And it speaks well for the enthusiasm of the teachers that these have been exceedingly well attended. But they have too often ended in smoke. A few teachers have gone away with definite ideas inspired by them ; but no widespread result has been secured.

What, too, can be said of the vast number of teachers who for various reasons never attend such conferences and never read the reports of them ? Those who keep in touch with the latest developments in educational thought and practice and also penetrate frequently into the elementary schools cannot fail to be struck by the wide gap which exists between thinkers and experimenters on the one hand and practical teachers on the other. There has, for instance, been much controversy and experiment in recent years with regard to the question as to how far subjects should be taught for the training or discipline of the mind and how far they should be attacked for their use in life. And very definite conclusions have been arrived at in some quarters. Yet there are thousands of teachers who, so far from knowing anything of the discussion, frequently show by their arguments and answers to questions that they are not even aware of the existence of the problem. When once all such discussions have a definite and certain bearing on the question of framing the curriculum for all elementary schools, a new and more vivid interest will be awakened in them.

In conclusion, it may be pointed out that in two of the subjects of the elementary school course—physical exercises and scripture— there is even now a standard syllabus. The reason is not far to seek. It does not lie in any outstanding difficulty in the selection and arrangement of the work in these two subjects. Nor does it consist of any necessity for a more rigidly fixed progression from one part of the curriculum to another. Will not every teacher admit that a " new " boy can adapt himself to the work in these subjects much more readily than in, for instance, geography or arithmetic ? The reason for fixing the syllabus in physical exercises and scripture is to be found in the apprehension that there is danger in leaving the selection and arrangement of matter to the predilections of the staff of each school. But if this is so for physical exercises and scripture, why not for geography and arithmetic ? And can anyone assert that the teaching of physical exercises and scripture is on the whole less successful than it would be if no definite lines were laid down ? We may all agree that the existing syllabuses in these subjects are susceptible of improvement. But few will deny that the work in these two subjects— though it may suffer a little in a small minority of schools in which there are experts with well considered views of their own who chafe under the limitations—is more thoroughly done throughout the system of elementary schools as a whole than it would be without any fixed syllabus. If, however, this is true for two subjects in which the demand for progressive elaboration is comparatively small, how much more necessary is it to fix the best conceivable plan of advance in those subjects in which the line of attack is of supreme importance ?

There will, it must be admitted, always exist some serious obstacles to the application of exactly the same curriculum to all schools.

The very small schools, for instance, present extremely great difficulties. In such schools the children cannot be divided up into the requisite number of classes for complete instruction in the work of each year. One way of dealing with these cases would be to amalgamate several small schools in a given area and to provide travelling facilities for the children attending them.

With a standardized curriculum in the chief subjects, there could still be some option with regard to the choice of certain additional subjects. It would be useless, for instance, under existing conditions, to prescribe gardening as a subject for all schools.

Again, in a subject such as English literature, it might be advisable to allow considerable latitude. Works for each standard could be *suggested* rather than *prescribed*. It might, for instance, be found possible to make for each class a large selection of works from which the teacher could be required to take a certain number. Or a small minimum of works could be set down for study in each class, the teacher being asked to add others of his own choice. It would probably be unadvisable to allow complete freedom of choice in all cases, though inspectors might be empowered to grant it where special reasons are given.

It would, however, be necessary to emphasize here what, let us hope, will be understood throughout, viz., that careful prescription need not imply exhaustive examination. In literature, more expecially than in any other secular subject, the fear of examination is only too liable to kill the spirit of appreciation. And in all the other subjects careful watch would be necessary to ensure that the increased facilities for definite testing of the work should not result in that tyrannical system of examinations which did so much to kill initiative and enthusiasm in the old days. * It should be an inspector's first duty to ascertain whether the various subjects are being taught on sound lines, with due regard to the development of interest.

Opponents of a fixed syllabus are only too likely to cite such evils as excessive examinations in order to arouse the strong prejudices of the past. Another method of attack will be to refer to the French Minister of Education who, sitting in his office in Paris, was able to say that at a given moment all the pupils in all the schools throughout France were being instructed in a certain prescribed topic. In answer to this last objection, it may be pointed out that the time table of each school may be immensely varied in spite of a fixed curriculum. Not long ago, Mr. Marshall Jackman, now a District Inspector under the London County Council, introduced into his school a time table which did not specify *when* the subjects should be taken, but only *how much time* should be given to each during the week. It would be quite possible to have such a time table in conjunction with a fixed curriculum. The *matter* might be fixed ; the *method* left largely to the teacher.

The Board of Education would also be well advised to permit the existence of a number of experimental schools in which variations from the prescribed curriculum could be made with a view to testing their results. The demonstration schools attached to training colleges could partake of this character.

Apart, however, from such exceptions as these, the crying need is for a much greater measure of standardization. At present, the ordinary teacher is confused and uncertain in his work, and is consequently in danger of becoming careless and indifferent in the execution of it. He requires a more clearly defined task.

And when this reform has been effected for elementary education, it may be possible to secure a similar improvement in our secondary schools. As a recent writer says :—

" No amount of tinkering with secondary education will avail till we have one definite system throughout the country, with definite types of schools working on definite programmes. Outside of this there is still plenty of room for individuality of tradition, but it ought to be possible, say, for a fourth form boy to be transferred to the corresponding form of another school of the same type without loss or confusion, without change of curriculum."—(" Magister " in the " Times Educational Supplement," 2nd August, 1917 ; p. 300.).

THE VOCABULARY OF A FREE KINDERGARTEN CHILD.

By JAMES DREVER, M.A., B.Sc., D.Phil., Lecturer on
Education in the University of Edinburgh.

IN the " Journal of Experimental Pedagogy " of March, June, and
December, 1915, the writer described the results of a study of
children's vocabularies, of which his own three children were the
subjects, and at the same time alluded to, and made some use of,
results obtained in an investigation, commenced at that time, into
the vocabularies of children attending the Edinburgh Provincial
Committee's Free Kindergarten at 46 Gilmore Place. The present
article is to be regarded as a continuation of the previous article,
and deals with the fuller results obtained in the Kindergarten
investigation.

Within recent years a fairly large number of detailed studies
of children's vocabularies have become available to the student of
child development through the work of Boyd,[1] Bush,[2] Miss
Drummond,[3] Gale,[4] Mrs. Nice,[5] Whipple,[6] and others. The type
of child studied is, however, in nearly every case the same—the child
belonging to a good home—and the conditions in such cases are
exceptionally favourable for the carrying out of a vocabulary investigation. The present study was carried out under somewhat
different circumstances. On the one hand it was carried out in the
school during a portion of the school period, and on this ground it is
not perhaps quite comparable with studies carried out in the home
under normal home conditions. On the other hand, the subjects
studied in this instance belong distinctly to a much lower social level,
a level at which vocabulary studies of the kind we know could be
carried out only under exceptional circumstances.

The children attending the Gilmore Place Kindergarten are
drawn mainly from one of the poorest localities in the city of Edinburgh.
They may enter the Kindergarten at the age of about two and a half
or three, and are transferred to the ordinary elementary schools of
the Edinburgh School Board at the age of five. Many of them are
of poor physique, and some of feeble or even defective mentality.
The Kindergarten life generally exerts a markedly beneficial effect
on their physical health, but nevertheless illness—epidemics are
fairly frequent—interferes to a considerable extent with their attendance. For this reason, in addition to those already indicated, an
investigation like the present is attended with not a little difficulty,
and is liable to defects which might be avoidable under better
conditions.

The present investigation, commenced some four years ago,
may be said to have had a threefold aim :—

1. In the first place to determine the normal extent of the
vocabulary of a child of five or under, living in slum conditions, to
determine also what might be considered the staple vocabulary, and
what might be regarded as the maximum vocabulary available for

1. Pedagogical Seminary, Vol. XXI. (1914).
2. Pedagogical Seminary, Vol. XXI. (1914).
3. Child Study, Vol. IX. (1916).
4. Pedagogical Seminary, Vol. IX. (1902).
5. Pedagogical Seminary, Vol. XXII. (1915).
6. Pedagogical Seminary, Vol. XVI. (1909).

such children. It goes without saying that the main interest is not in the mere vocables, but in the range of experience, circle of thought, forms of thought, and direction of interest, which the vocables represent. The educational importance of this problem, which is the only one studied in this paper, is apparent when we consider that the vocabulary of the child of five is the starting point for the linguistic development which the school undertakes, and the experience, circle of thought, and interests of the child the basis and foundation of its whole school education.

2. In the second place to determine by detailed analysis the nature of the vocabularies of individual children of different ages, and of the vocabulary of the Kindergarten child as a type, and also, if possible, the various influences which go to make the vocabularies what they are.

3. In the third place to determine, if possible, the effect which the life and work of the Kindergarten produces on the vocabularies of the children, again not with respect to the mere vocables, but with respect to the circle of thought, interests, and forms of thought, which the vocables represent.

The methods of investigation were practically identical with those described in the previous article. Selected students from the Educational Laboratory at Moray House—in the majority of cases Diploma Students, who had attended full courses in Psychology at the University and in Experimental Education at Moray House— were sent into the Kindergarten for one or two days a week during a period extending over from six to ten weeks according to circumstances. This duration of the period of study in the case of each vocabulary was what was practicable, rather than what might be considered desirable.

In all cases the students volunteered for the work. Before going to the Kindergarten at all they were asked to read the writer's previous article, and the method of investigation there described was discussed with them. The directions finally given them were, that they should follow that method as closely as possible, that they should try by every means they could think of to elicit from the child its stock of words, that they should get the child in as many different environments as possible, going for walks, excursions, visits to the Zoo and the like, that they should use pictures, models and whatever the resources of the Kindergarten could provide, get the children to talk with one another, watch them at their play, and so on, and record on the spot every word used by the child, but on no account suggest any word to the child or record any word if unintentionally or accidentally suggested.

There were twelve volunteers, and twenty-eight vocabularies in all were taken. Three of the students, however, have not handed in any returns, and only twenty-one vocabularies are therefore available for this study. The twenty-one represent thirteen boys and eight girls, the ages ranging from 27 months to 63 months. In selecting the children an attempt was made to get different ages and also different groups of children represented. In order to throw some light upon our third problem it was desirable that there should be at least three groups, children who had just entered the Kindergarten, children who had been in attendance for about a year, and children who were on the point of leaving after being in attendance for about two years. The results, however, can hardly be regarded as satisfactory from this point of view, owing to a variety of causes, the chief being the great variations in the periods during which children were in attendance at the Kindergarten.

The following Table (I.) shows the number of words obtained from each child. Unfortunately, owing to the absence of certain children, the ten periods regarded as the minimum during which children should be under observation, were only realized in about half the cases. In some cases, indeed, the periods of observation sank as low as two or four. These vocabularies, though obviously incomplete, are included, but are indicated by asterisks. All are boys.

TABLE I.

Subject.	Age in months	Nouns.		Verbs.	Adjectives.	Pron.	Adverbs	Prep.	Conj.	Mis. cell.	Total.
		Com.	Prop.								
BOYS—											
R. L.	36	108	9	43	27	14	14	11	2	3	231
J. S.	37	91	6	42	27	15	17	8	3	2	211*
D. B	39	373	16	107	49	18	24	16	2	6	611
J. M.	45	136	9	58	29	15	20	7	1	15	290*
T. W.	45	168	7	53	12	6	15	10	2	12	285*
R. M.	49	339	29	112	57	35	36	18	5	7	638
J. S.	53	304	17	92	55	14	18	9	6	5	520
C. McI.	55	332	32	85	40	24	28	15	4	5	565
W. S.	56	376	28	151	87	24	44	13	8	7	738
P. .K	57	195	10	66	30	7	13	8	4	17	350*
D. B.	59	387	20	106	64	14	15	8	4	7	625
E. C.	59	251	33	111	76	27	45	22	12	20	597
J. F.	62	380	19	98	44	16	15	13	8	4	597
GIRLS—											
A. H.	27	209	8	102	57	25	31	13	3	5	453
J. McI.	44	286	20	90	57	23	29	9	3	8	525
J. McI.	55	300	18	101	103	26	40	18	6	8	620
F. A.	56	218	18	83	55	24	14	7	5	1	425
J. McE.	56	370	5	143	49	21	12	18	4	2	624
A. C.	60	283	19	110	97	37	46	19	5	6	622
I. M.	60	307	25	129	82	31	46	19	7	10	656
M. L.	63	287	27	96	56	28	29	13	5	7	548

This Table shows that there were four children of ages varying between 27 and 42 months, five of ages varying between 42 and 54, and twelve of ages varying between 54 and 63. We may call the first the three-year group, the second the four-year group, and the third the five-year group. The first group gives us a total number of words 1,566, of which 820, or 54·4 per cent. are nouns, and the average number of words in the vocabulary at three is 376. The second group gives 2,256 words, of which 1,333, or 59 per cent., are nouns, and the average vocabulary at four is 451. The third group gives 6,966 words, of which 4,084, or 58·6 per cent. are nouns, and the average vocabulary at five is 580. The first two groups consist of so few cases that it is unsafe to draw any deductions from these figures. At the same time the percentages of nouns tend to support a conclusion arrived at in the previous article, viz., that nouns increase relatively to verbs between three and four, though the tendency may possibly be in the opposite direction earlier. It is interesting to note that the percentage of nouns at four and a half in the case of J. in the previous article was 59.

Table II. gives the full list of words obtained, with the exception of proper nouns and miscellaneous expressions, mostly exclamatory. It should be explained, however, that the lists compiled by the students have been edited, the following principles being applied :—Different parts of verbs are not separately recorded, except in cases like " be " and " was," or " go " and " went," where different stems are represented. Nouns used as adjectives, when coined for the occasion, as frequently happened with some subjects, are usually recorded as nouns and not as adjectives. There are special reasons for any exceptions to this rule. Scotch forms and words naturally bulk very largely among the words actually given, and some children gave both the Scotch word and its English equivalent, as " haud " and " hold," " sodger " and " soldier," " ain " and " own." In such cases the English equivalent only is given. Generally speaking, indeed, only such Scotch words as presented difficulties of translation are recorded at all, the English equivalents being recorded, though the Scotch words were actually given. Where the same vocable represents different parts of speech, it is recorded under each head if so used.

Each word has following it a number showing the number of children in whose vocabulary it appeared. The list is also arranged in such a way as to show : (1) what might be called the fundamental words in the vocabulary of the type of child studied. As such we may reckon, under the conditions of the investigation, all the words given by 75 per cent. of the children. In this instance we take 15 as representing 75 per cent. Considering that one child was present on only two occasions, and other two children on four, 15 is probably more than a fair 75 per cent. These fundamental words are shown in heavy type.

(2) What might be considered the full range of the normal vocabulary available, if one may so speak, for the type of child. As such we reckon all words obtained from at least 3 children. These are indicated in ordinary type.

(3) What might be considered as occasional rather than normal words, including words which might be described as " erratics," owing their presence in the vocabulary of individual children to more or less accidental circumstances. Some of these " erratics " it is quite easy to pick out. Other words, however, may also be " erratics " or they may come under the category rather of the merely occasional. Such are words given by one only or two children, and they are indicated by italics. The number of these words may seem considerable, but it must be remembered that practically every child gave some, and there were twenty-one children.

TABLE II.—Vocabulary.

NOUNS.—**Aeroplane** (18), air (4), angel (4), animal (4), apple (8), apron (4), arm (9), auntie (7), *age* (2), *airship* (1), *apple-tree* (2), *ark* (1), *arrow* (1), *artillery* (1), *ashes* (1), *ash-pan* (1), *axe* (2).

Baby (21), **bag** (15), **bairn** (15), **ball** (19), **barrow** (18), **basket** (17), **bead** (16), **bed** (20), **bell** (16), **bird** (18), **boat** (19), **book** (18), **boot** (21), **box** (18), **brick** (15), back (11), badge (5), bagpipes (3), baker (4), balloon (8), banana (5), band (8), bang (4), bank (10), barrel (9), basin (7), bat (4), bath (7), bathroom (6), bayonet (3), bean (4), bear (11), beast (11), bee (4), beef (8), beer (6), belly (3), belt (6), bench (6), Bible (3), bicycle (11), ' bike ' (4), ' birdie ' (3), birthday (3), biscuit (14), bit (14), blacking (3), blanket (7), blind (7), blood (5), blouse (10), board (8), bomb (6), bone (4), ' bool' (4), boot-lace (3), bottle (13), bow (6), bowl (6), boy (13), brae (8), bread (11), bridge (13), brooch (6), brother (9), brow (3), brush (13), bucket (7), buckle (3), bugle (5), bulldog (3), bullet (5), bun (12), bundle (4), bunny (4), bus (3), butcher (10), butter (14), buttercup (3), butterfly (9), button (11), button-hole (3), ' baby-dog ' (1), ' baby-school ' (1), back-green (2), bacon (1), ball-frame (1), bandage (1), bangle (2), banister (2), banjo (2), bantam (2), bar (1), barber (2), bark (1), barley (1), barracks (1), battery (2), battle (2), battleship (1), ' bealing ' (1), beanstalk (1), beard (2), beauty (1), beaver (2), bed-clothes (1), bed-time (2), beer-shop (1), berry (2), bill (2), ' billie ' (1), ' birlie ' (2), bite (1), black (1), blackbird (2), blame (1). block (1), blow (1), bluebell (1), ' bob ' (2), ' body ' (2), bog (1), bonbon (1), bonnet (2), ' booty ' (1), bottleful (1), bottom (2), bowling-green (2), ' bow-wow ' (1), braces (2), brake (1), branch (2), bran-scone (1), brass (2), breakfast (2), breast (2), briquette (1), bronchitis (1), bubble (1), ' buckie ' (1), bud (1), bug (1), building (2), bull (1), bumble-bee (1), bunch (1), bung (1), bunker (2), ' bun-shop ' (1), burglar (2), button-hook (2), buss (1), byre (1).

Car (19), **castle** (18), **chair** (18), **coal** (15), **coat** (16), **cow** (15), **cup** (15), cab (10), cabbage (4), cage (8), cake (8), calendar (4), camel (5), can (5), canal (9), canary (3), candle (4), cannon (8), cap (4), caramel (4), card (4), care (3), ' car-man ' (3), carpet (9), carriage (7), carrot (3), cart (5), car-ticket (5), cat (14), cave (3), chain (7), chalk (11,) cheek (4), cheese (4), chicken (5), chimney (8), chin (6), chocolate (14), church (7), cigarette (8), ' cloaker ' (4), cloakroom (3), clock (13), closet (7), cloth (6), clothes (14), cloud (3), coach (14), coal-man (5), cocoa (4), cold (5), collar (10), colour (7), comb (11), combinations (5), concert (3), ' cookie ' (3), cork (1), corner (7), couch (5), cough (5), country (5), cover (11), cow-boy (9), cradle (3), cream (3), crust (5), ' cuddy ' (7), currant (5), curtain (11), cubby (1), cabman (1), calf (1), camisole (1), candlestick (1), cane (1), canoe (1), cape (1), captain (2), caravan (1), car-island (1), car-line (1), car-rails (2), ' carry ' (2), castor-oil (2), ' catcher ' (1), cemetery (2), ceiling (2), chair-bed (1), change (2), chap (2), chemise (1), chemist (2). cheque (2), cherry (1), chest-of-drawers (2), chief (1), Christian (1), ' chuckie ' (1), church-bell (2), cigar (1), cinders (2), cinema (1), circus (1), clasp (2), class (2), claw (1), clay (2), climb (1), ' clip-shears ' (1), cloak (2), close (1), clown (1), coal-cellar (1). cock (2), cockatoo (1), cocoanut (2), coffee (2), coffin (1), collie (1) ' comic ' (1), company (2), conductor (2), cook (1), cord (1), corn (1), cotton-wool (1), counter (2), cousin (1), crab (1), crane (1), crib (2), cricket (1), cross (2), crowd (1), crown (2), crumb (2), crush (1), cub (2), cupboard (1), curl (1), cushion (1).

Dinner (15), **dog** (18), **door** (18), daddy (10), daisy (13), darkie (3), day (6), dicky-bird (3), dirt (11), dish (10), dish-clout (3), doctor (6), doll (13), donkey (6), drawer (6), dress (4), dresser (5), drink (10), driver (6), drop (4), drum (9), duck (11), dyke (4), daffodil (1), ' daftie ' (1), dagger (1), dairy (1), damson (1), dark (1), date (1), daylight (1), dear (2), deer (2), dentist (1), destroyer (1), dew (1), diamond (1), dining-room (1), dinner-time (1), dough-nut (1), ' doxie ' (1), ' doxiness ' (1), drag (1), drawing (1), drill (2), dripping (2), drummer (2), drumstick (1), duff (1), dummy (1), dumpling (2), dust (2), duster (2).

Ear (15), **egg** (15), **elephant** (15), **eve** (17), eagle (3), egg-cup (3), elastic (5), end (7), engine (11), earth (2), edge (1), elbow (1), emery-paper (1), empire (1), emulsion (1), enamel (1), engine-driver (1), entry (1), envelope (1), exercise (1).

Fire (17), **fish** (16), **flower** (19), **foot** (18), face (12), fan (3), farm (5), father (11). ' fattie ' (4), feather (14), feeder (3), fender (5), field (4), fight (3), finger (14), fire-engine (3), fireman (3), fireside (6), fisherman (3), flag (13), ' flitting ' (3), floor (10), flour (3), fly (5), folk (3), football (5), fork (5), frock (5), frog (3), front (3), funeral (4), fact (1), ' fag ' (1), fall (1), family (1), fare (1), farmer (1), farthing (1), fear (1), ' fever-motor ' (1), fiddle (1), fig (2), fighter (1), fire-station (1), fish-shop (1), fist (1), flat (2), flea (2), fox (2), Friday (1), friend (2), fright (2), ' front ' (clothing) (1), fun (2), funnel (1), fur (2), furniture (1).

Garden (17), game (3), garter (6), gas (11), gate (8), giant (4), ginger (5), ' gird ' (5), girl (4), glass (8), glasses (4), glove (10), God (3), golf (3), gramophone (5), grandfather (4), grandmother (4), granny (5), grape (3), grass (13), grave (3), grocer (3), ground (3), gun (14), gallop (1), ghost (2), gin (1), ginger-beer (1), gingerbread (1), giraffe (2), go-car (1), gold (2), golf-ball (2), golf-stick (1), goloshes (2), goods-train (1), goose-step (1), ' gounie ' (1), grate (1), grater (1), gravat (1), gravy (1), grease (2), green (2), grill (1), guidance (1), guide (1), gunner (1), gutter (2).

Hair (16), **hand** (18), **hat** (15), **head** (16), **hole** (15), home (16), horse (19), **house** (18), half-loaf (3), halfpenny (9), hall (3), ham (5), hammer (4), handkerchief (13), handle (11), hay (3), heart (3), height (3), hen (10), ' henner ' (3), hill (9), holiday (4), hook (3), horn (8), hospital (7), ' hurl ' (3), *hairpin* (1), *half* (2), *half-crown* (1), *hat-pin* (1), *haymakers* (1), *header* (2), *hearse* (1), *heel* (1), *herring* (1), *Highlanders* (1), *hit* (2), *hobbyhorse* (1), *hoist* (1), *hold* (2), *honey* (1), *hood* (1), *horseback* (1), *horse-shoe* (2), *hose* (1), *hose-tops* (1), *hotel* (1), *hour* (1), *hump* (2), ' *hurley* ' (1), *husband* (1).

Ink (8), iron (9), *ice* (2), *infirmary* (1).

Jacket (3), jam (14), jar (5), jelly (3), jersey (14), jug (11), *jack-tar* (1), *jam-tart* (1), *jaw* (1), *Jesus* (1), *jockey* (1), *jumper* (1).

Kettle (9), key (9), kilt (5), kiltie (5), kind (8), kindergarten (5), ' kist ' (5), kitchen (7), kitten (4), knee (6), knickers (3), knife (9), knot (4), *kangaroo* (1), *key-hole* (1), *khaki* (2), *kick* (2), *kid* (1), *king* (1), *kirk* (1), *kiss* (1), *kit-bag* (1), *kite* (2), *knitting* (1), *knock* (1).

Laddle (15), **lassie** (18), **leg** (15), laces (11), ladder (4), lady (3), lamp (6), lamp-post (6), leaf (11), lemonade (3), letter (12), letter-box (3), lid (8), light (6), line (5), lion (9), lip (3), looking glass (5), lorry (6), lot (11), ' lum ' (10), lump (4), *lamb* (1), *lane* (1), *lantern* (2), *leader* (1), *leek* (1), *lentil* (1), *length* (1), *lesson* (2), *liar* (1), *library* (1), *liquorice* (1), *lie* (1), *lighthouse* (1), *lightning* (1), *lining* (1), *links* (2), *load* (1), *loaf* (2), *loan* (2), *lock* (2), *love* (1), ' *lucky-bag* ' (1), ' *lum-hat* ' (1).

Man (20), **milk** (15), **mother** (19), **motor** (18), mammy (7), mangle (7), mark (3), master (3), match (8), meal (4), measles (3), meat (6), medicine (7), mess (3), message (7), middle (3), mill (4), mince (5), minute (7), Monday (6), money (11), monkey (12), moon (7), morning (11), moth (3), motor-boat (3), motor-man (3), mouse (8), mouth (8), muff (3), mug (3), mustard (3), *machine* (1), ' *magicals* ' (1), *mamma* (1), *mantle* (1), *mantlepiece* (1), *margarine* (1), *market* (1), *marriage* (1), *mask* (1), *mat* (2), *medal* (2), *message-boy* (2), *mew* (1), *milk-pitcher* (1), *milk-shop* (1), *minister* (2), *minnow* (1), *miss* (2), *mixture* (1), *money-box* (1), ' *morn* ' (2), *motor-ambulance* (1), *motor-bicycle* (2), *motor-bus* (2), *motor-engine* (1), *mountain* (1), *moustache* (1), *muffler* (1), *music* (2), *mussel* (1).

Nose (16), nail (finger) (7), nail (8), name (11), neck (11), needle (5), nest (4), night (12), noise (10), nurse (6), nut (3), *name-plate* (1), *navy* (1), *neb* (2), ' *necker* ' (2), *nib* (1), ' *nick* ' (1), *night-gown* (1), *night-time* (2), *number* (1).

Officer (4), oil (3), onion (4), orange (13), over-alls (12), ox (3), *oatcake* (1), *oblong* (2), *office* (2), *oven* (2).

Pencil (15), **penny** (16), **picture** (16), **piece** (15), page (4), pail (14), paint (3), painter (3), pair (6), paling (3), pan (7), pancake (5), paper (13), papers (news) (3), parcel (6), party (6), pavement (7), paw (4), pea (5), peacock (5), ' peerie ' (6), peg (4), pen (9), people (3), petticoat (6), photograph (10), piano (9), pie (8), pig (10), pigeon (5), pillow (9), pin (8), pinafore (3), ' pinkie ' (3), pipe (13), piper (4), pitcher (4), place (10), plant (4), plate (14), playground (6), pocket (12), ' poke ' (4), poker (6), polar-bear (4), pole (4), policeman (13), pony (5), porridge (3), postcard (7), postman (10), post-office (9), pot (9), potato (12), pound (4), powder (3), present (3), press (8), pudding (6), pulley (3), purse (8), pussy (9), *paint-brush* (1), ' *palmie* ' (1), *papa* (1), *parade* (1), *pardon* (1), *park* (2), *parrot* (2), *passenger* (1), *paste* (1), *path* (1), *peel* (1), *pelican* (1), *pend* (2), *pendulum* (1), *pen-nib* (1), *person* (1), *photographer* (1), *picture-book* (1), *picture-house* (2), *pillar* (2), *pillar-box* (2), *pills* (1), *pine-tree* (1), *pipe-clay* (1), *pistol* (2), *plaster* (1), *play* (1), *ploughman* (1), *plum* (1), *poison* (1), *police* (1), *police-office* (1), *polly* (2), *porter* (1), *post* (2), *potted-head* (1), *pound-note* (1), *pram* (1), *prayer* (1), *princess* (1), *prison* (1), *prisoner* (1), *prize* (2), *Punch-and-Judy* (1).

Quarter (1).

Rabbit (12), rail (3), railing (6), rails (8), railway (4), rain (7), rat (6), rhubarb (6), ribbon (12), ring (11), road (6), rock (5), rocking-horse (3), roll (4), roof (5), room (11), rope (12), rose (3), row (5), rubber (3), race (1), rag (2), rag-time (1), rainbow (1), raisin (1), rate (2), rattle (1), razor (1), record (1), register (2), rein (1), reindeer (2), rest (2), revolver (2), rice (2), rifle (1), river (1), rod (1), roly-poly (1), root (1), round (2), rubbish (1), rug (1), ruler (1).

School (18), **shoe** (16), **shop** (15), **smoke** (15), **soldier** (18), **spade** (15), **sweetie** (15), safety-pin (4), sailor (11), salmon (7), sand (14), Saturday (4), saucer (7), sausage (9), scale (4), scarf (6), school-bag (3), scissors (6), scone (10), scout (7), screw (3), sea (10), seagull (4), seal (3), sea-lion (3), sea-plane (3), seaside (3), seat (12), seed (3), shed (3), sheep (10), shelf (5), shilling (8), ship (12), shirt (5), shovel (12), shutter (4), side (7), signal (3), silver (3), sink (8), sister (11), sixpence (3), size (6), skin (3), sky (11), sleep (5), sleeve (5), slide (4), smell (6), snow (12), soap (10), sock (4), sofa (3), son (3), song (4), soup (11), sparrow (3), spider (4), sponge (5), spoon (8), spot (3), spur (3), square (3), ' squeaker ' (3), stable (3), stair (14), stamp (3), star (6), station (11), stays (3), steam (4), step (10), steps (4), stick (14), stile (4), stocking (14), stone (9), stool (5), store (6), story (7), straw (5), street (12), string (10), stud (3), stuff (3), submarine (3), sugar (12), sun (10), Sunday (10), Sunday-school (6), swan (3), sweep (5), swing (6), sword (7), syrup (4), *sail* (2), *sailor-hat* (1), *salt* (2), *salute* (2), ' *sammy* ' (1), *sand-tray* (1), ' *sanitary* ' (1), ' *scaffy* ' (1), *scent* (1), *school-bell* (1), *schoolboy* (1), ' *scooter* ' (2), *scraper* (1), *scratch* (2), *scream* (1), *scribbles* (2), *search-light* (1), *see-saw* (2), *semmit* (1), *sergeant* (1), *sewing* (1), *shame* (1), *shave* (1), *shaving* (1), *shaving-brush* (1), *shawl* (2), *shears* (2), *shell* (1), *shelter* (1), *shepherd* (1), *sherbet* (2), *shot* (2), *shoulder* (2), *silk* (1), *singer* (1), *skates* (1), *skirt* (2), *slap* (1), *slate* (2), *sledge* (1), *slice* (2), *slow-coach* (2), *smile* (1), *smithy* (1), *snake* (2), ' *sneck* ' (1), ' *snolter* ' (1), *snowball* (2), *snowflake* (1), *soak* (1), *soda* (1), *sole* (1), *somersault* (1), *soot* (2), *sound* (1), *spark* (1), ' *spats* ' (1), *speaker* (1), *spear* (1), *speed* (2), *sponge-cake* (1), *spy* (1), *spy-glass* (1), *stalk* (2), *starch* (2), *steam-boat* (1), *steamer* (1), *stitch* (1), *stock* (2), *story-book* (2), *stove* (1), *strainer* (1), *strap* (1), *strawberry* (2), ' *string-bed* ' (1), *strip* (1), *stripe* (1), ' *sugar-ally* ' (2), *sulphur* (1), *sum* (1), *summer* (2), *supper* (2), *surprise* (1), *sweetheart* (1), *swim* (1), *switch* (1).

Table (17), **tall** (16), **tea** (17), **teacher** (17), **time** (15), **train** (19,) **tree** (15), **trousers** (15), tam o' shanter (4), tank (3), tart (5), tea-party (3), teapot ((11), teddy (6), telephone (6), tent (7), thing (14), thread (5), threepenny (4), ticket (7), tiger (12), tile (10), tin (9), ' tinnie ' (3), toast (4), tobacco (5), toe (4), toffee (4), tongue (6), tooth (11), top (14), towel (13), town (3), toy (9), tray (7), treacle (6), trench (4), trumpet (11), trunk (3), tub (3), Tuesday (4), tumbler (5), tunnel (9), *table-cloth* (2), *table-cover* (1), *tablet* (1), *tailor* (1), ' *tanner* ' (1), *tap* (1), *tartan* (2), *tassel* (1), *taste* (1), *tea-leaves* (2), *teaspoon* (1), *tear* (2), *territorials* (1), *thief* (1), ' *thingummy* ' (2), *throat* (2), *thumb* (2), *thunder* (1), *Thursday* (3), *tie* (1), *tinker* (1), *tiptoes* (1), ' *toff* ' (2), *tommies* (1), *toot* (1), *tooth-brush* (2), *top-flat* (1), *torch* (1), *torpedo* (1), *tow* (1), *trail* (1), *tram* (1), *transfer* (1), *trap* (1), *trap-door* (1), *trick* (1), *trip* (2), *truck* (2), *tulip* (1), *tumble* (1), *turn* (1), *turnip* (2), *tusk* (1), *tyre* (1).

Umbrella (13), uncle (4), van (4), *Union Jack* (2), *vase* (2), *veil* (1).

Water (19), **window** (18), waistcoat (3), walk (7), walking-stick (6), wall (9), war (7), watch (7), watering-can (4), way (14), Wednesday (3), well (13), wheel (12), while (7), whip (6), whiskers (3), whistle (5), whooping-cough (3), wind (7), wind-mill (3), wire (7), wolf (6), woman (12), wood (10), word (3), work (6), worm (6), writing (4), *walnut* (1), *want* (1), *wardrobe* (1), *War Loan* (1), *war-time* (1), *warship* (1), *wash-house* (1), *washing-clout* (2), *waxcloth* (2), *weather* (1), *wedding* (1), *weed* (1), *week* (2), *weight* (1), *whiskey* (2), *whitening* (1), *wicket* (1), *wire-netting* (1), *wool* (2), *world* (2), *worsted* (2), *worth* (2).

Year (2), ' *yellie* ' (1).

Zeppelin (4), Zoo (10), *zebra* (2).

VERBS.—Am (10), are (14), ask (8), *add* (1), *apologize* (1).

Be (15), **break** (19), **buy** (16), bake (4), bark (3), bat (3), bath (3), beat (4), bite (13), bleed (3), blow (11), boil (3), bring (11), brush (6), build (4), burn (7), button (5), *bang* (1), *baptize* (1), *beg* (1), *belong* (1), *bend* (1), *bet* (1), ' *bide* ' (1), ' *big* ' (1), *blaze* (2), *bolt* (1), *bother* (1), *bubble* (1), *bump* (1), *burst* (2).

Can (19), **come** (20), **cut** (18), call (8), carry (9), catch (13), chase (3), choke (4), clap (3), clean (8), climb (13), comb (6), cough (3), could (6), ' coup ' (3), cover (4), crackle (3), creep (3), cry (3), ' *caa* ' (1), *caw* (1), *chain* (1), *chalk* (2), *charge* (1), *chew* (1), *chum* (2), *claw* (1), *clear* (1), *cook* (1), *count* (2), *crinkle* (1), *cross* (2), *crunch* (1), *cuddle* (2).

Do (21), dance (9), die (5), dig (7), dirty (3), draw (9), dress (3), drink (11), drive (5), drown (3), dry (6), *dash* (1), *doze* (1), *drop* (1), *drum* (1), ' *dunch* ' (1).

Eat (18), *empty* (1), *explode* (2).

Fall (18), fasten (3), feed (3), fetch (3), fight (13), fill (3), find (11), finish (4), fire (3), fling (11), flit (4), fly (6), forget (3), frighten (3), *fancy* (2), *fell* (1), *fence* (1), *fish* (2), *fit* (2) ' *fleg* ' (1), *flow* (1), *fold* (1), *fool* (1), *fry* (1).

Get (21), **give** (19), **go** (21), ' greet ' (12), grow (7), *gallop* (1), *gather* (1), *grate* (1), *greet* (1), *growl* (1), *guard* (1), *guess* (1), *guide* (2).

35

Have (18), hammer (3), hang (12), hear (14), help (3), hide (9), hit (8), hoist (4), hold (10), hop (3), hurry (9), hurt (13), *happen* (1), *heat* (1), *heave* (1), *hem* (1), *hook* (1), *hope* (2), *hum* (1), *hurl* (2).

Is (19), iron (4), *imagine* (1).

Jump (20), jag (4), *join* (1).

Know (19), keep (12), kick (5), ' kid ' (3), kill (14), kindle (3), kiss (4), knock (7), ' kep ' (2), ' kittle ' (1), *kneel* (2), *knit* (2).

Like (17), **look** (19), laugh (5), learn (3), leave (7), let (11), lick (3), lie (11), lift (7), light (5), listen (3), live (5), lock (5), lose (11), loosen (3), love (3), *lace* (1), *lay* (1).

Make (20), march (7), may (3), meet (5), mend (8), ' mind ' (5), *marry* (2), *matter* (1), *mean* (2), *might* (1), *move* (1), *must* (1).

Need (4), *nip* (1), *nurse* (1).

Open (13).

Play (19), **put** (19), paint (3), pass (6), pick (10), plant (3), please (4), poke (4), pour (4), pull (14), push (4), *paddle* (1), *paste* (1), *pay* (1), *peel* (1), *peep* (1), *poison* (1), *punish* (1).

Run (19), rain (7), reach ͵(6), read (10), ride (3), ring (10), rise (3), roar (4), roll (9), rub (6), *race* (2), *rap* (1), *rock* (1), *row* (1).

Say (18), **see** (20), **shut** (15), **sit** (20), **stand** (16), sail (3), salute (4), save (4), scrape (5), scratch (5), screw (7), sell (5), send (5), set (3), sew (5), shake (9), shave (4), shine (3), shoot (11), should (6), shove (3), show (9), sing (11), sink (6), sleep (13), slide (7), slip (4), smell (3), smoke (10), snow (3), ' sort ' (7), speak (5), spend (5), spill (3), spit (3), spread (3), stay (9), steal (3), stick (8), stop (14), sweep (8), swim (11), swing (3), *scatter* (1), *scent* (1), ' scoot ' (1), *scream* (1), *scrub* (2), *seem* (1), *shall* (1), *sharpen* (1), *shift* (1), *shout* (1), *shovel* (1), *signal* (2), *skin* (2), *skip* (1), *smack* (1), *smash* (2), *smile* (1), *smother* (1), *snap* (1), *soap* (2), *spell* (2), *split* (1), *spy* (2), *squeak* (1), *squeeze* (1), *stab* (2), *stir* (2), ' stot ' (1), *stretch* (1), *suck* (2), *sup* (1), *swallow* (2), *sweat* (1).

Take (20), tear (7), tell (12), thank (5), think (11), throw (5), tie (15), touch (6), tramp (3), try (7), tumble (4), turn (11), *talk* (1), *taste* (1), *tick* (2), *tickle* (1), *toast* (1), *twinkle* (2), *twirl* (2), *twist* (1).

Use (4).

Vomit (1).

Walk (16), **want** (20), **wash** (18), **write** (18), wait (13), waken (5), was (10), watch (8), wave (11), wear (5), went (6), whistle (5), will (14), wind (3), wish (4), work (8), would (6), ' wallop ' (1), *warm* (1), *waste* (1), *weigh* (2), *whack* (1), *whip* (2), *whisper* (1), *win* (1), *wink* (1), *wipe* (2), *wonder* (2), *wound* (1), *wrap* (2), *wreck* (1), *wriggle* (1).

Yell (1).

ADJECTIVES.—**A (an)** (15), **another** (15), **all** (14), alone (4), any (5), awful (5), *African* (1), *angry* (1), *asleep* (2).

Big (20), **black** (15), **blue** (17), **brown** (15), baby (5), back (3), bad (4), bare (3), best (better) (13), blind (4), ' bonnie ' (7), broken (13), ' bally ' (1), *bashed* (2), *batting* (1), *beautiful* (1), *Belgian* (1), *blazing* (1), *bleeding* (1), *boiled* (1), *bottom* (1), ' braw ' (1), *bright* (2), *burst* (1), *button* (1).

Cold (16), clean (13), curly (6), *Canadian* (1), *canvas* (1), *cheeky* (1), *cheese* (1), *cigarette* (1), *clear* (1), *clever* (2), *coal* (1), *cocoa* (2), *coloured* (1), *cool* (1), *crackling* (1), *cruel* (1).

Dirty (15), dark (8), dead (3), dear (5), different (5), drunk (7), dry (7), *daft* (1), *deep* (1), *dinner* (1), *doll* (1), *done* (2), *drunken* (1), *dull* (1), *dusky* (1).

Every (3), *early* (1), *easy* (1), *eight* (2), *eleven* (1), *empty* (2).

Funny (15), fair (4), fat (9), ' feared ' (6), fine (3), first (4), five (8), four (6), *far* (1), *farm* (1), *farther* (1), *fast(er)* (2), *father* (1), *flat* (2), *flowered* (1), *flying* (1), *free* (1), *fresh* (2), *front* (1), *full* (2).

Golden (3), good (6), green (13), *German* (2), *giddy* (1), *glad* (2), *grand* (1), *great* (1), *greedy* (1), *grey* (2).

Hard (6), heavy (5), her (13), high(er) (5), his (14), hot (6), hungry (3), *half* (2), *happy* (1), *hundred* (1).

Its (14), *ill* (1), *Indian* (2), *iron* (1).

' *Jaggy* ' (1).

Khaki (2), *kilted* (1).

Last (8), light (3), like (8), little (3), long (14), *laced* (1), *late* (1), *lean* (1), *left* (1), *lone* (1), *lost* (1), *lovely* (1), *lucky* (1).

My (20), more (9), mother (3), *magical* (1), *many* (2), *merry* (1), *middle* (1), *milk* (1), *mixed* (1), *monkey* (1), *much* (1).

Nice (17), next (3), new (13), no (11), *naughty* (1), *near* (1), *neat* (1), *nest* (1), *nice-like* (1), *nine* (2), ' *nippy* ' (1).

One (15), old (8), open (4), other (8), our (7), own (5), *only* (1), *orange* (1).

Pink (9), pretty (3), purple (5), *painted* (1), *paper* (2), *past* (1), *plain* (2), *poison* (1), *poor* (2).

Quiet (1).

Rare (5), ready (3), real (7), red (11), right (6), rotten (3), round (6), rubber (3), ' *raggy* (1), *rainy* (1), ' *rattly* (1), *Red-Cross* (1), *right* (hand) (1), *rough* (1), *rude* (1), *Russian* (1).

Sore (15), same (9), shining (3), sick (3), six (4), slippy (3), soft (3), some (12), sorry (3), strong (4), sunny (4), *sad* (1), *sailor* (1), *scented* (1), *Scotch* (1), *second* (1), *seven* (1), *shaky* (1), *sharp* (1), *shut* (2), *shy* (1), *silk* (1), *silly* (1), *silver* (2), *silvery* (2), *skinny* (1), *sleeping* (2), *sleepy* (1), ' *slidy* ' (2), *slow* (2), *snow* (1), *snowy* (2), *soapy* (1), ' *some* ' (1), *South African* (1), *squeaking* (1), *steady* (2), *stiff* (1), *straight* (2), *straw* (1), *summer* (1), *Sunday* (1).

That (those) (18), the (20), this (these) (17), two (16), tall (3), ten (4), ' thae ' (5), their (11), three (9), tired (6), torn (3), ' *tacketty* ' (1), *tartan* (1), *thick* (1), *thin* (2), *thirsty* (1), *tight* (2), *toasted* (1), *Tollcross* (1), *top* (2), *toy* (1), *twenty* (1).

Wee (21), white (16). warm (6), well (3), wet (7), what (10), whole (4), wooden (3), wounded (6), wrong (3), ' *wackly* ' (1), *waking* (2), *war* (1), *weak* (1), *which* (1), *wild* (1), *windy* (1), *worse* (2), *worsted* (1).

Your (15), yellow (11). yon (9), *yonder* (1), *young* (2).

PRONOUNS.—He (16), I (19), it (19), me (19), mine (16), one (18), that (18), this (15), what? (16), you (18), all (9), another (9), anybody (3), either (3), else (6), her (10), him (14), his (4), its (6), itself (6), myself (10), nobody (8), none (10), nothing (8), other (5), ours (4), same (3), she (14), some (5), somebody (7), something (5), them (14), themselves (4), there (3), these (7), they (14), us (9), we (12), who ? (6), whose ? (4), yours (8), yourself (4), *any* (2), *each* (1), *each other* (2), *everybody* (1), *hers* (1), *herself* (1), *himself* (2), *oneself* (1), *ourselves* (2), *ownself* (1), *someone* (2), *who* (1).

ADVERBS.—Away (18), down (18), no (15), not (16), now (17), out (19), there (18), where (17), after (5), again (13), ago (8), alone (3), along (3), already (4), always (3), as (3), ' aye ' (5), back (12), before (6), downstairs (8), far (8), fast (3), first (4), hardly (4), here (13), how (9), in (8), inside (7), just (14), like (3), maybe (4), more (5), much (3), nearly (3), never (9), off (13), on (4), once (5), outside (5), over (8), past (3), right (7), round (6), slowly (3), so (9), soon (3). then (3), to-day (3), together (4), too (3), to-night (5), under (4), up (14), upside-down (4), upstairs (5), very (4), when (13). why (7), yes (12), yet (9), yonder (8), about (2), *angry* (1), *anyway* (1), *awful* (1), *backwards* (1), *behind* (2), ' *ben* ' (2), *better* (2), ' *bonnie* (2), *brightly* (1), *early* (1), *enough* (1), *ever* (2), ' *fair* ' (2), *farther* (1), *forward* (2), ' *half* ' (2), *hard* (2), *high* (1), *home* (2), *late* (1), *likely* (1), *long* (2), *low* (1), *near* (2), *nicely* (2), *often* (1), *only* (1). ' *overheads* ' (1), *quickly* (2), *quietly* (2), *quite* (1), *sometimes* (2), *straight* (1), *sweetly* (1), *tight* (2), *thrice* (2), *through* (1), *to-morrow* (2), *twice* (1), *underneath* (1), *well* (2), *yesterday* (2).

PREPOSITIONS.—At (18), in (20), of (17), on (21), to (18), up (16), with (17), about (5), across (4), after (4), along (9), behind (4), beside (6), by (10), down (7), for (12), from (7), into (7), like (5), off (5), out of (5), over (12), round (6), through (7), under (8), *above* (1), *before* (2), ' *ben*,' (1), *below* (2), *except* (1), *near* (2), *next* (1), *past* (2), *underneath* (1), *without* (1).

CONJUNCTIONS.—**And** (17), **too (also)** (17), because (13), but (4), for (6), if (8), or (3), so (4), than (7), that (4), till (6), when (10), where (6), while (3), also (1), as (1), before (1), like (1), without (1).

MISCELLANEOUS EXPRESSIONS.—These form a rather motley crew, so that it hardly seems worth while to record them individually. Most of them are of an exclamatory nature, and some of them might almost be regarded as individually characteristic of certain children. Only three were given by more than five children, these being ' thankyou (9), ' hurrah ' (6), and ' good-bye' (6). About a hundred were recorded by the observers, but scarcely more than half of these could be admitted to the dignity of words. The numbers so admitted in individual cases are shown in the other tables.

Table III. is a summary of Table II., so arranged as to bring out more clearly its most interesting features by the separate tabulation of the number of words occurring in the vocabularies of practically all the children, the numbers occurring in the vocabularies of 75 per cent., in the vocabularies of 50 per cent., in the vocabularies of three, and in the vocabulary of only one child.

TABLE III.

	NUMBER GIVEN BY					Total No.
	19 subjects	15	10	3	1 only	
Nouns (Common) ..	12	72	190	625	400	1207
Verbs	19	32	72	212	104	361
Adjectives	4	20	35	112	122	275
Adverbs	1	9	16	62	21	104
Pronouns	3	8	18	42	7	54
Prepositions ..	2	7	10	25	5	35
Conjunctions ..	—	2	3	14	5	19
Interjections and Miscellaneous ..	—	—	—	17	25	61
TOTAL ..	41	148	345	1,109	689	2,116

As we have already noted the number of " interjections and miscellaneous unclassified expressions " might have been considerably greater, if we had included a number of imitative sounds and more or less characteristic individual exclamatory expressions, but these have been ignored owing to their doubtful status as elements of language proper.

The following is a list of the 41 words given by practically every child : Baby, ball, bed, boat, boot, car, flower, horse, man, mother, train, water. Break, can, come, do, get, give, go, is, jump, know, look, make, play, put, run, see, sit, take, want. Big, my, the, wee. I, it, me. Out. In, on.

A fuller analysis of the vocabularies must be reserved for another paper.

NOTES OF AN EXPERIMENT IN MIMING.

By WOUTRINA A. BONE.

AFTER reading Mr. Caldwell Cooke's account in the Play Way, of his experiment in miming with the boys of the Perse School, and seeing some clever miming in a London school, I felt I would like to try this means of expression for myself, so I spent ten afternoons in a Council School for this purpose.

I had three classes :—

    12 girls of 7 years from Standard II.
    12 ,, 8 ,, ,, III.
    12 ,, 9-10 ,, ,, IV.

They came for half an hour at a time, with a week's interval. Each group came separately.

I introduced the idea of language by gesture, and demonstrated by performing characteristic actions as beckoning, averting—also suggested attitudes, expressing sorrow, amusement, terror, expectations, etc. The girls were quick to take the initiative and almost every one volunteered to give some gesture. The younger children, however, found it very hard to translate into the probable words which would have been spoken, and only described the action. They said " Frightened " ins ead of " I am frightened," " Crying " instead of " I am sorry," and so on. This difficulty was felt all the way through the work with the younger children, and the experiment really remained at the level of a dumb charade. The older children, however, caught the further idea at once.

We then moved to the playing of a story, and " Cinderella " was suggested. The need of definite gesture was not realized at all ; the watchers knew the story, and could easily translate the vaguest actions,—the action seen was what they expected to see, the visit of the fairy godmother, etc.

This was pointed out, and the children set to work to find characteristic gestures for definite actions. A problem like :— " How can we show that Cinderella *was sitting in front of the fire* " ? had to be met. She must do *more* than just sit on the floor ; the gestures of sweeping the hearth, poking the fire, etc., were at once quickly forthcoming.

The question of how to represent the godmother's warning was passed over in this first attempt, to be revived later in the term, but the critical fact of the striking of 12 o'clock while Cinderella was at the Ball, was too important a part in the whole story to be left out. All conversations were practically omitted for some weeks, and the girls seemed completely satisfied with this rather meagre outline.

So long as the story was represented by dumb actions only, very little progress was made, and the experiment showed no great possibilities of educational value, but directly the idea of translating the words the people of the story really said to each other, was attempted to be illustrated, the possibilities grew with each attempt. The younger children, however, hardly reached this stage at all. To expect Council School children of 7 years to translate the actual words was rather premature, I found, though they were quite ready to do the actions straight away.

In the next stage a halt was called in the miming of the stories when the players were baffled for want of a gesture ; and the problem was presented to the whole class ; for instance :—How can we represent the fact that it is now 12 o'clock, the fateful hour in he Cinderella story ? Among the suggestions were—the pointing to the real clock, followed by holding up of two fingers side by side to represent the position of the two hands at midday and midnight But the clock might not always be there, and we felt that we must have a more reliable sign. The drawing of a circle in the air, and holding up the two hands for 10 and two fingers for 12, satisfied for a time, till the question was raised " Are we to understand 12 noon or midnight " ? We were rather bound throughout by the actual surroundings—and the girls decided to point to the window side of the room to represent " day," and the opposite wall when they meant " night."

The rest of the Cinderella story proceeded by means of dumb show of actions alone.

I found that with the older children they really searched in their minds for meaningful signs, and criticisms and comments were abundant.

All the girls were eager to try to act little scenes of their own composing, and three half-hour periods were given to these. They were markedly of the same type. Dumb show of little scenes in the girls' own lives. Two children going to shop—or to school—a friend going to tea with another—children playing together, picking flowers in the country—a mother teaching her girl to sew—and dust. Simple little dialogues were introduced and were understood by the watchers.

The other type belonging to this period of free choice of subject in miming, was evidently influenced largely by what these little girls of nine and ten years had been reading, perhaps in penny books out of school :—a midnight elopement, a deceived parent, and a happy reunion, formed the subject of one mime—burglaries, and lovemaking, delightfully childishly represented, were frequent subjects. At my suggestion, a Greek story was chosen, read and studied among the girls, and they mimed Baucus and Philemon in class the following week. The first part of this was really well mimed with dignity and smoothness. Some of the watchers, however, who did not know the story could not follow the entire plot. They realized that the two old people, a man and a woman, entertained two strangers in their cottage on the hillside, and that the playing children stoned them during their journey. The episode of the hospitality of the old couple being recognized and repaid by the heavenly strangers by a continual supply of food and drink, was well shown. The fate of the hostile village below was not possible to follow in detail, but all those who watched, realized that the valley people were punished by death. It was the last part of the story which was obscure—no sign for " trees " had been decided on, and a considerable amount of muddling took place here.

The miming of this story was, however, a very great advance. The girls seemed to realize the different quality in the subject matter from the little commonplace scenes they had offered before, and in addition to this, the preliminary practice they had already had in miming was beginning to show in the more rhythmic movements.

The need of distinguishing the characters made itself felt quite soon and resulted in the leader introducing each character. This meant the coining of new signs, and signs for " man," " woman," " boy," " girl," " baby " were evolved ; the short hair of the man was recognized from the long hair denoting the woman, by pointing to the neck in the first place, and to the shoulders in the second. The two further signs of lifting the hand to indicate " tall " or " grown-up," and lowering it to show " short " or " not grown-up " made the distinction between " woman " and " girl " and the " man " and " boy."

We quickly moved to the same sign as the Perse schoolboys in denoting " King," " Queen," " Prince " and " Princess " by drawing a circle round the head to indicate the crown. A reminder of the stately character of these personages was needed sometimes, as the children throughout tended to give their actions at far too great a speed.

In this respect the difference between individual children was very marked. some presenting very jerky movements and others showing real beauty, both in isolated and continuous action.

" Fairy " proved a difficulty for a little while. A girl wished to show—

" Oh ! how pleased I am to see you, dear fairy ! "
She showed the emotion well enough and combined it with a pretty gesture, large and stooping—the hands coming in welcome almost down to the ground. The criticism, however, brought out that this was not distinctive enough—any beautiful and charming thing might be welcomed in this way. So we had to search for a sign for " fairy." We decided the characteristic smallness should be represented, and a little space between the first finger and the thumb was selected ; this was accompanied by a particularly pleased and alert expression.

The idea " Far away in China " was once expressed by the reiterated backward wave of the hand, followed by the finger indicating the upward slant of the eyes characteristic of the Chinaman's face.

The relationship of " Twins " was carefully represented by pointing to two girls of the same height who belonged to the same mother. " Mother " was distinguished from " woman " by the extra gesture of pointing to her in connexion with the child described —and so on.

Later on we had to further distinguish our characters. At first the girls used to draw objects in the air with the finger, but it was found to be too vague, and was abandoned for much more particular and distinctive gestures—for instance, one girl tried to represent a doctor by drawing a medicine bottle in the air, after the accepted sign for man, and strengthened the part by miming the man carrying a bag. We failed to recognize these complicated actions, and later simplified them to the one characteristic action of the doctor, *i.e.*, the play of the fingers of the one hand on the wrist of the other (taking the pulse) after the sign for " man."

" Soldier " was easily evolved by a very erect attitude, and with the " present arms " movements.

"Sailor," "the man who by night and day is on the sea," was shown by a billowing movement of the hand, followed by indications of night and day, these two movements elaborating the first sign for "man." This was a very charming little flow of mime. Indeed, some of these explanatory introductions were full of grace and were very pleasurable to watch when they were undertaken by the abler children.

The Priest or Minister was shown by "the man who read from the open book."

The schoolmaster or mistress, sad to say, was unhesitatingly represented, and instantly and unanimously recognized as the person with an emphatic forefinger ! !

The "witch" was represented by the shaping of the hands in the air to make a pointed cap and wand after the sign "woman."

The experiment certainly made me feel that miming might, with real value to the teachers and the scholars, have a place amongst the other means of expression used in the school. It was often illuminating to catch a glimpse of the concept which the child had, and which can only more rarely be shown by the words he used in his composition. We continually found ourselves sorting the accidental from the essential characteristics in a really meaningful way.

The words "rich" and "poor" had to be mimed. Several attempts were given—a number of children assumed a lounging attitude with hands in pockets to represent the out-of-work man, and the rest associated "poor" with abject misery—a poor man seemed necessarily a miserable one. "Rich" was by practically all the class associated with the fur-collared coat and cigar-in-mouth type.

The children began to grow more critical of the actual style during the later part of this experiment. They began to recognize some of the qualities which make for pleasurable and beautiful miming. They told me that purposeless gestures obscured the meaning, and that smoothness and dignity added greatly to the general effect.

Miming took us into a situation where we wrestled with difficulties as they arose in the need to communicate an idea or series of ideas to our comrades, in the medium of movement.

Of course, it is true that the richer the store the mimer has to draw upon, the better his miming will be, and it would be unfair to expect these little Council School girls to evolve as suggestive and wide a vocabulary as did the "Little men" of the Perse School.

But the experiment certainly seemed to me very well worth trying by the class teacher in the ordinary class-room of the Middle School.

THE SCHOOL AND THE COMMUNITY SPIRIT. II.

A SERIES of papers on this subject in these days hardly needs an apology even in a Journal primarily devoted to the cause of educational research. The community spirit must sooner or later influence the life of the school, and educational experiment in recent times has already been affected by that spirit in its modern form, though in the main our schools continue to reflect the social atmosphere of a bygone period. Even in the interest of experimental effort, it is important that the essential features of the communal outlook should be sympathetically understood by those who are going to be teachers, and perhaps the best approach will be to consider some of the ways in which thoughtful men have been driven by experience to think about society in the hope either of explaining or improving it or of doing both. We shall, however, leave aside at any rate for the moment the political philosophy of the Greeks and Romans though much of what is best in the most modern writers has its roots in Plato and Aristotle.

In my previous paper, attention was called to the fundamentally social nature of man, and to the fact that although he has always lived in some sort of society, man has not always been aware of the ultimate meaning of his social life. After all, this will not surprise you for, as you know, most men are still unaware of its final significance. You yourself have in all probability taken the world as you found it for granted. You have had your rough times at home perhaps, but you have never seriously questioned the rights of your parents or the nature of your duties to them. And the relations of the individual to the great society are for the most part accepted in much the same way. Were it not so, no society could be stable and an unstable society means wretchedness and misery for its members.

On this point of stability, human societies, however, are incomparably inferior to those, for example, of the honey bee. A colony of bees is organized on precisely the same lines to-day as it was in what we call the ancient world, just because individual bees have never failed to accept the group organization as they found it. For them the laws of the group are the laws of life. Their organic nature finds complete satisfaction in the group, into the fixed form of which the bee fits exactly. There is for them, therefore, no call for reflection on the constitution of their society. Bees do not think in that way, because there is nothing for them to think about.

Although human societies have never been quite so rigid in form as that of the bees or the ants, men have for long periods accepted unquestioningly the life into which they were born. They have for long ages rendered to Cæsar the things that were Cæsar's and to God the things that were God's. They did not ask who Cæsar was, nor why they should pay tribute to him, nor did they challenge accepted views about God and what was due to Him. So long as life went smoothly, so long as food and shelter were fairly assured, so long as lords and masters cherished and protected those dependent upon them, men did not recognize their bondage. There was no call for social questionings. Even when disaster came it was generally accepted as the sinister action of Fate, or as a Divine punishment for sin—a situation against which revolt was not thought of.

This attitude of mind is not wholly absent from the world of to-day, but as men grow in social comprehension, they tend to look for sources of misfortune in themselves and to seek to avoid them, not by appealing to Divine assistance, but by setting their house in such order as is best adapted to the circumstances of the time. Even to make this step forward is not easy. It is possible to recognize the fact of distress without being active-minded enough to look for a cause and seek a remedy. In times of war especially distress abounds, and it is in times when trouble is acute that men are stirred into thinking. The havoc wrought on men's domestic life and happiness must produce disintegrating effects, and the present moment is the best illustration we could have of the fact. " Social Reconstruction " is the order of the day. The whole fabric of society is shaken and men are thinking more about society and less about themselves to-day than ever they were before—a hopeful sign. Yet the war of 1914-18 is not the first misfortune which humanity has suffered, though it is perhaps the greatest, nor is it the first time that men have noted these misfortunes, mourned them and sought a way out.

> "And have you not heard
> That the Prime Minister of T'ien-Pao, Yan Kuo-chung
> Desiring to win Imperial favour, started a frontier war ?
> But long before he could win the war, people had lost their temper ; "

So wrote a Chinese poet in the ninth century. Men had of course made great advances in social comprehension before they could think like that. It is the peculiar service of the poet to see and record things in this large way, to give direction to the thought of humble individuals in the crowd of sufferers who, each of them, finds only—

> "To the north of my village, to the south of my village the sound of
> weeping and wailing.
> Children parting from fathers and mothers ; husbands parting from
> their wives "

It is some consolation for the grim horror of war, that it compels men sooner or later to take stock as it were of themselves. Oftentimes in their desperate struggle for a life that was worth living, men plunged out of the frying pan into the fire, or exchanged the chastisement of whips for that of scorpions. The drama of history has been a long one, but we can trace a line of progress in its tortuous movement. It was not a poet but a politician who first raised the question—

> " When Adam delved and Eve spun
> Who was then the gentleman ? "

Much water had flowed under the bridges before such a challenge could echo in the hearts of men and produce a revolt amongst the peasantry. When power is concentrated in the hands of a few, abuse is sure to arise. This thing is as old as the hills.

> " For men's quarters and monks' cells ample space is allowed,
> For green moss and bright moonlight—plenty of room provided ;
> In a hovel opposite is a sick man who has hardly room to lie down.
> I remember once when at Ping-Yang they were building a great man's house.
> How it swallowed up the housing space of thousands of ordinary men."

An old Chinese poet again ! Have we not heard the like complaint in our own time ? We may quote from the same source the reflection

of a farm hand who passed through the market when the rich folk
were competing with each other for the purchase of fine peonies—

> " For the fine flower—a hundred pieces of damask,
>   For the cheap flower—five bits of silk."
> "The farm labourer bowed his head and sighed a deep sigh :
>   But this sigh nobody understood.
>   He was thinking, ' A cluster of deep-red flowers
>   Would pay the taxes of ten poorhouses.' "

I have quoted freely from these far-eastern poets[1] who flourished
in a past millennium to illustrate some of the things which have led
men to look at society and ask hard questions about it. Asking
difficult questions is not solving them. Chinese civilization and
Chinese society went on unchanged for hundreds of years after great
poets had raised these issues. Social tradition and social habit die
hard especially where the mass of men is entirely illiterate. Even
in Western Europe, society was, essentially feudal until near the
end of the eighteenth century. So unsatisfactory did Rousseau find
it, that he startled the world by his fiery denunciation of the bonds
which men had made for themselves in their societies. True, he
was not the first modern to think and write about the problem, but
he caught the ear of Europe and gave a turn to what was known as
the doctrine of the *Social Contract* which has been an inspiration
to most modern political thinking.

Before there was a science of Anthropology, and before men
had learned clearly to distinguish between Myth and History, there
had in point of fact been a good deal of speculation about the origin
of society and the relation of government to the people.

This was especially the case in Ancient Greece, where the state
was just a city often smaller than one of our own provincial towns.
This nearness of the government to the people made all the difference.
What we know intimately and at first hand we can grow warm about
when what is remote leaves us cold. As a member of a cricket or a
hockey club you have an immediate interest in the conduct of its
affairs. Our partnership in church or chapel touches us directly,
and a man's Trade Union is a reality before which a national Parliament
is only a pale reflection of a world to which he scarcely feels an attach-
ment. That is why, during these centuries when the modern nations
of Europe were in the making, man's political sense faded as his
direct concern with government grew slighter. At that time ordinary
men and women were bred in a loyalty which expressed itself chiefly
in direct services rendered in return for a right to cultivate the
lands. They had, of course, to take their part in the quarrels of their
lords. This they took to be in the nature of things—a duty attaching
to the station to which it had pleased God to call them. They were
no doubt dimly conscious of a big world beyond—a world in which
Kings and Emperors, Bishops and Popes moved, but Rome and Paris
and London were a great way off in times when railways and newspapers and telegrams were undreamt of. Great things were happening
in this big world which sometimes tore the countryman from his home
to fight in his lord's train for King against Emperor or for Emperor
against Pope. We can see now the tremendous significance of those
events, but amongst the rank and file it was the personal loyalties
that counted rather than the political ideas which were the motive
forces—often implicit rather than explicit—that stirred their Masters.

[1] v. 170, Chinese Poems, translated by Arthur Waley (Constable & Co.)

In point of fact, Western Europe was for many centuries torn by a struggle between two great ideas about society—should the Pope or the Emperor, the layman or the Churchman—one or other be supreme, or should men's lives be lived as it were, in two compartments, over one of which the Pope held final sway and over the other the Emperor. The details of the struggle do not concern us, but the fact of it was the theme of political discussion which occupied men's minds for several centuries, and upon its right solution the social and political progress of the nations depended. Which loyalty was final—that to Pope or that to King? Imagine England under the Interdict at the time of King John if you would realize what the issue meant. Great names are linked to each side of the controversy. Thomas Aquinas, for example, argued for the Pope, and Dante took the side of the Emperor.

When men's thoughts are directed by their sympathies for a particular standpoint, they are always apt to be blind to the things that tell against them, and the partisan spirit was too strong in the thirteenth century to allow of men bei. g critical either of "facts" or arguments which seemed to favour their own view. The controversy was not, however, a wholly idle one, as both parties to it were seeking a principle of peace and happiness amongst men. They saw, as it were, two orders of men—the governors and the governed. The multitude had nothing to do with government, but the peace and happiness of the multitude was desirable, and to accomplish that some principle of finality in government should be found. That was their problem, and it was no small gain that these great writers should regard the well-being of the common people as the object of government. You will notice that their problem was an international one, though the story of Thomas à Becket will remind you that the struggle between Emperor and Pope was repeated at a lower level within the boundaries of nations.

The controversalists of that time differed from those of a later date in seeking the origins of government, not in the nature of men but in what they believed to be the ordnances of God. The weakness of such a position is that it can be used quite honestly in support of any form of society in which a person sincerely and profoundly believed.

A new spirit must enter the discussion before any finality can be reached, and this we find in the great political writings of the seventeenth and eighteenth centuries—a period often called the period of the Enlightenment for that reason. By this time, the nations of Europe had taken definite form and the most interesting political problems arose out of national life, and especially out of English national life expressed as it was in the conflict between the Stuarts and the people.

The philosopher Hobbes was an Englishman of that kind who showed the spirit of the Enlightenment in his way of looking at the political problem, although he was concerned like Dante to seek a type of government which would bring the blessings of peace to a land harrowed by civil war, and although like Dante he found the solution of his problem in a strong lay government, his method of establishing his case breathes a wholly different spirit. His book, "The Great Leviathan" (this being Hobbes's picturesque name for the State) opens with a little treatise on psychology. In other words, he is concerned to find the foundations of society in the necessities of human nature. With characteristic disregard of history he draws a picture of man as he must have been before he hit upon the device of an ordered society under authority. Hobbes did not invent the idea of a state of nature, but he pictured it in a new way. In a famous chapter of his book, he describes how this state of nature must have been a state of war—a war of each against all, when each man's hand was against every other, and in consequence "the life of man was solitary, poore, nasty, brutish and short." From such a position there was no escape, for men were by nature equal ; not equal in power of mind or body, but equal in their rights one against the other, thus " if any two men desire the same thing which both cannot enjoy, they become enemies," and endeavour to destroy one another. Even if there never had been a time when individuals stood in such relation one to another, he pertinently points to the fact that his description corresponded to the relations actually existing between " Kings and persons of sovereigne authority."

Yet he finds in the nature of man a way out. Certain native passions incline men to peace—these are the " feare of death ; the desire for such things as are necessary to commodious living and a Hope by their Industry to obtain them."

These passions are universal amongst men, and by combining them with the inherent rights which are common to all men, he arrives at what he calls the Laws of Nature, the existence of which leads men " to seek peace and follow it, to defend themselves, to be ready, for the sake of peace and self defence, to renounce any of their native rights when others are equally ready to do the same and to be content with so much liberty against other men as they would allow other men against themselves." Granted that all these inclinations are in men by nature, the step into a society is an easy one. Men come to some agreement amongst themselves and desire a means for making that agreement " constant and lasting," and the only means to that end is to set up a common power to keep them all in awe. Here, then, was the origin of the idea of a State which men brought into being by a solemn contract amongst themselves. All this means that in Hobbes's view, the existence of a state implies the existence, actual or tacit, of an agreement of this kind, not between the state and the subjects, but between the subjects themselves. In Hobbes's view this agreement or contract runs like this:—

" I Authorise and give up my right of governing myselfe to this Man, or to this Assembly of men, on this condition, that thou give up thy Right to him and Authorise all his actions in like Manner." When this is done, the Multitude is united in one Person and is called a Commonwealth.

It was no doubt due to the circumstances of the time that Hobbes conceived the agreement in those particular terms. He was concerned to establish two very far-reaching principles. You notice that the covenant was between the parties seeking peace. They entered into certain obligations one to another, but made no contractual obligations as between themselves and the power they set over them. They placed it outside their own control because they imposed no duties upon it except that of maintaining the peace between them and defending them against external enemies. Thus the government was absolute. Again, it followed from the nature of the contract, that in handing over their rights to this superior power, they did what could not be undone. The subjects could not change the form of the government ; the rights conferred upon the sovereign power could not be properly taken away on account of any breach of contract on its part, as it had entered into none ; its actions were not therefore controlled by any sense of responsibility. "A soveraigne power may commit Iniquity ; but not Injustice or Injury in the proper signification," for both these imply the breach of a covenant. You see it was the Stuart *régime* that Hobbes had in mind, and his longing for a stable government and the blessings of peace led him into a position which exalts the state into an irresponsible and permanent authority which ordinary men and women must for their own sakes accept unquestioningly as a final product of the wisdom of their ancestors. This authority makes the laws, it is for the people to obey them.

And yet James I would not have found this great book comfortable reading. He would have put his finger upon the weak spot straightway. It was a defence of absolute and inalienable power certainly, but Hobbes found the source of that power in the original good sense of the people themselves. Dante's Monarch held his authority direct from God without even the intervention of the Church. So James I believed of himself, and the doctrine of the Divine Right of Kings, to which Hobbes dealt so cruel a blow, has perhaps only recently been finally overthrown in the rude awakening of the German Kaiser. Hobbes' gave a new stimulus to political thinking and his conception of a contract between man and man as the basis of the modern state has been fruitful beyond measure in spite of the fact that it was an abstract political idea invented for purposes of special pleading and not the outcome of historical research.

The notion of a " social contract " did not keep the form which Hobbes gave it. If we imagine society to begin with a bargain, we can make the terms of that bargain what we please just to suit the circumstances as we imagine them when the bargain was made and to suit the circumstances of the moment in which we are living. This was what both Hobbes and Locke did. Locke turned the idea of the contract into a very different instrument of political thought when he undertook the defence of the Revolution of 1688. That great event was, of course, in direct violation of Hobbes's doctrine of the inalienable nature of the Rights conferred upon the Sovereign by the contract. To make it clear that Hobbes was wrong and the Revolution right, Locke made a new attempt to describe the state of nature and the necessities which drove men out of that state into a state of society. For him the state of nature was not a state of war, but rather one governed by man's native reasonableness.

" To understand political power right and derive it from its original, we must consider, what State all men are naturally in, and that is, a State of *perfect freedom* to order their actions, and dispose of their possessions and persons as they think fit, within the bounds of the Law of Nature, without asking leave, or depending upon the Will of any other man." But their state of liberty is not a state of licence ; it is obedient to the law of nature, and " reason which is that law, teaches all mankind, who will but consult it, that being all *equal and independent*, no one ought to harm another in his Life, Health, Liberty or Possessions."

It is perhaps a little difficult to see at once the difference between Locke's natural man and man in such a society as Locke knew, or rather, to understand why from Locke's standpoint peace-loving and reasonable men whose native rights to life, liberty and property were accepted should ever desire more. But Locke had to account for the existence of the state and for the people's right to change the organ of government within the state, a right which they had just assumed. He found the blissful state of nature deficient only in one thing—some instrument for administering the law of nature which gave men those rights in equal measure. In spite of the fact that each man had the law of nature in his heart, there were differences amongst men—*e.g.*, of intelligence, and of personal interest, which made for trouble, for in the state of nature, " every man hath a right to punish the offender, and be executioner of the law of Nature." But for men to be judges in their own case was to court mischief, and the *need of a common judge with authority* led men to form a society on the principle that each man should give up his own natural right to administer the law of nature and his right to punish those whom he believed to offend against it. This right is resigned to the community as a whole, and the community is entrusted with the problem of deciding what are offences against the natural law and what shall be the punishment in such cases. So the state arose and so its functions are defined. The community as a whole remains supreme. It must act through duly appointed officers whose responsibility to the community is implied in the original contract. Government exists to protect the lives, the liberties and the properties of the individual members of the community. It is the organ of the whole community, the essence and union of which lies in the fact of its having one will. A people which cannot in some way or other speak with one voice cannot form a society, and in practice the only way of bringing this about is to admit the rule of majority.

In this way Locke satisfied himself in his Treatise on Civil Government that the Stuarts were rightly driven from the throne, and that such action was always justifiable if and when the community lost confidence in the integrity or in the competence of those who conducted the government in its behalf. It is a great advance upon the political theory of Hobbes who carried his notion of contractual obligation to such absurd lengths. Once and for all Locke laid down what has not since been seriously disputed as an essential feature of our own state—the final supremacy of the people. •

But we have moved a long way since Locke's time. Locke's state was just a big policeman who punished people when they transgressed. Except to see that men played the game of life fairly, it had nothing to do with the problem of how to make life happier for the mass of men. The number of men who made up the community to which the government was responsible was an extremely small proportion of the adults who were affected by it. We are still a long way from the twentieth-century notion of a democracy and of the duties of a government.

REVIEWS AND NOTICES OF BOOKS.

The Port-Royalists on Education. By H. C. Barnard, M.A., B.Litt. (pp. 276). Cambridge University Press. 7/6 net.

SOME five or six years ago Mr. Barnard gave us in his *Little Schools of Port-Royal* a careful study of the educational work of the Port-Royalists. He now supplements that work by laying before the English reader translations of some of the original sources ; and a useful and welcome supplement it will be found by students of the history of Education.

Much care has been taken to supply the " apparatus " needed. There is first an Introduction of fifty-six pages, in which comes first a necessarily brief sketch of the condition of education in France in the 17th Century, then notes on the chief Port-Royalist writers on education, then Bibliographical Notes referring to generally available books which deal with the subject, lastly a List of Dates illustrative of the Introduction.

This ended, we reach the body of the book, which consists of extracts translated 'from Port-Royalist writings, classified under the four heads— Educational Theory, General Educational Methods, Particular Teaching Methods, The Port-Royal Girls' Schools.

Then follow a couple of pages in which, in six columns, the arrangement of a day in the Little Schools of Port-Royal, the Oratorian Schools, Lancelot's Regulations for the Prince de Conti, a Modern French *Lycée*, the Port-Royal Girls' Schools, and the Girls' School of Saint-Cyr, founded by Madame de Maintenon, are shown side by side.

Lastly, come some three dozen pages of notes, which the student would doubtless have found more useful had references to them been placed in the text, and an adequate Index.

The book is thus similar in construction and utility to Cadet's *L' Education à Port-Royal*, though, both as a whole and in the particular extracts given, it is much briefer.

We have thought it best to indicate fully what the reader will find in Mr. Barnard's book. We would add that the extracts are selected with judgement, and in the mass enable the student to estimate the permanent value of the contributions to education of the famous community.

It may well be that many will not regard those contributions as of such high and permanent worth as Mr. Barnard himself does. They will be impressed by the repressive character of the whole, a natural result from the theological position of the solitaries. Of the girls Jacqueline Pascal says " they are told that the less the work which they do pleases them, the more it pleases God " (p. 201), and this gives the key-note of the whole theory and practice, with boys as well as with girls. The doctrine that children are naturally inclined only to evil (p. 73), is, indeed, a hopeless foundation for either true theory or sound practice in education. From it followed constant and minute supervision. With the boys " there is always one of the masters who never loses sight of the children " (p. 137) ; with the girls " we must keep unfailing watch over the children, never leaving them alone wherever they may be " (p. 224), while " everything that they say should be audible to the mistress " (p. 209). Even had the teaching methods advocated been more perfect than these extracts show them to have been, such unjustifiable intrusion into the sacred temple of a child's inner life condemns the educational doctrine and practice based on it as unsound in its very essence.

But Port-Royal has to be reckoned with in education as in other departments of life and thought to which its contributions were truer and wiser, and students will thank Mr. Barnard for the help he has given them in his two books, which should be studied side by side. J.W.

Comparative Education. Studies of the Educational Systems of Six Modern Nations. By H. W. Foght, A. H. Hope, I. L. Viandel, W. Russell, Peter Sandiford. Edited by Peter Sandiford. F. W. Dent & Sons, Ltd. 1918. Price

THE appearance of this book is timely. In the days before the War, England was somewhat inclined to look enviously on the educational systems of other nations, but to think that for some reason or other, whatever it might regard as ideally the best in education, it was unable to attain it. Yet along with this feeling there went a half-unconscious attitude that after all it did not much matter ; we get along quite well with a second best system, and there was a tinge of self-satisfaction in the thought that there must be something in our hereditary gifts which enabled us to dispense with a better. The War has altered our traditional attitude in every respect. We have done that which we hoped we should never be compelled to do ; we no longer believe in the impossibility of doing things which we wish to do. We find ourselves not the least member of a triumvirate which must settle the World ; we are unwilling to be behindhand in settling our own affairs. We have beaten the nation which we were disposed to regard as our intellectual superior ; and we believe that it was a wrong intellectual ideal which drove it along the path of madness which ended in disaster.

Henceforward, it seems as if we should attempt to develop an educational system which shall be based on our own ideals ; for those ideals have been tried in the fire and not found wanting. Imitation will not be adoption of foreign institutions, but adaptation. When we see something in the educational system of another country which appears to be good, we shall ask ourselves what is its basis in the ultimate aim which the statesmen of that country have set before themselves, and whether it fits in with our own aims. We have risen to a practical realization that machinery has no merit in itself, that the most highly organized system is not necessarily the best system, that we need also to consider what the organization is seeking to accomplish. Life without organization is better than organization without life ; but a combination of both is the only thing which should satisfy us.

The six articles in this book are equally divided between British and American writers. The editor writes on England and Canada ; he has taken part in the training of teachers in both countries. Mr. Hope is not writing for the first time on French Education. Of the American writers, Mr. Russell, Dean of the College of Education in the University ot Iowa, describes American education ; Mr. Kandel, of the Teachers' College, Columbia, German ; Mr. Foght, Specialist in Rural Education to the Bureau of Education, Danish. It is a happy division of labour ; for, vastly as the educational machinery of Great Britain and the United States differ, the ideals of the two peoples are at bottom largely the same ; and the criticisms of all the writers are unmistakably inspired by a common outlook. They see in the systems of the larger European nations an over-elaboration of the machine, in those of the Anglo-Saxon peoples an unwillingness to throw themselves whole-heartedly into the cause of education with all their resources, financial and otherwise. They believe that the State has much still to do in supplying educational facilities unstintingly, and that its central executive and its inspectors can investigate, spread information and be suggestive, but that true efficiency rests on the originality of the teachers. This is not new, but a comparative criticism of educational systems from this standpoint in the limits of a single volume will enable many readers to realize the meaning of this difference of function in its applications more clearly than they ever did before.

Mr. Sandiford's article on English education was written before the appearance of Mr. Fisher's Bill, and an additional section is added dealing with the Bill as it eventually became law. Most of the criticisms which were made in the original article are met by the Act, but it is a far cry from an Act of Parliament to the realization of the aims which inspired its promoters ; and the passing of the Fisher Act makes it doubly necessary for British educationalists to consider the difficulties which every one of the progressive nations is experiencing in translating aspirations into fact and the extent to which any nation has solved them. For the moment Comparative Education is perhaps the most fertile field of educational study.

The book is necessarily long, and different readers will naturally select the parts with which they are most concerned. It is also written from a particular standpoint, but this standpoint is one from which most British educators of the present day would choose to survey the education of our own and other countries. We feel in reading the book that we are dealing with live problems, not with mere information. Not that we cannot get information more easily from the book than from other sources. The fact that there is much about American education which we could not obtain from the Report of the Moseley Commission is evidence enough on this score. Many readers, too, will gather information in a compact form from this book which they would previously have had to seek with greater labour from the Special Reports of the Board of Education. Its use is twofold ; its tables and details will make it a valuable book of reference to persons engaged in solving particular problems of organization ; while the reader who wishes to form a clear view as to the outstanding differences of aim and method in the systems of the six nations can find his need satisfied by a rapid reading which will omit such details.

Though it is not over-emphasized, one of the conclusions which forces itself more and more on the reader as he proceeds is that the nation which desires a good education must be prepared to pay for it. The articles on France and Germany leave the impression that efficiency has come rather in spite of centralization and elaborate control than because of them. The French and Germans were in earnest ; thence sprang the willingness to pay, the social prestige attaching to the teacher, and the control ; and the former advantages have outweighed the last-mentioned hindrance. If this be a true interpretation, Anglo-Saxons have been on the wrong tack for the last two decades ; they have been trying to imitate the bad result of the enthusiasm, and neglected both the enthusiasm itself and its good results. Fortunately our innate dislike of government control has acted as a brake. But we were always thinking that the success of other nations must be due to some quality which we could never possess, and such a quality was docility. Enthusiasm, generosity, respect were not foreign to our nature ; therefore we did not realize that what we needed was to expend these feelings on education.

Except in the article on France, Universities are not treated ; the exception is due to the fact that university teachers in France are selected from the pick of teachers in the *lycées*. The article on Denmark is mainly included in order to familiarize English-speaking readers with the Danish folk-schools. We doubt whether the Englishman is sufficient of a humanist for any exact counterpart of these schools to be possible ; the W.E.A. appears to be the English equivalent, but differs because for the last hundred years politics have furnished the British working-man with his primary intellectual interest. Wales, with the popular love of music and the national literature and antiquities, may produce a much closer approximation.

With these two exceptions the account of the systems of the different countries deals mainly with the same topics and in the same order. Perhaps the most striking contrast between nation and nations concerns the relation of elementary and secondary schools. In the United States and Canada, secondary education is superimposed on elementary ; in France and Germany the two are distinct from the beginning. In England we really have the two systems side by side. The former system is democratic ; but unfortunately the latter is more efficient. Can equality of opportunity be attained without lowering the opportunity ? It is interesting to see that Canada, which began by thinking equality everything, is now realizing the more complex nature of the problem. We have lately lived under an equality of food rations ; but we should hardly be content with that as a permanent arrangement.

The reader will probably be struck by the comparative newness of the continuation school. Germany set the pace, but the other nations have not been slow to follow on her heels. To our minds the essential problem which emerges from the account is the supply of teachers, especially for the practical subjects. The article on Germany is instructive on this point. Are we to take an expert and train him as a teacher or to take a teacher and train him as an expert ? Whatever we do, don't let us pretend to teach these subjects unless we have persons who are both teachers and experts to teach them. Probably we should add, to inspect them too. It seems to be realized everywhere that the new pupils will be of secondary school age and accustomed to even more independence than secondary school pupils, and that discipline will have to be on secondary school lines.

The problems to which we have alluded are those which appear to be most pressing from our new point of view inspired by the War. The War has made explicit much that was previously only implicit. We were democratic in a sense but had no clear theory of democracy, except that it meant that every man should have a vote. We now see that a greater approximation to intellectual equality—more than this is of course impossible owing to differences in inherent ability—is an essential means to solve any problem concerned with equality of any kind. The more capacities are equalized, the more will remunerations tend to be equalized. The more judgment is equalized, the safer becomes counting votes as a means of deciding national policy. Education lies at the bottom of social reconstruction. But the competition of the nations will in the future be a competition of brains. Hence we are entering on an era of increased competition between the nations in educational efficiency. Everyone must be nearer the top, but the top must be higher. This book would not have been written exactly as it is before the War, nor would the reader have approached it in the same spirit.   R.L.A.

The Psychology of Special Disability in Spelling. By Leta S. Hollingworth, Ph.D., assisted by C. A. Winford. (vi. +105 pp.). Teachers' College, Columbia University.

THE continuous publication of educational researches by the authorities of Teachers' College is rendering great service to the scientific study of educational problems, not only by the actual additions to knowledge which are made from time to time, but also by the contributions to method which the various volumes present. Even when the results are not startling in their novelty, the statement and analysis of the problem, the review of the literature bearing upon the problem and the objective spirit in which the investigation is conducted are valuable. The particular research before us shows all these qualities, and although it leaves us with the sense of an unsolved problem, one cannot read it carefully without realizing more clearly the complexities involved.

The enquiry concerned a group of children selected from fifth-grade children in a large New York school as being deficient in not more than two school subjects, of which one was spelling. These children were taught spelling systematically and by the use of a great variety of devices to make spelling interesting. The children were studied individually with the object of finding out any physical, temperamental or psychological characteristics which might account for their disability. They were tested for improvement, their failures in spelling were analytically considered—the whole object being of course to remove the causes of failure.

A preliminary investigation into the correlation between Intelligence and spelling capacity led the authors to suggest that this might be high if children were taken *at random*, but that in a group specially selected as theirs was, there is no clear connexion between the two.

Every teacher knows that you may lead a child to spell a word correctly one day, and the next day or the next week, he lapses. This phenomenon was most carefully examined. The children were taught a group of words (25) in December. After the Christmas holidays they were tested in two ways—by dictation and by requiring each word to be recognized in a group of three possible spellings (two of which were wrong), *e.g.*, cashear, cashier, kashier. The same test was repeated a week later, and again three months afterwards— the list having been left entirely out of mind in the meantime. In general they found recognition gave fewer errors than recall in all three tests, but, curiously enough, the ten children who took all three tests made fewer errors in recall in April than they had made in January (72 as against 89). This inquiry was repeated with greater elaboration. Three groups of ten words were learned so thoroughly that a child was only regarded as knowing them when he had written them out five times on five successive days without error. They were then tested for recognition and recall for ten successive weeks. Nine children wrote in all 2,700 words (thirty words ten times each), and made 148 mistakes in recall altogether—only 5.4 per cent. of error. The degree of error was neither progressive nor regular, however. Children would spell one word right nine times out of ten and so on quite ' 'unaccountably." The same general result was true also of recognition, tested very severely this time by putting the right spelling in a group of ten, nine of which were wrong.

An interesting chapter deals with these " unaccountable " errors, which are classed as pure " lapses," due to wandering attention, idiosyncrasies (*e.g.*, persistently writing intrusive letters or adding an *e* to the end of words), &c. Analysis also showed that long words were more often misspelled than short ones, but that all misspelled words showed *some* similarity to the right form. Even the worst spellers would nearly always get the first letter right, and the second and third letters were much oftener right than those which came later in the word. Further inquiry showed that all the children but one tended to misuse the words they could not spell—to know the meaning of a word, to be able to use it rightly seems then to be an element counting in favour of correct spelling. May this not be due to the establishment of a direct " bond " between the auditory verbal image and the writing act, instead of or in substitution for the bond between the usual symbol and the motor response necessary to produce the written word ? As I write at this moment, visual imagery plays no part in the conscious process. Auditory imagery and kinaesthetic imagery precede the written word and determine it in line so to speak with the current of thought which they symbolize. The investigators' analysis of the process of learning to spell stops short of this last step in the process, though it is surely the final mark of efficiency. Whether we get there necessarily by the paths they indicate is at least not certain, and possibly the two or three girls who proved most inaccessible to treatment might have been more successful had they received special training designed to discover a shorter route to the path which must finally be fixed. Oral spelling is a luxury. Spelling at the finger tips is the end to be reached. Some may get there in one way, some in another, and some not at all. This particular aspect of the problem is not discussed here. In spite of this, the research is interesting and suggestive to a degree far greater than it is possible to indicate in a short notice. J. A. G.

Ancient Indian Education. By the Rev. F. E. Keay, M.A. Oxford University Press. (pp. 191). 4/6 net.

A History of Education in Ancient India. By Nogendra Nath Mazumder, M.A., B.T. Macmillan & Co. (pp. vii. + 128).

Mr. Keay truly remarks that " the history of the ancient education of India is to a large extent an unexplored tract." These books do something to remove the reproach, and each in its way shows that the tract is well worth exploring. Though dealing largely with the same matter they do so on very different lines, and so are complementary rather than competitive. Mr. Keay traces the history, describes the educational work in some detail, but treats only briefly, and that in the last chapter, of the principles. On the other hand, Mr. Mazumder lays the chief emphasis on the fundamental conceptions of life and education, and gives much less of the history in the common acceptation of the term. Each book deserves study, but the English reader will do well to begin with Mr. Keay's, where he will find the probably needed explanation of many terms and allusions which the Hindu writer, writing primarily for Hindus, naturally takes for granted.

For all who have control over the schools and universities of India a study of the culture which has been indigenous for over three thousand years should be regarded as essential. Sir W. M. Ramsay is quoted by Mr. Keay as saying : " The ignorant European fancies that progress for the East lies in Europeanizing it " (p. 183), and assuredly English administrative action in organizing elementary schools for Hindus has not avoided that delusion. " If a system is to be evolved for India, it must, while assimilating much that is Western, also gather up what is best and most useful from its own ancient systems and weave them into the complex whole that is being built up " (*Keay*, p. 7).

But it is not only the Indian administrator and teacher who will profit from a study of these books. They have much of value for the modern European student of education. He will find how ancient some of his most cherished " modern " theories really are ; but, far more important, he will be strengthened in his grasp of the ultimate verities by learning that they were as clearly apprehended in the dim past of the East, as they are in our own day and country. On the other hand, another object lesson is given him, and that on an unusually large scale, of the inevitable decay of the external body, when the inner spirit is sterilized. " The ideal of the Hindus was not a life of inaction and contemplation, but the attainment of divine wisdom through a self-controlled and self-active life of action " (*Mazumder*, p. 61), and Mr. Mazumder quotes Hindu texts which he is able so to interpret as to support his contention that " the principal philosophical ideas underlying modern pedagogy are found in the religion and philosophy of the Hindus " (*ib.* p. 65). Among these not the least important is the emphasis laid on discipline conceived as a means of training the will. Doubtless, much of Hindu culture was killed by the Muhammadan invasion, but Mr. Keay gives an interesting through brief account of the attempts of Muhammadan rulers in India to develop culture, a topic excluded from the scope of Mr. Mazumder's work. But, apart from this external cause of decay, increasing formalism and narrow utilitarianism did their evil work, and India —like Greece—finds its golden age of culture and of the education of the young in the past. The great problem now is to secure that the assimilation of what is known as " Western civilization " may not kill the spirit of the culture which was evolved from, expresses, and finds fruitful relations, in the traditional Eastern life, so stable in its essence. It is in a development of Indian culture, not in a substitution for it of European culture, different in origin and in parentage, that the future salvation of India should be sought. As Mr. Mazumder says, " By embracing its *spirit* we shall surely exalt our life and character " (p. 87).

To this needful constructive work each of the books before us makes a valuable contribution, and our one regret in laying them down is that those contributions are not on a larger scale. Even as it is they furnish a conclusive answer to those who deny the practical value of the study of the history of education to men and women who are preparing to take an active part in educational work, whether as teachers or as administrators. J. W.

TRAINING COLLEGE ASSOCIATION.

MORNING SESSION.

Rev. Canon H. WESLEY DENNIS (President) in the Chair.

(1) The minutes of the last Annual General Meeting were read and confirmed.

(2) It was decided to send to the President of the Board of Education the hearty congratulations of the Association on the passing of his Education Bill.

(3) The Annual Report and Cash Statement for 1918 were adopted.

(4) On the motion of Prof. Green it was unanimously resolved :—

"That this meeting heartily approves the proposals of the Executive Committee *re* the working of the Constitution, and welcomes the alteration in the subscription to 7s. 6d."

The following are the proposals referred to :—

(i.) The Treasurer of the Association shall be authorized to pay out of its funds to any member of the Committee who attends a meeting of the Committee and who makes application for such payment, third-class return railway fare between the town in which his college is situated and the place of meeting.

(ii.) In order to meet the additional expenditure that will be incurred through the payment of expenses of the members of the Executive Committee, and possibly in other ways, the rate of annual subscription be increased to 7s. 6d.

(iii.) That in consequence of the above changes a good deal of additional work must in future attach to the Treasurership of the Association, the office of Treasurer and that of Secretary shall not be held by the same person.

The appointment of a part-time Secretary at a salary of £50 is recommended.

(iv.) That besides the Secretary, Assistant Secretaries shall be elected as occasion may require ; but that in order to prevent the official element from being too prominent in the Committee, such Assistant Secretaries shall not be members of that Committee unless they are elected as such.

(5) In accordance with the above, Miss M. B. Synge, 24, Royal Avenue, Chelsea, S.W.3, was appointed Secretary.

The President for 1919 (Miss W. MERCIER) here took the Chair.

(6) On the motion of Rev. V. W. Pearson, the following alterations in the Rules were carried :—

Rule xx. to read : The Officers of the Association shall be a President, a *Vice-President* . . . .

Rule xxi. : All the Officers shall retire at each Annual Meeting, but shall be eligible for re-election. Except in the event of the re-nomination for special reasons of the President, *the Vice-President* shall be elected . . . .

Rule xxii. : The Vice-President (a man and a woman in alternate years), the Treasurer, the Secretary . . .

(7) The following elections for 1919 were declared :—

Vice-Presidents :—Miss A. LLOYD EVANS.

Rev. Canon S. BLOFIELD.

Hon. Treasurer :—Major H. E. GRIFFITHS.

Executive Committee :—

Group I.	Mr. T. RAYMONT (Goldsmiths').
	Mr. H. E. J. CURZON (Goldsmiths').
	Mr. W. P. WELPTON (Leeds University).
Group IIA.	Miss S. M. SMITH (Hereford).
	Miss WALKER (Bingley).
Group IIB.	Rev. V. W. PEARSON (Sheffield City).
	Mr. T. P. HOLGATE (Leeds City).
Group IIIA.	Rev. H. A. BREN (Cheltenham).
	Rev. R. HUDSON (St. Mark's, Chelsea).
	Major H. E. GRIFFITHS (St. John's, Battersea).
	Mr. J. W. JARVIS (St. Mark's, Chelsea).

Group IIIB. Miss M. M. ALLAN (Homerton, Cambridge).
Rev. Canon M. STEVENSON (Warrington).
Miss NOAKES (Whitelands).
Miss G. OWEN (Mather College, Manchester).

(8) A hearty vote of thanks was accorded the President and other outgoing Officers on the motion of Rev. Canon Stevenson and Miss Hawtrey.

(9) The following resolutions were carried, on the motion of Miss Graveson and Dr. White :—

(a) That the T.C.A. be asked to make arrangements for the regular holding of sectional meetings on every subject, or group of allied subjects, included in the T.C. curriculum, these to be in London or elsewhere from time to time as the needs of the subject demand.

(b) That every lecturer in the special subject, being also a member of the T.C.A., be *ipso facto* entitled to attend the sectional meetings in his subject.

(c) That each section be required at one of its meetings to elect not more than twelve members to represent it on occasions when the interests of the special subject are under consideration by the Board of Education or other educational authority ; and that a certain proportion of these twelve resign each year, their places being taken by newly-elected representatives.

(d) That at the Annual Meetings of the T.C.A. a session be reserved for the annual meetings of these Special Subject Sections, these being open meetings or not as the respective sections may decide.

(10) The President then delivered the Presidential Address.

(11) Dates for Meetings were decided upon as follows (Rule xv.) :—
Next Annual General Meeting, January, 1919, in Conference Week.
Ordinary Meetings for 1919 :—Saturday, March 22nd and Saturday, October 25th.

(12) Canon Dennis reported the reply he had received from the Board of Education on the question of Demobilization, and it was decided to send a letter to the Board from the Association asking for full information at once as to the returns of demobilization as regards students.
Rev. R. Hudson and Mr. Henry to draft the letter.

(13) Rev. R. Hudson and Rev. V. W. Pearson brought up their Report on the Teachers' Superannuation Act.
It was decided :—
(1) That this report should be at once referred to the Committee of the Association for them to decide which of the points shall be adopted by the Association.
(2) That the Board be asked to receive immediately a small deputation, so that the views of the Association may be considered before the " Rules " are finally drafted to be submitted to Parliament.
(3) That the Committee consider the question of appointing a small Standing Sub-Committee on " Superannuation " that could deal with such special cases that members like to submit for their opinion ; and that the Board be invited to deal with such Sub-Committee in arriving at a decision to such cases.

(14) An address was given by Mr. George Lansbury on
" Labour Looks at Teachers and the Schools."
A discussion followed in which the President, Rev. V. W. Pearson, Rev. Preb. Hobson, Mr. T. Raymont took part, and a hearty vote of thanks was accorded Mr. Lansbury on the motion of Prof. T. P. Nunn and Miss Dunlop.

(15) The Secretary reported having written to University Day Colleges to inquire whether there are or are contemplated in these Colleges Special Third-year Courses. There were nine replies, mostly in the negative.
It was decided to extend the inquiry to the ordinary Two-year Colleges.

(16) With regard to the proposed B.A. Course for Teachers, the following resolution was passed on the motion of Prof. Nunn and Mr. Curzon :—
" That, in view of the needs of teachers in training for elementary, central and continuation schools, this Association endorses the recommendations to the Senate of the University of London adopted at the Conference recently convened by the Froebel Society, and instructs the Executive Committee to take with reference to the other Universities, such action in the sense of the recommendations as may seem to them desirable."

Teachers' Registration Council,

Representative of the Teaching Profession

(Constituted by Order in Council, Feb. 29, 1912).

———

In accordance with the above Order, a

REGISTER OF TEACHERS

is now maintained by the Council.

———

For Information apply to:

THE SECRETARY, TEACHERS' REGISTRATION COUNCIL,

47 Bedford Square, London, W.C.1.

═══════════

The Journal of

Experimental Pedagogy

AND

Training College Record.

═══════════

THE Journal is published three times a year (March, June, and December). Annual Subscription (3/-) may be sent to the Editor, who will forward post free; or the Journal may be obtained through any bookseller.

A few complete sets of Vols. I, II, and III are still on hand.

Single copies of most back numbers may also be had, either from the Editor or the Publishers.

Vol. 5, No. 2.   June 5th, 1919.

THE STANDPOINT OF EDUCATIONAL PSYCHOLOGY.

(The substance of a lecture delivered before the College of Preceptors.)

By Professor H. BOMPAS SMITH.

THE purpose of the following pages is to urge the importance of developing the science of educational psychology more definitely than heretofore as a special branch of knowledge with aims and methods of its own.

An effort in this direction appears to be demanded in the interests both of educational theory and educational practice. So far as our practice is concerned the present position is far from satisfactory. In spite of all our progress, a very large proportion of the children in our infant, our elementary, and our secondary schools are having their mental life deformed or stunted because their teachers do not understand their needs. The schools need all the guidance and inspiration they can derive from an educational psychology which quickens sympathetic insight into the needs of boys and girls of every age and class. But speaking generally and with some notable exceptions, both teachers and administrators are guided more by unintelligent tradition, unsystematized experience, or unco-ordinated theories than by insight illuminated by scientific knowledge. Similarly, if we consider the average well-meaning parent, we find the same lack of practical understanding. The old system of home-training under which children were told that they should be seen and not heard is breaking down. In many cases discipline has grown lax. But no sound educational tradition has taken the place of that which ruled the homes in which our parents were brought up. Among the many problems which confront our time few are more urgent than that of establishing an educational tradition both in our homes and in our schools, as generally accepted as was the tradition now outlived, but more in accordance with our fuller knowledge and the new conditions of our day.

Our present failure to establish the educational tradition of which we stand in need is not due solely to our ignorance of educational psychology. The failure has far deeper causes, which do not concern us here. Nevertheless, one source of weakness is the comparatively small influence which psychology has so far exerted outside a relatively narrow circle, and our hope for the future must include the diffusion of an effective acquaintance with psychological facts and laws. For while a sound educational tradition will be primarily the fruit of a serious effort on the part of parents and teachers to sympathize with and understand their children, this effort will be successful only if it is enlightened by thought and knowledge. It is here that psychology can help, provided that it is a psychology specifically adapted for the purpose. In the form of a reasoned body of knowledge it will be the possession of the few, but any great system of knowledge affects the outlook and the practice of many to whom its scientific basis is unknown. In this way an educational psychology, embodying a definite standpoint and developed in close touch with life, will under favourable conditions give rise to an educational tradition accepted by the great body of intelligent parents, teachers, and administrators. Moreover, we must not underrate the possibility of spreading among a large section of the community some acquaintance with technical psychology. We know how keen is the response of teachers and students, and also of working-class and other parents, to any reasonable attempt to expound an educational psychology which appeals directly to their interest in their children.

The success of these attempts to expound a true educational psychology is full of promise for the future, but at present it forms a striking contrast to the more general failure of educational psychology as currently understood to give us the inspiration and the knowledge we require. This comparative failure I attribute largely to the fact that the educational psychology of many text-books and some Training Colleges is educational in name but not in deed. It is rather general psychology with an educational bias, or with educational applications and examples. But the educational psychology for which I plead will be a real branch of the science of education. Its purpose will be to develop our insight into our children's minds because such insight is essential if we are to educate them aright. It must therefore be organically connected with the science of education as a whole.

And further, such a development of educational psychology is as needful for educational science as it is for educational practice. Our theory no less than our practice requires that the sympathetic insight into our children's minds, which is the natural gift of all true teachers in the home and in the school, should be deepened and enlightened by psychological knowledge. But the psychology which will serve this purpose must be definitely developed with this specific aim. It must help us to understand our boys and girls as growing human persons. It must not deal with mental processes as such, but with the value of mental processes as elements in concrete human lives. Moreover, it must view these mental processes not merely as given facts but also as modifiable, so that their value may be increased. Thus a boy's telling of a lie must not merely be explained, we must also know how its repetition can be prevented.

In the sequel I shall try to give more precision to the point of view thus indicated, but before doing so we must meet an objection which, if it could be sustained, would cut away the ground beneath our feet. The distinction you are drawing, I may be told, is altogether illegitimate. Psychology, whether educational or other, is still psychology, of which the aim is the pursuit of truth and not the edification of your boys and girls. Any admixture of extraneous motives will result in a hybrid compound, which is neither scientifically valid nor practically useful.

This objection has a value as a protest against any relaxation of scientific rigour, but it is based upon an inadequate conception of logical methods. It is not possible to discuss the question fully,[1] but I must be content to indicate the general line of argument by which the objection may be met. The objection apparently assumes that there are certain objective facts which it is the sole purpose of science to discover. Any other motive is illegitimate and must be excluded. This assumption, however, is mistaken, for three reasons. First, we cannot dissociate facts from the mind that knows them. Facts have

[1] I may refer to Joachim: *Nature of Truth*, p. 104 ff, and Baldwin: *Thought and Things*, vol. III, chap. v, among other writers, for fuller discussions of the points at issue.

no meaning except as objects of knowledge. A science is a systematic effort to know, or more generally to appreciate, some aspect of reality. This effort is the expression of some interest in that aspect of reality ; it therefore seeks to know or appreciate it from a definite point of view. The meaning of reality, e.g., of a group of mental processes, is inexhaustible, and aspects of this meaning may become the subject matter of different sciences, or different branches of one science. There may legitimately be a science of educational as well as of " pure " psychology. Secondly, facts are not isolated things which can be learned one by one. A fact depends for its meaning upon the whole context to which it belongs. Hence no judgment is in any valuable sense true in and by itself. Its degree of truth is determined by its place in a whole system of knowledge. If I say " ' a ' is ' b,' " my statement is worthless except as an element in a train of inference involving, at any rate, some acquaintance with the meaning of " a " and " b." Our critic's objective facts are therefore fictions if they are conceived as separate and unchanging entities. Thirdly, no science deals merely with existence as distinct from value. Even when a science, such as pure mathematics, is concerned with truths in abstraction from their value for practical life, there is always an appreciation of the worthwhileness of the investigation which would otherwise never be undertaken. And, as we see in the historical development of any science, the sense of value which leads to the pursuit of knowledge may be a sense of the value of this knowledge for some practical purposes. Such a practical interest need not and ought not to detract from the logical rigour of the science, but it may determine the field in which logic is applied. The science will aim at being, within its proper limits, a coherent whole, but that whole will not be the same as it would be if the practical interest were not present. We may, for instance, compare pure mathematics and engineering. The illegitimate procedure is to take over the selection of material and the detailed methods of one branch of science, and force them into the service of some distinct but kindred interest, without effecting the modifications which are required. This course is, however, frequently adopted in the case of educational psychology, which is treated as a mere sub-division of general psychology, instead of a relatively independent branch of knowledge with its own special interest and point of view.

It follows, therefore, that we need not be deterred by theoretical considerations from endeavouring to develop an educational psychology which shall be the scientific embodiment of our interest in understanding and sympathizing with our children. We must now attempt a more definite description of the standpoint which such a psychology will adopt. But here we must confess that our discussion can only be very tentative. The science of educational psychology which I have in mind is still in its early stages, and its point of view will grow clearer and more comprehensive with each fresh advance. But with this explanation I will for the sake of brevity dogmatically enumerate some of the principles upon which educational psychology ought in my opinion to be based.

The first principle is that of Value. As we have seen, we shall fix our attention on mental processes not merely as objective facts, like the phenomena of natural science, but upon the value of these processes for the boy's mental life.

The second principle is that of Growth. We shall view the boy's mind as a growing organism, and measure the value of mental processes by their function in promoting or retarding growth.

The third principle is that of Mental Unity. Growth we shall regard as progress towards completer coherence and harmony of mind.

The fourth principle is that of Freedom. It is by the boy's own self-determination that the growth in unity and value can be accomplished.

The fifth principle is that of Reality. It is by actual concrete experience, by the appreciation of various aspects of reality, that this freedom can be gained and exercised.

The sixth principle is that of Individuality. Each boy and girl is a unique personality, and must be known as such.

The last principle is that of Experience. Our science must explain and develop our actual experience of education at its best, and must stand the test of that experience.

These principles do not exhaust the characteristic features of our science, but they indicate the point of view from which its subject-matter will be approached.

It will have been noticed that in stating these principles I have assumed that education deals primarily with individual boys and girls. It would take too long to justify this assumption, so I will employ the simple method of assertion and say that all educational problems, whether of teaching, discipline, administration, or social organization and culture, depend ultimately for their solution upon the right treatment of boys and girls as persons.

Now, my criticism of our current educational psychology is that it is not always sufficiently inspired by an educational interest. It therefore tends to disregard the principles we have mentioned as embodying this interest. I cannot justify this criticism at length, but I will illustrate the common failure of educational psychology to do justice to the principle of Value, or, in other words, its tendency to concentrate attention upon mental processes as such and not upon their significance for the boy's whole mental life.

This tendency affects both the selection of material and the mode of treatment. Thus, for example, one popular textbook of considerable merit, after a preliminary chapter, discusses the relations of mind and body, distinguishes cognition, feeling, and conation, and then gives chapters on sensation and perception. A short chapter on imagination is followed by three long chapters on ideation, after which comes memory, then discussions of conation, instinct, the sentiments and will, and finally two chapters on attention. That such topics treated in this order may be the right ones for a treatise on pure psychology I do not here dispute. But they seem to me inappropriate in a book for teachers. The centre of interest should be the active, living, growing boy, with his main concrete interests, his mental struggles, his self-determination, his widening outlook; not an analysis of abstract mental processes with applications to class-teaching. I presume that the un-educational character of much educational psychology has been one reason why American Training Colleges have come to abandon their courses in psychology altogether. Whether this action is justified or not, it is at any rate significant.

Further, this failure to appreciate the principle of Value has led educational psychology to deal mainly with questions of instruction or àdministration, instead of coming to grips with the central problem of gaining insight into the boy's life as a whole. A proof of this tendency may be found in almost any list of new books on educational psychology. By far the larger number deal with such questions as I have mentioned. The work they represent is of very great importance, but to suppose that it will of itself suffice to give us a true educational psychology seems to me as mistaken as it would be to imagine that experiments with pigments will enable a man to paint a noble picture. Again, illustrations of the intellectualist or class-room bias of much current educational psychology might be drawn from almost any text-book. There are some notable exceptions, but as a rule such books seem still to suffer from the tradition that the teacher does little else than give instruction.

Further, the comparative disregard of the value of mental processes leads too often to superficiality of treatment, and superficial treatment is rarely of much practical utility. Consider, for example, two typical problems of extreme importance. The first is, how are we to help a boy who has little determination to develop strength of will? The second problem may be thus stated : Most men's morality and religion are largely a reproduction of a traditional system. But this system is breaking down. How are we to avoid intellectual and moral anarchy? At present the elementary schools hardly introduce their boys to any effective system of belief and conduct. The secondary schools tend to perpetuate the traditional system. What changes do we need?

It is obvious that psychology cannot of itself provide an answer to these and similar problems, but it ought, at any rate, to give us some of the data upon which our answers may be founded. It will not do this by vague generalities about the training of character and the like, but only by the systematic investigation of concrete facts in the light of a definite conception of the problems to be solved. Our educational psychology must consciously assume definite conceptions of the value and end of life, of the nature of society, and the like. Unfortunately, too many books fail to deal with any concrete problems other than superficial ones of teaching and class management, and seem quite unconscious of the deeper issues everywhere at stake.

These criticisms of some features of traditional educational psychology may give rise to the impression that I am advocating a quite new departure. On the contrary, the changes I desire are in the direct line of recent psychological advance, and an educational psychology based upon the principles we have laid down will, I believe, be more in harmony with the best thought on the subject than the traditional form of educational psychology can ever be. The static, descriptive, purely analytical psychology, Dr. McDougall tells us, is giving place to a dynamic, functional, voluntaristic view of mind, and it is just such a view of mind that is assumed in the educational psychology I am demanding.

The close connexion of our reformed educational psychology with the advance McDougall describes may be illustrated by considering the debt which our psychology will owe to the progress which has been made in other branches of psychology.

We may take first the line of investigation known as Child Study, in which so much valuable work has been done in recent years.

It may, indeed, have seemed as if my description of educational psychology were really a description of an enlarged and glorified Child

Study, and to a certain extent I should be prepared to accept this view. Among the characteristic methods of educational psychology will be the careful and systematic observation of individual boys and girls or of small groups of children, and this is the method of which Child Study has taught us the importance. Moreover, many of the results which Child Study has attained will certainly be incorporated in our science. I may mention, for example, the light that has been thrown upon the characteristics and significance of various periods of physical and mental growth. I have not, however, given the name of Child Study to the science we are discussing mainly for two reasons. First, Child Study, as usually understood, is concerned chiefly with young children ; and, secondly, Child Study tends to be too empirical for our purpose. It has probably been wise in confining itself mainly to the collection of data, and has been less active in investigating underlying principles. For this reason it has never been regarded as in itself a satisfactory substitute for a more general study of the mind, and since for educational psychology the scientific evaluation of mental processes is of primary importance, Child Study in its present form is inadequate for our needs. If the term were given a wider connotation, a good deal might be said for its adoption.

A second branch of psychological research from which an important contribution may be expected is that of psycho-analysis. I am not suggesting that teachers as a body should become psycho-analysts in the technical sense. Such a consummation is both impossible and, in my opinion, highly undesirable. I mean rather that psycho-analytic methods in the hands of Freud and his co-workers have thrown important light upon the nature of our mental processes, and that their point of view and many of their results are of great significance for educational psychology. The validity of the detailed theories which these investigators have propounded need not be here discussed. We may hold that many of their interpretations are inadequate or misleading, and yet welcome the light they have thrown upon the effects produced by mental processes of which the mind itself is quite unconscious. We may also regard the greater precision given to our conceptions of mental conflict, symbolism and other mental mechanisms as an important gain to science. Moreover, the work of psycho-analysts has a special significance for our purpose in that it emphasizes and applies our principle of Value. Instead of treating mental processes in relative isolation, these processes are considered largely in their bearing upon mental health, and mental health, again, is viewed mainly from the standpoint of mental unity. In this way the attitude of psycho-analysis towards mental phenomena is very similar to that of the educational psychology I advocate. It is true that psycho-analysis has so far been concerned primarily with medical psychology, and that much of its literature is more suitable for doctors than for teachers. A good deal remains to be done before its potential value for education can be realized. That this value is very great has been shown by the educational writings of Pfister, Ernest Jones, and other psychoanalysts, and the tendency to speak of the aim of psychiatry as re-education is evidence that the two branches of psychology are likely to be brought into still closer relations with each other.

Psycho-analysts, however, are not alone in emphasizing the organic or vital unity of mind. This mode of treatment is common to psychological writers belonging to many schools. Whether we call our psychology genetic or functional or social, we are coming more and more to deal with living human beings and less with abstract mental processes and abstract mental laws. Just as the old classical political economy has been transformed into a more human science, so the purely analytical psychology is giving place to a deeper and more concrete view of mental happenings. The prominence now given to instinct and emotion is only one among many indications of the change which is taking place.

As a third illustration of the help which educational psychology may gain from recent psychological researches, I may mention the interesting results obtained by Ach and others in their experimental investigations of the act of willing. They have, for instance, shown us the importance of the sense that it is we ourselves who are effectively active when we make a voluntary decision. They have suggested the possibility of forming so strong an association between will and deed that the transition from the act of resolving to the practical carrying out of our resolve may insensibly become almost automatic. They have taught us the significance of determining tendencies, and latent adaptations. I cannot discuss the educational applications of these and similar doctrines, but I think they provide us with a starting-point from which we may hope to develop a system of training character based upon a clearer insight into the processes involved.

These illustrations will, I hope, be enough to show that our principles of Value, Mental Unity, and Freedom are in harmony with the present position of psychological thought. It would be possible similarly to illustrate the way in which our other principles are endorsed by psychological research. I cannot, however, linger over this point in my argument, and will only suggest in passing that the general point of view we are considering appears to be consonant not simply with the accepted doctrines of psychology, but also with some of the most characteristic tendencies of contemporary thought. We seem to be passing beyond a merely mechanistic or analytical view of life, and to be substituting more organic and teleological conceptions. We can trace this movement, for instance, in biology and also in philosophy. To give one example only, the idea of value has assumed a new prominence in the writings of philosophers, to whatever school of thought they may belong. "At the present day," says Prof. Pringle-Pattison, "philosophical discussion is carried on more explicitly in terms of value than at any previous time." I do not imply that because a view is fashionable it is necessarily true, but the fact that our point of view represents in its special field tendencies which are making themselves thus widely felt may legitimately encourage us to pursue our investigations.

Our argument so far has been mainly concerned with prolegomena. We have provisionally indicated some of the general principles by which educational psychology should be inspired. We have criticized the traditional presentation of the subject. We have reminded ourselves of some of the resources upon which we may draw in our efforts to build up a more coherent and effective science. The next step would logically be to sketch the form which this science should assume. Such a sketch, however, I cannot here attempt. I can only illustrate the mode of treatment which appears to be demanded by drawing some general deductions from the principles of Value and Mental Unity. My suggestions will be obviously and confessedly provisional, though for the sake of brevity I shall dogmatically state conclusions which have taken shape in my own mind. My aim is to give possible examples of a point of view, not to lay down conclusions to be accepted as they stand.

In order to give a more definite shape to our principle of Value, it will be convenient to raise two questions. First, how are we to tell whether a mental process is valuable or not? And, secondly, what is the source or ground of the value we thus recognize?

Our answer to the first question will be derived from the general observation that a mental process is always an element in some interest. By an interest I mean a mental attitude or activity directed towards making some felt potential value actual. I look at a picture because I feel that the picture has some beauty or meaning of which the appreciation is worth while. My looking is an element in my interest in the picture. I achieve my interest in the picture when I identify myself with the active attitude which is my interest in it. Now this achievement of an interest, this realization of some potential value, is normally accompanied by a sense of satisfaction, and we may take this sense of satisfaction as the sign that the interest does in fact make some potential value actual, or we may say is itself valuable. We must add, without discussing the point in detail, that the satisfaction must be permanent and not merely fleeting, to be followed, e.g., by remorse. We conclude, then, that we know a mental process to be valuable when it is an element in an interest of which the achievement is accompanied by permanent satisfaction.

A point to be noted in passing is the relation between satisfaction and success. If my interest is in the appeasement of my hunger, success is clearly essential to my satisfaction. But in the case of what I may vaguely call the higher interests, achievement and the resulting satisfaction do not depend upon success. A mother achieves her interest in her child by nursing it through a fatal illness. "Beatudo," says Spinoza, "non est virtutis præmium sed ipsa virtus."

Before dealing with our second question, I will say a few words about the general attitude of mind to which this conception of value corresponds. It would lead the school to find its main purpose in the development of keen interests in worthy ends; to encourage freedom in the sense of self-determination; to place endeavour above success—

> To set the cause above renown,
> To love the game beyond the prize.

And this attitude surely is in accordance with our best experience.

So far we have been speaking of the test by which the value of an interest or mental process can be known. We come now to our second question: In what does the value thus known consist? My answer is that an interest is valuable in so far as its achievement is the realization by the mind of its own potential value, or, we may say, in so far as it promotes the mind's development in unity, comprehensiveness, and strength, the distinction between these two questions and their answers is one of considerable theoretical and practical importance. It saves us from the necessity of basing our valuation upon subjective feeling. An interest gives us permanent satisfaction because it is itself valuable. It is not valuable because it gives us satisfaction. Similarly in practice it leads us, for example, to try and make our lessons valuable in the confidence that they will then be interesting, and not to think in the first place of how interesting we can make them. At the same time, the test of a good lesson will be the interest it arouses.

In order to simplify the discussion, I shall assume that an interest is valuable when it tends to promote mental unity, omitting the other aspects of mental growth. The achievement of an interest promotes mental unity if two conditions are fulfilled. First, the interest itself must be a true interest of the whole self, including, e.g., its nisus towards perfection; and secondly, the whole of the self must be identified with this interest. Suppose, e.g., I begin to read a book. The book may be a novel and distract me from my proper work. In that case my interest in it is not a true interest of my whole self. Or the book may be one I ought to read, but I look at it half-heartedly. In that case I do not identify my whole self with my interest. There is no sovereign specific for securing that the interests which a boy achieves should be the interests of his true self. Whatever enthusiasts for certain methods may assert, there are not Morison's Pills in education. But educational psychology ought to throw light upon the character of the interests stimulated by specific types of school organization and discipline, or by specific methods of teaching and subjects of instruction. Here, however, I cannot enter upon this fruitful field, but must be content to summarize some general considerations.

In the first place, then, an interest cannot be a true interest unless its object is felt or appreciated as real. An interest is always an interest in the value of its object, and an object without reality can have no value. Ultimately, I suppose, an object is real for us just in so far as we appreciate its value, actual or potential, but its objective reality is felt to be the condition of its value. It is because the objects of our interest are not our own creation, but have in a sense an independent being of their own, that we can take an interest in them.

This principle is of great importance for our teaching and education generally, and it is also fundamental for our point of view. Our mental life is not self-centred, and it can develop only by contact with realities recognized as not ourselves.

The more obvious educational applications of this principle are familiar, but have not always been rightly understood. We may emphasize the importance of things as compared with words, of the concrete before the abstract, of example rather than precept; but we must remember that words, abstract ideas, and precepts may have meanings which are intensely real, while material things gain reality and meaning only in so far as they are elements in a more inclusive world, objects of affection, for example, or of scientific knowledge, or of æsthetic appreciation.

But the principle of Reality has a wider application. We must abandon the idea that mental training can be given otherwise than by bringing boys into contact with real things, real persons, real facts, and problems. I believe that one source of our social and intellectual troubles is the fact that our culture is primarily a culture characteristic of brain-workers and not of hand-workers also. Our thought therefore tends to lack a basis of concrete reality. Hence, for instance, our general weakness in æsthetic appreciation and our bondage to officialism. On the other hand, a large proportion of our people who deal chiefly with concrete things (e.g., the manual workers), are cut off from a culture which is alien to their modes of thought and feeling. This state of things the schools must help to cure.

Again, an interest is always an interest in an object as an element in a larger whole. We know things in their relations, and the same principle holds good also of our feelings and our actions. I may refer to the investigations of Külpe and his co-workers for experimental evidence that our minds deal always with wholes of related objects, with complexes, as this school understands the term. And further, our system of interests as a whole finds its counterpart in an environment of which we are constantly endeavouring to appreciate the coherence. The world of our experience we feel must be ultimately one. It follows that if an interest is to be an interest of our whole self, its object must be implicitly appreciated as an element in a comprehensive unity. Here I can only indicate this general point of view without illustrating it in detail or discussing its difficulties and limitations. It is, however, interesting to note that the old conception of the unity of knowledge has lately been emphasized afresh in educational literature. " There is only one subject-matter of education," says Dr. Whitehead, " and that is Life in all its manifestations."

The moral for our schools and universities is the need to avoid the narrow academic spirit, and teach and think in terms of the great human interests. Further, since the object of an interest must be appreciated as real, our interest must do justice to each of the three ways in which reality is experienced—by thought, emotion, and conation. Each interest, that is, must have cognitive, affective, and conational elements. This principle is a commonplace, but we do not always realize how greatly our culture, our social order, and our individual lives now suffer from the too frequent divorce, both in different social classes and in individual minds, between knowledge and emotion or conation. This weakness is reflected in our schools, and our psychology should point the way to its removal.

Again, since an interest aims always at the appreciation of the value of its object, our whole system of interests, and within limits each separate interest, must lead to an appreciation of the three types or aspects of value which we find in our environment. Speaking roughly, we may say that any object of an interest has for us a personal, a social, and an objective value, each of which implies the others. Take, for example, a boy's interest in playing football. His interest, in so far as it is achieved, involves a realization of the value of the game from three points of view. First, the game is of value to him personally. It satisfies some of the demands of his own life. He enjoys the game, for instance, and feels the better for it in body and in mind. Secondly, the game is of value in itself apart from any benefit he may derive. The game is part of the school's life or of a social order. In particular, it is valuable for people other than himself. Thirdly, the game has value as a symbol or embodiment of the ideal. " Games," says a wise schoolmaster, " have in a boy's eyes certain high-spirited affinities which are missed by our older selves. In his inner thought they have a sacred character, just as with primitive man, and this is the cause of his deep seriousness on the subject." He feels that every deed of pluck or cowardice, every unselfish pass or wrongful keeping of the ball, is an act done in the sight of heaven, an act of loyalty or treason to its laws. We have still much to learn about the relations between these three types of value, but I believe that the recognition of their importance will save us from some of the dangers into which educational reform is apt to run. It will save us, for instance, from exaggerating the personal aspect of value, as Mr. Edmund Holmes apears to me to do, or from laying too exclusive a stress upon the objective or social aspect, like, for example, Professor Dewey. It will also help us to solve such problems as that previously mentioned, the substitution of what we may call in Calvinistic language experimental morality and religion for the mere acceptance of tradition.

Such are some of the considerations which we must bear in mind if we are to help our boys and girls to develop interests which shall be interests of their whole selves. We come now to the second of our two conditions of mental unity, namely, that the whole self must be identified with the interest it is achieving. With this part of my subject I have left myself with but little time to deal. Not because I consider it unimportant—I believe its importance is difficult to exaggerate—but because it has seemed impossible to treat it at all adequately within the limits of my paper. The great weakness of our lives is surely due, not to the lack of the right interests, but rather to our failure to devote ourselves whole-heartedly to the interests we approve. We do not love the good with all our hearts and with all our minds and with all our strength. Consider, for example, the double-mindedness which comes from worry or from fear. The Freudian doctrine of mental conflict has thrown much light upon the causes to which this double-mindedness is due, but I can only refer to this branch of our science as one which will take a foremost place in the educational psychology we desire.

Here I must end my attempt to illustrate the standpoint of educational psychology. Upon the details of my discussion I lay no stress. As I have already said, any forecast of our science must be in a high degree provisional. It is the underlying attitude of mind which seems to me of importance. It is this attitude which must find expression in a wise and healthy educational tradition, and for this reason amongst others must be embodied in a real science of educational psychology.

In many departments of our common life we are faced by a lack of harmony between science and daily life, between our intellectual interests and other fundamental human needs. Our theology does not always correspond to our religion, nor our political economy to our social aspirations. Our industrial methods are not always scientific, nor have our artistic theories completely beautified our homes. It was no doubt essential that our interest in knowledge should be developed in relative independence of other equally-important motives, and that science should, in the first instance, be the possession of the few. But this phase is not the final one, and we are now called upon to solve the problem of restoring unity to our individual and our social life by making our scientific interest an organic element in our system of interests as a whole. Towards the solution of this problem progress is being made in many fields, but such progress must be effected largely by education. Hence, education is more especially bound to put its own house in order. If education is to help to save our nation, our strong interest in our children's welfare must be guided and enlightened by educational science, while that science in its turn must live not only in the study or the laboratory, but also in the people's homes and schools. It must become more truly scientific by growing more broadly human. It is towards this transformation of educational psychology that I have tried to make a tentative contribution.

THE DEVELOPMENT OF REASONING IN SCHOOL CHILDREN.—I.

By CYRIL BURT, M.A.

THE tests appended to this article were devised for two purposes: first, to ascertain the mode in which the reasoning capacities of children develop from year to year; secondly, by means of their reasoning capacities, to estimate the level of general intelligence among older or brighter children attending ordinary elementary schools.

The latter problem forms the subject of the first portion of this article. Whatever may be thought of the commoner mental tests as measurements of capacity or deficiency among the young, the dull, or the defective, they are beyond question unsatisfactory for measuring the abilities of children in the upper standards or classes. No one could award junior county scholarships by means of the Binet scale. In an earlier paper in this *Journal*, I reported a series of experiments which seemed to show that "of all the tests proposed for this purpose, those involving higher mental processes, particularly those involving reasoning, vary most closely with intelligence."[1] This conclusion is in harmony with results more recently described by other investigators in this country, in America, and elsewhere.[2] Those who originally proposed to measure intelligence by means of simple sensory tests— such as the discrimination of weight, of pitch, or of touch, or by means of simple motor tests, such as tapping or reaction-time experiments— have ceased to maintain that these elementary processes have a high diagnostic value. Tests of more complex mental processes are almost universally preferred. With the exception, however, of one or two more elementary forms, reasoning processes are still undervalued or ignored.

Of the reasoning tests described in my earlier article, perhaps the most promising was that termed "the syllogism test." Superficially, this test would seem to involve reasoning in its most typical and familiar form. Yet the simpler test which I designated "Analogies" has been far more extensively preferred.[3]

[1] "Experimental Tests of Higher Mental Processes," *Journal Exp. Ped.*, 1911, Vol. I, No. 2, p. 101. cf. also "The Experimental Study of General Intelligence," "Address to the Manchester Child Study Society," October, 1909, published in *Child Study*, Vol. IV, Nos. 2 and 3. See especially p. 93 *et seq*.

[2] See, for example, Wyatt and other references cited in the following note.

[3] S. Wyatt and W. Vickers, "Grading by Mental Tests," this *Journal*, Vol. II, No. 3, 1913, p. 195 (gives sample tests). Also S. Wyatt, "The Quantitative Investigation of Higher Mental Processes," *British Journal of Psychology*, 1913, Vol. VI, Pt. 1; cf. p 116-130. R. S. Woodworth and F. L. Wells, "Association Tests." Psychological Monographs, No. 13, 1911 (gives a standardized procedure). M. E. Bickersteth, "The Application of Mental Tests to Children," *Brit. Journ. Psychology*, 1917, Vol. IX, Pt. 1; cf. p. 45 (gives norms for different ages).

The test has been embodied in revisions of the Binet scheme, e.g., in Yerkes's Point Scale and in Otis's Absolute Point Scale for Group Measurements (*Journ. Educ. Psychol.* 1918, Vol. IX, Nos. 5 and 6; cf., p. 242). It is also inserted in the second edition of Whipple's *Manual of Mental and Physical Tests* (Test 34a, Vol. II, pp 89-94; perhaps the best description of procedure and results). Sheets containing stimuli, selected from those originally employed by Mr. Moore and myself in the Liverpool experiments, can be purchased from Messrs. C. H. Stoelting & Co., of Chicago. A defect, however, in the earlier test-sheets is that the fourth term can often be guessed from the third without looking at the first two. This can usually be remedied by merely re-arranging the order of stimulus-words. The Analogies test has been used upon an extensive scale in the test-series devised for examining recruits for the American Army. Two modifications have been introduced. First, instead of a blank space for the answer to be written in by the examinees, three or four alternative answers are printed, one of which has to be marked as correct—a modification comparable to that found desirable in the case of the Syllogisms test; in the second form, used for foreign or illiterate examinees, the stimuli are presented in pictorial form instead of in words—a modification to that described below in the case of both Syllogisms and Absurdities tests.

For those interested in the comparative merits of the tests in question, I may add that in a recent investigation I tested several groups of school children with the Inferences test appended, with Analogies, with Completion and Absurdities, in both verbal and pictorial forms, and found that although the reliability and intelligence correlations furnished by the Analogies were high, those furnished by the present test were almost invariably higher.

It is true that the latter furnished higher correlations, both for reliability and for intelligence. But, as was noted in the course of the original experiments, the procedure adopted with the former left considerable room for improvement. "If," it was observed, "we allow for the unreliability of the method, the intelligence coefficient would become one of the highest of all."[1]

Further experience has corroborated this estimate of the high value of brief logical arguments and inferences as tests of intelligence. Various modifications, however, have proved necessary, both in the material and in the form of the test-questions. Before renewing the inquiry, a great variety of the problems were collected and tried out upon preliminary groups of children. In compiling this initial list an endeavour was made to construct examples illustrating all the more important types of logical fallacies and inferential principles; and at the same time to avoid any problem depending for its solution upon specific information outside the scope of the children tested. Where school knowledge is required—for example, familiarity with the points of the compass, or with simple arithmetical computation—this should be always well below the level of the weakest child upon whom the test is likely to be tried.

The problems printed at the end of this paper are samples of the more satisfactory types. The questions retained are graded roughly in order of difficulty. An attempt has been made to select from the most satisfactory tests six for each mental age from seven to fourteen. The addition of one or two extra for the higher and lower ages brings up the number in the entire series to fifty questions.

The whole investigation has involved three sets of experiments. First, the initial collection consisting of 250 questions was set to miscellaneous groups of children and adults, with a view to arranging them in order of difficulty, and incidentally eliminating obscurity and ambiguity in phraseology. Secondly, sections of the entire series were given to complete age groups, to determine which could be answered by approximately fifty per cent of the children at each age, and incidentally to observe which questions were on the whole answered successfully by the brightest members, and unsuccessfully by the duller. Thirdly, the final list was given to median children in median schools to determine more precisely the norm for each age, and to entire age-groups to determine the standard deviations.

The results of the experiments provide a rough, schematic picture of the development of the reasoning capacities of an average sample of London children. To make this picture more definite the list appended is subdivided into sections which are assigned successively to the various ages from seven to fourteen. The assignment of any one section does not imply that the problems it contains are peculiarly appropriate to the year specified; but merely that between forty and sixty per cent of a random sample of London school children at that age may be expected to solve them. Unless the child is behind or ahead of the average of his fellows, the preceding problems are well within his power, and the succeeding problems well beyond it. The reader who has in mind the development of "the normal child" will probably be surprised at the ease of the problems allotted. He should remember that among the elementary schools of a city like London, the large proportion coming from poor and uncultured homes drags the actual mean below the ideal norm.

[1] This *Journal*, loc. cit., p. 101.

The scale is presented merely as a preliminary and illustrative result. Measured in terms of their S.D. values, the increments of difficulty between succeeding tests prove to be more unequal than the preliminary computations suggested. Both in form and in substance, many, if not most, of the problems are still somewhat imperfect. But it is only at the end of a long series of experiments that one discovers exactly the location and the source of such unsatisfactoriness.

· It will be noticed that certain types of subject-matter and certain types of inference tend to recur. This is, indeed, one of the more serious defects. In the original list a variety of types were represented, and several specimens of each type were deliberately included. Contrary to expectation the preliminary trials eliminated all the samples of certain types, and allowed nearly all the samples of certain other types to survive. Perhaps because of its familiarity, perhaps because of its intrinsic interest, or for various other reasons not difficult to conjecture, test matter dealing with geography, with the detection of crime, with simple computations, appeared to give steadier results than many of the other topics originally selected. Forms, too, involving the elimination of alternatives appeared to give steadier results than syllogistic deduction, reasoning as to causes, or generalizing from particulars. These peculiarities are, perhaps, in part the result of limitations in the specimens originally used. But in part they are also due to the nature of the mental processes involved. At first sight it might appear that the perception of some general rule or principle, such as that underlying an algebraic series (cf. tests 40 and 42), or a "law" of chemistry or physics (cf. tests 43 and 50), would constitute an excellent test of intelligence. But even with the brightest child an element of chance is risked in hitting upon a suitable hypothesis, before the reasoning process proper can test that hypothesis by applying it to the premises given. Hence, in brief tests it proves a better maxim of procedure to state explicitly three or four alternative conclusions, and allow the child to select the only one which fits the data.

The test-questions are intended to be given to each child individually and orally. In my own experiments each problem was type-written upon a separate card; a fresh statement commenced on a fresh line; and by means of indentation and spacing, question and premises were distinguished from each other. A card is handed to the child with the following instructions:—"Will you read this little puzzle? There is an easy question at the end. When you have read the question, read carefully again what is printed above, and try whether you can think out the answer." The younger and duller children should read the test-questions aloud; and with the youngest and dullest of all, the examiner should read the questions with or to the child. Children of higher levels (Standard III) need only read aloud the first few questions. Any child who is unable to read a particular word or to comprehend its meaning should be freely helped. The graver incongruities between difficulty of phrase and difficulty of logic have been eliminated. In a perfectly revised list they should never occur. A bright young child is occasionally puzzled by such words as "sub-tropical," and "emotion," although competent to follow the reasoning. When it is clear that the child understands his task, he should be left quietly with the card, forgetful if possible of the examiner's presence. The emotional confusion, the "examination paralysis," that so commonly embarrasses an oral interview is by this means largely avoided. When the child gives an answer, it is invariably received with a word of praise, whether right or wrong; and the child is asked to give his reason.

One mark is given for each test correctly answered and correctly reasoned. Where necessary, the child may be given additional trials, not exceeding three in all for any one test. But for each unsuccessful attempt a quarter of a mark is deducted. A fraction—as a rule, a quarter, a half, or three-quarters respectively—is also deducted for an ill-expressed reason, an inadequate reason, or no reason at all. In the cross-examination as to reasons lies the most valuable part of the test. The examiner gleans considerable information, not only about the knowledge and intellectual procedure of the child, but also about its temperament and disposition so far as they affect his intellectual efficiency. In a final estimate of the child he would take into account both these broader observations, and in particular the speed with which the child has worked. In the actual marking no allowance is made for such latter factors; nor is any time-limit assigned. Could scores be corrected on the basis of the general impressions incidentally gained, the correlations with ability, high as they are, would be still further raised.

For a child to work steadily through a series of fifty reasoning tests until he breaks down would, at any rate, for the brighter and older children, be a slow and fatiguing process. A short series has therefore been constructed by selecting every third test in the full series. The short list thus contains only seventeen questions, two for each age except the first, which has three.

In the full list appended (p. 73 *et seq.*) these selected questions are marked with asterisks. They have been more carefully chosen, more extensively used, and more thoroughly revised. For practical purposes, indeed, the short list will be sufficient, since this allows a rough and rapid determination of mental age. Where, however, it is required to obtain a more exact estimate of a child whose mental level is already approximately known—for example, in testing children within the same school standard—the full list is indispensable, since with the short list no member of a fairly homogeneous class could be expected to differ from the others by more than one or two marks.

Children should be tested with the short list first. Even the oldest and brightest should begin with the easiest test. They should be carried through the series until they have broken down with three consecutive tests. The supplementary questions should be given subsequently, and upon a different day. Here it will be expedient to start, not at the beginning of the series, but about four tests below the level of the first serious failure made on the short list; and the child should be carried through until he breaks down on at least six tests consecutively.

The reliability of the test as now revised is high. If the whole series is, as it were, split lengthwise, and the marks obtained on the even numbers are correlated with those obtained with the odd numbers, the reliability coefficient for children of all ages and standards combined proves to be ·93. The short list correlates with the supplementary list to the extent of ·89,[1] in a group of 108 children of all ages and standards, and to the extent of ·75 to ·78 with the several standards taken separately.[2]

[1] P.e., ± ·01.   [2] P.e. ± ·04 to ·06.

The correlations with intelligence are also high. With separate standards or classes the correlation with intelligence ranges from ·64 to ·78.[1] Here the children are already partly selected for intelligence, and in consequence the correlation must be reduced. With an un-selected age-group, consisting of all the children aged 11 last birthday, the correlations rise to ·81.[2] These coefficients refer to groups numbering about forty to sixty children; and the members in any one group were all taken from the same department and were estimated by the same teacher. It is, however, not sufficiently recognized that a test which furnishes a high correlation with a group attending the same school, living and taught under approximately the same conditions, may have very poor diagnostic value when employed with identical standards or criteria for children in different schools. Speed and quality of handwriting, for example, furnish positive correlations with intelligence so long as the correlation is limited to children from a single department. But it would be impossible to diagnose high ability in one child from school X or mental deficiency in another child from school Y, because the writing of the former surpassed, and that of the latter fell below, the norms obtained in a third school chosen as typical. In this respect the test here described appears satisfactory. Together with other criteria it was used in an oral examination of 243 children aged 10 attending 26 different departments or schools. The children of this age had been tested in a preliminary examination for Junior County Scholarships, and the brighter children were subse-quently tested in the final scholarship examination. The oral examination was conducted by Mr. G. F. Daniell, Chief Examiner for the London County Council, and myself. At each school a certain number of children were interviewed by both examiners to keep the standard of marking equivalent from school to school and from examiner to examiner; all doubtful cases were also interviewed by both; and the child's work during the term and the views of the head teacher and class teacher were at our disposal when required. There were thus unusual opportunities for checking the trustworthiness of the test. The correspondence was excellent. Although the methods of instruction, the standards of the teacher, and the social status of the children varied considerably from school to school, yet the marks obtained in the test correlated very closely with both the written and the oral examinations. The agreement between the results of the test and the final examination appeared high, but the cases were too few for correlation. The correlation with the marks of the preliminary examination was ·79; that with the marks given in the oral examina-tion was ·84.[3]

The test has proved equally satisfactory in examining the vocational aptitude of young adults. Figures will be given elsewhere, when the examination of larger numbers has been completed.

(To be continued.)

---

[1] P.e., ±·04 to ·06   [2] P.e., ±·03.   [3] P.e., ±0·2.

APPENDIX.
GRADED REASONING TESTS.
7 YEARS.

*1. Tom runs faster than Jim: Jack runs slower than Jim. Who is the slowest—Jim, Jack, or Tom?

2. All wall-flowers have four petals: this flower has three petals. Is this a wall-flower?

3. It looks like rain: but I shall stay indoors. Shall I want an umbrella to-day?

*4. Kate is cleverer than May: May is cleverer than Jane. Who is cleverest—Jane, Kate, or May?

5. It is Sunday: and on a Sunday afternoon Ada usually takes the baby out, or goes by herself to the pictures, or walks over to see her aunt, or else goes by tram to the cemetery. To-day she had no money with her: and the baby is asleep upstairs. Where do you think she has probably gone?

6. Tom said to his sisters: "Some of my flowers are buttercups." His sisters knew that all buttercups are yellow. So Mary said: "All your flowers must be yellow." Grace said: "Some of your flowers must be yellow." And Rose said: "None of your flowers are yellow." Which girl was right?

*7. I have bought the following Christmas presents: a pipe, a blouse, some music, a box of cigarettes, a bracelet, a toy engine, a bat, a book, a doll, a walking-stick, and an umbrella. My brother is 18: he does not smoke, nor play cricket, nor play the piano. I want to give the walking-stick to my father and the umbrella to my mother. Which of the above shall I give my brother?

8 YEARS.

8. All great men work hard and long every day: Sir John Smith worked three hours a day. Was Sir John Smith a great man?

9. Peter has a half holiday on Wednesdays and Saturdays, and a whole holiday on Sunday. I am at work all day, except on Monday, Wednesday, Friday, and Sunday. I want to take Peter to the tailor's to buy a new suit. Which afternoon could we go together?

*10. I don't like sea voyages: and I don't like the seaside. I must spend Easter either in France, or among the Scottish Hills, or on the South Coast. Which shall it be?

11. Ethel has twice as many apples as John: Lucy has half as many as John: Lucy has 10. How many has Ethel?

12. Edith is fairer than Olive: but she is darker than Lily. Who is darker—Olive or Lily.

*13. The person who stole Brown's purse was neither dark, nor tall, nor clean-shaven. The only persons in the room at the time were—1. Jones, who is short, dark, and clean-shaven. 2. Smith, who is fair, short, and bearded. 3. Grant, who is dark, tall, but not clean-shaven. Who stole Brown's purse?

9 YEARS.

14. C is smaller than B: and B is smaller than A. Is A greater than C?

15. A burglar entered my room at the Hotel Splendid last night. The windows were all securely fastened on the inside, and the fastenings and the window-panes are undisturbed. The opening up the chimney is only nine inches square. The door opening into the main corridor was locked, and the key left on the outside. The ceiling, walls, and floor have no other openings, either secret or forced, through which he could have entered. How did he get in?

*16. Three boys are sitting in a row: Harry is to the left of Willie: George is to the left of Harry. Which boy is in the middle?

17. If I have more than a shilling I shall either go by taxi or by train: if it rains I shall either go by train or by 'bus. It is raining and I have half-a-crown. How do you think I shall go?

18. On one side of my street the houses all have odd numbers, beginning with the grocer's, which is number one. On the other side, the numbers are even, number two, the baker's, being opposite number one. My house is

number 16. Walter is my next-door neighbour : you pass his house as you come up from the baker's just before you get to mine. What is the number on his door ?

*19. In cold, damp climates, root crops like potatoes and turnips grow best : in temperate climates there are abundant pastures, and oats and barley flourish : in sub-tropical climates, wheat, olives, and vines flourish : in tropical climates, date-palms and rice flourish. The ancient Greeks lived largely on bread, with oil instead of butter : they had wine to drink and raisins for fruit. Which climate do you think they had ?

10 YEARS.

20. Some children were asked : "Why are towns nearly always more un-healthy than the country?" They gave the following replies :—1. "Some country places are by the seaside." 2. "There are more doctors in the towns." 3. "The smoke of the houses and the breath of the people prevents the air from being fresh." 4. "The cottages in the country are dark, tiny, and badly built." 5. "Disease spreads where people are crowded together." Which two children gave the best answers?

21. "Drinking the sea dry." "Catching the wind in a cabbage net." "Gathering grapes from thistles." "Washing a blackamoor white." "Touching the end of a rainbow." All these sayings mean something that is——? (Give the meaning of all of them in one word.)

*22. The doctor thinks Violet has caught some illness. If she has a rash, it is probably chicken-pox, measles, or scarlet fever. If she has been ailing with a cold or cough she may develop whooping-cough, measles, or mumps. She has been sneezing and coughing for some days, and now spots are appearing on her face and arms. What do you think is the matter with Violet ?

23. "I sprang to the stirrup and Joris and he :
     I galloped, Dirck galloped, we galloped all three."
What was the name of the person referred to as "he" in these lines of poetry ?

24. The Duchess of Dustiland's diamonds have been stolen. After the ball at the palace she gave them to her manservant to take home, with instructions to hand them over to her maid at once. When he was half-way home he met a friend, and a few minutes afterwards a man in blue uniform and helmet came up to them and said : "I arrest you for stealing the Duchess of Dustiland's jewels." They were taken to a large building outside which a blue lamp was hanging with the words "Police Station" printed on it. Here another man in uniform took possession of the diamonds, and locked up both the manservant and his friend in a small bare room for the night. When day dawned, hearing nobody about, they climbed out through the window, but could see nothing of either the lamp or policemen. The Duchess is still looking for her jewels. Who do you think was the thief ?

*25. There are four roads here. I have come from the South and want to go to Melton. The road to the right leads somewhere else : straight ahead it leads only to a farm. In which direction is Melton—North, South, East, or West?

11 YEARS.

26. A man was found nearly dead with his throat cut, and on the back of his left arm there was a blood-stained mark of a left hand. The policeman says he tried to kill himself. Do you think the policeman was right ?

27. C is West of B : B is West of A. Is A to the North, South, East, or West of C ?

*28. Father has just come home in a brand new overcoat : there is clay on his boots and flour on his hat. The only places he can have been to are Northgate, Southgate, Westgate, or the City. He has not had time to go to more than one of these. There is no clay anywhere in the streets except where the pavement is up for repair. There are tailor shops only in Southgate, Westgate, and the City. There are flour mills only in Northgate, Westgate, and the City. I know the roads are not being repaired in the City, though they may be in the other places. Where has father been ?

29. The following are some of the occasions on which people shed tears :—People laugh till they cry. When they are very unhappy they weep. A fly in the eye makes the tears flow. Peeling onions, scraping horseradish, going through

smoke, a cold wind in the face—all make the eyes water. These instances suggest two general causes which produce tears. What are they? Choose your answer from the following phrases :—(1) Moderate happiness. (2) Bright colours such as red and green. (3) Germs. (4) Violent emotions. (5) Irritation of the eyeball. (6) A warm temperature.

30. In our school a third of the school play football, and a third play cricket. (1) Are there any who play neither football nor cricket? (2) Are there any who play both? (If it is impossible to tell without asking further, say so.)

*31. Where the climate is hot, aloes and rubber will grow · heather and grass will only grow where it is cold. Heather and rubber require plenty of moisture : grass and aloes will grow only in fairly dry regions. Near the river Amazon it is very hot and very damp. Which of the above grows there?

12 YEARS.

32. My brother writes :—"I have walked over from Byford Wood to-day, where I had the misfortune yesterday to break a limb." Can you guess from this which he probably broke—his right arm, left arm, right leg, or left leg.

33. In the old world the most thickly-populated parts have usually been India, China, and the South and West of Europe. In India and China the rainfall is high in the summer : on the shores of the Mediterranean it is high during the winter : on the shores of the Atlantic it is fairly high all the year round. In the deserts of Russia, Persia and Africa, it is dry all the year round. Africa is very hot : India and China very warm : South and West Europe rather warm : the deserts of Russia cold. What kind of climate seems to have helped the growth of civilization most of all—cold and dry, warm and dry, or hot and dry ; cold and wet, warm and wet, or hot and wet?

*34. Field-mice devour the honey stored by the humble-bees : the honey which they store is the chief food of the humble-bees. Near towns there are far more cats than in the open country. Cats kill all kinds of mice. Where, then, do you think there are most humble-bees—near towns or in the open country?

35. My birthday is on December 27 : and I am just four days older than Tom. This year Christmas Day comes on a Tuesday. On what day of the week is Tom's birthday?

36. If the train is late he will miss his appointment : if the train is not late he will miss the train. We do not know whether the train was late or not. Can we tell whether he kept his appointment?

*37. I started from the Church and walked 100 yards : I turned to the right and walked 50 yards : I turned to the right again and walked 100 yards. How far am I from the Church?

13 YEARS.

38. Explain how the following code is worked :
Message (in code) - - dpnf up Mpoepo bu podf
The same (translated) - come to London at once
What is the secret letter for " x " in this code?

39. Dismal Johnny said to Sunny Jim—"If I marry I shall be miserable, because I shall be bothered with looking after my wife : if I don't marry I shall still be miserable, because I shall have no wife to look after me. So in either case I shall be miserable." Sunny Jim replied—"On the contrary, you ought to be happy in either case ; for, if you do not marry, you will be happy, because you will not be bothered with looking after your wife, and——" How do you think he finished his argument?

*40. A pound of meat should roast for half an hour : two pounds of meat should roast for three-quarters of an hour ; three pounds of meat should roast for one hour : eight pounds of meat should roast for two hours and a quarter : nine pounds of meat should roast for two hours and a half. From this can you discover a simple rule by which you can tell from the weight of a joint how long it should roast?

41. I walked 10 yards down High Street : I turned to the left and walked 15 yards down Thomas Street : I turned to the left again and walked 10 yards down James Street : I turned to the left again and walked 15 yards down another street : I turned to the left again and walked 10 yards down that street : I turned to the left again and walked 5 yards. What street was I in?

42.   1   is 1, that is 1 times 1
    1 & 3   added together are 4, that is 2 times 2
    1 & 3 & 5   added together are 9, that is 3 times 3
    1 & 3 & 5 & 7 added together are 16, that is ————?

Look at the above carefully. Can you see a simple rule for guessing the answers without adding up the figures? Work the following sums yourself : this will help you to find the rule. (i) 1 & 3 & 5 & 7 & 9 added together are——, because this is——times——. (ii) What do the first seven odd numbers (1, 3, 5, 7, 9, 11, 13) come to when added together? This is——times——.

Use the rule to find how much the first hundred odd numbers would come to if added up.

*43. What conclusions can you draw from the following facts? Iron nails will not float in a pool : a cup of pure gold dust weighs nearly twenty times as much as a cup of water of the same size : if you drop a silver sixpence or a copper coin into a puddle, it will sink to the bottom : a cubic inch (about a table-spoonful) of water weighs less than half an ounce, a cubic inch of brass weighs over two ounces : a leaden weight will drop to the bottom of the ocean. Sum up all these observations in one short statement of the following form : " Most—— are—— —— ——."

14 YEARS.

44. When you enter my house you will find a window on your right in the side wall of the passage. When the sun sets it shines straight through this window on to the wall opposite. What direction are you facing, when you stand in the doorway and look across the street?

45. If the A's have a bigger Army than the B's we ought first either to fight the B's, or attack the C's by sea, but not attack the A's : if their army is smaller we should attack the A's first. If the C's have a bigger navy than we, we ought to fight either the B's or the A's, but not the C's. If their navy is smaller, we should first attack the C's by sea. The size of their armies and navies is as follows :—

	Men	Ships
A.	7,000,000	300
B.	5,000,000	400
C.	4,000,000	500
Ourselves.	6,000,000	200

Whom should we attack first?

*46. John said : " I heard my bedroom clock strike yesterday, ten minutes before the first gun fired. I did not count the strokes, but I am sure it struck more than once, and I think it struck an odd number. John was out all the morning : and his clock stopped at 5 to 5 the same afternoon. When do you think the first gun fired?

47. Mary has just taken a penny ticket. The trains from this station all stop at Euston : but after that some go to Chalk Farm and Golders Green, others go to Kentish Town and Highgate. They stop nowhere else. The fare to Euston, Chalk Farm, or Kentish Town is a penny : to Highgate or Golders Green two-pence. Mary did not get in the Golders Green train. To what station do you think she is travelling?

48. They say that in Dodoland hundreds of years ago all the kingfishers had legs about six inches long and beaks about two inches long : and they used to wade in the water to catch fish for food. The individual birds might differ from one another in the length of their beaks and legs by about half an inch or so— not more. But the offspring of the birds with the shortest legs or beaks would inherit legs and beaks equally short, though again the brothers would differ a little from each other : and similarly with the birds whose parents had longer legs and longer beaks. And the same happened with each succeeding generation. Now, in those days the pools were only four inches deep. But they got gradually deeper and deeper : and to-day, where the fish swim, the water is always a foot deep at the very least. Kingfishers of the ancient kind would nowadays either drown in the deep water, or starve for lack of food : for they could never learn to swim. What, then, do you think has happened to these wading birds in the course of centuries?

*49. Captain Watts and his son James have been found shot—the father in the chest and the son in the back. Both clearly died instantaneously. A gun fired close to the person—as, for example, when a man shoots himself—will blacken and even burn the skin or clothes : fired from a greater distance it will leave no such mark. The two bodies were found near the middle of a large hall used as a rifle range. Its floor is covered with damp sand which shows every footprint distinctly. Inside the room there are two pairs of footprints only. A third man standing just outside the door or window could aim at any part of the room : but the pavement outside would show no footmarks. Under Captain Watts's body was found a gun : no such weapon was found near James. In each case the coat, where the bullet entered, was blackened with gunpowder, and the cloth a little singed. Captain Watts was devoted to his son, and would have died sooner than harm him purposely : hence it is impossible to suppose that he killed him deliberately, even in self-defence. But some think that James secretly disliked his father, and hoped to inherit his fortune at his death. (1) Was Captain Watts's death due to murder, accident, or suicide ? (2) Was James's death due to murder, accident, or suicide ?

50. The crust of the earth—that is, the outer layer down to at least fifty miles below the top—consists chiefly of rock and stone. Rock and stone weigh about three times as much as a bulk of water of the same size. The heaviest materials found in the crust of the earth are metals ; but in the outer layer of the earth these are, of course, comparatively rare. The earth as a whole weighs over five times as heavy as a globe of water of the same size. What does this suggest that the interior and middle of the earth are mainly composed of—water, rock and stone, metal, or hot gas ?

A NOTE ON PICTURES IN TEACHING HISTORY.

It is, we believe, the orthodox view that copies of contemporary pictures are more useful in teaching history than modern imaginative pictures. Little account is often taken of the pupil's age when this view is laid down; correctness is everything, and the pictures are necessarily of individual persons and objects more often than of complete scenes. Is it not possible that those who give this advice are doing what we are always warning students against doing, viz., thinking exclusively of the subject-matter and not at all of children's way of regarding things ? Correctness of detail is with younger children of no importance compared with a correct general impression. Imaginative work which makes an age live is surely tolerable even if it involves details of which we cannot be sure as to the accuracy.

The following incident which has just occurred is the occasion of writing this note. A class, aged about nine, was receiving a series of lessons on Henry V. The teacher stated that he was a handsome man. She also showed a copy of an original portrait in an extract-book. Shortly afterwards she stated that his queen was a beautiful woman. Immediately a girl in the class objected. If people thought Henry V a handsome man " when he was really so ugly," could we be sure that Katherine was really a beautiful woman because they thought so ? The picture may have been a stimulus to historical criticism, but surely it missed the aim for which it was shown. It had lowered Henry V in the child's opinion beyond hope of recovery.   R.L.A.

AGE SCALE METHODS OF MEASURING INTELLIGENCE.

By R. C. MOORE, M.A., M.Sc.

I.—Introduction.

In 1905 Binet and Simon[1] published a set of serially graded tests. The tests were devised with the object of assisting an examiner in diagnosing the grade of intelligence of children. Sante de Sanctis[2] also brought out a set of tests to assist in the same object. In 1908, Binet and Simon[3] evolved an extended series of tests based on the 1905 series, but altered and extended on the results of further experience. As the result of still further trial, Binet and Simon[4] again revised their scale and the revision was published in 1911.

These scales attracted great attention, and they were soon put into use by other psychologists. As the results of these latter investigations were published, quite an extensive literature grew up on the subject. A number of the experimenters were not quite satisfied with the Binet Scales, and drew up revised scales which they considered of more value. Hence there are now in existence a number of serially graded tests scales of intelligence, e.g.:—

1. Binet and Simon's 1905 Scale.

2. S. de Sanctis' Scale.

3. Binet and Simon's 1908 Scale.

4. Binet and Simon's 1911 Scale.

5. Winch's Scale.[5]

6. Goddard's Scale.[6]

7. A Point Scale for Measuring Mental Ability,[7] by Yerkes, Bridges and Hardwick.

8. Terman and Child's Scale.[8]

9. The Stanford Scale[9], and others.

Since the great majority of the scales have been drawn up on the results of experiments on foreign children, it is advisable to try them

[1]Binet, A., and Simon, T., (a) " Sur la nécessité d'établir un diagnostic scientifique des états inférieurs de l'intelligence "—L'Année psycohologique, 1905, 11, 163-190.

(b) " Méthodes nouvelles pour le diagnostic du niveau intellectuel des anormaux," ibid., 191-244.

(c) " Application des méthodes nouvelles au diagnostic du niveau intellectuel chez des enfants normaux et anormaux d'hospice et d'école primaire," ibid., 245-336.

[2]S. d. Sanctis. "Types et degrés d'insuffisance mentale."—L'Année psychologique, 1906, 12, 70 83.

[3]Binet, A., and Simon, T. " Le développement de l'intelligence chez les enfants."—L'Année psychologique, 1908 14, 1-94.

[4]Binet, A., and Simon, T. "La mesure du développement de l'intelligence chez les jeunes enfants."—Bulletin de la Société libre pour l'Etude psychologique de l'Enfant, 1911, 11, 187-256.

[5]Published by Ralph, Holland & Co., 35 and 36 Temple Chambers, London, E.C.

[6]Goddard, H. H. " Two Thousand Normal Children measured by the Binet Measuring Scale of Intelligence." Ped. Sem., 1911, xviii, 232-259.

[7]Yerkes, R.M., Bridges. J. W., and Hardwick, R.S. " A Point Scale for measuring Mental Ability." Published by Warwick & York, Baltimore, 1915.

[8]Terman, L. M., and Childs, H. G. " A Tentative Revision and Extension of the Binet-Simon Measuring Scale of Intelligence." J. Ed. Psych., 1912, III, pp. 61-74, 133 143, 198-208, 277-289.

[9]Terman, L. M. " The Measurement of Intelligence," Published by Houghton Mifflin Co., Boston, 1916, also " The Stanford Revision and Extension of the Binet-Simon Scale for Measuring Intelligence." Published by Warwick and York, Inc., Baltimore, 1917.

on normal English children. In this way they would be standardized and their values compared.

With this purpose in view, the author tried on normal English children three of the best known of these scales, viz. :—

    1. Binet's 1908 Series.
    2. Binet's 1911 Series.
    3. Goddard's Series.

The experiments were carried out in an elementary school in the Liverpool district. Table I shows the number of boys and girls tested at each age.

TABLE I.—THE CHILDREN TESTED.

Age.	Boys.	Girls.	Total.
4 years ..	11	14	25
5 ,, ...	34	33	67
6 ,, ...	42	39	81
7 ,, ...	29	30	59
8 ,, ...	35	33	68
9 ,, ...	29	31	60
10 ,, ...	15	14	29
Total ...	195	194	389

The tests were carried out in a quiet room reserved for the purpose.

In each of the test series, tests are given for each age up to ten years. After this age, the test series are not directly comparable from the standpoint of computing mental ages, on account of tests not being given for certain ages, e.g., in Binet's 1908 series no tests are given for Age 15 and the Adult Group ; in Binet's 1911 series no tests are given for Age 11 and Age 13 ; in Goddard's series no tests are given for Age 13, Age 15 and the Adult Group. Even the mental ages deduced for Age 10, and to a less extent for the lower ages, will be somewhat influenced by the lack of tests for certain of the higher ages. This is especially so in the case of Binet's 1911 series, owing to there being no tests for Age 11.

On account of the differences in the omissions of tests for the ages higher than ten, no children above this age were tested.

II.—The Test Series.

Each of the three series of tests differs considerably from the others. Before going further it is advisable to consider these differences. A summary of the three scales is given in Table II.

TABLE II.—SUMMARY OF SYSTEMS OF TESTS.

	Binet's 1908 Series.	Binet's 1911 Series.	Goddard's Series.
Age 3	Shows nose, eyes, and mouth. Repeats two digits. Enumerates object in picture. Gives family name. Repeats sentence: 6 syllables.	Shows nose, eyes, and mouth. Repeats two digits. Enumerates objects in picture. Gives family name. Repeats sentence: 6 syllables.	Shows, nose, eyes, and mouth. Repeats two digits. Enumerates objects in picture. Gives family name. Repeats sentence: 6 syllables.
Age 4	Gives own sex. Names key, knife, and penny. Repeats three digits. Compares two lines.	Gives own sex. Names key, knife, and penny. Repeats three digits. Compares two lines.	Gives own sex. Names key, knife, and penny. Repeats three digits. Compares two lines.
Age 5	Copies two weights. Copies a square. Counts four pennies. Game of patience: 2 pieces.	Compares two weights. Copies a square. Repeats sentence: 10 syllables. Counts four pennies. Game of patience: 2 pieces.	Compares two weights. Copies a square. Repeats sentence: 10 syllables. Counts four pennies. Game of patience: 2 pieces.
Age 6	Morning or afternoon. Defines in terms of use. Compares faces. Three commissions. Repeats sentence: 16 syllables. Right hand, left ear. Knows own age.	Morning or afternoon. Defines in terms of use. Copies a lozenge. Counts 13 pennies. Compares faces.	Morning or afternoon. Defines in terms of use. Three commissions. Right hand, left ear. Compares faces.
Age 7	Omissions in pictures. Number of fingers. Writing from copy. Copies a lozenge. Repeats five digits. Describes pictures. Counts 13 pennies. Names four common coins.	Right hand, left ear. Describes pictures. Three commissions. Value of 9 halfpennies: 3 double and 3 single. Names four colours.	Counts 13 pennies. Describes pictures. Omissions in pictures. Copies a lozenge. Names four colours.
Age 8	Reading and report: 2 items. Value of 9 halfpennies: 3 double and 3 single. Names four colours. Counts 20—0. Writing from dictation. Compares two remembered objects.	Compares two remembered objects. Counts 20—0. Omissions in pictures. Gives day and date. Repeats five digits.	Compares two remembered objects. Counts 20—1. Names days of week. Gives value of stamps, 1 1 1 2 2 2. Repeats five digits.

TABLE II.—SUMMARY OF SYSTEMS OF TESTS (continued).

Age	Binet's 1908 Series.	Binet's 1911 Series.	Goddard's Series.
Age 9	Gives day and date. Names days of week. Gives change. Defines in terms superior to use. Reading and report: 6 items. Arrangement of five weights.	Gives change. Defines in terms superior to use. Names pieces of money. Enumerates the months. Easy questions.	Gives change. Defines in terms superior to use. Gives day and date. Enumerates the months. Arrangement of five weights.
Age 10	Enumerates the months. Names pieces of money. Uses three words in two sentences. *Questions {Easy. {Difficult.	Arrangement of five weights. Copies drawings from memory. Criticizes absurd statements. Difficult questions. Uses three words in two sentences.	Names pieces of money. Copies drawings from memory. Repeats six digits. *Questions {Easy. {Difficult. Uses three words in two sentences.
Age 11	Absurd statements. Uses three words in one sentence. Names at least sixty words in three minutes. Definition of abstract terms. Arranging words in a sentence.		Absurd statements. Uses three words in one sentence. Names at least 60 words in 3 minutes. Gives three rhymes. Arranging words in a sentence.
Age 12	Repeats seven digits. Gives three rhymes. Repeats sentence: 26 syllables. Solves problem from several facts.	Resists suggestion (lines). Uses three words in one sentence. Names at least 60 words in 3 minutes. Definition of abstract terms. Arranging words in a sentence.	Repeats seven digits. Definition of abstract terms. Repeats sentence: 26 syllables. Resists suggestion (lines). Solves problem from several facts.
Age 13	Solves the paper cutting test. Re-arranges a triangle. Distinguishes between abstract terms.		
Age 15		Repeats seven digits. Gives three rhymes. Repeats sentence: 26 syllables. Interprets a picture. Solves a problem from several facts.	
Adult		Solves the paper cutting test. Re-arranges a triangle. Distinguishes between abstract terms. Solves the question about the president. Thought of Hervieu.	

*For comparative purposes this test has been considered as two separate tests.

1.—BINET'S 1908 AND 1911 SERIES.

The 1911 series was developed on the results of experience from the 1908 series. An important alteration, that was developed in the 1911 scale, was the arrangement of an equal number of tests in each age group. In the 1908 series the number of tests in the different age groups varied considerably, there being as many as eight tests for age seven, and only three tests for age thirteen. In the 1911 series five tests were allotted to each age, with the exception of age four which was left with only four tests.

In the 1908 series, a child's mental age was considered to be the highest year in which he passed all the tests, or all the tests save one, plus one year for every five higher tests passed. In the 1911 series the mental age of a child was calculated as the highest age at which he passed ALL the tests plus one year for every five higher tests passed.

There are 57 tests in the 1908 series, and 54 in the 1911. There are considerable differences in the arrangement of the tests in the two series. Twenty-three tests are common to both series, and are also in the same age group in each. The distribution of these twenty-three tests is shown in Table III.

TABLE III.—DISTRIBUTION OF TESTS WHICH ARE COMMON TO THE SAME AGE GROUP FOR EACH PAIR OF TEST SERIES.

Test Series compared.	Number of Common Tests for each Age Group.													
Binet's 1908 and 1911 Series.	5	4	4	3	1	2	2	2	—	0	—	—	—	23
Binet's 1908 and Goddard's Series	5	4	4	5	4	3	4	4	4	3	—	—	—	40
Binet's 1911 and Goddard's Series	5	4	5	3	2	3	3	3	—	2	—	—	—	30
Age Groups	3	4	5	6	7	8	9	10	11	12	13	15	Adult	Total

Twenty-five other tests are likewise common to each series, but do not occur in the same age groups. In the 1911 series, sixteen of these tests have been put in a higher age group than the one they were in in the 1908 series, while nine have been put in a lower age group.

Thus, altogether, there are forty-eight tests common to the two series.

The greatest number of transfers to higher ages occurs in ages eleven, twelve, and thirteen. The tests for these ages (with the exception of the absurd statements test) on further trial were found too difficult. Hence in the 1911 series they were given as tests for higher ages. Four of the 1908 eleven-year tests are transferred to the twelve-year group. The whole of the twelve-year tests are transferred to the 1911 fifteen-year group, and the thirteen-year tests are all included in the 1911 adult tests.

Table IV gives the analysis of these transfers.

TABLE IV.—DISTRIBUTION OF TESTS WHICH ARE COMMON TO
EACH OF A PAIR OF TEST SERIES, BUT WHICH DO NOT
OCCUR IN THE SAME AGE GROUP.

1908.	Tests transferred from Binet's 1908 series to other groups in 1911 series.		
Age Groups.	Number of Tests transferred.	Transfers to higher age groups.	Transfers to lower age groups.
3	0	—	—
4	0	—	—
5	0	—	—
6	2	2 to age 7	—
7	4	2 to age 8	2 to age 6
8	2	—	2 to age 7
9	2	1 to age 10	1 to age 8
10	3	—	3 to age 9
11	5	4 to age 12	1 to age 10
12	4	4 to age 15	—
13	3	3 to adult group	—
Total......	25	16	9

1908.	Tests transferred from Binet's 1908 series to other groups in Goddard's series.		
Age Groups.	Number of Tests transferred.	Transfers to higher age groups.	Transfers to lower age groups.
3	0	—	—
4	0	—	—
5	0	—	—
6	0	—	—
7	1	1 to age 8	—
8	1	—	1 to age 7
9	1	—	1 to age 8
10	1	—	1 to age 9
11	1	1 to age 12	—
12	1	—	1 to age 11
13	0	—	—
Total......	6	2	4

1911.	Tests in Binet's 1911 series which are allocated to other age groups in Goddard's series.		
Age Groups.	Number of Tests differently allocated	Allocations to higher age groups.	Allocations to lower age groups.
3	0	—	—
4	0	—	—
5	0	—	—
6	2	2 to age 7	—
7	3	1 to age 8	2 to age 6
8	2	1 to age 9	1 to age 7
9	2	2 to age 10	—
10	2	1 to age 11	1 to age 9
12	3	—	3 to age 11
15	4	—	1 to age 11 / 3 to age 12
Adult	0	—	—
Total......	18	7	11

There are nine tests in the 1908 series which do not appear in that of 1911; while six tests occur in the later series which are not included in the earlier. These tests are given in Table V.

TABLE V.—DISTRIBUTION OF TESTS WHICH ARE NOT COMMON TO EACH OF A PAIR OF TEST SERIES.

Tests occurring in the 1908 but not in the 1911 series.		Tests occurring in the 1911 but not in the 1908 series.	
Age Group.		Age Group.	
6	Repeat sentence : 16 syllables.	5	Repeats sentence : 10 syllables.
6	Knows own age.	10	Copies drawings from memory.
7	Number of fingers.	12	Resists suggestion lines.
7	Writing from copy.	15	Interprets a picture.
7	Names four common coins.	Adult	Solves question about president.
8	Reading and report : two items.	Adult	Thought of Hervieu.
8	Writing from dictation.		
9	Names days of week.		
9	Reading and report : six items.		

TABLE V (continued).

Tests occurring in the 1908 but not in Goddard's series.		Tests occurring in Goddard's but not in the 1908 series.	
Age Group.		Age Group.	
6	Repeats sentence: 16 syllables.	5	Repeats sentence : 10 syllables.
6	Knows own age.	10	Copies drawings from memory.
7	Number of fingers.	10	Repeats six digits.
7	Writing from copy.	12	Resists suggestion lines.
7	Names four common cotns.		
8	Reading and report : two items.		
8	Writing from dictation.		
9	Reading and report : six items		
13	Solves the paper cutting test.		
13	Re-arranges a triangle.		
13	Distinguishes between abstract terms.		

TABLE V (continued).

Tests occurring in the 1911 but not in Goddard's series.		Tests occurring in Goddard's but not in the 1911 series.	
Age Group.		Age Group.	
15	Interprets a picture.	8	Repeats days of week.
Adult	Solves the paper cutting test.	10	Repeats six digits.
Adult	Re-arranges a triangle.		
Adult	Distinguishes between abstract terms.		
Adult	Question about the president.		
Adult	Thought of Hervieu.		

The tests in the 1908 series, which were not included in the 1911 series, were largely left out because they rather tested scholastic knowledge or acquired information than general intelligence.

The tests " Resists suggestion lines " and " Copies drawings from memory " are included in the 1911 series. These two tests occurred in the 1905 series, were left out in 1908, and included again in the 1911 series.

2.—Binet's 1908 and Goddard's Series.

Goddard's series of tests, like Binet's 1911 series, was drawn up on the results of the experience gained in using the 1908 series. The great majority of the tests remain in the age groups to which they were assigned in Binet's 1908 series.

Out of the 50 tests in Goddard's series, 40 occur in the same age groups as in Binet's 1908 series. This fact and the distribution of these tests are shown in Table III. There are six other tests common to the two series but which are not in the same age group in each series. These are shown in Table IV. There are eleven tests in the 1908 series which have been left out by Goddard when compiling his series, but he has included four tests which do not occur in Binet's 1908 series. For the names and distribution of these tests see Table V.

Writing in reference to his series Goddard[1] states, "The new scale will simply be more convenient because it will obviate straggling; that is, where a child, for example, stops at seven years, but gets enough credits to make him eight, some of these credits coming from nine and some from ten. The tendency under the new scale will be to answer the eight-year questions and stop there, doing none in nine or ten."

In Goddard's series, a child's mental age is calculated as being the highest age at which all the tests in a group are passed, plus one year for every five higher tests passed.

3.—Binet's 1911 Series and Goddard's Series.

In each case many of the 1908 tests have been adopted, but some have been transferred to different age groups and others have been omitted. Binet's 1911 series contains 54 tests, and Goddard's series contains 50. The number of the tests which are common to both series and are also in the same age groups are shown in Table III. These tests are thirty in number. In addition to these there are eighteen common tests, which are not distributed in the same age groups in the two series. The distribution of these tests is shown in Table IV. For the ages three, four, and five, the tests are exactly the same in the two series. In Binet's 1911 system there are six tests, and in Goddard's two tests, which do not occur in the other system. These tests are shown in Table V. It will thus be seen that the suggested improvements over the 1908 system are far from being identical in the two series.

[1] Goddard, H. H., "The Binet-Simon Measuring Scale for Intelligence," p. 10. Published by The Department of Psychological Research, The Training School, Vineland, N.J.

III.—The Evaluation of the Data.

The Relation between Chronological and Mental Age as shown by the Three Systems of Tests.

The mental age, as derived from the results of each series of tests, is greater than the corresponding physical age for the lower ages tested ; but tends to become greater than the corresponding physical age for the higher ages. This matter has been discussed in a previous paper.[1]

Binet's 1908 series yields the highest mental ages (except for ages three and ten) corresponding to given physical ages, while Binet's 1911 series gives the lowest mental ages (except for age ten) of the three test series. The results from Goddard's series lie in between those of the two Binet series except for ages three and ten. This is shown in Table VI.

TABLE VI.—PHYSICAL AND MENTAL AGES.

Physical Age.	Average Mental Age.		
	Binet's 1908 Series.	Binet's 1911 Series.	Goddard's Series.
4·4	5·1	5·0	5·1
5·2	6·0	5·7	5·8
6·3	7·5	6·9	7·1
7·5	8·3	7·8	8·0
8·6	8·6	8·3	8·5
9·5	9·5	9·2	9·4
10·3	10·4	10·4	10·3

The Distribution of Mental with Physical Age.

The experimental data, arranged to show this distribution, are given in Table VII. Figure I shows graphically the distribution of ability for each age and for each series of tests. Figure II shows the percentage of all the children who are at age, and also those who are advanced or retarded by one or more years, for each test series.

The number of children, who are at age, corresponds fairly closely for each series of tests. The number is lowest for Binet's 1908 series, and highest for Binet's 1911 series. Binet's 1908 series gives the greatest number of advanced children, while Binet's 1911 series gives the greatest number of children who are retarded. If we consider the children as being backward[2], normal or gifted, we find that the greatest number of normal children is given by Binet's 1911 series.

[1] Moore, R. C. " The Application of the Binet-Simon Scale to Normal English Children.' —This *Journal*, 1917, 114-116.

[2] Goddard suggests that " backward " children should be considered as those who are more than one year behind their age, " normal " children those at age or only one year in advance or behind their age, and "gifted " children those who are more than one year advanced.—*The Pedagogical Seminary*, 1911, 236-237.

FIGURE 1. Percentage of Children at Age, Advanced and
Retarded for each Age Tested.

BINET'S 1908 SERIES.　　BINET'S 1911 SERIES.　　GODDARD'S SERIES.

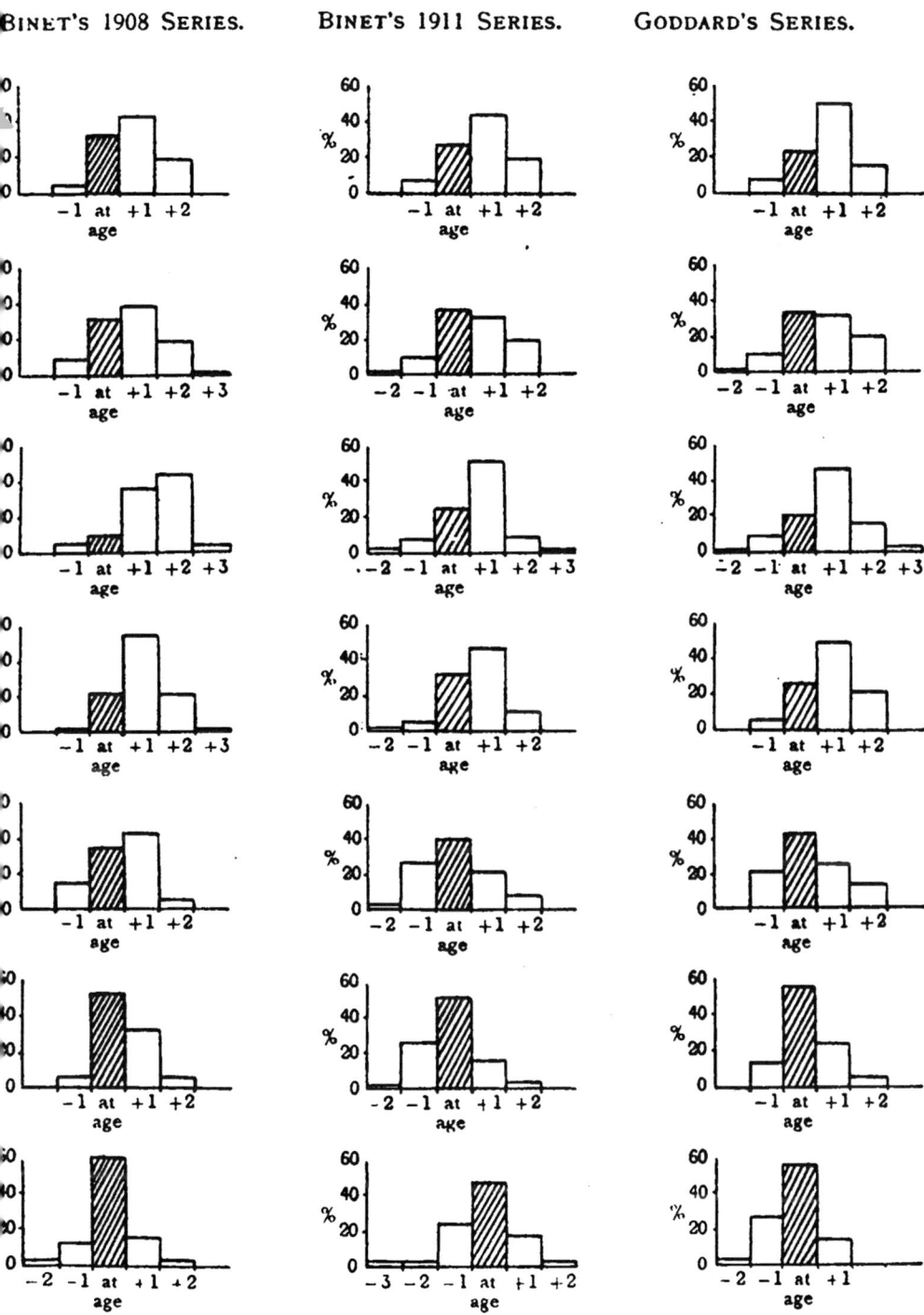

FIGURE. 2.   Percentage of Children at Age, Advanced
and Retarded for all ages.

BINET'S 1908 SERIES.

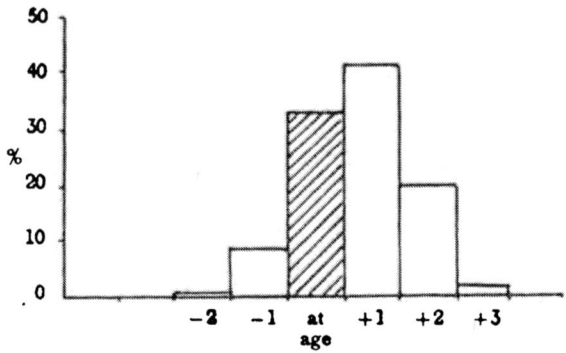

BINET'S 1911 SERIES.

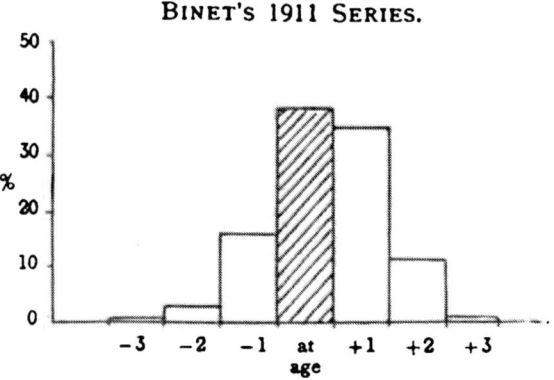

GODDARD'S SERIES.

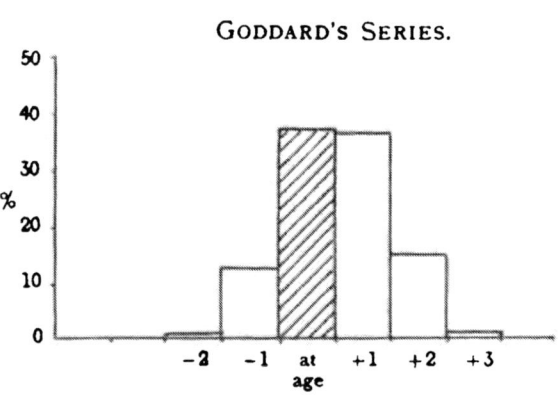

TABLE VII.—DISTRIBUTION OF MENTAL WITH PHYSICAL AGE.
BINET'S 1908 SERIES.

Phys. Age.	Mental Age.															Total.	At Age %
	1	2	3	4	5	6	7	8	9	10	11	12	13	14	15		
4			1	8	11	5										25	32·0
5				6	21	26	13	1								67	31·3
6					4	8	30	35	4							81	9·9
7						1	13	32	12	1						59	22·0
8							11	24	29	4						68	35·3
9								4	32	20	4					60	53·3
10								1	4	18	5	1				29	62·1
Totals			1	14	36	40	67	97	81	43	9	1				389	

BINET'S 1911 SERIES.

Phys. Age.	Mental Age.															Total.	At Age %
	1	2	3	4	5	6	7	8	9	10	11	12	13	14	15		
4			2	7	11	5										25	28·0
5			1	7	25	21	13									67	37·3
6				2	7	20	42	8	2							81	24·7
7					1	4	19	28	7							59	32·2
8						2	19	27	14	6						68	39·7
9							1	16	31	10	2					60	51·7
10							1	1	7	14	5	1				29	48·3
Totals			3	16	44	52	95	80	61	30	7	1				389	

GODDARD'S SERIES.

Phys. Age.	Mental Age.															Total.	At Age %
	1	2	3	4	5	6	7	8	9	10	11	12	13	14	15		
4			2	6	13	4										25	24·0
5			1	7	23	22	14									67	34·3
6				1	8	17	38	14	3							81	21·0
7						3	15	29	12							59	25·4
8							14	28	17	9						68	41·2
9								8	35	14	3					60	58·3
10								1	8	16	4					29	55·2
Totals			3	14	44	46	81	80	75	39	7					389	

Binet's 1908 series supplies the largest number of gifted children, whilst Binet's 1911 series gives the greatest number of backward ones. A summary of the results in this connexion is given in Table VIII.

TABLE VIII.—DISTRIBUTION OF ABILITIES.

THE PERCENTAGE OF THE CHILDREN.

			Backward.	Normal.	Gifted.
Binet's 1908 Series	...	...	0·3	79·1	20·6
Binet's 1911 Series	...	...	2·3	86·4	11·3
Goddard's Series	....	...	0·8	84·1	15·2
			Retarded.	At Age.	Advanced.
Binet's 1908 Series	...	...	8·2	31·9	59·9
Binet's 1911 Series	...	...	18·3	36·8	45·0
Goddard's Series	...	...	13·6	36·0	50·4

A comparative study of Binet's 1908 nnd 1911 series has been carried ont by McIntyre and Rogers[1], and also by Berry[2]. In each case, it appears that a greater percentage of children was graded as normal by the 1911 series than by the 1908 one. Both investigators also showed that the number of children graded as gifted was lower in the case of the 1911 series than when the earlier series was used. McIntyre and Rogers found that the number of children classified as backward was greater for the 1911 tests, while Berry noticed that the number of backward children was the same for both series.

When the children were classified as retarded, at age and advanced, it was found in both the case of the Scotch and American children, that the number of children graded as retarded by the 1911 series was greater than by the 1908 scale. Whilst the number of children graded as advanced was larger for the 1908 series. McIntyre and Rogers found that slightly more children were graded at age by the 1911 series than by the 1908 tests. Berry found the reverse of this.

A summary of the results (in this connexion) of these workers is given in Table IX.

TABLE IX.—COMPARATIVE RESULTS OF OTHER INVESTIGATORS ON THE DISTRIBUTION OF ABILITIES.

Investigators.	Test Series.	Percentage of Children.			Number of Children Tested.
		Backward.	Normal.	Gifted.	
McIntyre & Rogers	1908	0·7	83·6	15·7	140[1]
	1911	2·1	90·0	7·9	140
Berry	1908	4·8	88·1	7·1	42[2]
	1911	4·8	95·2	0·0	42

1 Only those children of ages four to ten years inclusive are here considered.
2 These children were between the ages of six and ten years inclusive.

[1]Rogers, A. L., and McIntyre, J. L. "The Measurement of Intelligence in Children by the Binet-Simon Scale."—*British Journal of Psychology*, 1914, 265-299.
[2]Berry, C. S. "A Comparison of the Binet Tests of 1908 and 1911.—J. Ed., *Psych.*, 1912, 444-451.

TABLE IX.—*Continued.*

Investigators.	Test Series.	Percentage of Children.			Number of Children Tested.
		Retarded.	At Age.	Advanced.	
McIntyre & Rogers	1908	12·1	38·6	49·3	140
	1911	30·0	40·0	30·0	140
Berry	1908	23·8	47·6	28·6	42
	1911	45·2	45·2	9·5	42

THE PERCENTAGE OF THE SUBJECTS WHO PASSED THE TESTS CORRESPONDING TO THEIR OWN AGES.

We may consider the suitability of the tests from another stand-point. In each test series the tests, allocated to a particular age, are deemed suitable for that age. The suitability of a test for a given age is usually decided by ascertaining what percentage of children of that age succeed in passing the test. When 70—75% of the children of the required age pass the test, the test is judged to be suitably placed. The exact percentage required for this allocation varies somewhat with different investigators.[1] The criterion here taken is that a test is suitably placed in an age group when 70% of the children of that age pass the test.

Each of the test series[3] can now be considered from the standpoint of this criterion.

Binet's 1908 series contains two tests which are too difficult for the ages in which they are placed; fourteen which are too easy[2], and twenty-four which are in their right age group.

Binet's 1911 series contains three tests which are too difficult, eleven which are too easy, and twenty tests which are suitable.

Goddard's series contains two tests which are too difficult, twelve tests which are too easy, and twenty tests which are rightly placed.

These facts are shown in detail graphically in Fig. 3. The black columns represent tests which are too difficult, the shaded columns tests which are too easy, and the remaining columns tests which are suitably placed.

Goddard adopts 75% as the criterion of suitability. If this standard had been adopted instead of the 70% value the results obtained would be as shown in Table X.

When the 75% criterion is used we get, as might be expected, the tests which are too difficult increased in number, and those which are too easy decreased.

It is noticeable that of the tests which are misplaced, the majority are too easy for the allotted ages. This is so whichever criterion is used. The number of the tests which are too difficult is practically identical in each of the three test series. Binet's 1911 series has the fewest tests which are too easy. On the basis of the 70% criterion

1 Goddard uses the 75% criterion. *Ped. Sem.*, vol. xviii, No. 2, p. 240. Rogers and McIntyre use the 70% criterion. *Brit. J. Psych.*, vol vii, No. 3, p. 283.

2 A test is considered as being too easy for a given age when 70% or more of the children of a lower age succeed in passing it.

3 Tests for ages four to ten inclusive are only considered here as these correspond to the ages of the children tested.

FIGURE 3. The Percentage of the Subjects who Passed the Tests Corresponding to their own Ages.

(a) BINET'S 1908 SERIES.   (b) BINET'S 1911 SERIES.   (c) GODDARD'S SERIES.

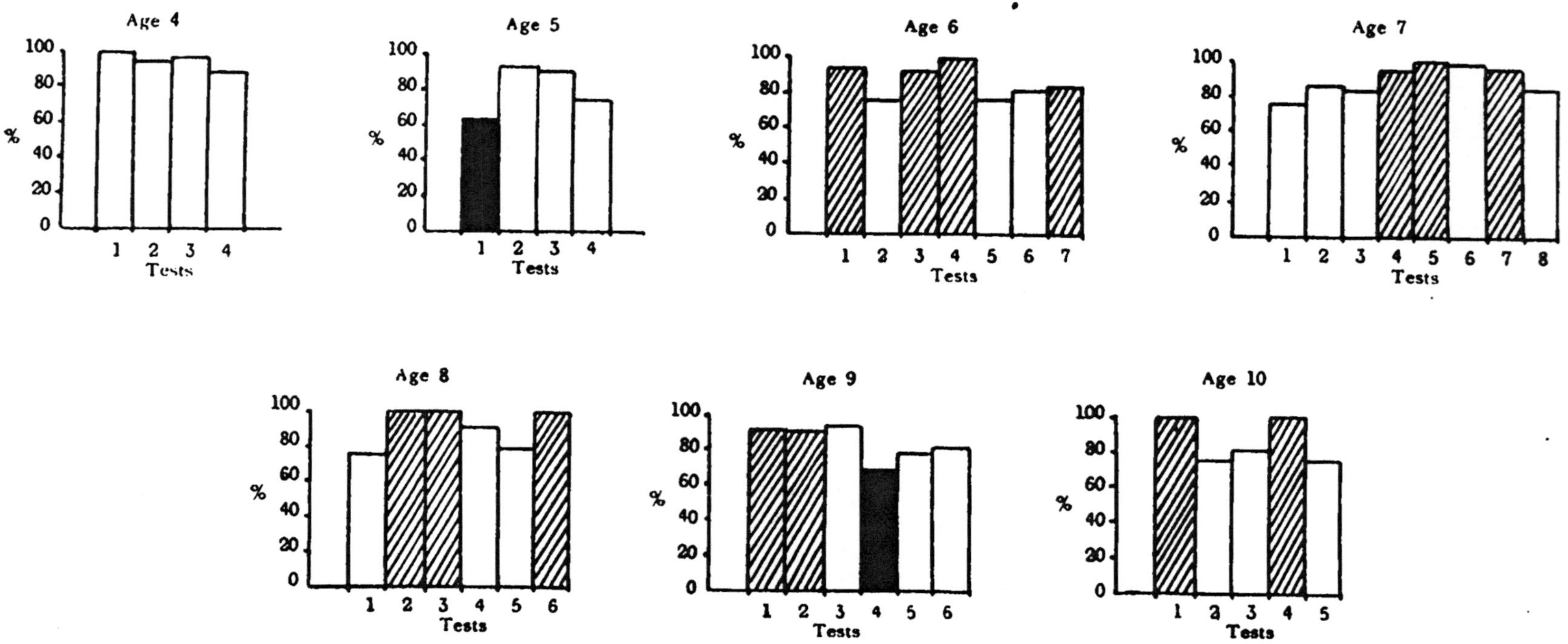

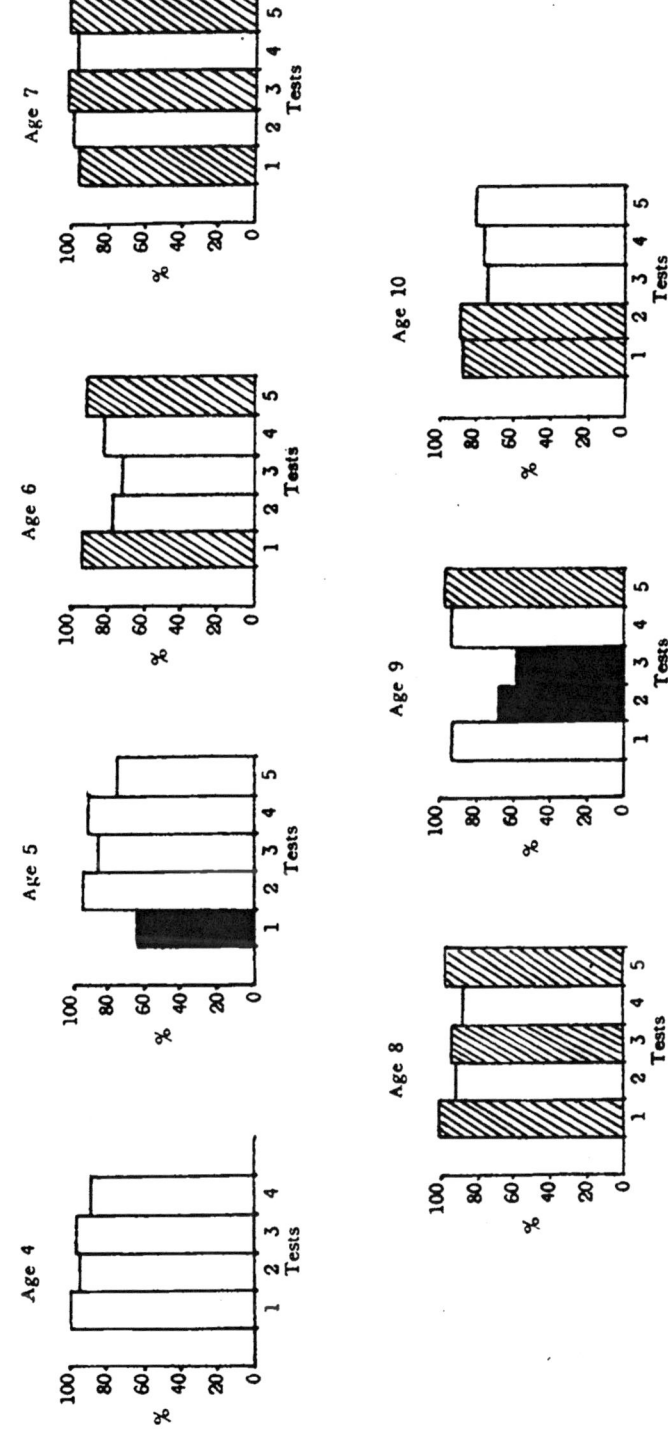

(b) BINET'S 1911 SERIES.

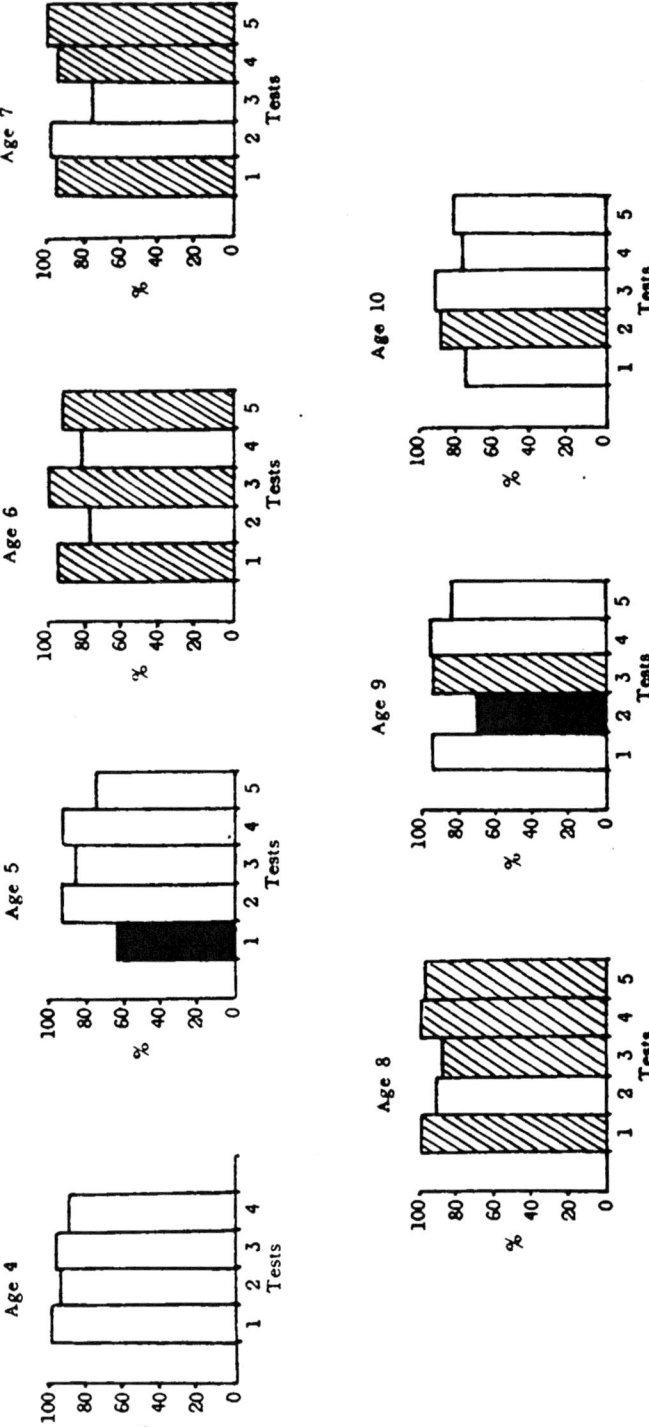

(c) GODDARD'S SERIES.

TABLE X.—THE SUITABILITY OF THE TESTS BASED ON
GODDARD'S CRITERION.

Test Series.	Test Ages.	Tests which are			No. of Tests.
		Too difficult.	Too easy.	Suitable.	
Binet's 1908 Series.	4	—	—	4	4
	5	2	—	2	4
	6	—	2	5	7
	7	1	3	4	8
	8	—	3	3	6
	9	1	2	3	6
	10	1	2	2	5
	Total ...	5	12	23	40
Binet's 1911 Series.	4	—	—	4	4
	5	2	—	3	5
	6	1	1	3	5
	7	—	3	2	5
	8	—	2	3	5
	9	2	1	2	5
	10	1	2	2	5
	Total ...	6	9	19	34
Goddard's Series.	4	—	—	4	4
	5	2	—	3	5
	6	—	2	3	5
	7	1	3	1	5
	8	—	3	2	5
	9	1	1	3	5
	10	1	1	3	5
	Total ...	5	10	19	34

Binet's 1911 series has 58·8% of the tests correctly placed, Binet's 1908 series 60%, and Goddard's series 58·8%. When the 75% criterion is used, Binet's 1911 series has 55·9% of the tests correctly placed, Binet's 1908 series 57·5% and Goddard's series 55·9%. Thus, in the case of each criterion, Binet's 1908 series has a slightly greater percentage of suitably placed tests than the other two series, which are equal to each other in this respect.

Instead of considering each test in a series separately, we may consider the average results obtained from all the tests in a given age group. The results of this procedure are shown in Table XI.

It will be noticed that the average percentage of children who pass the tests for their own ages is very similar for each of the three series. It is highest for Goddard's series and a little lower for the two Binet series.

TABLE XI.—THE AVERAGE PERCENTAGE OF CHILDREN
WHO PASS THE TESTS FOR THEIR OWN AGE.

Age.	The Average Percentage of Children who Pass the Tests for their own Age.		
	Binet's 1911 Series.	Binet's 1908 Series.	Goddard's Series.
4	95·2	95·2	95·2
5	81·8	80·9	81·8
6	82·9	86·5	89·0
7	97·3	89·0	92·5
8	94·0	91·1	95·6
9	82·0	84·7	86·0
10	81·3	85·8	81·8
Average ...	87·8	87·6	88·8

THE AGE ALLOCATION OF THE INDIVIDUAL TESTS.

The age to which a test is allocated in each of the three series of tests, and also the age to which it corresponds, from the results of the present research, are shown in Table XII. We have thus four different distributions of the tests. Out of the forty-four different tests which occur in the three series for the ages four to ten inclusive, the age allocation of thirteen is unanimously agreed to in the four distributions. There are ten other tests which do not occur in each of the test series, but where age allocation is also unanimously agreed upon, by the present investigation and those series in which they occur. There are sixteen tests which differ in their allocation by one year; four tests which differ in allocation by two years; and one test which differs in allocation by three years. The last named test is " The naming of four colours." Binet's 1908 series places it in Age 8. Binet's 1911 and Goddard's series place it in Age 7; while the results of the present research allocate it to Age 5. Several other investigators have also found the test to be suitable for Age 5. Referring to this test Terman[1] states " Binet originally placed this test in year 8, changing it to year 7 in the 1911 scale. Goddard places it in year 7, while Kuhlmann omits it altogether. With a single exception, all the actual statistics with normal children justify the location of the test in year 5. Robertag's figures are the exception, opposed to which are Rowe, Winch, Dumville, Dougherty, Brigham, and all three of the Stanford investigations."

IV.—Conclusions.

1.—The arrangement of Binet's 1911 and Goddard's series, so that the same number of tests occurs in each group (except age four), is a decided improvement over Binet's 1908 series.

2.—Binet's 1911 and Goddard's series do not contain several 1908 tests which are especially liable to school or home training. This is an advantage.

3.—The methods of estimating mental age in Binet's 1908 series is not as good as that adopted in the two later systems.

1 Terman, L. M., "The Measurement of Intelligence," p. 165. Published by Houghton, Mifflin & Co., Boston.

TABLE XII.—THE AGE ALLOCATION OF THE INDIVIDUAL TESTS.

Test No.	Test.	Age to which the Tests are allocated.			
		Binet, 1908	Binet, 1911	Goddard	The present research
1	Gives own sex	4	4	4	4
2	Names key, knife, and penny ...	4	4	4	4
3	Repeats three digits	4	4	4	4
4	Compares two lines	4	4	4	4
5	Compares two weights	5	5	5	6
6	Copies a square	5	5	5	5
7	Repeats sentence : 10 syllables	—	5	5	5
8	Counts four pennies	5	5	5	5
9	Game of patience	5	5	5	5
10	Morning and afternoon... ...	6	6	6	5
11	Defines in terms of use	6	6	6	6
12	Copies a lozenge...	7	6	7	6
13	Counts 13 pennies	7	6	7	6
14	Compares faces	6	6	6	5
15	Three commissions	6	7	6	5
16	Repeats sentence : 16 syllables	6	—	—	6
17	Right hand, left ear	6	7	6	6
18	Knows own age	6	—	—	5
19	Describes a picture	7	7	7	7
20	Value of nine halfpennies ...	8	7	8	7
21	Names four colours	8	7	7	5
22	Number of fingers	7	—	—	7
23	Writing from copy	7	—	—	7
24	Repeats five digits	7	8	8	6
25	Omissions in pictures	7	8	7	7
26	Names four common coins ...	7	—	—	7
27	Compares two digits	8	8	8	7
28	Counts 20—0	8	8	8	8
29	Gives day and date	9	8	9	8
30	Reading and report : two items	8	—	—	8
31	Writing from dictation	8	—	—	8
32	Repeats days of week	9	—	8	7
33	Gives change	9	9	9	9
34	Defines superior to use	9	9	9	10
35	Recognizes English coins ...	10	9	10	10
36	Enumerates the months... ...	10	9	9	9
37	Easy questions	10	9	10	8
38	Reading and report : six items...	9	—	—	9
39	Arrangement of five weights ...	9	10	9	9
40	Memory drawings	—	10	10	9
41	Absurd statements	—	10	—	10
42	Difficult questions	10	10	10	10
43	Three words in two sentences ...	10	10	10	10
44	Repeats six digits	—	—	10	10

4.—The mental ages derived from the use of Binet's 1911 series most closely resemble the corresponding physiological ages. Goddard's scale ranks next in this respect.

5.—The percentage of tests suitable for the ages in which they are placed is very similar for each series.

6.—In each of the series there are a number of tests which are not in the right age groups for English children.

7.—Binet's 1911 and Goddard's series both appear better than Binet's 1908 series, and, of the two, Binet's 1911 series is if anything the superior.

HAS EDUCATION PROGRESSED?

By DOUGLAS WAPLES, M.A.

PERHAPS the first negative reply to this question by a zealous educator was made by Ratke, when to obtain his release from prison he was forced to give Prince Lewis of Anhalt-Koethen a signed statement of failure to carry out his educational reforms. Yet Ratke by no means stands alone in his failure, and educational disappointments occurring periodically since his death in 1635 have kept the question alive. The present is an era of hope. Public opinion and consequent political reactions[1] both indicate a measure of confidence in educational aims. It is true that this confidence is not shared by numerous sceptics like Shaw[2] nor by a few of the better informed, but both the variety and extent of recent educational experiments give rise to the popular notion that "there may be something in it."[3] One authority sees evidence in the popular use of the term "New Education" that such is at least desired.[4] This being true, the hostile critic must assume the burden of proof on the principle of *judex damnatur cum nocens absolvitur*, and a dispassionate evaluation of educational progress is both possible and harmless.

In attempting to distinguish those elements of the educative process which may progress from others which may not, it is wise to proceed along very general lines. "Has education progressed?" seems to herald a comparison between the results of past and present methods for which, strictly speaking, there are no valid criteria; nor is it safe to restrict the inquiry to comparison of methods, for the value of results is inseparable from the idea of progress. The simplest course therefore would seem to be a search for analogies in other social activities which, as regards progress, hold about the same place as education. Clearly, those activities in which progress is most apparent are such as benefit most directly by additions to empirical knowledge. Activities which lag farthest behind are those least benefited, and activities which fall by the wayside, e.g., necromancy, alchemy, and primitive religions, are those opposed by advancing knowledge. From this point of view it may be inferred that activities like education in which social interest appears permanent, while not uninfluenced by scientific advance, must somehow derive their vigour from forces at present beyond scientific control. It also follows that these forces must be of psychic origin like assumptions as to the rationality of the universe,[5] that underlie all scientific thought, and which science, by hypothesis, is therefore unable to deal with.

This conclusion, expressed in terms of social activities whose progress admits of debate, amounts to the statement that new knowledge in each field must improve the psychic faculty before any clear gain is discernible. In these activities it is proposed to distinguish the scientific from the psychic factors in their relation to progress, and

---

[1] For illustrations see President's address to Training College Association, *Journal of Experimental Pedagogy*, March, 1919.

[2] cf. *Man and Superman*, p. 25.

[3] i.e. Along commercial, industrial, political and social lines as well as in strictly experimental pedagogy. Note particularly the advance of adult education in America and England, and the extent of academic instruction in Allied Military Forces overseas.

[4] John Adams, *The New Teaching*, p. 1.

[5] cf. John Adams, *The Evolution of Educational Theory*, 78 ff.

then to consider to what extent these same psychic factors appear in education. Inasmuch as this consideration will require frequent reference to "the psychic factor which affects progress" in each activity discussed, it will prove convenient to attach this meaning to the term *psychic variable,* which, as we shall see, applies to various faculties depending on the nature of the activity. In selecting certain activities for purposes of illustration, it will be noted that there are three general classes distinguished by the type of social interest pursued, for the cause of social like that of individual activity is the prosecution of interest.

These three types of interest, allowing for difference of term, are generally accepted to be the æsthetic or intrinsic, the practical or extrinsic, and the intellectual or cognitive types.[1] The first seeks intrinsic worth; the second seeks usefulness, and the third seeks meaning. As best representing these social interests, we may then select as corresponding activities—creative art, politics, and normative criticism,[2] and examine each briefly for a definition of the psychic variable involved.

Rather for its clearness than for its depth, the following testimony[3] offers a convenient approach to the psychic variable in art: "So far as art is dependent upon any form of exact knowledge, so far as it is of science, it is capable of progress. So far as it depends upon mind and soul it is dependent upon the greatness of mind and is incapable of progress." And later the familiar remark,[4] "the one essential prerequisite to great art is a great man." We have adduced here an argument from authority. Though begging the most venerable question of academic dispute as to the effect of training on genius, it does indicate the nature and importance of the psychic variable. However hard it is for critics to draw the line between training and genius, all are substantially agreed that the greatest art owes its greatness to genius as distinct from training.[5] Specific reference to classic opinion on this subject is therefore unprofitable, but such opinion can be inferred, if required, from passing acquaintance with the writer's life and artistic standards. One might assume from very slight reading, for instance, that Longinus, Boileau, Goethe, and Dr. Johnson emphasize training; and that Aristotle, Rousseau, Schiller, and Byron emphasize genius. It is safer to decide from the nature of the case that while some training may develop artistic expression to the extent of capacity, no training can do more. Art as

1 Though generally accepted as above, many authors employ a dual classification, e.g., Herbart distinguishes æsthetic, empirical, and speculative interests as derived from nature, from religious, social, and sympathetic interests, derived from man. cf. W. Mitchell, *Structure and Growth of the Mind,* 380 ff. who distinguishes mental types as above, each implying different combinations of thought, desire, and interest, from the interests themselves. See also J. Welton, *Psychology of Education,* 198 ff. for a similar classification.

2 Science, though the most obvious expression of both practical and intellectual interests, would not serve as well as politics and criticism, for progress in Science results from accumulated results of experiment, and does not involve the question of the effect of experiment on the mind so clearly as in the activities chosen.

3 Kenyon Cox, *The Illusion of Progress,* N.Y., p. 87.

4 ibid, p. 96.

5 For significant remarks by one artist on genius and training, see Sir Joshua Reynolds's statement (quoted and attacked by Hazlitt, *Collected Works,* Waller & Glover, Edition VI, p. 122) "You must have no dependence on your genius. If you have great talents, industry will improve them; if you have but moderate abilities, industry will supply their deficiency. Nothing is denied to well directed labour, nothing is to be obtained without it." And compare this with the following (Reynolds, *Discourses on Art,* E. G. Johnson, Ed., Chicago, 1891, p. 185). "It is not easy to define in what this grand style consists; nor to describe by words the proper means of acquiring it—*if the mind of the student should be at all capable of such an acquisition.* Could we teach taste and genius by rules, they would be no longer taste and genius."

a result can never rise above the capacity of the greatest artist, nor has this capacity increased perceptibly since the age of Pericles. It follows, then, that genius, or the creative æsthetic faculty, is the form of psychic variable appearing in art. The attempt is made later to identify this faculty with persuasive force in education. For both, while faithful to empirical fact, stimulate the emotions[1] by a super-rational appeal.[2]

Mr. Graham Wallas, in his *Human Nature in Politics*,[3] is a safe guide to illustrations in his field. His careful analysis of the relation between instinctive and rational inference, indicated in the following extract, views the question of progress most impartially. The proposition is stated thus:—[4]" Men often act in politics under the immediate stimulus of affection and instinct, and affection and interest may be directed toward political entities which are very different from those facts in the world around us which we can discover by deliberate observation and analysis." And in the subsequent inquiry, " How far is it true that men, when they do form inferences as to the result of their political actions, always form them by a process of reasoning ? " To which the reply is "almost never." Two facts help to mitigate the depressing effect of this conclusion. First, without sufficient quantitative evidence, qualitative methods of reasoning cannot lead even the expert's mind to correct inferences.[5] And, second, even in evaluating past events the historian is to such an extent influenced by habitual preference that two minds commonly draw conflicting inferences from the same body of facts.[6] When party feeling is involved in current issues, even the most obvious facts are ignored.[7] The hope for political progress then lies in the development of quantitative research to facilitate rational inference. Mr. Wallas finds justification for this hope[8] in attempts such as were made by the Poor Law Commission of 1905 to estimate quantitatively the relative industrial effectiveness of health, hope, and imaginative range resulting from education, together with " the ' purely economic ' motive created by ideas of future pleasure and pain." If in addition to the problems now solved by statistics and other means of exact comparison,[9] problems involving social motives as tenuous as these may be attacked on the same footing, the sign is of good omen. With the general acceptance of a standard classification for political facts,[10] science may in time lay before both voter and politician all the facts required to decide a point on its merits. Yet even when this end is reached, the welfare of all concerned must depend essentially on the collective capacity to act from rational as opposed to

1 cf. Aristotle, *Poetics*, Chap. VI. "And the end is the chief thing of all, " i.e., the end of *purposeful*, not adventitious action.

2 Evidence of the superrationality of the "grand style" is found in the failure of critics, from Longinus to Matthew Arnold, to explain it in rational terms. The grand style is more easily illustrated than described.

3 Constable, London, 1908.

4 ibid. p. 98.

5 ibid. p. 142.

6 cf. Max Nordau, *The Interpretation of History*, trans. M. A. Hamilton, London, 1910, p. 77. " This teleological philosophy of history has no scientific value, and may be completely neglected by any reasonable man."

7 The " surprise " of the Italian Peace delegation at Mr. Wilson's decision with regard to Fiume, published April 22nd, ignored his previous memorandum to them of April 14th, which set forth his reasons and intention to make this decision. Second memorandum published April 25th.

8 op. cit. p. 157.

9 e.g., Photographs. ibid. p. 162.

10 see proposed classification, ibid. p. 122.

non-rational motives which the mere availability of evidence cannot determine. " The limits of our conscious conduct are fixed by the limits of our self-knowledge."[1] The psychic variable, then, affecting social progress along lines of practical interest, is a faculty of deliberate analytic judgment, to be recognized in the educative process under the head of intellectual discipline.

The transition from politics to our next topic—the art of normative criticism—may well be made by a final quotation from the authority so closely followed in the last.[2] " The political thinker has indeed sometimes to imitate the cabinet maker, who discards his most finely-divided numerical rule for some kinds of specially delicate work, and trusts to his sense of touch for a quantitative estimation." It is precisely this sense of touch which in cognitive terms is known familiarly as the critical acumen. Pascal distinguishes in this faculty two main elements—"l'esprit de géométrie" and "l'esprit de finesse." These may be interpreted as "the sense of logical distinction" and "the sense of æsthetic unity," which Dr. Johnson combines without losing the distinction into "intuitive good sense." This, he insists, is more than a logical process. The ideal critic[3] must possess this intuitive good sense to the full, and apply it in the formation of critical standards. In that criticism fairly represents social interest in the creation of standards by which to judge self-expression, it falls well within the intellectual sphere. Criticism therefore receives less than art from science, for the effects of drama and painting, at least, are intensified by improvements in materials and stage settings. Like the artist's training and the politician's analysis of social forces, the critic is helped to recognize distinction by study of his field, and the methods of such study become increasingly quantitative. This much is of science. But just as extensive reading in history does not of itself give the power of accurate forecast, the study of criticism does not of itself give intuitive good sense. Setting its compass by the laws of thought, criticism in society cannot progress beyond the rationality of popular philosophies, nor in the individual beyond his intuitive good sense. This psychic variable is also related to mental discipline.

" The critical spirit is thus the moulding of human experience from age to age. It is therefore identical with education."[4] While criticism and education have this aim in common, education must do more than label human experiences. Indeed, education must often create experiences for the pupil to teach him what the labels mean, or, in heuristic terms, that he may choose his own labels. To adapt Lincoln's epigram, education is the moulding of the pupil, by the pupil, and for the pupil— under the educator's direction. And here, again, appears the reflex mental action of impulse upon experience which tends to discredit progress in the fields of art, politics, and criticism. Further, since the educative process involves correspondence between two minds, one may expect to come upon the psychic variable in each mind.

The common distinctions drawn between teaching, instruction, and education serve the present purpose by separating those elements

1 ibid. p. 181.

2 ibid. p. 162.

3 cf. Irving Babbitt, The Masters of Modern French Criticism. Boston. 1912. p. 392. "Our ideal critic, then, would need to combine the breadth and versatility and sense of differences of a Sainte-Beuve with the elevation and insight and sense of unity of an Emerson. It might be prudent to add of this critic in particular what Emerson has said of man in general, that he is a golden impossibility."

4 Paul E. More, Essay on Criticism, Shelburne Essays, VII Series.

whose object is to impart and arrange knowledge from education proper, which aims to modify character by applying knowledge, to activities. Though perhaps never entirely separate in the class room, this distinction helps to mark off the province in which the psychic variables predominate ; namely, in the deliberate modification of character.

In the first division of the process, the acquisition and arrangement of knowledge, we deal with processes almost entirely under scientific control. The fields of research contributing to these processes are three ; namely, study of pupil, study of subject matter, and study of teaching methods. As affecting the extent of such processes, the science of school administration should also be mentioned. The outstanding achievement of research in child study is mutual saving of energy through the discovery of psycho-physical laws. Correspondence between teacher and pupil is vastly improved when by mechanical means[1] the teacher can test and compare his pupils' power of attention, sense discrimination, motor reaction, memory, association, fatigue endurance, and even interest.[2] The classification of pupils by aptitude has already entered schools of vocational training through the Taylor system of scientific industrial management, and may, by universal adoption, eventually eliminate the "misfit." When to these has been added scientific arrangement of conditions under which the pupil works, and of the tools he uses, enough has been said to suggest the wealth of knowledge to be applied. Similarly as regards the preparation of material for study, the pupil receives prime consideration in the form of text-books, graphic illustrations, and in the increasingly-united efforts of teachers to offer the proper subject, and indicate how it may best be studied.[1] With regard to method, the case is only slightly less clear. The fact that recent innovations in practice appeared long ago in theory does not argue lack of progress, for "each reappearance of an old method finds it treated on a higher plane."[2] In fact, it is on compromises effected between individual and collective teaching, humanistic and handicraft subjects, instinctive and social interests, that the claim for progress is chiefly based. The science of school administration has brought these advantages to an ever-increasing proportion of the population. Science, thus far, has left comparatively little to chance.

It is only when we pass to the other aspect—purposive modification of character—that science is clearly beyond her depth, but even so, there is some resistance to the drift of wind and tide. In the application of knowledge to activities, the educator must decide what interests and activities to recommend. He must logically demonstrate their superiority to other interests and activities which, because more instinctive, are easier to acquire and perform. Further, he must teach mental discipline,[3] which requires that the pupil's mind shall distinguish between the teacher's thought and his own thought regarding an object, and also

---

1 see Chas. Myers, *An Introduction to Experimental Psychology*, Chap. VI, and references p. 153.

2 see E. L. Thorndike's results, *Popular Science Monthly*, N.Y., Vol. 81, 448 ff. (19-2), article on *Permanence of interests and their relation to abilities*. cf. Myers, op. cit. p. 150 for contradictory statement.

1 John Adams, *The New Teaching*, p. 12 [quotes from report published *The School Review* (Chicago) March, 1917]. Extra period of 45 minutes set aside each fortnight to teach how to study that subject.

2 ibid. p. 4.

3 see development of this distinction in W. Mitchell. *The Structure and Growth of the Mind*, p. 64, which justifies the use of the term discipline in the above sense.

between both thoughts and the object itself. In each of these processes the educator obtains much help from empirical knowledge. Philosophy and ethics though social science appraise interests and their appropriate activities by standards of social worth. Psychology provides material to support these judgments, and formal logic furnishes laws and suggestions in the method of proof.

If this much be granted sufficiently true in theory, two desiderata remain, in each of which appears the psychic variable. First, having logically demonstrated the relative merits of two equally possible courses of action, the educator may not rest content with the academic distinction. He must, by force of emotional appeal, see to it that the better course is acted upon. If the issue lie between drunkenness and sobriety, the educator's exposition, through fidelity to fact, must arouse associations to make the public house uninviting. It is this educative power to determine action by faithful representation of fact which I have identified with the creative æsthetic in art. In the educator the art is histrionic, and varies in excellence from the town crier to the finished player of Hamlet's description; but whenever the educator, by setting values in true proportion, modifies character through "warmth and intimacy" of presentation, he approximates the homeopathic treatment of emotion which Aristotle conceived the end of dramatic art.[1] Progress, then, for the educator is determined by inherent power of emotional appeal.

The second desideratum left by science is the means of acquiring discipline. This obviously concerns the pupil, and at first seems little else than the power of response to the appeal just described—Ruskin's "happy flexibility." However much the educator welcomes this quality, it lacks the permanence of real discipline. In practical matters of conduct, the pupil's thoughts of an idea such as plagiarism, for example, must be sufficiently distinct from the desire to appear learned, to prevent his taking credit for work not his own. He has thus to compare his own thoughts of plagiarism with the educator's thoughts, and distinguish both from the cold idea of literary dishonesty. In the purely intellectual sphere the same degree of permanence is required. When the educator, let us say, tries to convey the idea of infinity which he symbolizes by ∞, suggests by extending parallel lines on the same plane, and finally visualizes by placing a light between two mirrors, he fails unless the pupil's mind fuses these impressions into a lasting concept. Such examples as these, taken at random, will suggest many more to indicate that the pupil must possess something of the politician's analytic judgment and the critic's intuitive good sense before his mind can be capable of discipline.

The strength of these faculties—for persuasion and for acquiring discipline—has been said to depend on psychic variables beyond social control. One is then forced to conclude that the pupil's knowledge cannot be applied to his activities beyond the educator's power of stimulation and the pupil's own powers of self-command and intuition. Beyond these limits, education as a social interest has not progressed.

Yet justice to experimental pedagogy requires even so theoretic a discussion as this to moderate the finality of the last statement. Though education may logically be bound within the stated limits, there is every reason to suppose that the profession has a long way to travel

---

1 *Poetics*, Chap. VI, ethical interpretation of Catharsis. cf. also Plato, *Republic, Bk. IV*, for further discussion of ethical discipline.

before these limits are reached. There is also ground for hope that the resisting organisms may eventually be modified in the direction desired. The first point is difficult to argue for lack of evidence, yet the fact of tremendous acceleration in the development of empirical knowledge since the race has come to self-consciousness implies that such progress has only just begun.[1] It is therefore entirely probable that through public opinion and State support education may attract more vigorous minds than the profession contains now. This must favourably affect the progress of the pupil, but to a less degree than organic modification. Since this latter end lies before the greater part of research in medicine, criminology, sociology, eugenics, and their new sister euthenics, some progress is likely to result   The New Teaching seeks this end by arousing interest to produce volitional attention by which discipline is realized.[2]

Saint-Beuve quotes a saying of Pascal that "the inventions of men increase from age to age, but that the goodness and badness of the world remain in general the same."[3] My feeling is that the majority of educators, while accepting the generality, would render a more hopeful verdict considering the many promises of escape from the fiat of biological inheritance.

1 See the striking illustration quoted by John Adams, *Evolution of Educational Theory*, p. 86. The 240,000 years of human life are crowded into a 12-hour day, in which at twenty minutes to twelve the earliest vestiges of Egyptian and Babylonian civilization begin to appear " Before this, " for over eleven and a half hours there is nothing to record."

2 cf.   Irving Babbitt, op. cit. p 349, note   This quality of mental strenuousness, the " unre. mitting exercise of the active will " is the chief of Buddhist virtues. " This Oriental strenuousness one should hasten to add, is directed toward self conquest and not, like the Occidental variety, toward the conquest of the outer world."

3 Ibid. p. 135.

CONCERNING CATCHWORDS.

(A prevented Address to the Education Society of the University of Leeds.

By GERALDINE E. HODGSON, Litt.D.

THE seventeenth century, among other notable and choice gifts, left us two warnings concerning language. Said Thomas Hobbes: "Words are wise men's counters, they do but reckon by them; but they are the money of fools."[1]

Blaise Pascal buried amid the devastating dialectics of *Les Provinciales* this illumined reminder :—*Le monde se paye de paroles : peu approfondissent les choses.*[2]

Yet the mass of mankind went unheeding on their way, until about the middle of the last century, Mr. John Morley pulled them up once more with his terse witticism : "Labels are devices for saving talkative persons the trouble of thinking."[3]   If ordinary words have, as Hobbes and Pascal urge, their hidden traps and dangers, how much worse are these "labels," *catchwords*, which the Oxford Concise

[1]*Leviathan*, ch. ii.

[2]*Lettres Provinciales*, ii :—" The world pays itself with words · few men look deeply into things."

[3]*Miscellanies*, Vol. 1, p. 142.

Dictionary defines as "influential temporary phrases in politics, religion, &c.," whose distinguishing mark, perhaps, is superficiality rather than mere evanescence. The true catchword, or catch-phrase, is so rather by its use than in its essence; hence it is relative to its employer. We cannot, at any rate as a rule, take a word and say—this, *semper, ubique, et ab omnibus*, is a catchword. A may employ a given word, no matter how hardly worked a one, wisely and with suggestion; while B flings it about with little meaning, and that a wrong one. In attempting some illustrations, I will resist the impulse to select *pacificist* or *bolshevist*; not because they might raise a storm, since some storms are more fruitful than some calms, nor because I doubt the mischievous taste of some here for provocative topical terms, it being entirely true that

> The fighting races don't die out
> If they seldom die in their bed ;

nor because I think these two poor examples of their kind, for in fact they are excellent, specially in their ugly corruptions "bolshies" and "conchies." I reject them because I am inclined to suppose that they may prove more temporary (and therefore less truly catchwords) than those which I propose to attempt to discuss. Yet before I sweep them aside I will use them as an illustration of a minor point, viz., that they are painful and striking examples of literary and etymological poverty—specially in their corrupt, popular, shortened form—poverty verging on bankruptcy. In this they are typical of a grave danger. In the *Times Literary Supplement* last autumn, Professor Postgate started a correspondence on the "Corruption of English." In the course of it I contributed a quotation from one of Milton's "Letters." As I think this letter cannot be too widely known, too carefully considered, I will quote part of it again now. Writing to a Florentine friend, Benedetto Buonmattai, engaged at the moment on a Tuscan grammar, Milton wrote —

> " I hold him to deserve the highest praise who fixes the principles and forms the manners of a state, and makes the wisdom of his administration conspicuous both at home and abroad. But I assign the second place to him who endeavours by precepts and by rules to perpetuate that style and idiom of speech and composition which have flourished in the purest periods of the language. . . . . If we compare the benefits which each of these confer, we shall find that the former alone can render the intercourse of the citizens just and conscientious, but that the latter gives that gentility, that elegance, that refinement which are next to be desired. The one inspires lofty courage and intrepid ardour against the invasion of an enemy ; the other exerts himself to annihilate that barbarism which commits more extensive ravages on the minds of men. . . . . It is the opinion of Plato that changes in the dress and habits of the citizens portend great commotions and changes in the state ; and I am inclined to believe that when the language in common use in any country becomes irregular and depraved, it is followed by their ruin or their degradation. For what do terms used without skill or meaning, which are at once corrupt or misapplied, denote but a people listless, supine, and ripe for servitude ? On the contrary, we have never heard of any people or state which has not flourished in some degree of prosperity as long as their language has retained its elegance and purity."

It is obvious that our everyday speech is becoming more and more deteriorated by slang, slang without either traceable meaning or charm. We have not yet forgotten *Punch's* recent subaltern who, being asked to interpret the adjective "posh," explained that it is "slang for 'swish.' " The accompanying picture was admirably drawn ; yet underneath lay the indigenous stupidity ; and even while one laughed at the draughtsman's wit, down the ages rang those warning words, "What do terms used without skill or meaning, which are at once corrupt or misapplied, denote but a people listless, supine, and ripe for servitude?"

It is not as if the slang-mongers were damaging a bad tool. English is neither poor nor unexpressive. What can surpass such passages as—

" A man shall be as an hiding-place from the wind, and a covert from the tempest ; as rivers of water in a dry place, as the shadow of a great rock in a weary land ;"

or

> Sunset and evening star,
> And one clear call for me.
> And may there be no moaning of the bar
> When I put out to sea.
> But such a tide as moving seems asleep,
> Too full for sound or foam,
> When that which drew from out the boundless deep
> Turns again home.

I chose these particular passages because they are pure English ; their melody and dignity owe nothing to elaborateness or any recondite factor.

It may be urged that, however beautiful these passages are, we cannot all, all the time, live on the level of the Authorized Version or Tennyson's Swan-song.

While that is true and obvious, I should like to urge that there are other alternatives than senseless slang. Cockney dialect was once made the vehicle of one of the most moving little poems in any form of our English tongue, when Rudyard Kipling wrote " Danny Deever." No one can pretend that is classical speech, but it is human poetry. There is an alternative, indeed there are many, between the grand manner and meaningless slang.

Of course, new words must come into the tongue of every nation which is not stagnating, which is ever going on into new spheres of activity, material and non-material. By no possibility can such new coinages be condemned, so long as they are coined on intelligent lines : for new things new names must be found. Yet, it remains true that senseless slang degrades the common speech.

Now I must turn away from slang to the matter in hand. The two words I have criticized are, from an etymological standpoint, rather poor and ugly than actually senseless ; but besides that they are used with that extreme degree of superficiality and recklessness which reduces them to the status of catchwords.

The examples I propose to take have a wider application, consequently more interest. The first is the phrase " We moderns." It has a ring of Nietzsche about it. Yet, let us remember that if on that ground we condemn it wholesale, we ourselves are "catchwording." Those of us who think most severely about him must admit that he had lucid moments. Surely, few among us mortals are homogeneously, universally mad or bad, without any respite at all ?

The objection to this phrase " We moderns " should rest not on the user but the use. "I" is employed nowadays, constantly, in season and out, and with bludgeoning finality. It seems, very often, to be assumed that everything "modern" is *ipso facto* beyond challenge; and, equally, that "we moderns"

> are the men, and wisdom will die with us,
> And none of the old seven Churches shall vie with us.

But, in good sooth, who are "we," and what is the meaning of "modern"? Surely if "we" cover the whole population, then no one pretends that "we" are all agreed about anything, save such settled and incontrovertible matters as that, other things being equal, "fire burns."

We hear, even *ad nauseam*, of the "modern man"; but who is he? Are all the multitudes we pass in the street, sit with in crowded trains and tramcars, live our daily life with,—"modern"? If so, have they all one agreed philosophy, religious, political, social? Have they even agreed on such twopenny-ha'penny matters as which is the best evening paper or the most suitable pudding for Sunday? I trow not. First and foremost, beneath this catchword is the monstrous fallacy that we think and feel in agreed herds. Again, what do we mean by the very word "modern"? There is no one definition which even those who use it and apply it to themselves will all accept.

It is a catch-phrase, employed perhaps consciously, more probably unconsciously, to win a concensus of opinion which does not exist; sometimes even to suggest that such a concensus is already won. It is as much and as dangerous a catchword as our antique acquaintances, "All intelligent people know," or "All honest men maintain," phrases which, on analysis, dwindle down to include those who happen to agree with the user of the phrase. Yet one of the commonplaces of manuals on logic is a warning against the employment of "ambiguous or question-begging terms," of which class catchwords form a large part. "We moderns" is the sin of the hasty journalist. Our old friend Gigadibs would have revelled in it till some dread hour when Blougram made mincemeat of it and him.

It may be more than worth while to pause and ask ourselves if it may not be at least as foolish, as unintelligent, as disastrous to wish to change everything as to refuse to change anything.

The second which I have chosen is not solely journalese: it is also the error of literary and historical people, who should know better:— it is *mediæval*. Even in learned and scholarly books it is not uncommon to find this word used as a comprehensive and decisive term of condemnation; one used to connote—in a superb uprising of contempt—ignorance, credulity, vice.

Yet the cadence of a great line steals on the ear, lingers in the memory of some among us; a line not only exquisitely musical, but full of meaning, and surely full of truth—

> Le moyen âge énorme et délicat.

In a flash it recalls the stupendous majesty of Reims, that tapering slender *flèche* of Amiens. People are careless about precise limitations; but whatever their delimitation, the Middle Ages must surely include the twelfth and thirteenth centuries. Well, the great achievement of St. Thomas Aquinas belongs to them. People talk and write contemptuously of Scholasticism, but they are not often those who have studied it. So far, no system of Philosophy has answered all our questions nor satisfied all our needs; in that, Scholasticism shares the common fate. But it must take a stupid person indeed to dismiss the *Summa* of St. Thomas as ignorance or credulity.

But I will take an example of the creative power of the Middle Ages, viz., the Gothic Cathedrals, an example not only more within the general reach, but perhaps more profoundly typical, for no less a critic than Mr. Arthur Symons declared that "Every age has its own symbols, Gothic Architecture remains the very soul of the Middle Ages." Possibly, he had not studied Scholasticism sufficiently to perceive the relation which some have discerned between it and the great Cathedrals.

Now, in sober truth, could men guilty of ignorance, credulity, or vice, or even of general incapacity, have built the west fronts of Amiens and Reims; have raised the vast, solemn, awful nave of Chartres; have created the dreaming, soaring, lace-like grace of Beauvais; or the symmetry, the white perfection of Soissons, now more than half destroyed ? Could such people have schemed the procession-path at Wells, the retro-choir of Chichester, or the shimmering beauty of Gloucester's choir ? The mere suggestion is ridiculous.

But Gothic Architecture is as much a proof of mediæval *intellect* as of the mediæval taste for and sense of beauty. The *raison d'être* of Gothic Art, as everyone may learn from any competent book on architecture is that nothing in it ever is merely beautiful, but everything has a reason and a use.

Writing of the windows of the two Sainte-Chapelles of France— at Paris and at St. Germain—Mr. West says :—"Like everything else in Gothic Art, they are the result of subtle reasoning and exquisite artistic taste."[1] "Everything else !" The *whole* of Gothic Art is a blend of intellect and taste.

"Mediæval," Gothic Art most certainly is; the *soul* of the Middle Ages," according to Mr. Symons, who is not solitary in his view. Can anyone afford to dismiss contemptuously "the result of subtle reasoning and exquisite artistic sense" ? I can hardly think so.

While I leave on one side here and now all that vast side of it which is spiritual, I venture to ask what possibility is there that an age should be ignorant, stupid, credulous, futile when *its most characteristic work* can be described as subtly reasonable, artistically exquisite. Nor is this all. While the great master builders wrought in stone, the artists in glass added their aid. True, the great west window of Reims is gone beyond repair ; but Chartres remains still more glorious, and more complete, that twelfth and thirteenth century glass which Huysmans called "La folle splendeur de ses vitres," which he compared to a "glowing furnace of precious stones."[2]

To enter Notre Dame de Chartres, passing from the dazzling sunlight of the bare, exposed little *Placc*, passing through the rich sculpture of *le Portail Royal*, is to experience a sensation comparable with few, if any others. Slowly, out of the stupendous gloom, emerge those jewelled windows, sparkling, scintillating, twinkling like stars set in the deep darkness of a moonless night.

[1] *Gothic Architecture in England France*, by G. H. West, p. 131.
[2] *La Cathédrale*, p. 163.

You may find some faint analogue of the brilliance in the glorious vestibule of the Chapter House in York Minster, but there the splendour lacks that mysterious setting of Chartres' sombre vastness. It is so light at York.

Now, all this, which I have tried inadequately to describe, and far, far more than I have attempted to include, is the work, the inimitable work of the ages often scornfully dismissed in the epithet *mediæval*, an epithet which has lost its primary meaning, and has become in the mouths and on the pens of many a mere damaging catchword. When people fling these adjectives about at random, surely they forget Mr. Symons's pertinent reminder: "Every age has its own symbols," a statement which does not necessarily mean, as is not infrequently supposed, that the symbols of one age are useless to another, but means that each age develops certain traits peculiarly its own. The more one reads history the more one is inclined to discredit these harsh sweeping judgments on the centuries, even on the tenth, "the age of iron, lead, and gloom," as one described it. The same is very generally true of harsh personal judgments. Putting aside the irreclaimable few in all classes, the more we know of our fellows the more keenly we appreciate each one's peculiar difference. *Tout savoir c'est tout pardonner.* But how seldom we know *all*.

I have dwelt at length on this term mediæval, because, as I have said, it is a catchword of the educated, and one of which they should not be guilty, just so little knowledge proving it a catchword.

My third example shall be drawn from current social life. We all know that not in this country alone, but all over Europe, there is great disturbance, discontent in the industrial world. Apart from real, solid grievances, grievances which can be put into words and amended by legislative and social arrangements, administered by good will, there is a fringe of indefinite aspiration, of partly diagnosed dissatisfaction. When those who harbour these feelings are pressed to explain themselves, I suppose the most usual phrase which comes to their lips is, " I have a right to be as well off as other people." Superficially, it may sound reasonable, but it is a catch-phrase, containing three most ambiguous epithets—" right " (with which I have not time to deal now), " other people," and " as well off."

Now, as a matter of fact (and facts *have* value), who are these "other people "? How "well off " are they? Lastly, if some are well off, how far is their condition due to their own lawful efforts, strenuous efforts, perhaps, which the grumblers may not be at all willing to make? To ask these questions is not to pretend that there are no members of the community who grow rich and wallow in comfort at others' expense, there are too many of such ; nor is it the smallest attempt to deny or underrate the undeserved misery to which the selfishness and greed of some of our fellow-creatures condemn others.

But the catch-phrase, " as well off as others," if it is to mean anything, implies that equality of condition is a mechanical thing, and that conditions could be equalized by external means, a view which I think is contradicted by History and Political Science. A blend of many causes is requisite to secure even *equality of opportunity*, i.e., the real enabling of every child to make the best of himself and his life according to his personal ability and bent.

The present time is guilty of a dangerous catchword—*Reconstruction*. It is strewn all over the dailies and monthlies; conversation is peppered with it. It is a genuine instance, being used to cover every kind of idea, and half idea, and no idea, and yet as if it had one meaning and only one, and that so clearly defined and proclaimed that no one can remain ignorant of it. Yet nothing of the sort is true.

Doubtless many changes are vitally necessary; quite certainly we have tolerated too long many indefensible conditions of life, but they are not all of one kind, nor amenable to a single remedy. We must first tackle the complementary relations of the individual and of the community of which he is a unit—a complicated problem that. Further, the individual must be considered on all his sides: industrial, sociological, intellectual, emotional, moral, spiritual. Since the community is composed of such individuals, its characteristics must be similar. Nor is it enough to deal with the individual or community of *to-day*: the problem includes history of the past as well as intelligent, close, alert observation of the present. To-day is the fruit of all the yesterdays; we are, in fact and not rhetorically, inheritors of the ages, custodians of the passing present, and, to no small extent, architects of the future.

People who so lightly and with such almost vulgar assurance bandy about this catchword *reconstruction* seem scarcely to realize the prerequisites of its fruitful use; e.g., the intellectual effort necessary to grasp the historical, philosophical, and practical factors involved, so much of this not to be learned from books, but from the slower process of mastering our contact with men and affairs; or the long discipline needed in justice, self-control, patience, foresight, insight; or the slow training of passions and emotions in the transforming light of a great ideal; or the refining fire of spiritual achievement. People too often speak and write as if the entire life of a great and mixed race could be cast down and remoulded as irresponsibly as our old friend Balbus, of the discredited Latin exercise book, went and built his ever-recurring wall.

All catchwords are intrinsically mischievous, most of all those which, whether literary or sociological, possess that bit of truth which Tennyson branded when he wrote—

A lie which is half a truth is ever the blackest of lies.

When words like reconstruction have some shred of meaning, then the great mass hurries off with them, and, not analysing their context, either weaves them into fantastic, impossible theories, or, disillusioned by difficulty, dismisses the whole idea and possibility of human improvement.

Mr. Morley gibbetted another damaging quality; they "save the trouble of thinking." While all capacity grows and is enriched by effort and exercise, the love of ease, the failure of endurance, the deliberate avoidance of difficulty, the shirking of responsibility are all fostered by this heedless, facile use of catchwords, terms which sound as if they mean something, which may be capable of meaning, but which have none to those who snatch them up and employ them without reflection. All distinctions, qualifications, saving circumstances, modifications, and the like disappear in the mental and moral mist of these sounding but empty words; we are left, as Henri de Regnier said, with

Les contours indécis des choses incertaines
(The blurred outlines of doubtful things).

Locke, in the *Essay on the Human Understanding*, wrote:—
"There is nobody in the Commonwealth of Learning who does not profess himself a lover of Truth, and there is not a rational creature that
would not take it amiss to be thought otherwise of. And yet for all
this, one may truly say that there are very few lovers of Truth for
Truth's sake." In his short fragment "On Study," he wrote:—"It is
a duty we owe to GOD as the Fountain and Author of all Truth, Who
is Truth itself; and it is a duty also we owe to our own selves, if we
will deal candidly and sincerely with our own souls, to have our minds
constantly disposed to receive Truth wheresoever we meet with it. . . . .
Our first and great duty is to bring to our studies and inquiries after
knowledge a mind covetous of Truth, that seeks after nothing else,
and after that impartially, and embraces it, how poor, how contemptible,
how unfashionable soever it may seem."

To sound, clear thought, sharp edges, defined divisions, precise
accuracy, articulation of parts, logical sequence are essential. The
strength and coherence of reasoned discourse are dissipated and dissolved by the kaleidoscopic indefiniteness of catchwords, its lucidity
dimmed by their mist and fog; in short, they undermine our whole
intellectual life. Locke's words are at least as true now as when they
were written. In an era when few desire Truth with what the
Economist would call an "effectual demand," i.e., ability and intention
to pay the irremovable cost, even though large demands are made for
popular education, it cannot be too widely taught and learned that the
pursuit of Truth, the acquisition of knowledge and sound judgment are
costly processes, not only in money, the least part both in amount and
importance of the total outlay, but in time, unremitting, often uphill,
sometimes painful effort, intellectual, moral, spiritual effort, and, occasionally, in the more terrible cost of temporary doubt, uncertainty,
clouds, and darkness.

Book-learning may possibly be bought at a less price, but not
Truth, nor the power of sound judgment. Just to safeguard my meaning, let me say that catchwords—offering a shadow for substance, pre-.
tending to be something when they are nothing, inasmuch as being led
astray is worse than being left alone to grope our way in the difficult
twilight we call Life—catchwords must not be confounded with those
technical specialized terms which are essential to philosophy and
science. Nor is condemnation of superficiality to be regarded as an
attack on Authority. Dr. Creighton's test of education, viz., "Ability
to discern the true core of a problem," i.e., to disentangle the main proposition from its corollaries, is not more searching than the perhaps
rarer ability to distinguish legitimate from false authority. This taste
for current catchwords, for the passing hour's unthought-out fashions
may be classed with those labour-saving devices and mental short-cuts
which the charlatan is ever ready to offer to the idle and half-educated.

In the present welter of views, theories, and passions, when everyone talks and argues, when those who have thought least seem most
positive about all things in heaven and upon earth, it is specially in-
cumbent on all who care about the nation's mental and moral life to
insist on accuracy of observation and statement; to urge strict
sequence in inference, and justice in implication; to increase, train,
and develop to the utmost the rare power of sound judgment.

Since diagnosis of a thing's cause is often a necessary preliminary to its alteration or eradication, it may not be impertinent to inquire into the source of this taste for catchwords. Of what are they the outcome ? No doubt, as I have already suggested, they spring from a blend of ignorance and laziness, causes which, not improbably, are persistent and indigenous in the human race. But have there not been, say in the last fifty years, special causes at work, new circumstances changing the whole surface of our English life, and, in some measure, our ways of thought and speech ? Surely yes.

The demand for " more education," attempted in the legislation of 1870 and the subsequent amplifying Acts, have accustomed us to the idea of education.

The effort to spread it has, however, been unaccompanied, too often, by a just, widely disseminated appreciation of education's highest aims and proper contents. The power to read written and printed matter has become the property of all and sundry ; but alongside and with it have not gone the development of judgment and the cultivation of taste. The mere ability to read, unguided, uncounselled, uninformed, afforded, among its other baneful results, a potent encouragement to the catchword habit.

Once more, with the spread of so-called education, the notion seems to have arrived that one person's opinion is as valuable as another's. This does not obtain in academic or in cultivated circles; but the Universities, even the Provincial ones, are apt to forget how isolated they are, how small is their effective influence ; how few they really reach and touch.

Among the ordinary mass, accustomed through the power of reading to that amalgam of fact and fancy, of half-formed opinion and sheer invention, of rhetoric and emotion, which form the material of all save our very best journalism, among that ordinary mass there seems to be little or no idea of the long discipline, the hard work, the self-denying ordinances of a scholar, or of any man or woman whose opinion on a matter of any importance is to be worth the breath with which it is uttered.

Further, the tendency of present-day education is rather to satisfy the receptive than to develop the creative, active, judging capacity of the mind. Then again, as it has been well said, and that before the war, " We live in an age of unparalleled distraction."[1] Possibly, we scarcely realize how hard it is amid a mass of impressions, and amidst their variety, to remain fresh enough to judge as well as to suffer them. This multiplicity and variety fatigue the senses and blunt the mind's fine delicate edge.

To distraction is added hurry. There is so much to know; so many of us are expected to know it, and time is short. As a philosoper, recently dead, once wrote: " We have no time to think things out, and yet are expected to have an opinion."[1] Is it surprising, in such circumstances, if the teacher cater for human receptivity, or if the taught snatch at ready-made opinion and the current catchword ? It is not surprising; that they should not do so is only possible at the cost of great pains, exerted at the prompting of unusual insight and foresight.

[1] J. R. Illingworth.

Are there, and this is my final point, any remedies? May I suggest three?

The first is the restoration of the almost lost love of fine workmanship, not for the sake of any possible reward, but for itself. May I, for a moment, return to Gothic architecture as a type of fine work? Often the names of the great cathedral builders cannot now be found; they seldom put a name or even an initial to their work. An exception at Notre Dame at Amiens occurs to me. On one of the exquisite stalls there, those carved stalls of which Ruskin said their young-grained oak seemed "under the carver's hand, . . . to cut like clay, to fold like silk, to grow like living branches, to leap like living flame," there is a figure, doubtless the carver's portrait, and his name. Yet the name is appended not as an advertisement, but as a prayer; as the craftsman left his beautiful work he cut out the words—"Jean Trupin, DIEU te pourvoie." Those stalls are not mediæval, but flamboyant, of the late fifteenth century. Of the mediæval *builder* of Amiens, Ruskin wrote:—"The actual man who built scarcely cared to tell you he did so. . . This is probably the first time you ever read the name of Robert of Luzarches. I say he 'scarcely cared,'—we are not sure that he cared at all. He signed his name nowhere that I can hear of. You may perhaps find some recent initials cut by English remarkable visitors, desirous of immortality, here and there about the edifice, but Robert the builder—or at least the Master of Building, cut *his* on no stone of it."

In Carlisle Cathedral, on the back of an exquisitely carved leaf, so placed that no eye can see it, but that a rightly-guided hand can feel it, is a sculptured beetle. "Useless," no doubt is the utilitarian's verdict. But is it? Is it not a fine proof of that craftsman taste which finishes and perfects work, whether it be seen or unseen? This lover-like work is almost unknown to-day.

The second remedy I would suggest is the making of a dead set against luxury and ease, in and for themselves. Recreation, rest, amusement are, we all agree, neccssaries, "necessaries of efficiency," is the Economist's term; but luxury, for luxury's sake, is an enemy of all fine achievement. It may be said that the hardships of war have inured us to difficulty, have dragged us out of that slough of ease into which we were falling. Have they? Is there no danger of a reaction all the deeper because we have been uncomfortable? Can we not easily foresee the possibility of the temptation to most of us, when the opportunity comes to us at last to say, "Oh! we have borne enough, let us have a little ease, a little peace, a little freedom to do just as we like?" An insidious temptation because it does not lack some shred of justification.

Do not the books advocating *pleasant* methods of education which still pour from the Press show that a relapse into luxury is by no means impossible? There is no reason in the world why learning should be turned into drudgery, why education should be made a painful nuisance. But learning cannot be easy: all excellence is bought at a price, a great price of effort and self-sacrifice. "The gods sell us all things for labour," wrote Erasmus to William of Gouda; and Erasmus was at once a fine scholar and an indefatigable worker.

¹J R. Illingworth.

Lastly, I would suggest the restoration of legitimate authority. I will explain what I mean by the old saying, *Cuique in sua arte credendum est.* At present, we are often unwilling to believe the expert, and, which is sillier and more disastrous, we are willing sometimes to believe an expert in one thing when he handles another. Perhaps it is time that chemists gave up making catechisms, and novelists ceased from posing as political scientists. A restoration of authority to its rightful place, a place where it neither claims too much nor is awarded too little, would indeed be a salutary change in matters of mind, morals, art, and letters.

I have only to add that the aim of this paper is not to attempt to exhaust the subject, but to suggest some lines of reflection to those who soon must be making or marring this country of ours.

REVIEWS.

Education and Social Movements, 1700-1850. By A. E. Dobbs. (xiv + 257 pp.) Longmans, Green & Co., 1919. 10/6 net.

OF recent years the literature bearing on the History of Education in England has been greatly enriched by a variety of social, political, and economic studies like Mr. Graham Wallas's *Life of Francis Place*, and Kirkman Grey's *History of English Philanthropy*, and *Philanthropy and the State*. Mr. Dobbs's book, the first of two volumes of a history of English popular education in modern times, has, in the words of the preface, " special reference to movements of democratic origin and tendency." It is written largely from an economic standpoint and under the stimulus of the W.E.A. movement. To it students of education will extend a warm welcome. It is hardly possible to have too many monographs from experts in these fields. Every subject benefits by being viewed from a new angle, and none more so than education. No one nowadays wonders that William of Wykeham should have emphasized the importance of manners in the making of man, that Elyot concentrated on the training of the ruler for social service, that Rousseau pleaded passionately for the development of human personality, or that Ruskin taught that social service is an obligation and a privilege of every member of the community. To study the history of education means much more than getting up the doctrines of reformers or reading of the schooling of an earlier age. Educational creeds and practices are the expression of ideals and social forces. The student to-day realizes that the education and schooling of the eighteenth and nineteenth centuries, for example, have no meaning apart from the religious, economic, and political beliefs of the time. Unless the philosophy of life that animates an age or party is known, it is difficult to grasp the contemporary attitude towards instruction. It is to be hoped, therefore, that Mr. Dobbs is mistaken in thinking that the title of his book—*Education and Social Movements*—" may suggest a broader field of inquiry than is commonly associated with the subject of education." It is just the broad view that is wanted. Indeed, the criticism that is most likely to be brought against the book is that it does not sufficiently break away from tradition,—Chapters II and IV, for example, add nothing new,—and does not show as clearly as could be wished how economic thought as elaborated, for instance, by Adam Smith, Malthus, and Ricardo, has reacted on popular education.

The reader must not expect to find here a complete account of the circumstances that moulded popular education up to 1850. This would have required a much fuller consideration of religious and political thought than the author has found room for. On the other hand, there is a good deal of suggestive material in the account of economic conditions up and down the country that calls for attention when the reasons why education prospered in one area and lagged behind in another come under consideration.

It is somewhat unfortunate that the volume dealing with conditions since 1850 should not have appeared simultaneously. It might, perhaps, be asked whether under the circumstances it would not have been well to break off the narrative in the thirties. That this decade marks the rise of a new spirit in every sphere of education cannot be doubted.

The book is copiously supplied with references, and most clearly printed. Altogether it is a welcome addition to the educational literature of the period.

C. BIRCHENOUGH.

Experimental Education. By Robert R. Rusk, M.A., Ph.D.- (pp. 346). Longmans, Green & Co., 1919. 7/6 net.

DR. RUSK first published his *Introduction to Experimental Education* in 1912, basing it on Meumann's well-known *Vorlesungen*. He has now revised, brought up to date, and considerably altered what was the first comprehensive English text-book on the subject. At the same time extensive additions have been made, so that now the book is nearly twice its original size, in words if not in pages. The general scope and arrangement is naturally still largely Meumann's, but many of the best parts of the book are Dr. Rusk's own.

The two short new chapters, one on "Thinking, Reasoning, and Speech;" the other on the Psychology and Pedagogy of subjects other than reading, writing, orthography, and arithmetic, enhance the value of the book, and it is to be hoped that in any future editions these subjects will be treated more adequately.

The outstanding fault of the former book was the lack of discrimination shown in estimating the relative value of experiments that have been performed. Although there is quite an improvement in this respect in the present edition, yet Dr. Rusk proves himself far too modest. This is a great loss. Such a large proportion of the work that has been done in experimental education is so entirely useless and shows such a waste of energy, that if the scientific study of educational problems is going to be treated seriously, then comprehensive text-books setting out the results obtained in each line of investigation must show the operation of an intense critical spirit. Experimental results are quoted without mention of the necessary data by which the results can be interpreted, and usually without any estimation of their scientific value (e.g., Stanley Hall's work, p. 78). It may be objected that to do this at all adequately a volume many times the size of the present one would be needed. Possibly so. Yet, on the other hand, much that now appears would with advantage have met a well-earned death. Examples of this may be found on most pages. For example (p. 86), the methods and results of Lobsien's experiment on the special memories of children are accepted uncritically. The results of the testing of a child's immediate memory of lists of words denoting emotions cannot surely be interpreted as measuring the "memory for emotions." "Touch, temperature, and muscular experiences" are mentioned, without remark, as being the basis of a "special memory." This gives a false sense of security to the uninitiated, for what psychologist can delimit our "special memories," or say with certainty that these delimitations when found would apply to everybody?

Dr. Rusk has wisely limited his book in the main to the analytical aspect, for the time is not yet ripe to encourage synthetic work, and what has been done is of little value. In fact, the most common error made by investigators at the present time is insufficient analysis of their problems and matter. Few pedagogical deductions are made; again, wisely. The more experimental education limits itself in its practical applications to the points it has proved up to the hilt, as, e.g., in the more simple rules as regards learning by heart, the more respect will it gain even from its prejudiced opponents.

In future editions, which, one hopes, will be called for, it would be an improvement to add an analysis of chapters in the table of contents.   W. V.

An Advanced History of Great Britain, from the Earliest Times to 1918. By T. F. Tout, M.A., F.B.A., with 63 Maps and Plans. Longmans' Historical Series for Schools, Book III, New Edition. Longmans, Green & Co., 39 Paternoster Row, London. 1919.

THE special interest of this new edition of Professor Tout's valuable *Advanced History of Great Britain* lies in the author's attempt to bring his book up to date by the inclusion of chapters dealing with the reigns of Edward VII and George V. The history of England since the death of Queen Victoria has been so crowded with great happenings, both political and military, that no narrative of these events can fail to be of interest, as well as value to the historical student. If Professor Tout had elected to close his story at August 4th, 1914, his experiment might have been described as markedly successful, for his account of the bitter party struggles of the years 1901-14 is both clear and impartial—some may think too impartial in view of the significance of those struggles as a contributory cause of Armageddon. On the other hand, it is doubtful whether the writer has been well advised to pursue the story beyond the outbreak of the war. The terminus chosen, viz., the Armistice of November 11th, 1918, is not satisfactory. It has yet to be seen whether the war really came to an end at the Armistice ; and, in any case, if it was desirable to present a summary of the war, it would surely have been preferable to wait a few months longer, so as to include, at least, a word of reference to the terms of the Peace. The account of the actual military operations suffers from having been composed too early, the consequence being that the writer is compelled to refer to the great battles of August–November, 1918—the most glorious in the annals of the British Army—in vague language (e.g., " the tide of war swept eastwards beyond Cambrai and St. Qnentin "), instead of by the names by which they will live in history.   M.L.R.B.

Civic Biology. By Clifton F. Hodge and Jean Dawson. (x + 381 pp.) Guin and Co. 7/- net.

THIS admirably illustrated volume is a new departure in the literature of nature study. As suggested by its title, it is a study of living things which affect human life very closely, and which can only be dealt with by intelligent co-operation. The whole scheme gives a particular practical direction to " nature study," which might well be adopted in the higher classes of our elementary schools and in the new continuation classes. To study flies " for their own sake " may appeal to some boys and girls, but the ordinary youth is more likely to be keen about the work when he realizes that the object of it is to make human life healthier. The book has a wide range. Noxious insects, destructive fungi, disease-carrying bacteria, and the like are, of course, included, but the authors also discuss such problems as the preservation of wild birds and wild flowers, the more complete utilization of the land, landscape gardening, &c. It is really impossible to cover so much ground adequately in so small a space, and the authors are inevitably led into a rather technical and summary treatment which would require considerable filling out to make some parts of the text intelligible to an uninstructed reader. It is written with American conditions particularly in mind, but it is suggestive enough to make it a valuable addition to the library of any teacher who is responsible for this department of school or training college work.

Outlines of European History. By A. J. Grant, M.A. ; with illustrations. New edition. Longmans, Green & Co., 39 Paternoster Row, London, 1919.

PROFESSOR GRANT has enlarged his *Outlines of European History* by the inclusion of chapters dealing with the History of the British Isles, which found no place in former editions, and with the causes and antecedents of the Great War of 1914. The chapters relating to English History have been not unsuccessfully welded with the rest, and the author has succeeded in keeping them within good proportions. . . . . The concluding chapters are less satisfactory, and cannot be said to have enhanced the value of the book. Professor Grant has avoided the pitfall of attempting to give an account of the war before the time has come when it will be possible to review it in its true perspective ; but his summary of the events preceding 1914 is sketchy and disconnected, and disfigured by serious chronological inaccuracy. Thus, we are told that the Tsar's invitation to a Disarmament Conference at the Hague was issued in 1908 (instead of 1898), and that the quarrel between France and Germany over Morocco was " in 1912 and 1913 " (instead of 1905 and 1911). Other instances of similar carelessness might be quoted. The illustrations are well reproduced, and the maps will be found useful by students.   M.L.R.B.

BOOKS RECEIVED.

Le Scarabée d'Or (*Baudelaire's* translation of Poe's *The Gold Bug*).

Lettre de Mon Moulin (*A. Daudet*), Les Jumeaux de l' Hôtel Corneille (*E. About*). The first three volumes in Harrap's new Bilingual Series. Text and Translation on opposite pages. Paper covers. Each 1s. 6d. net.

Britain in the Middle Ages. A History for Beginners. By Frances L. Bowman. (120 pp.) Limp cloth. 3s. net. Cambridge University Press.

The Experimental Psychology of Beauty. By Prof. C. W. Valentine. (Revised Edition.) (128 pp.) T. C. & E. C. Jack. 1s. 3d.

Everyday Stories to tell Children. By Mrs. H. C. Cradock. (256 pp.) Harrap & Co. 5s. net.

America at School and at Work. By H. B. Gray. (xx + 172 pp.) Nisbet & Co. 5s. net.

Numerical Trigonometry. By P. Abbott. (vii + 163 pp. and supplement 32 pp.) Longmans, Green & Co. 5s. net.

Mathematical Tables and Formulæ. By P. Abbott. (iv + 58 pp.)

The Measurement of Intelligence. By Lewis M. Terman, with an Introduction by J. J. Findlay. (xix + 362 pp.) Harrap & Co. 5s. net.

Test Material for the Measurement of Intelligence. By Lewis M. Terman. Harrap & Co. 3s. 6d. net.

Problems of National Education, with Prefatory Note by the Right Hon. Robert Munro. By Twelve Scottish Educationists ; edited by John Clarke. (xxvi + 368 pp.) Macmillan & Co. 12s. net.

The Education Problem in Leeds. (95 pp.) Education Offices, Leeds.

The following publications of the General Education Board have been received :—

Reports 1902-14, 1914-15, 1916-17. 1917-18.

The Gary Schools. Seven volumes of reports : A *General Account*, by A. Flexner and F. P. Bachman ; *Industrial Work*, by C. R. Richards ; *Organization and Administration*, by G. D. Strayer and F. P. Bachman ; *Physical Training and Play*, by L. F. Hanmer ; *Science Teaching*, by O. W. Caldwell ; *Household Arts*, by E. W. White ; *Costs, School Year, 1915-16*, by F. P. Bachman and R. Bowman.

Public Education in Delaware. A Report to the Public School Commission of Delaware.

Occasional Papers: *The Country School of To-morrow*, by F. T. Gates; *Changes needed in American Secondary Education*, by C. W. Eliot; *A Modern School*, by A. Flexner; *The Functions and Needs of Schools of Education in Universities and Colleges*, by E. A. Alderman; *Latin and the A.B. Degree*, by C. W. Eliot.

Pamphlets:

Malnutrition and Health Education. By D. Mitchell. (Reprint from *Pedagogical Seminary.*)

The Essentials of English Teaching. By Members of the English Association. (12 pp.) Longmans, Green & Co. 1s.

The Teaching of Children as to the Reproduction of Life. By Beatrice Webb, M.D. (15 pp.) National Council for Combating Venereal Diseases. 3d.

The Incidence of Venereal Diseases and its Relation to School Life and School Teaching. (15 pp.) National Council for Combating Venereal Diseases. 2d.

TRAINING COLLEGE ASSOCIATION.

At the Ordinary Meeting, on March 22nd, of the Training College Association, the following were elected Conveners of the Special Subject Sections:—

1. *English.*—Miss K. T. Stephenson, St. Gabriel's College, Culham.

2. *History.*—Miss H. M. Davis, Whitelands College, Chelsea, S.W.3.

3. *Geography.*—Mr. T. Fairgrieve, London Day Training College, Southampton Row, W.C.1.

4. *Mathematics.*—Professor T. P. Nunn, London Day Training College, Southampton Row, W.C.1.

5. *Science.*—Miss Little, Whitelands College, Chelsea, S.W.3.

6. *French.*—

7. *Principles of Teaching.*—Miss Catty, Goldsmiths College, New Cross, S.E.14.

8. *Hygiene and Physical Training.*—

9. *Drawing.*.—Miss Sharp, Whitelands College, Chelsea, S.W.3.

10. *Music.*—Dr. R. T. White, Goldsmiths College, New Cross, S.E.14.

11. *Handwork and Needlework.*—Miss S. E. Fisher, Training College, Stockwell Road, S.W.9.

All communications should be addressed to the Convener of the Section.

A Sub-Committee on Salaries has been elected, and held its first meeting on May 24. Mr. H. E. J. Curzon (Goldsmiths College) has kindly consented to act as Secretary to this Committee, and all communications on the subject should be addressed to him.

Those serving on the Committee are :—

Group I.—Miss M. H. Wood (Cambridge), Prof. A. E. Dean (Exeter), Mr. H. E. J. Curzon (Goldsmiths College), Mr. Welpton (Leeds).

Group IIa.—Miss Lloyd-Evans (Furzedown College), Dr. Sleight (Graystoke Place).

Group IIb.—Principal Harris (Bangor), Mr. Holgate (Leeds City).

Group IIIa.—Rev. H. A. Bren (Cheltenham), Major H. E. Griffiths.

Group IIIb.—Miss Allan (Homerton), Miss Mercier (Whitelands College), Miss Jenkins (Edge Hill, Liverpool), Miss S. Walker (Darlington).

The names of the Standing Committee on the Superannuation Act are :— Principal Hudson, Miss Mercier, Mr. T. Raymont, Rev. V. W. Pearson, Mr. W. P. Welpton.

The Secretary of this Committee is M. B. Synge (Sec. T.C.A.).

NOTICES.

Readers should take note of the new development of the British Psychological Society. Under the inspiring guidance of Dr. C. S. Myers, F.R.S., the Society is taking a great leap forward. Three sections are being formed, devoted respectively to Medicine, Industry, and Education. No doubt further sections will develop, but the Educational Section should attract many readers of this *Journal.* Those who wish to become members, and who do not know any existing members who would be able to propose and second their nomination, should write to the Honorary Secretary, British Psychological Society, Psychological Laboratory, University College, London, W.C.1, for further particulars.

The publication of the third article on the " School and the Community Spirit " has had to be deferred until the next number, owing to limitations of space. It is still impossible to return to the original size of the *Journal.* Although paper is cheaper, the cost of labour is more than doubled, and printing is in consequence even more expensive than ever.

The Sixth Annual Conference of New Ideals in Education will take place at Cambridge, from July 25th to August 1st, on " The Creative Impulse and its place in Education." The inaugural address will be delivered on Friday, July 25th, at 8.15 p.m., by Mr. Henry Wilson, the Earl of Lytton presiding. Captain Brock will speak on "The Effect of Handcraft on Mind and Body," Viscount Haldane presiding; Professor Rothenstein on "Drawing and the Imaginative Side of Education," Professor Lethaby on "Craft and Culture," Mr. Geoffrey Shaw on "Nationality in Music," Miss Swanson on "Needlecraft," Madame Mairet on "Weaving," &c. Application to be made to the Secretary, 24 Royal Avenue, Chelsea, S.W.3.

The Journal of
Experimental Pedagogy

AND

Training College Record.

THE Journal is published three times a year (March, June, and December). Annual Subscription (3/-) may be sent to the Editor, who will forward post free; or the Journal may be obtained through any bookseller.

A few complete sets of Vols. I, II, and III are still on hand.

Single copies of most back numbers may also be had, either from the Editor or the Publishers.

THE DEVELOPMENT OF REASONING IN SCHOOL CHILDREN.—II.

By CYRIL BURT, M.A.

(Continued.)

The averages obtained with the short list and with the full list, respectively are given in the table below. The figures for ages seven and fourteen are untrustworthy. The standard deviations are based on data from complete age-groups from four schools or departments. The averages are not the strict arithmetic means for these age-groups, but means calculated by averaging medians for these and seven other departments.[1] In selecting the medians an allowance, doubtless insufficient, has been made for the brighter children of the older age-groups who were recorded as having been transferred to central or secondary schools. No such allowance was made in

TABLE SHOWING NUMBER OF PROBLEMS ANSWERED
AT EACH AGE.

| Age (last birth-day.) | SHORT LIST. | | | | | FULL LIST. | | | | |
| | Averages | | Sug-gested Norms | Standard Deviation | | Averages | | Sug-gested Norms | Standard Deviation | |
	Boys	Girls		Boys	Girls	Boys	Girls		Boys	Girls
7	1·6	2·1	2	1·5	1·7	3·8	6·2	6	4·1	4·7
8	4·1	3·8	4	2·1	1·9	11·8	10·1	12	6·0	5·5
9	6·2	5·7	6	2·7	2·4	18·1	16·3	18	7·8	7·2
10	8·5	8·1	8	2·6	2·8	24·6	23·9	24	7·5	8·1
11	10·5	10·2	10	2·3	2·5	31·0	29·0	30	6·8	7·3
12	11·2	12·3	12	1·9	1·8	33·2	35·1	36	5·7	5·4
13	13·7	13·4	14	1·6	1·7	38·8	39·4	42	4·9	5·3
14	15·3	14·9	16	1·4	1·3	45·3	44·1	48	4·5	4·1

calculating the standard deviations. It will be seen that the differences between the averages for the two sexes are extremely small. The figures, however, agree with my general impressions. These are that (1) in the infants' school sex-differences in reasoning proper are undiscernible, but that, owing to a slight precocity in ability to read and use words, the girls appear slightly superior towards the age of six or seven; (2) from the age of eight to eleven, a slight superiority on the part of the boys, probably an inherent sex-difference, manifests itself; (3) at about twelve, the earlier pre-pubertal

[1] For this reason the figures headed "standard deviation" cannot strictly be used to determine the sampling errors of the figures headed "averages." I calculate, however, that with the average for the short list a difference of about 0·5 or more would be significant, one of 1·0 or more would be fairly reliable. For the full list the differences should be about three times this size. Hence, differences between the age averages are reliably demonstrated in every case: differences between the sex-averages are significant in but one or two.

acceleration of general mental growth once more gives the girls a transient superiority; (4) about the school leaving age the superiority of the boys reasserts itself, and increases progressively, until, with post-adolescent students and young employees, the divergence is, as a rule, fairly well-marked. At this age, however, the differences are largely social: for example, in Training Colleges where the women are, on the average, from homes economically somewhat superior to those of the men, the differences in reasoning are reversed.

During school age, however, sex-differences are extremely small. In mixed departments, where the boys are taught the same curriculum by the same teachers, the differences are so minute as to defy demonstration until very large groups have been tested. Throughout, sex-differences appear more clearly in particular aspects of the reasoning processes than in reasoning as such. Girls excel in patient and persevering analysis, in attention to minutiæ and details, in jumping to presumptive conclusions, in constructing concrete hypotheses or picturing definite situations by the aid of the imagination, and, above all, in rapidly extracting the meaning of printed statements and in formulating their solutions in words. Boys tend to be more methodical in their thought processes, and more critical of their own conclusions; they are less wordy and less diffuse; they appear less prone to commit logical fallacies, and more resistant to the suggestions embodied in phrase and form of statement. Interest and familiarity with subject-matter has a noticeable influence. In mathematical, mechanical, and out-of-door problems girls are often clearly penalized. Teaching efficiency, as commonly judged, appears of itself to affect performances in reasoning but little. General culture, whether acquired at home or at school, has a considerable influence. But of all environmental factors the most powerful appears to be the degree of freedom and independence accorded to the child in its life both in class and without.

The differences, however, between the sexes are in no way so marked as to entail separate tests or norms for girls and for boys. For both sexes the annual increment may be taken as, approximately, 2 marks with the short list and 6 marks with the full list. With the short list, the norm for any age is approximately twice the corresponding school standard. Thus, a child aged ten, who would normally be working in Standard IV, should answer the first 8 questions in the short list and about 22 in the full list.

The standard deviations given in the table are also suggestive. The average of the younger children is too near the zero point of the scale for their variability to be clearly expressed. On the other hand, the older age-groups have already given up a large proportion of their brighter members to central and secondary schools. With the middle age-groups the standard deviation is about one-and-a-third times the annual increment. In educational attainments, as I have elsewhere shown, the standard deviation is about equivalent to the annual increment about this period. In these tests, therefore, individual differences are far more apparent. The inferences may be, first, that children of a given age vary more in reasoning capacity than they do in educational attainments; and, secondly, that age, even scholastic age, affects the child's performance less in proportion than do inherent differences in mental capacity. Several very bright nine year old children have, in my experience, reached a score equivalent or superior to the average marks attained at the age of thirteen.

One unusually brilliant girl, aged $10\frac{2}{13}$, succeeded with practically every test-question ; she obtained a score of $16\frac{3}{4}$ with the short list, and $48\frac{3}{4}$ with the full list, the deductions being due not to erroneous answers, but to slight inadequacies in the reasoning. On the other hand, the most highly developed "defective" I have found in a London special school, a boy of $14\frac{7}{13}$, who with the Binet tests reached a mental age of nearly 11, and could read fairly fluently, proved unable to do more than three of the simpler reasoning tests allotted to ages 7 or 8.

A perusal of the tests, as graded in the form of a rough age-scale, suggests interesting features characterizing the development of reasoning in children of school age.

The most obvious difference between the problems solved at an early age and those solved at a later consists in the increase of complexity. A conspicuous consequence of this general principle is the increasing length of the test problems. It would be difficult to devise a test which should at once be as short as the first four tests for age seven (tests 1 to 4) and at the same time be of diagnostic value for age fourteen. Conversely, it would be difficult to devise a test which would be as lengthy as tests 48 or 49, and yet easy enough for an average child of seven to solve. The enlarging span of apprehension is thus an important factor in the development of reasoning capacity. The enlargement depends apparently upon two closely connected functions. In the first place, the child's immediate memory for significant verbal material—"logical" memory, as it is sometimes infelicitously termed—increases very considerably during school life. Binet, for example, found that, immediately after reading his report of a fire, children of eight could reproduce 2 items, children of nine as many as 6 ; and later investigations have found a further increase at older ages. But the solution of a logical problem depends upon something more than the mere retention of the individual data. The data have to be grasped as a single coherent whole, each understood in its bearing upon the other. This requires a retentive memory, but it also requires an extensive scope of attention. The dull child may re-read the problem until he knows the premisses off by heart. But he cannot envisage them as a unity. When the details accumulate beyond a certain minimal amount, his span of apprehension —stretched too wide— breaks down, and bursts like an over-inflated soap-bubble.

A second difference, hardly less obvious, is the increasing variety of subject matter. The subjects about which the older children can reason would be, in many cases, entirely unsuited to the younger. The present tests do not give a fair indication of this increase in general knowledge, since the topics were so chosen as to be well within the experience of even duller children at each stage. Hence, the difficulty of the subject-matter is far less than the difficulty of the reasoning required. The influence of subject-matter, therefore, emerges most clearly in the comparatively narrow circle of ideas to which tests for younger children have to be confined.

Neither of these differences, however, is essentially logical in character. Are there any types of argument, which a child cannot follow at an early age, which he yet can employ with increasing facility as he grows older? At the age of seven, the average child can do little more than solve simple syllogisms, containing for their premisses simple categorical propositions (tests 1, 2 and 4). He is able, however, to supply one of the premisses himself, and to resist the suggestion contained in a proposition whose relevance is apparent only (test 3). Before reaching the age of eight, he can attempt compound disjunctive syllogisms, containing numerous alternatives, and involving parallel pro-syllogisms with suppressed major premisses (tests 5 and 7). Hypothetical propositions occasion difficulties but little, if at all, greater than those occasioned by disjunctive propositions. But the union of the two forms of statement in a single argument, and especially in a single proposition, at once augments the difficulty of inference (e.g., test 22). Dilemmas (compound syllogisms containing a disjunctive proposition as the minor premiss and two hypothetical propositions as the major) are apt to be extremely confusing to the child until a comparatively late stage (cf. tests 36 and 39, although these are not straightforward instances). Other forms of the compound syllogism, analogous in structure (e.g., tests 17 and 22, which contain as the major premiss two propositions, each in form both hypothetical and disjunctive), cannot, apparently, be solved before the age of nine, however simple the subject and however brief the argument (test 17). If in a train of argument the prosyllogisms are serial (e.g., tests 34 and 42) rather than parallel (e.g., test 7)—the whole forming a sorites—a child under twelve finds considerable difficulty in correctly carrying on the inference through one suppressed conclusion to the next over more than three steps. Induction, in the sense of discovering a general rule from a number of particular instances (tests 38, 40, 41, 43; cf. also 29), is rarely accomplished successfully until near the end of the elementary school career; but where the argument proceeds by eliminating in succession each of a number of given alternative hypotheses, except the one consistent with the given data, there the induction can be accomplished almost at the beginning of the school career (tests 5 or 6). In the former case, the difficulty arises from the child being left to invent the hypothetical generalization as well as to verify it. In the latter case, the methodical child has merely to weigh each alternative, as he points to it with his finger tip.

None of these developments, however, implies the mastery of a logical process of a new kind. Indeed, most of the inferences involved might be reduced to a single syllogism or to a system of interdependent syllogisms. And the syllogistic form is, as we have seen, well within the capacity of the youngest age-group tested. The increase in difficulty is thus due to increase in complexity rather than to change in kind.

But there are other ways in which inferences may be classified, in the hope of eliciting differences in kind among the reasoning powers at different ages.

The original series of problems was very largely compiled by taking, one by one, the classical fallacies and the general princples of inference, and constructing syllogisms to illustrate each from approximately the same subject-matter. The subject-matter consisted of elementary judgments about the more familiar properties, (such as colours), of the more familiar objects (such as flowers), and generally about those daily events in the life of school children which are of greatest interest to the children themselves. By re-classifying the problems according to inferential types and calculating the average age at which each type was correctly answered by 50 per cent of the children, it was hoped, incidentally, to gain further information as to the general course followed by the development of the child's logical abilities.

These mechanically constructed problems, however, proved to be the least satisfactory. The fallacy tests, in particular, proved to entail all the disadvantages that are notoriously characteristic of examination questions involving traps and catches; none, therefore, was retained in the final test-scale. The following was the order of difficulty actually given by the various types of fallacy used; the figures in brackets indicate the average age at which five comparable examples, used to illustrate each type, were solved by approximately 50 per cent of the children. Illicit process (age, 8.2), undistributed middle (age, 8.7), *petitio principii* (age, 9.5), fallacy of division (age, 10.5), imperfect enumeration (age, 10.9), ambiguity of terms (age, 11.0), *ignoratio elenchi* (age, 12.1), fallacy of composition (age, 12.4), *argumentum ad hominem* (age, 12.9), *a dicto secundum quid ad dictum simpliciter* (age, 13.7), *fallacia accidentis* (age, 14+), *non causa pro causa* (age, 14 +), false analogy (age, 14+). But, if put in a sufficiently glaring form, nearly every fallacy can be detected and avoided by children of seven; if sufficiently disguised, each will entrap even children of fourteen. The formal character of the fallacy has thus only a small influence upon the age at which it can be perceived. And such an order as the preceding means very little apart from the actual problems from which it is computed.

The same may be said, though not quite so emphatically, of the tests constructed to exemplify the various principles of inference. The classification used was that suggested by F. H. Bradley[1]. Ten instances were used for each type. A few gave sufficiently steady results to be retained in the final test-scale. Most of them, however, being of the "yes or no" type of question, proved unreliable. Synthesis of subject and attribute (e.g., test 2) appears to be the easiest type (age 7.2). Synthesis of identity[2] is nearly as easy (age 7.5). Synthesis of degree (e.g., tests 1, 4, 12, 14) is somewhat harder (age 8.1). Synthesis of space is very definitely harder still (age 9.8). The ages assigned to tests 16 and 27 are unexpectedly late, although these, of course, are not stated in the simplest possible form. Synthesis of time appears slightly harder than synthesis of space wherever the arguments attain some degree of complexity (age 10.1). Tests 35 and 46, for example, though not included in the group on which the age-average for this type is based, nevertheless illustrate by their position the curious difficulty of moderately complex arguments as to time. It is possible, however, that the equivalent arguments in spatial form unintentionally involved other difficulties besides those due to change of category. In the simplest types of syllogism the mere fact that time is one dimensional, while space admits of two or three, makes the former type appear easier; further, "before" or "after" occasion far less confusion than "right or "left." Synthesis of cause and effect is hardly parallel to the foregoing types; it involves an abstract conception which (if

---

[1] *Principles of Logic*, p. 244.
[2] E.g., " Mary's dress is the same colour as mine : Kate's dress is a different colour to Mary's : Is my dress the same colour as Kate's, or not, or can't you tell? " No example appears in the final list.

human causation be disregarded) is only recognized by the child at a comparatively late stage. It is, too, almost impossible, to construct syllogisms of this type which shall be at once as simple and as brief as the easier examples of other types, and yet avoid language unfamiliar to the younger children. Hence, synthesis of cause appears to be the latest of the half-dozen main types of inference to be satisfactorily performed (age 12.6).

Stern, it will be remembered, in his analysis of children's capacity to "report" (Aussage), distinguished distinct stages, according as the child attends to objects in isolation, their actions, their relations according to space, time, cause, and finally their attributes or qualities. In the development of the child's capacity for formal reasoning no such distinct stages are discernible. The differences between the age-averages cited above are, on the whole, small, and doubtless not entirely attributable to change in form.

Logical form, therefore, is of far less importance than either the amount or the kind of subject-matter.

Indeed, there is but one other factor which in importance appears to be at all comparable with these two. This is linguistic form. Verbal phrasing and verbal arrangement are second in importance to subject-matter alone. Take, for example, test 16. In its present form it is answered correctly by almost exactly fifty per cent of the children aged nine. If, however, the order of the two premises is inverted, so that the test reads: "George is to the left of Harry; and Harry is to the left of Willie," the test at once becomes easier, and is passed by sixty-one per cent of the same age-group. If again it reads: "George is to the left of Harry; Willie is to the right of Harry," it is passed by sixty-eight per cent, and becomes suitable for age eight rather than age nine. Test 14 would also be transferred to age eight if the question read: "Is C smaller than A?" or which is the smallest of the three?" Test 27 would be made easier by nearly two years by simply asking "Is C to the North, South, East, or West of A?" instead of "Is A to the North, South, East, or West of C?" Read in conjunction with the questions given, certain forms of phrasing are apt to have what may be termed a "suggestive dominance." With the statement "Jack runs slower ... " ringing in the memory, a child asked "who is the slowest?" naturally tends to say "Jack is slowest," or at least to try that statement as a hypothesis, and, finding nothing in the other premiss to contradict it, easily solves the problem. This is the sole reason that test 1 is easier than test 4. To ask "Who runs fastest?" would make it easier still; since, in reading the test through, the first premiss, "Tom runs faster ... ," together with the boy's natural interests, tends to make him select Tom as a fast runner from the outset, and Tom's name the most prominent one to bear in mind in answering questions on this topic. Again, in test 12, the statement, "Edith is darker than Lily," suggests that both Edith and Lily belong to the dark group, Edith being merely more intensely marked by the special character of that group. Hence, the child is apt to select Lily as the dark one, when asked if she is darker than Olive. The problem has only to be re-phrased, "Lily is fairer than Edith; Edith is fairer than Olive; Who is the fairest—Lily or Olive?" for the question to be answered by seventy-two per cent. aged eight, instead of only forty-six per cent. In relating the results

127

of introspection nearly every child who answers correctly states that
he actually converted the disparate premiss in this way, so that all
the statements referred to different degrees of the quality mentioned
in the final question ("darkness" in the original form). It is this
extra step, necessitated by the form of the statement, which increases
the difficulty of this intance of what is practically the same syllogism
as tests 4 and 1. The "suggestive dominance" of unessential
portions of the premisses is responsible for many of the errors at
every stage.[1] In test 3, the mention of "rain" in the first premiss,
remaining unrelated to the second premiss (which should dominate
over the first), suggests "Yes, I shall want an umbrella." In
test 37, the numbers tend to dominate the attention; "turning to
the right" is inhibited; hence, the child simply adds up the numbers
and replies "250 yards." A lucid writer so phrases and arranges
his statements that the critical points tend naturally to dominate in
virtue of the emphasis given them by position or other device. The
reader's "sagacity" (as James[2] would call it) is by this means econo-
mized. Lucidity is thus a factor of considerable moment in influencing ease or difficulty. And, generally, it appears that linguistic form
is of far greater importance than logical form.

The conclusions tentatively suggested by this preliminary survey
of the development of reasoning may be summarized as follows:—
All the elementary mental mechanisms essential to formal reasoning
are present before the child leaves the infants' department, i.e.,
by the mental age of seven, if not somewhat before. Development
consists primarily in an increase in the extent and variety of the
subject-matter to which those mechanisms can be applied, and in an
increase in the precision and elaboration with which those mechanisms can operate. The difficulty of a test depends upon its complexity, that is, in the main upon four points: how many connexions
have to be made between one idea and another—only three, as in the
ordinary syllogism, or four, or more? How many of these connexions has he to supply himself? How closely are these connexions
to be knit together—in parallel, in series, or in a more or less intricate
system? How far do they fall into the same category—of time,
space, number, &c., or differ one from another? Other points, what
is the precise nature of these connexions—temporal, spatial, numerical,
causal, &c.—and of their interconnexions—hypothetical, disjunctive,
&c.—are of little importance.

A child's reasoning ability thus appears to be a function of the
degree of organic complexity of which his attention[3] is capable, or
in Stout's phrase—of his capacity for "noetic synthesis." And
the development of reasoning appears to consist essentially in an
increase in the number, variety, originality, and compactness of the
relations which his mind can perceive and integrate into a coherent
whole.

[1]In test 46, as printed in the preceding number of this *Journal*, an unfortunate error in trans-
cription has provided an excellent illustration of this point. The word "bedroom" is, of course,
irrelevant, and should be deleted. (Its insertion was due to a reminiscence in the transcriber's
mind of an earlier form of the problem, where the hours related to a nocturnal air-raid: I much
regret that it escaped correction in the proof). Reading the test as printed, the examiner is apt to
be dominated by the suggestion contained by the word "bedroom," and so to name an hour
during the night or early morning—a time excluded by other details in the question.
[2]*Principles of Psychology*, Vol. II., p. 343. "The power to extract the right characteristics
for our conclusion;" "the ability to pounce on the essential attribute."
[3]I use attention in the sense in which it is used by the teacher, rather than by the
psychologist. It includes marginal as well as focal awareness: and awareness as sustained over
long periods not as occurring in brief pulses. "Apprehension" would be a more accurate
technical term.

A CHILD'S FEARS.

By WILLIAM BOYD, M.A., B.Sc., D.Phil.

THE fears of children present problems of extraordinary interest to all who are concerned with their mental development. Most intelligent parents have confirmed for themselves Professor Sully's graphic description of childhood as the time of battle with the fears, and have realized, in some measure, that the issues of this battle are of great consequence in moral education. But the interest is by no means confined to the practical question as to the best methods of dealing with the fears that distress one's children in the early years of life. The long-standing discussion of the parts played by heredity and environmental influences on mental evolution and the more recent discussion, initiated by Freud, regarding the relation of fear to the sex life both raise crucial questions in the matter of fears.

On the practical and on the theoretical side alike much more knowledge than we yet possess is needed before anything like an adequate answer can be given to these questions. There are required further collective inquiries like that of Dr. Stanley Hall. Still more are required carefully recorded studies of the fears of individual children in their context over a considerable period of time.

The notes here presented are intended as a contribution to the study of fear from the latter point of view. They have been extracted from a diary recording a little girl's mental development from three to seven-and-a-half, which was kept conjointly by her father and mother, supplemented by occasional notes made at both earlier and later years. All through the child's fears were made a special subject of observation and the more outstanding manifestations of fear were regularly recorded at the time of their occurrence. In addition, a number of related facts, drawn from a mass of observations on other aspects of the child's behaviour, have been included in the present survey. The most important of these is a series of ninety dreams at different ages, one-third of which were fear dreams.*

The child's main fears may be most conveniently set forth in the first instance in certain large groups according to the nature of the objects inspiring fear.

A.—Persons.

(1) *Strangers.*—During the period under observation there was only one case of the fear of strangers which appears in most children in the early years of life. One day, when out walking with her parents (36 months), she was asked her name by a man. She turned shy and hid behind her father, saying, "You tell him." Next morning, while still but half awake, her first words were: "I don't want to be seen."

(2) *People in masks, &c.*—When her father put on a black-faced mask belonging to herself at Hallowe'en—the one time in the year when masks make their appearance in Scotland—she cried and hid behind her mother (40 months). When he covered himself with

---

* All the dreams up to those of the 76th month are given in "A Study of a Child's Dreams," *Child-Study*, October, 1915.

a rug and pretended to be a lion, the effect was the same (40, 42). Her mother thought that if she put on the rug the child would not be afraid, but she was. By the middle of her fifth year this game had nearly lost its terrors. Occasionally she showed a slight fear, but generally greeted the lion with a shout of laughter.

(3) *Sickness and old age.*—A strong objection to the sight of sick people, suggesting fear, showed itself in two cases in the 43rd month. When the proposal was made that she should be taken to visit a girl bed-ridden with arthritis, she protested again and again that she did not wish to go, and during the visit she asked repeatedly: "When are we going out?" A day later her mother took her to see a very old woman All the way she kept saying that she did not want to go in. "I don't want to go in. I don't want to see that old lady. I'll wait outside the gate." In the latter case the fear may have been due to the connexion between old age and death. See below D (1).

(4) *Robbers.*—The fear of robbers was only one among many imaginary fears which took possession of her in the 51st month, and the slightest of them all. It came by way of infection from another child who was obsessed by it, and it made no lasting impression. The only later reference made to it occurred one night at bedtime three months after.

(5) *Germans.*—The fear of Germans was similar in character to that of robbers, but struck far deeper. The talk she heard about the war and the stories of a maid-servant about Germans peeping in at the window made a strong impression and produced a whole crop of fears. These appeared first about March, 1915, when she had a "dreadful dream" about shells falling into the garden (68). This fear turned up in a more specific form in a later dream about "Germans dropping bombs" (71), and in the statement that she was frightened that the Germans would drop bombs (80). Simultaneously, the Germans began to figure among the bedtime fears. See A (8) below. "There is a German with his feet peeping out under the bed." (68). "When I shut my eyes I see pictures of tigers and lions and wolves and Germans" (72).

(6) *Tramps, drunk men, &c.*—The fear of badly-dressed people, induced in her by a little companion of her own age (74), was comparatively slight, and showed itself chiefly in the avoidance of certain roads. It did not completely disappear until the second half of the tenth year.

(7) *Bullying children.*—The bullying of boys of her own age and of older girls developed one of the strongest and most persistent of her fears, dating back to the 4th year and still in evidence in the 10th. At ordinary times this manifested itself mainly in the refusal to go into the village near which she lives when there was even a remote chance of meeting her persecutors. In the 51st month—a time of many fears—she lived for a whole fortnight in dread of a boy who had threatened to shoot her, and had to be continually reassured that he had only spoken in fun. In the 71st month occurred a dream about an older girl whom she specially feared, and in all she had six dreams during the next twelve months, either about children hitting her or about children who had hit her. The fact is

the more striking because she rarely referred to the matter in ordinary conversation.

(8) *Absence of persons.*—The most intense and enduring of all the child's fears have been those that came when she was alone. Darkness, which is sometimes regarded as a cause of fear, did not, in this case, make much difference. The fears that troubled her when left alone at the bedtime hour, though accentuated, were similar in kind to which arose when she happened to be alone at other times. No note was made of the genesis of these fears in the first year or two, and it is therefore impossible to say how far they could have been prevented or minimized by different treatment in the first instance. It is conceivable that if she had been left more to herself in babyhood than an only child of comparatively leisured parents is generally left, loneliness would have had fewer terrors for her. The most notable fact about these fears was their vagueness. Being alone created a state of panic, and an active imagination supplied some object of fear. Going along a road for a short distance herself, she suddenly stopped and broke out crying. "A lady was coming after her"; an explanation suggested by an innocent old lady some way off (38)). Passing from room to room or into an uninhabited room, she had to be reassured periodically that someone was at hand; she heard "wee noises" (42, 58, 59), suspected the presence of "wee mice" (42, 56), "thought there was a robber coming upstairs" (54), heard the noise of somebody "breathing" in a room she had to pass (66), saw "two green eyes," and feared wolves (periodically from $5\frac{1}{2}$ to 7 years), thought a man would spring out on her (75, 81), heard a "sh, sh" upstairs during a storm. The bedtime fears were for the most part of a man "tip-toeing about the room" (68), a German below the bed with his feet sticking out (68). All these fears were most intense in the 5th year, and had lost much of their power by the 7th. Even at 9, however, they occasionally revived, and at bedtime she suspected a man behind the screen or under the bed. The gradual escape from fear showed itself in occasional explanations which she herself knew to be ridiculous. ["There's a tiger in my bed: it's biting my toes." (60)]; and in the avowal that she did not know why she was afraid when put to bed in a strange house. "I feel a fear I cannot explain. Why do little girls sometimes have a frightened feeling?" Then, a day later: "I feel the strange fear I felt last night. I don't know what kind of fear it is. It is because I am in a strange bed. I am strange and lonely in this house." (84)

B.—Animals.

(1) *Dog.*—The first sign of fear appeared in the 16th month—for no obvious reason. She has always been very fond of dogs, but can never suppress a slight apprehension.

(2) *Cow.*—Her attitude to the cow is not unlike that to the dog. At 36 months she ran up a bank to look at some cows, but one of them turned its eyes on her, and she cried out at once for her father to take her down and carry her home. It was not till she was seven that the slight fear that their great bodies evidently inspired passed away with the familiarity that came from helping in the work of a farm.

(3) *Horse.*—When she was about three she had a misadventure with a horse which affected her so deeply that she told the story in

graphic terms when she was 7½ and again when she was 9. A large white horse had broken out of a field on a farm adjoining her house and was coming along the road where she was at play with another little girl. Immediately, both took to their heels and made for the safety of the house. The first signs of the horse obsession appeared in a story told by her in the 38th month. "There was a little girl, and she was baking scones in the kitchen for her mother, and a big horse came up the steps and ate all the scones." Two months later the same story was told three several times with variations. A lion, a tiger, and a bear in these cases played the leading rôle, and it was the little girl and not the scones that was eaten up. Four months later an echo of the story was heard in a tale about a fearful and wonderful animal called the "corksporks," that lives in India and eats little girls. In addition to this, the identical horse turned up twice in dreams (50, 69). When walking along a road where a horse was standing she always took care to get someone between her and the animal.

(4) *Tiger, lion, bear, crocodile.*—These animals were all spoken of quite vaguely, and chiefly among the fears that possessed her when alone. For example, she ran away from her father and mother one day (59) but soon returned with all the signs of fear. When asked what was wrong, she answered first that she had heard "little noises," then that there were lions and tigers in the wood near by. The tiger was most fearsome of them all. Besides figuring in a fear dream (50) it was mentioned on half-a-dozen occasions as an object of dread. The crocodile was only mentioned once (51), and then in a list of fear-inspiring animals.

(5) *Wolf, fox.*—The fear of the wolf was the strongest of all the animal fears. It was so far individualized that generally, when it was mentioned between the 62nd and the 84th months, reference was made to "green eyes." The origin of this fear is quite unknown, and it is difficult to explain its intensity. The fox also produced a strong reaction. When told a story about foxes in the 45th and again in the 74th month she became greatly excited, and finally closed her ears and refused to listen. Yet, curiously enough, the fox was never mentioned by her as a fearsome animal. On the contrary, after beginning to tell a story about a tiger and a baby (56), she changed the tiger into a fox because "foxes are frightened for people."

(6) *Mouse*—She would never confess herself afraid of mice. But she kept back from a mouse hole (42), saw an imaginary mouse run across the floor (52), and several times professed to hear mice at bedtime. The reason of her fear is perhaps given by the remark that "they gnaw things" (56); that is, it was the fear of teeth.

(7) *Flies, worms*—She has always taken a delighted interest in all the smaller animals, and handled spiders, blue-bottle flies, &c., without the slightest sign of fear. The mild fear shown in regard to crabs (61) and wasps (75) was obviously due to the danger of taking liberties with them, and did not prevent her catching them in play. The two exceptions were flies and worms, and even in the case of these the fears were transient. Ordinarily, she handled worms freely from the earliest years. Only once did she show fear (58) and would not lift them with her hand, because they were "like little snakes." Fear of flies was more pronounced, but, again, temporary. When about two years old she showed herself afraid of flies on the window pane. At 56 months she

was thrown into great terror by a sudden imagination. One day she lost sight of a fly she had been watching. Immediately she began to wonder if it had gone into her eye and got into her head. She came to her mother with a woe-begone face and told her about this fly " with a thin body and tiny thin legs," and asked if she thought it was in her head. " How could it get into your head ? " asked mother. " Through this little part," pointing to the eye near the tear gland. Even the story of a little boy who ate flies with no dire consequences but a dose of castor oil did not remove the dreadful suspicion. She returned to the subject at night with the question : " What if the fly did get into my head ? " In spite of this episode there was no subsequent recurrence of the fear of flies in any form.

C.—Natural Phenomena.

(1) *Sea.*—When taken a walk near the sea at 33 months she showed herself vaguely apprehensive, would not go near it, and finally insisted in walking away from it. At 38 months she was taken to bathe in the sea, but was very reluctant to go in even before feeling the cold. A year later she had overcome this reluctance, and ever since has been exceedingly fond of the water.

(2) *Woods.*—A walk through a wood when she was about five produced a vaguely subdued feeling, showing itself mainly in a lowering of the voice and the desire to get out into the open. For some considerable time after she kept back from the woods, but by nine this feeling had completely passed and given way to a keen delight in woodlands.

(3) *Thunder.*—There has been a slight fear of thunder and lightning all along, which once or twice has become serious. At 38 months she was excited on hearing a gunshot which she mistook for thunder. At 52 months a thunderstorm evoked various fears. " Will the lightning make the house tumble down ? Do some people with an umbrella get killed by lightning ? " At 59 months she heard of a church steeple being damaged and a man killed in a thunderstorm. She remembered this and referred to it several times later. So far as outward appearances went, however, her own fears were but slight. In the course of a thunderstorm in the 74th month she was afraid to go upstairs alone, because she heard a sound like " sh, sh." In another thunderstorm during the same month she went below a table with other children, but while they cried she laughed—which was probably her way of showing a fear more moderate than theirs. Three months later she dreamed that she was caught in a storm of pelting rain with thunder and lightning, and that she ran into the scullery to hide.

(4) *Wind.*—The sound of wind made her greatly afraid in the 45th month, but did not do so a month later. The autumn winds renewed her fears. She was afraid the windows might be blown in, and she looked forward dolefully to the winter because there was so much wind then. " Why," she asked, " is it not always summer?" At night she prayed that there might be no wind in the coming winter. Her mother suggested that she should rather pray to be made brave, and her father pointed out that the wind made the air fresh for the city children. She recalled the latter point a month later. " Do you know what I said to GOD ? I said : ' Give far more storms than last year, and far harder storms.' " In the 58th month she was again afraid.

She was frightened for the noise, she said; and she refused to go upstairs herself. "When I hear little noises, I'm frightened." The fear of wind has long since vanished.

(5) *Earthquake.*—Among other imaginary fears of the 57th month was the fear of an earthquake, probably connected with the fear of the house falling down. See F (4).

D.—Death and Disease.

(1) *Death.*—Several times in the course of the second half of the 4th year there was an unaccountably strong fear of death. Care had been taken to prevent her getting any knowledge of death up to this age. The only dead thing she had seen was a dead bird on the roadside in the 21st month. This made a considerable impression on her at the time. She went over the various parts of the bird—head, legs, wings, tail—saying of each : " It does not move." She spoke of it again about a year later when passing the spot where she had seen it, though no reference had been made to it by herself or anyone else in the interval. The first sign of repugnance at the thought of death appeared in the reproduction of a story by her in the 41st month. In the original version mention had been made of motors and of the death of a sheep. In her story there were no motors and "the sheep did not die." In the following month, when one of her aunts was telling her about grandmas becoming old and dying, she said vehemently : " I don't want to die." This personal note was repeated in the 45th month with added force. Her mother had been telling her about the death of Livingstone. " The black men," said mother, " were very sad when he died." This provoked many questions. " Why were they sad when he died ?" " He could not speak any more to them and tell them to be good." " Why could he not speak to them ? " " Because he was dead." " Can you not speak when you are dead ? " " No." " Well, I don't want to be dead, mother." Then she added through her tears : " I don't want to be dead, because if I died you would not have any other wee girl." The idea stuck in her mind and she said again and again : " I don't want to die." Mother, comforting her, said that that was a foolish thing to say. " Dying is just like a big deep sleep, and when you waken up, instead of father and mother being beside you there is GOD." Then said the child in a tone of infinite relief : " It is not really dying at all. People don't die." " Yes," said mother, "it is really dying. But you must not think that dying is terrible. Lots of people who are old and frail are glad when the time comes to die." " But I don't want to die and I don't want to get old," she said, "and you know, mother, if I died you would not have any wee girl." Then there was an outburst of tears and broken-hearted weeping. About the same time as this took place one of her conversations with a maid was overheard regarding the death of the maid's father after illness. Speaking of this to her mother, she said : " You know, mother, you die when you are very ill. You get worse and worse and then you die." A casual reference to death in a story told her three weeks after the Livingstone episode brought back the same fear. Mother tried to divert her mind from it by telling her that every animal and plant dies, and added that the plants come up again. " If I die," she asked, " will I come up again ? I don't want to die." Then she repeated to herself two or three times : " Death is only a very deep sleep." On two occasions in the following months

(46, 47) she had long conversations with her mother on the subject, but by this time the fear had greatly moderated. " Do doctors never die ? " she asked (47). Then she added : " Dying is only a deep sleep. Afterwards you become alive again and have a new life." To all outward seeming the fear completely disappeared after the fifth year. When told of the death of a much loved grandfather in the 54th month she commented on the matter without any emotion.

(2) *Disease.*—The fear of ill persons in the 43rd month has already been noted. The first indication of a personal fear of disease occurred in the 69th month. At a time when measles was rife her father told her a story about a girl who had measles. At bath time she said she was not feeling well and was afraid that she had measles. In the 87th and 88th months she had dreams about festering sores on her legs, but as she had already had a sore of the kind these dreams may have been due to repugnance rather than fear. In the 75th month when mother was taking a thorn out of some one's hand, she turned away her head at the sight of a few drops of blood. This was the only occasion on which the sight of blood disturbed her in any way.

E.—Fear for Parents.

A most interesting group of fears were those for her parents. The earliest case was in a dream she had when on a seaside holiday in the 61st month. " Do you know what I dreamed about you ? " she asked her father, " You went out in a boat and the boat capsized, and you swam back to us all safe." In the 72nd month she had another fear dream about her father. One morning she woke sobbing. When asked what was wrong she said that she had dreamed that she had got another father. Half an hour later she expanded the dream. " I dreamed that my father had gone away and that I had got another father." She subsequently recalled this dream on two or three occasions —the last time in her tenth year—and interpreted it as meaning that her father had gone away as a soldier. But the obvious interpretation is that she had been dreaming that her father was dead. Her fears for her mother were less pronounced. In the 55th month she heard an account of a stormy night at sea. When, following this, her mother talked about going on a sea voyage, she became greatly distressed. " Don't sleep on a boat," she implored. " Why not ? " asked mother. " Because the boat might get wrecked, and you would be drowned, and I would have no mother." In the 75th month she dreamed about her mother " going away." " Last night," she told her mother at bedtime, " I dreamed that you were going to leave daddy. I was clinging to your hand and crying." She declared that if mother went away she would go with her. But the real thought behind the dream was perhaps revealed in a conversation a week before. She said that she meant to marry father when she grew up. The objection was made that her father was married already. " But mother . . ." (hesitating) " mother might go away." The psycho-analytic implication of the dream as a sub-conscious wish for the death of the mother is patent. In two instances her fears for her parents were connected with the fears of falling houses. See F (4). When her father and mother were climbing up an old castle, she refused to go with them and remained in an unhappy state of mind at the foot till they came down (69). In the

84th month she began to whimper and cry when her father was climbing up a ruined castle which, according to a notice board at the foot, was dangerous.

F.—Miscellaneous Fears.

(1) *Cobwebs.*—One day in the 37th month, when she was blowing away a cobweb in a doorway, she blew some of it on her cheek. She rushed to an aunt in considerable distress to get it wiped off, and for a time she was afraid to pass out of the door where the cobweb had been. This fear, however, soon vanished, to reappear no more.

(2) *Noises.*—Though showing no fear of noises in streets and railway stations, and indeed seeming to enjoy them, " little noises " have figured largely in her bedtime fears (41, 58, 59, 66). One of the reasons for her fear of the wind seemed to be the noise it made.

(3) *Trains and Motors.*—She has never been afraid of railway trains. On one occasion, however, when a train in which she was, stopped in a short tunnel and another train rushed past, she nestled in close to her father. She explained afterwards : " I hided from that thing." (36). In the 4th and 5th years motor-cars inspired a great dread. When one drew near she shrank back and insisted on the person with whom she was, keeping well back from the roadway. The fear which had been inculcated in her in the interest of safety was considerably intensified by her seeing a dog killed by a motor when she was about 4½. The fear has long since lost its keenness, and the episode of the dog was no longer in her conscious memory in the 10th year.

(4) *House falling.*—A most persistent fear, for which it is impossible to account, is a fear of the house or some part of it falling. It seemed to date back to a casual sight of an old castle from the train, which provoked many questions, early in the 4th year, but nothing was said at the time which could have caused the fear. In the 43rd month she had the following dream : " I dreamed that all our pictures were broken and our walls were broken and our house was broken, and we were all dead." (All this was said laughingly). Among the host of fears that beset her in the 51st month was this fear of the house falling. She asked repeatedly how old the house was and how long it would be before it fell down. A week or two later she noticed a small crack in the stonework above a window in a house in which she was staying for a few days, and she cried because she thought the house might be on the point of falling. When a thunderstorm came on here the main disturbing thought was that the lightning might knock the house down. In the same month she saw a burst water pipe being repaired. She became greatly afraid that the pipes in her own house would burst, and said, " I don't want the winter to come. The pipes might burst and the water would drown us." Repeating this, she said, " The water would drown *me*." On this occasion, however, the fear was comparatively slight and was easily allayed. The fear of the house falling reappeared in the 57th month when she saw a piece of cement that had fallen from the fireplace. At once she became alarmed about the possibility of the fireplace falling. This was the last exhibition of this particular fear. In the 59th month she saw once more the crack that had made her apprehensive in the 51st month, and recalled her former fears with a smile. The fear of the burst pipe, however, remained much longer. In the 78th month she was made anxious by an over-flow of water from

a cistern, and the sight of water dripping from a burst pipe in the 107th month made her rather uneasy.

Education with regard to the fears.

The methods adopted to keep the child's fears within moderate limits were quite simple.

(*a.*) The greatest care was taken, especially in the early years, to prevent apprehension rising to the emotional violence of terror. Stories like Bluebeard, likely to provoke a strong reaction and to stimulate fearsome imaginings, were vetoed. Red Riding Hood's wolf was slain before it could eat anybody, and the Babes in the Wood were rescued before anything serious could befall them. References to deformity, disease, death or any other facts with ugly associations were generally avoided. When they could not be avoided they were left as vague and innocuous as possible. Careful watch, which, as the record of fears has shown, was not always successful, was kept on the conversations and stories of maid-servants and companions.

(*b*) When, in spite of all precautions, strong fears did arise, every effort was made to allay them. It was kept clearly in mind, however, that this could only be done to good purpose if she faced and overcame them herself. At night when left alone to go to sleep she always had a night light burning till the time came when, in response to constant suggestion, she declared that she was no longer afraid, and begged that it be taken away to let her prove her courage. When the fears recurred, the light was restored, and the surrender of it was repeated several times till in the end it was no longer needed. Only when the fears were exceptionally bad did anyone sit with her till she fell asleep, and even then the watcher generally sat in an adjoining room to prevent too great dependence on companionship. The usual compromise with her night fears was the arrangement that all doors except that of her bed-room and of the room in which the older people were sitting should be shut, so as to give her the moral support of remote company. Other fears were dealt with in a similar way. When she had to leave the security of downstairs on a journey upstairs she was enjoined to sing, " Fear not, oh little flock," being the favourite song to charm away evil. At other times some one sang as she mounted upwards to give her comfort and suggest the nearness of help, if need arose.

(*c*) All through, the attempt was made to reason away her fears. "There are no wolves (lions, bears, &c.), in this country," she was told again and again. "There used to be wolves here a very long time ago, but they were all killed. Aren't you glad you don't live in a country like Africa where there are still wild beasts?" When the fear of the man hiding somewhere in the room was to the fore, pretence was made of searching every corner for him and assurances then given that all was well. "This is the safest house in the world," she would be told, "with father and mother protecting you, no one can possibly do you any harm." On several occasions when a thunderstorm was raging, she was taken to the window and her attention called to the beauty and grandeur of the scene. All these things were done without any delusion as to the powerlessness of reason to subdue fear at the time of its occurrence. The immediate object was to divert the mind from its obsessions by means of calm speech. But beyond that was the hope and expectation that ideas counter to the fears would be established in the texture of mind through sustained suggestion, and would ultimately moderate the fears and prompt to right conduct in spite of them.

The Waning of the Fears

Whether as a result of the measures taken, or by reason of natural development, or, most probably, because of the two combined, the fears gradually decreased in intensity and in frequency, until, near the age of ten, they had ceased to play any considerable part in the child's mental life. The one that lingered longest in a serious form was the fear of being alone, and that disappeared as an obvious fear quite abruptly in the sixth month of the tenth year. For the first time in her life she was prepared to go upstairs by herself at any hour of the day, and to traverse alone after nightfall a rather dark road leading up to the house. . This change of mind, which has continued for over a year, with one or two slight lapses, seemed to be connected with some deep physical change. As there began about the same time (or shortly after) a very marked increase in weight—steadily maintained ever since—which is in striking contrast with the rate of growth in the three preceding years, the presumption is that this is the beginning of the pre-pubertal growth. If this is correct, we may perhaps get from this single case the suggestion of a generalization : that, given proper training, fear should end with the period of childhood (that is, the period of slackened growth in height and weight, which is followed by the rapid growth of pre-adolescence).

The progressive decline in the frequency of the fears from year to year is illustrated in an interesting way by the collection of dreams, to which reference has already been made. In spite of the fact that these were for the most part only noted at irregular intervals, and that the number recorded before five and after seven was small, they serve to give a rough indication of the rate of decline.

Age.	Fear Dreams.	Other Dreams.	Percentage of Fear Dreams.
4-5	4	1	80
5-6	8	7	53
6-7	13	30	30
7-8	3	6	33
8-9	2	15	12

The Nature of the Fears.

It must be said right away that the facts concerning the various groups of fears which have been set forth above do not seem to warrant any very definite conclusions as to the essential nature of childish fears. But perhaps it may be found on a careful scrutiny of the data that some light is thrown on the main questions at issue in regard to fear.

The first point that calls for note is that in a considerable number of the child's fears the emotional disturbance was far greater than can readily be explained by personal experience and environmental conditions. The fear of the horse (B3) or of persecutors (A7) is quite understandable. She actually got a bad fright from a horse, and lived in apprehension of hurt from certain bullying children. But what about the much deeper fear of wild animals—especially the wolf? Or of the man hiding in the room? or of buildings falling down? or of the wind? or of death? There was no obvious reason in the manifest facts of her life for these fears, and yet they were very real fears for her.

It may be said that though there was never any known shock to create and maintain the state of fear in these instances, fear may have been due to contagion: that, for example, she may have heard fear-inspiring stories or remarks, have been in the company of older persons whose fears she adopted by sympathetic induction, or have got a fright that was outwardly so slight that it was not appreciable even to a close observer. It is of course impossible to rule out such an origin for the fears altogether. Emotional influences are so subtle that particular fears, or even the the general condition of fearfulness, may conceivably be produced by an unknown infection, just as measles or any other germ disease may be. It is not easy, however, to accept this explanation in the case of a child under constant observation, who has been carefully guarded against externally suggested fears. It might account for some of the fears; it can scarcely account for all. And in view of the fact that the few fears (A 4, 6, for example) which were known to have been prompted by companions were slight and unimportant, it is doubtful whether it actually accounted for any.

Another possibility, which will occur at once to anyone acquainted with psycho-analytic phenomena, is that those fears which have an intensity and frequency greater than seems warranted by experiences within the range of the ordinary conscious life, are the outcome of some deep perturbation of a quite different character in the sub-conscious mind. It can certainly not be denied that some of the irrational obsessing fears of the child are very much like those adult phobias which Freud has so brilliantly shown to be pathological substitutes for the normal activities of sex, when the fundamental impulses of life are thwarted. This suggests that the fears in question owe their excessive intensity to some similar repression of the child's impulses; and the view may seem to be confirmed—in part at least—by the fact that, in the present case some of the fears admit of the psycho-analytic inter-pretation. The fears for the parents (E), for example, were of this kind, and so were one or two of the dream-fears in which the manifest content of the dream was at variance with the emotion associated with it. The slight lapse into night fears in the eleventh year (mentioned above) was also most obviously in the category, having followed directly on a minor conflict with the father. But while it is possible that some of the unexplained fears were the results of deep-seated mental stresses, the comparative simplicity of the child mind forbids any wholesale reference of them to this source. It is difficult to believe, for example, that the dread of death towards the end of the fourth year (D1) was determined in this fashion. The repressive process by which the child is socialized certainly begins earlier than this, but the fact that infantile dreams are normally direct expressions of unfulfilled wishes (as Freud himself allows), or repeat the day-time fears with but little change, implies that repression does not upset the mental balance of the child as it does in the adult.

All things considered it seems to me that the simplest explanation of these particular fears is to be found outside the individual experience altogether, in the hypothesis of a spontaneous appearance of racial fears. Even if it be contended that the child's fears would not arise without the stimulus of external infections or internal repressions, some such hypothesis is necessary. If the tendency to fear were not present, the fears of other people would not find a sympathetic response in the child, nor could a thwarted impulse mask itself as a fear. Fear, in short, must be postulated as a primitive element in the soul, inherited from the past like all the primitive elements.

This at once raises the question as to what exactly it is that is inherited. Is it specific fears or merely a vague undifferentiated impulse to fear? The answer on the scanty evidence immediately before us is that the child's inheritance includes both specific fears and the general disposition to fear. On the one hand, there are in the list of this particular child's fears some that appear to be survivals from a remote past: notably the fear of eyes (the gaze of the stranger, A1, the cow, B2, the green eyes of the wolf, B5), the fear of teeth (the mice that *gnaw* B6), the fear of the serpent (worms like little snakes B7), the fear of great wild animals and especially of the wolf (B4), the fear of the wind and the sea (C1, 4), perhaps also the fear of death (D1). On the other hand, there are other fears, which, though presumably having primitive constituents, are plainly not themselves primitive: such, for example, as some of the bedtime fears (A8), the fear of the fly that might get into the head (B7), and the fear of the house falling (F4). In this latter group of fears, an indeterminate state of fear has become determinate by projecting itself into various fanciful forms, suggested by some fact in the immediate environment. Why it should take the particular forms it actually takes in the individual child, it is ·impossible to say on data such as have been presented. That is the kind of problem for which we must look for a solution from psycho-analysis.

HISTORY LESSONS IN AN ELEMENTARY SCHOOL.

By F. L. BOWMAN, M.Ed., Homerton College, Cambridge.

It is a school without equipment of any kind, but there is one large room and the sun comes through high windows and makes pathways across the floor all the year round, the red virginia creeper taps at the window pane on windy days and the raindrops run along the ledges to the great delight of all within. It is surrounded by the meanest of streets and crowded homes, yet the names of the children occur in the parish records three hundred years ago and more, and the words they use daily have long since been lost to our speech.

It is in this school also and among these children that students of history are to be found.

Caldicott is nine years old. In a ragged jersey and boots tied together with string, he pipes on a tin-whistle at all hours of the day, carefully secreting it beneath his jersey in school hours. Up at five in the morning to help with the milk round, running, often dinnerless, to carry out the basket for the chemist between the hours of twelve and two. At four o'clock, wrestling for a share of the evening papers to sell, helping at the market stalls from dawn till dusk on Saturday. He is already a wage-earner, with a life of high adventure.

If you watch him in school, he is careless of a text-book, full of words and things he does not understand. He had been hearing the tragedy of the Norman Conquest, listening eagerly to the chronicle, and spelling out the pictures of the Bayeux Tapestry with delight. Turning to the history reader, he found the usual bald statement in it, and with fallen countenance muttered, "Tain't there, they don't seem to know about it!"

He is equipped with the best selection of cigarette cards, "wot show you history pictures," and a private notebook, in which he was found writing a descripton of Thomas More, "In case I should forget that chap."

He is alert and eager for every story, weaving his fancies round about it, pursuing with pitiless logic and ruthless questioning the tangle of human affairs as they unfold before him. "Taillefer, the minstrel, rode at the head of the army singing:—

"De Karlemaigne et de Rolant
Et d'Oliver et des vassals.
Qui morurent en Roncevals."

"What's that they say?"

"A song in French about Roland and Oliver."

"They won didn't they?"

"Then I don't understand because we did fight the French at Crecy and we are fighting with the French now."

To his teacher, he is a fine educaton, challenging beliefs and traditions and facts, in singleness of purpose and an urgency that admits of no excuse.

He has the spirit of a scholar, too, and has spent many an hour comparing pictures of castles in books, making plans of drawbridges and doors and windows, using all his resources to construct a castle out of old boot boxes, with a drawbridge "wot works" and a well. This has become a toy in common use.

It was his neighbour, Wilson, with whom he keeps up a "friendly" relation by frequent challenges to "oblige" (wrestle), who equipped the class in secret with bows and arrows and arrow-cases, and with words, and was found, on the first half-holiday of the term, trespassing in a deep wood, some miles away, acting out the joys of Robin Hood on the most perfect of stages.

Ashley cleans the stables in his spare time and has a large acquaintance with camps and is of the company of dreamers. He makes his own poems. "Poetry is what makes you more sad or more happy than what goes straight on," he once remarked, and he sings of the willow catkins, dropping on the water and floating down stream in the sunshine, and of deeds of chivalry.

History is for him a storehouse of treasures, more precious than the Arabian Nights, for they are "true stories."

"They do say they're true too!" he says, triumphantly, as he pores over the chronicles of Froissart or the adventures in the new world.

Ward is just "striking fourteen," when he must take his chance in the world. He is already a man of affairs, with considerable business capacity. He has gauged the situation, created by the miserable dearth of literature and the deserts of "readers" in the classroom, and being a capitalist, he originated the brilliant plan of buying paper-covered fairy tale books and old histories from the market stalls and lending out at a ½d. a reading. He is very popular and drives a roaring trade.

"Jolly fine, them tales of discoverers and traders, I'm pertickly intrested in them," is his comment, "because I'm going to sea—a fine life is a sailor's"—"Top-hole history for telling you things you want to know."

He is quick to grasp the significance of facts. Hearing the story of the Hudson Bay Company and the French trappers, one day, with a flash of joy, he shouted "Now I see it." He has discovered the meaning of the fall of Quebec, the only part of this history the books usually give.

His eager mind jumps to problems of government and suggests, before you have time to arrange the evidence, the possible development of markets and the need for a change in finance. He is already aware of economic law.

Ridley, in the same class, is different. He has come from South Africa and has already planned to return to work on the land there, and one day, perhaps, to own a farm. He follows the fortunes of planters and settlers breathlessly and has views about slave labour.

He has a fine sense of humour, chuckling aloud, as he reads over Anthony Parkhurst's letter in Hakluyt, on the fisheries of Newfoundland. "These be the fishes which (when I please to be merry with my old companions) I say, do come on shore when I command them in the name of the five ports and conjure them by such-like words . . . These be also the fishes which I may sweep with brooms on an heap and never wet my foot, so they hear my voice . . . For the squid, whose nature is to come by night as well as by day, I tell them, I set him a candle to see his way, with which he is much delighted or else cometh to wonder at it as do our fresh water fish.''

"Didn't he have 'em just!''

He is always arrested by the ethical aspect of the story, and ponders thoughtfully the disconcerting differences between public and private morality. He is full of admiration for the fine mettle of a pirate, and like the biographer of Cortès feels that, ''it was perhaps intended he should receive his recompense in a better world, for he was a good cavalier and most true to his devotions.'' At the same time, he is haunted by the tragedy of Montezuma and levels searching questions at the grown-ups as to their views about such actions, distinctly relieved when the centre of interest passes to the less difficult events in the search for the North-west Passage.

He is the proud possessor of an elephant's foot, ''stopped at many a port'' before it reached him, he likes to think, and he has lately acquired a gasolene cinema and a history film is in progress for this.

He is an insatiable reader, devouring two books a week, if you can provide them, and, just now, begging, borrowing, filching any picture of colonial life that will suggest a subject for the film.

These are children living in a very poor district and attending school with the minimum of equipment, yet the problem is much the same from whatever point of view we regard it, for the laws of mental development apply equally to all alike and there is no distinction of sex or class.

Some differences, of course, there must be, arising out of their environment, for such children have a variety of experience in a great world beyond the school doors and little enough help in co-ordinating it. They have been thrown so often on their own resources that response has quickened, and their teachers are often startled by their judgments on problems that have never even entered the horizon of the more sheltered child. All the same, their demand on life is just as eager, just as urgent as any other child's, and the rival claims on their attention in a crowded day leave no room for irrelevances. Like the Little Brothers of S. Francis, they live joyously, unembarrassed by legacies of material goods or the prejudices of their fathers.

It is in the company of these critics that we begin to realize how irrelevant the subjects of our syllabuses really are. We have made them with an eye to the ''notes'' we possess rather than an appreciation of the demands of our children to know and to understand ''what came before.''

II.—Sequences of thought.

We had talked of the gods of the northmen and listened to some of their stories. We had a thrilling moment when the missionaries came, for the gods had become dear to the children also and they understood. It was after that I took them a model of a timber church for their village. These children were eight to ten years old.

"Were there any bells in the tower?"

"Who made them?"

"The bells on Sunday always say now, '*Do* come to church,'" someone said.

"The bells on Sunday used to say, 'It is time to come to church,'" was the answer.

Here is the material for an interesting comment.

"How often did they go to church? Twice on Sunday, like us?"

"The goose-boy would have to hurry, he had a long way to come." The pictures were very clear in their minds. There was the boy with his rattle, hurrying his flock over the meadows homeward, to get to prayers in time.

"What prayers did they say?"

"They were in Latin."

"My brother talks Latin at the Perse. Is it the same?"

"Show us what it looks like."

"They say Latin prayers at the Catholic Church now, don't they?"

"They were the same perhaps?"

"Were they Catholics then?" and their own answer forestalling mine,

"You said the missionaries came from Rome."

"Roman Catholics. And were they Catholics then?"

"Was there only one church?"

"Weren't there any chapels?"

"Did the Saxons learn Latin then?"

"Did they make the Saxons priests?" Here is another point. We are almost ready for some of the problems of organization.

At this moment they returned to the detail of the model.

The mental rhythm becomes interesting. The child's attention swings from the particular to the universal, to and fro, from the little thing to the great thing. He is busied in relating the present and the past, his experience and the experience of others, in associating thought with thought, and action with principle.

"How thick was the door? Had it a bolt?"

"I saw one at Peterborough with iron bars."

"When did they make iron bars like that?"

"Why did they make them?"

"It would be a good place to hide in if the enemy came. There we have rights of 'sanctuary.'"

"Did they go to church when it was dark sometimes?"

"Had they lamps?" We can answer this ourselves.

"Where did they keep the precious books?"

"I should put them up where everyone could read," was the suggestion and the rapid comment from the child, too.

"They were in Latin, though."

"Did they turn them into Saxon."

"Alfred, King, turned each word of me into English and sent me to his writers, north and south, and bade them make more such copies that he might send them to the bishops." This is one of the uses of a source.

"Who is he?" We shall have to turn to this again.

"Have you seen one?"

With reverence and joy, they thumbed an old sheet from a psalter, where centuries ago others had turned it and left traces of their use. Here we set out on a new track of interests that led us, for several lessons, into the scriptorium, into monastic life and far beyond.

If we begin with the history of material things, we inevitably find ourselves engaged with the manifold activities of man. It is as impossible to separate one aspect of history from another as it is in life. Yet the sequences become important. We have emphasized, and quite rightly, the necessity for beginning our study with social economic facts, but in so doing we are in danger of forgetting that this is only the jumping-off place, that a knowledge of this aspect of history involves us in other consideratons, and enables us to discover meanings in political and constitutional history.

The child leaps from the material object to the stars, passing, not by slow stages at different periods in his career but by the constant rhythm of his mind, between particular and universal, between the illustration and the principle, relating all in one universe of thought.

Here is an instance of the way in which he can grasp political issues after a real study of social conditions.

We have made the village. Let us clear the floor and have a game there.

Here ran the river, that was the best place for fishing. Here was the mill and there the lord's house, over there, the woodlands, the pigs feeding, the villagers gathering fallen timber, the stranger blowing his horn three times.

"What did the people look like?"

The folk can tell us themselves. There is an old calendar, showing the occupations for every month in the year, ploughing, sowing, harvesting. We can study them.

"What did the people think about it?"

They can tell us. There is Ælfric's Dialogue and that tells you what work they did. The ploughman says:—"I work hard. I go out at daybreak driving the oxen to the field and I yoke them to the plough. Be it never so stark winter I dare not linger at home for awe of my lord, but having yoked my oxen and fastened share and coulter, every day I must plough a full acre or more. I have a boy driving the oxen with a goad-iron, who is hoarse with cold and shouting, and I do more also. I have to fill the oxen's bins with hay, and water them and take out their litter. Mighty hard work it is, for I am not free."

There is much besides. "Let's pretend" or "Do you know any stories that happened?"

There was domesday book. The King sent his messengers to inquire in all the land:

"How much land have you?"

"Who gave it you?"

"What services do you owe?"

"Have you a mill?"

"Have you a fish pond?" The children can frame these questions themselves.

"So narrowly did the king make them seek all this, that there was not a single yard of land (shameful it is to tell, though he thought it no shame to do), nor one ox, nor one cow, nor one swine left out, that was not set down in his rolls, and all these rolls were afterwards brought to him." We shall have to go on to the Court of Exchequer.

These are political and economic questions. It all becomes quite intelligible when the village has been built up under our eyes and we are so familiar with the detail. We are, too, getting an introduction to some of the most vital and difficult subjects of history not peculiar to our own country.

From whatever point of view we start in the story, the child's ultimate concern is the thoughts of men about life. He finds rules of conduct and he is in search of principles and motives. History should leave him with the conviction that our thoughts have a past no less interesting than the story of material objects.

We may begin by building a castle in clay and discussing its defence, but we are led to other issues before the end.

"Some of these men were very cruel. Were they Christian?"

There is the great story of chivalry, and the material for it is found in the beautiful prayers, used when the knight made his vows and went forth "to keep the good peace of the LORD his GOD," and in the songs and stories of those days. Literature is one of the evidences of history.

"Did they find the Grail?"

"What happened when they saw it?"

"Then began every knight to behold other, and either saw other, by their seeming, fairer than ever they saw afore."

The Crusades follow out of this naturally enough.

"Which way did they go?"

"How long did they take?"

"Who went with them?"

"Did they get the Holy City?"

Always, there comes into their minds, sooner or later, the question "What was the use?"

This inqury, in the early stages, is of much the same nature as that other one, "Was he a good man?" the answer growing more and more difficult as the child developes.

It may be that in this study he finds real values and learns to set his needle for a great voyage of discovery.

AN EXPERIMENT IN TEACHING ELEMENTARY GEOMETRY.

By KATHARINE STEINTHAL.

THIS is an account of an experiment in teaching elementary Geometry at a preparatory school for boys and girls. The class concerned consisted of a dozen children of about twelve years of age. Some of them had learnt Geometry for three terms and some for five. The year's work began with the consideration of brown paper parallelograms and the equivalent rectangles obtained from them by cutting off a triangle and replacing it in a different position. After four weeks work during which paper, scissors, diagrams on the blackboard and diagrams on the floor had been used, the fact that a parallelogram and a rectangle on the same base and of the same height are equal in area was not a belief of the class as a whole.

M's doubt was patent, so I said: "I have tried everything I can think of, but I can't make M. understand, will one of you take my place?"

E. came out, drew a parallelogram and a rectangle on the board, talked a little, grew confused, lost the confidence of the class, and was replaced by C.

He put questions to M. to find the point of disagreement. M. did not believe that the two triangles were equal. Several children called out "but they were the same piece of paper," C. said "look M., that side's equal to that side, that side's equal to that side, and that side's equal to that side, so the triangles must be equal." No work on congruent triangles had been done by the class: M. seemed convinced. I said "Oh, is that all right, are two triangles always equal if three sides of the one are equal to three sides of the other?" Opinion varied, many children thought such triangles could be different in area and some thought their angles could be different. After a short discussion this question was written on the blackboard:

"Can two triangles have their three sides equal and differ in angles or in area?"

This was to stay up until the class could answer yes or no to it unanimously.

Each member of the class agreed to make at home a set of six paper triangles, each set with equal sides.

At the next lesson each child made a formal report to the class. "I made six triangles with sides 6, 5, 4 inches long, and found that they did not differ in angles or area." One or two children reported differences, their triangles were examined by the class and shown to be inaccurate. During such an examination I asked whether one exception would matter. The children who realized the importance of this were so emphatic that it was not possible to judge the general feeling of the class apart from their influence. The further question "How many instances would be necessary to prove the impossibility of a difference in angles and area?" was answered by H.: "If you made a million sets, you wouldn't have proved it, but even now we should be jolly surprised to see an exception."

One of the reports ran "I said I would make six triangles with sides 4, 1, 8 cms., but they wouldn't come." This led to an investigation and quickly to the agreement that any two sides of a triangle are together greater than the third. This fact was considered by the class to be proved. This time, they explained, you could see the triangles growing smaller and smaller until there was one "without any area at all" and after that no more, whereas in the case of the triangles with equal sides they had not been able to arrange snch a series.

Next week one child had a new method of proving the original proposition of the equivalent parallelogram and rectangle. It was unsuccessful, but it introduced the statement, familiar to those of the class who had learned Geometry for five terms, that the angle sum of a triangle was equal to two right angles. Doubts of this led back to parallel lines and angles made by transversals. All the doubters were encouraged to give their opinions, because I never expressed mine so that there was no authority to whom appeal could be made. The stupid children gave a training in thought and exposition to their quicker classmates and were themselves enjoying the lessons and their own importance. When they had led the class back to the statement that two adjacent angles together form two right angles, the lessons were changed.

It seemed time to introduce the idea of drawing conclusions from data. After a few examples outside Geometry, these statements were put on the board :—

DATA.

$$A + B = 180°$$
$$A = B$$

Each child was to copy the statements and to write below them some conclusion drawn from them. Each child came out before the class and read his conclusion. Then he asked "Is it true?" If the answer of the class was not unanimous, the question was discussed until agreement was reached. Then the further question was asked, "Is it relevant?" In this first example the word relevant was not strictly applicable. Such conclusions as "they are both angles" were excluded as irrelevant. In practice this use of the term did not seem to obscure its correct use a little later on, but it would possibly be better to alter the wording. The answering of this second question produced some of the best work of the class. Perhaps it would be better to make two questions of it: "Is it a conclusion from the data," and then "Is it relevant." The third question could then be introduced a stage later.

Problems of this kind occupied the class for several weeks. After a time I began to ask whether the conclusions were applicable only to the particular case, or could be enunciated as a general law. A few such were enunciated, for instance "triangles of the same perimeter can have different areas."

The next change turned the lessons into a tournament. A king was elected and chose a herald and a scribe. Volunteers were called for to take the part of knight challenger who was to propose statements and to maintain them against all opponents. The first of these lessons was fairly successful. After it I met the king and herald, and we drew up a few rules of procedure for which we had felt a need.

I will report at length one of the simplest of these contests.

B., as knight challenger, asked the herald to write up, " Any two straight lines cannot enclose a space." To my surprise several opponents appeared when she asked " Does anybody disagree ? "

The people who drew curved lines were soon dealt with, but M. spoke for several when she drew two straight lines meeting at a point and said :

" Look, there's space between those straight lines."

" Yes, but it's not enclosed."

" It can't get out."

" What prevents it ? "

" Why, all this space here."

" Yes, but I didn't say two straight lines and space couldn't enclose a space : I said two straight lines couldn't "

M. was satisfied, but C. said:

" If you had a garden with a wall round it and the gate was open, you could still say it was an enclosed garden."

B. answered, " When I say enclosed, I mean shut in all round."

There was a short discussion on parallel lines, resulting in the decision that the space between them could " flow out at both ends " and then the class accepted the statement. According to the rules the herald now began to dictate the statement, but the challenger herself called out " Wait, there's something wrong, we don't need that ʻany.' "

The tournament went on till the class seemed ready to work at the conditions of congruence of triangles. I brought to the lesson a closed envelope containing a paper triangle. I told the class that I wished for an exact copy of the hidden triangle, that I would tell them any of its measurements they wanted, and that the problem was to see how few measurements were necessary. The class worked in couples and the work of each couple was registered for all the class to see, thus :—

Name.	Number of Measurements.	Measurements.	Report.
M. R.	3	A, B, AB. (2 angles and included side)	Success.
B. O.	2	AB, area (1 side and area)	Failure.

Most of the children assumed the necessity of three measurements, but a few of the best workers made persistent efforts with two. When several successful attempts had been made, the problem became to find which groups of three measurements gave successful results.

During this work I was asked whether there was any way of drawing the triangle or triangles with given base and given vertical angle. At the time I thought the children could not solve this, so I promised them some work leading up to it. (With another class the following method has been used. The children cut out pieces of paper with the given vertical angle, opened their dividers to the length of the given base, and pricked off different positions of the base. The triangles

were all cut out and superposed, and their vertices were seen to lie on
the arc of a circle.) For this purpose the children drew circles and a
diameter in each, joined the ends of the diameter to points on the
circumference, and measured the angles. Some of the children were
quickly ready to extend their investigations to angles in major and
minor segments. As soon as all the children had made some way with
the first exercise, a tournament was held at which the statement that the
angle in a semicircle is a right angle was discussed and approved.
There was difficulty in wording this statement.

As the time for examinations had come, the following paper was
given to the class.

1. Draw a circle.
    Draw 3 chords in it.
    Find the midpoint of each chord.
    Join the midpoint of each chord to the centre of the circle.
    Measure the angle made with each chord by the straight line
        joining its midpoint to the centre of the circle.
    Write a report of your experiment.

2. Draw 3 circles.
    Draw a chord in each.
    Find the midpoint of each chord.
    In each circle join the midpoint of the chord to the centre of
        the circle.
    In each circle measure the angle made with the chord by the
        straight line joining the midpoint to the centre of the
        circle.
    Write a report of your experiment.

3. AB and AC are two straight lines meeting at A.
    AB is $4 \cdot 2$ cms., AC $3 \cdot 8$ cms., A is $56°$.
    Find the midpoints of these two straight lines.
    If the two straight lines are chords of a circle, draw the circle.
    Describe carefully your method of constructing this circle.
    Measure the angle in the major segment cut off by AB.
    What is the size of the angle in the minor segment cut off by
        AB.

Four of the ten children present answered the paper correctly except
for errors of detail, the other six failed to apply the experience of the
first two questions to the solution of the problem. Four of the six
answered the first two questions well, three of these made guesswork
attempts at the problem. Two papers were worthless.

In the remaining lessons the four who had solved the problem and
one other who had talked the matter over with them afterwards worked
apart. Working together, without help from me, they drew the series
of triangles having a fixed base and a fixed vertical angle, and also
worked out a proof of the proposition that in a circle the straight line
joining the midpoint of a chord to the centre of a circle is at right angles
to the chord They were told that the proof had two stages, and were
directed a little at the beginning of their discussion. They wrote out a
correct proof. The rest of the class spent these two lessons working
through the examination paper.

The work described was spread over a school year in weekly
lessons of forty minutes.

THE SCHOOL AND THE COMMUNITY SPIRIT.[1]

III.

In the last paper on this subject, we described the efforts of various philosophers, to show how the relations actually existing between subjects and sovereign in a modern State, were founded on reason. Locke's arguments were arrayed in defence of the Revolution of 1688, and since his time nobody has seriously questioned the right of the people to choose their own sovereign, at any rate in our own country. It was, however, left for a French writer to lift the whole subject out of a position in which the State was no more than a necessary evil—a convenient device for protecting men from each other,—a device which had a very limited use. As the subject of a State, the individual retained all his primitive rights except that of being the judge in his own case. It was thought extremely important that individual freedom should be interfered with as little as possible; freedom meant the absence of restraints. The less government the better. You have the individuals on the one side and the ruling authority on the other. Their interests were naturally opposed to each other, and until a totally new conception of society was reached, the jealousy of the subjects against the encroachments of the ruler was a prime factor in the politics of the market place. It was, for example, no business of the State, as Locke conceived it, to concern itself with education. The compulsory schooling of children was an invasion of the rights of parenthood; firmly rooted as they were in the Law of Nature, these rights were inalienable and quite outside the range of the State's authority. True, some States had, under the influence of Protestantism, made attendance at school compulsory, but that was an arbitrary act, inconceivable in a free country.

Except for purposes of national defence or of national aggrandisement, there was no community spirit in the large sense that we understand it to-day. Of course there were communities, some of which, like the Church, extended beyond the boundaries of the State, and all of which expressed in some measure the social nature of man. The Church took special charge of his spiritual welfare. Guilds of various kinds looked after the interests of crafts and trade. Each society called for loyalty from its members within the range of its objects. The Church alone had any claim to cover the whole of life and as then conceived, it was the function of the Church to provide such education as was necessary for men's spiritual well-being. The State was merely a secular institution, with very restricted functions, and it was inconceivable that, as such, it should be charged with any positive direction of the individual life. The school was therefore not its concern.

The whole position was reflected in the school itself, and the old tradition is not altogether dead. The spirit of both Church and State was disciplinary and individualistic. Rewards and punishments were the chief appeal, tempered with the hope of achieving social or official distinction in one or other public capacity—administrator, legislator, soldier or parson. The schoolmaster was an autocrat, often "a beast," at his best "a just beast," as autocrats everywhere are likely to be. There was no hope for a higher development than this until a new spirit was breathed into society itself.

[1] A series of short papers for young teachers and students in training.

The difficulty came from the failure to realize the true meaning of society in its relation to the individual, and it was Rousseau's penetrating genius that first threw light upon the problem. In the short space of twelve years (1750-1762), he wrote a series of small books, all of them contained in a single volume of the Everyman Library, which were destined completely to transform men's ideas on politics and education. Hitherto, books on political and social questions appealed to a very small public. They were often dry-as-dust treatises of an abstract kind which either had little bearing upon the practical questions of the moment or were too dull and intellectual for the mass of men to grasp. Rousseau wrote with a passionate conviction which carried men off their feet. In fact a new era in literature as well as in politics had dawned when in 1750 he carried off the Dijon prize by an essay designed to show the disastrous effects which progress in the Arts and Sciences had had upon men's morals. It was a literary bombshell hurled at a complacent society which was soon to be shaken to its foundations by the new doctrine and by the new spirit which Rousseau gave to the world during those fateful years.

Perhaps the most important points in his message were reserved to the last, for it was in 1762 that Rousseau published the *Social Contract* and *Emile*. We are concerned, of course, with the first of these. As its title tells us, Rousseau is considering the same problem as Hobbes and Locke had written about. Like them he imagines a State of Nature as a condition preliminary to the Social State. We need not concern ourselves about the peculiarities of his conception, as it does not really affect the problem he set himself to solve. He had in his essay on the *Origin of Inequality amongst Men* contrasted very unfavourably the social man as he knew him with the "noble savage" as he pictured him, but in the Social Contract he set himself a more serious task. Whether or not man ever led the happy and dignified but isolated life he described as a state of nature, Rousseau admits to be doubtful, but the bondage of his social chains could not be questioned. His condition was evil beyond remedy unless we could come upon a new interpretation for society and for the relationship of individual men to it. It was precisely this that he sought—and found.

Adopting the idea of a compact as the basis of society—an implied if not an historical agreement—he defines it in these words: "Each of us puts his person and all his power in common under the supreme direction of the general will, and, in our corporate capacity, we receive each member as an indivisable part of the whole." His object had been to find a form of society "which would defend and protect with the whole common force the person and goods of each associate, and in which each, while uniting himself with all *may still obey himself alone, and remain as free as before.*" He sought an interpretation of society which would revolutionize the individual man's attitude to it and its attitude to the individual man. He believed that any society divided into a governing and a governed class was in a fundamentally false position and that the future depended upon the acceptance of the idea of society as an organic unity. He couched his doctrine in the terms of a compact in conformity with current ideas, but the terms of the compact as he phrased it expressed a relationship which seemed to Rousseau in closest conformity with human nature. There should not be, there cannot be, when the social ideal is reached, any opposition between the individual on the one hand and the State on the other. The compact, says Rousseau, "creates a moral and collective body" in which each member is an indivisible part of the whole.

It is the conception of society as a moral person which has made his doctrine so fruitful of political consequences. This is the seminal idea which steadily made its way into the nineteenth century politics of our own country, and which finds at least tacit acceptance in the hesitating opportunism of much of our modern political activity. Once we grasp the moral purpose of society, we can set no limits to its authority, so long, that is to say, as it remains moral, and it remains moral so long as it is inspired by a "general will"—that is to say, so long as it seeks the well-being of all its members, so long as it strives for "the common interest" and not for the interest of sections.

It is not our business to follow out the details of Rousseau's political theory. The details might not all be acceptable even to those who accept unreservedly the basic doctrine. Society is too complex a structure for us all to agree about specific proposals for its betterment, though we may all be equally anxious to reach a form of social organization in which privilege has disappeared and in which equality of opportunity is as nearly achieved as nature herself will allow. It is, however, an urgent need that we should be clear about some, at least, of the implications which attend to this notion of society as a moral person.

In the first place, of course, a moral person is one whose conduct is under the control of an ideal held as firmly as human weakness will allow. He may not, he does not, achieve his ideal, indeed his ideal is ever advancing. It is not momentary convenience, but principle which guides him in all the real issues of life. He seeks the right unfailingly. His knowledge is limited and he makes mistakes, but he is ever extending the one and he learns from the others.

All this applies with steadily increasing force to a society which is gradually becoming conscious of a moral *raison d'être*. We shall see it endeavouring to set its house in such order that the end for which it exists may be reached. Governments, institutions, even the particular form of State which it "enjoys" are each in turn brought into the common crucible of critical discussion. Do they help or hinder the achievement of the moral aim of the community? Whether we call it evolution or revolution does not matter, but as surely as night follows day everything which stands in the way of the ultimate "moralization" of society will sooner or later be removed. Any particular community may in this process make mistakes so gross as to lead to its own undoing. Its knowledge is imperfect, and its judgment may err. The community is, in this regard, in no better case than the individual. The great fact is the steadily advancing recognition of the moral purpose of an organized society. This is the new community spirit which is slowly penetrating the schools.

(To be continued.)

REVIEWS.

The English Elementary School: Some Elementary Facts about it. By
A. W. Newton, M.A., formerly Inspector of the Board of Education.
Longmans, Green & Co. 6/- net.

MR. NEWTON'S book is "something between a history and a guide book," as he
says himself in his introduction. It does not contain, as some reviewers seem to
have expected that it would, the mature reflections of an education official on his
career. Still less does it enunciate a new theory of education like the famous work
of Mr. Edward Holmes. Indeed, Mr. Newton's cautious and sceptical mind will
not allow him ever to proclaim himself as a prophet, or even as the fervent
supporter of any school of thought. In matters controversial, which a writer on
elementary education is bound to encounter, he strives to present rival views with
painstaking fairness, though here and there his own bias may be faintly perceived.
Nor is the book in any sense a text-book in the history of education for the student
who is taking this as a subject in his course. It should no doubt be on the shelves
of the Training College Library, but for reference or for consulting, not for study.

Yet openly and avowedly as a "guide book" it has very great value. It
presents an admirable summary of facts about the English Elementary School,
with just so much relevant history as is necessary to explain them. It
ought to be of much service to members of Education Committees and of
the general public who take an intelligent interest in popular education, and
to officials and teachers whose main concern may lie with other branches of education, and elementary teachers themselves, even of long experience, may derive
advantage from reading the book, if only that they may learn something of the
origin and history of many practices and regulations they cannot understand ; and
perhaps the younger generation may realize the pit out of which they have been
digged. Mr. Newton does not seek to defend the elementary school system except
in so far as showing what are the real facts, and not the imaginary facts of the
critic, and how most of them have an historical justification constitutes a defence.
There is no antiquarianism in the book, and the reader would look in vain for any
attempt to trace in a philosophical spirit the development of ideas. But as a plain
account of the work of the Elementary School in 1919, Mr. Newton's book would
be hard to surpass.

In this Journal it is fitting to refer especially to the chapter on the Training of
Teachers, for this is the essential part of the Elementary School Scheme. The
author is particularly clear and well-balanced in his description of the Pupil
Teacher system, and his judgment of it. He does not assume the attitude of the
superior person who applies an ideal to all stages of struggling progress, and who
grows more and more contemptuous the further from the ideal the particular
subject recedes. Yet the *laudator temporis acti se tirone* will find very little
comfort in the book. Mr. Newton gives the Pupil Teacher system its meed of
credit and also the criticism it deserves.

After explaining the mode of training teachers in the ordinary Training College
at the present time, and showing how it has arisen and what justification it has in
history if not as an ideal plan, Mr. Newton devotes a chapter to training in
University institutions. Here, although he balances the pros and cons with a
great show of impartiality, he is patently himself very critical. He states with
fairness and clearness the aims of the Universities to give a philosophical basis to
training : "the teacher," in the view of the Universities, "should ground his
practice on principles which he acquires at the outset of his career." At the same
time the doubts of the critics whether formal instruction in philosophy or
psychology in the history of education is any help to the beginner in teaching are
very forcibly presented. Mr. Newton appears to lean to the intermediate view
that University studies in education are rather for the teacher of experience than
for the student "at the outset of his career."

In a short review there is no space to examine the question at length. But, perhaps, one may ask: how should the training of a teacher be conceived? and put the previous question, what is a teacher? Is he a kind of craftsman to be taught to acquire a certain skill in imparting knowledge and in cultivating mental intelligence, shaping the scholar's mind? If so, his training will be a training mainly in skill and technique. Even so, his technique need not be of the "tips and dodges" order, and he can take an intelligent interest in the nature and effects of his own skill. But he hardly needs philosophy of a mature kind or the history of education. Is he, on the other hand, in a position like that of the clergyman, but with more definite duties, a man whose main care is the right development of the personality of the pupil on all sides, and not the intellectual alone? If so, he should know the foundations of the philosophy of his craft, and learn how others in the past have envisaged his task. Analogies are apt to be misleading, but it appears to us that the analogy of the training of the physician has too often been applied to the teacher's case, as if the teacher were only a kind of practitioner whose training should be of a highly practical kind. But is not the teacher more comparable with the clergyman or minister? Does the clergyman get his training only in the details of parochial work or in the technique of preaching? Does the theological college really "train" at all, as some critics would have the Training College train or as the Hospital trains the doctor? Perhaps the truth is that many teachers are destined by the limitations of their native endowment to be only practitioners, who should be trained as such. But the University, it seems to us, is bound to provide for the nobler type, and perhaps therein lies the justification of much in the University courses that appears so remote from the immediate business of the classroom.

This chapter and others also will set people thinking not only of the present but of the future. Mr. Newton has made one curious omission which may have considerable significance in the future. He has no allusion to Experimental Psychology, though courses in this are to be found in the Training Departments of many Universities. It would have been interesting to have even the provisional views of a man of scientific and mathematical turn of mind, like Mr. Newton, on this new claimant for a position in the studies of the teacher in training.   X.

New Town: A proposal in Agricultural, Industrial, Educational, Civic, and Social Reconstruction. (141 pp.) Published by Dent. 2/-.

THE dynamic principle of life is shown in two ways, by the spirit of unrest and dissatisfaction with life as it is generally lived to-day, which finds its expression in breaking down, and by the creative spirit with its cry of reconstruction. Sometimes this spirit works among the debris and ruin of failure brought about by the clash of individualistic material aims, and tries by legislation to remedy, or at any rate better, the old conditions, and then there are many notes in her cry: "Back to the Land, Housing Reform, Physical Fitness, Higher Wages and Shorter Working Hours, Longer School Life, Revival of Village Life and Cottage Industries," &c.

But now and then a golden day dawns when the creative spirit breaks away from the ruins and failures, and starts afresh. Here is the animating force of those who colonize overseas ; there is everything to make, there is not only vision in the heart *but power in the hand*, and all reconstructive notes are found in the full chord.

It is this characteristic in the proposed New Town experiment which makes it so full of promise. The creative spirit, working in the first place through some practical idealists belonging to the Society of Friends, has unity of purpose, though it is necessarily manysided in development.

New Town is an attempt, not only on paper but already in the initial stages of being, to create a City of Joy on the green countryside of England, where the main principles of Co-operative enterprise, particularly in agricultural and industrial life, will be adopted and extended. By gradually building a new Country Town, free from the almost irredeemable evils of existing city life, it is hoped to show that an enlightened democratic community (educated for democracy) inspired by high ideals and the spirit of Co-operative service may redeem industry from materialistic aims, restore agriculture to her right position, and make of the day's work a dignified and joyous expression. The motive power in factory, farm, and store, municipality, home, school, and club, will be that of service to the community, and not only in material things but in the deeper values of life, for it is realized that "man does not live by bread alone."

Three thousand acres of land, yet to be located, is to be bought by a Trust Company, whose Board of Directors is already active, and gradually to become the property of the ten to twenty thousand residents. £12,500 has already been subscribed, and the remainder to £75,000 is offered for subscription to the public in shares of £1 each, and two kinds of Loan Stock, that bearing Interest of 4%, and Non-bearing Stock. The land when bought will be vested in a Limited Liability Company, whose first business will be the foundation and equipment of the town: in course of time the body will become more and more definitely representative of the growing city. It will let land on leases with conditions framed to safeguard the city against exploitation for private gains, it will help and offer facilities for schemes of democratic control, and carry on, at any rate at first, the civic work generally done by a progressive Town Council.

Subsidiary Companies who will be associated to the Parent Company will have the special work of the development of agricultural and industrial enterprise, housing, transport, &c. ; the Farming Company will naturally be the most important, controlling, as it will, the main experiment in agriculture. The spirit of Association animates the scheme, the experience of Co-operative enterprise enlightens it, we see some of the best features of the Mediæval Guilds Organization in the Open Markets, a hint of Gary's educational policy in the school, we find a city largely dependent, though by no means entirely, on the agriculture carried on within her borders, and electric heating and labour saving devices in the homes. The buildings are not to be put up under a contract system, but by a self-organized Guild of Builders, whose only competition will be that of service and beauty of expression.

The ground plan of New Town must necessarily be conditioned by the ultimate site, but a little picture may be roughly sketched :—the Urban district has the group of associated Central Buildings—the Town Hall with its pleasant Committee rooms for craftsmen, farmers, &c.—the People's House of Recreation, Museum, Library, and Open Market—and these stand in a spacious green park. The Schools with their workshops and playing fields come next, and then the homes looking "as though some heart was in their stones," for all classes of the community—with no social East and West end.

Beyond these, and taking a third of the entire area of New Town, are the small holdings and large farms, the food crops, pasture for the dairy herds, and orchards stretching away to the woodland boundaries. It is not difficult to see that the townsman will live in the country and the farmer in the town, while the schoolchild will be as familiar with the farm as with the store ; the world in miniature lies before him.

There is no outward church, the city will build it if it feels the need. Meanwhile, the expresssion of the inner spirit of New Town is holinesss in a very real sense of the word, for it is not in organization by itself that social salvation is to be wholly found, but only so far as it is inspired by love, faith in, and respect for the neighbour. This is the inner light by which energy may be directed, knowledge applied, and a breadth of vision kept.

The city is to be no paradise of saints, isolated and complacent in a green retreat, but a vigorous community seeking to produce for the world more than it consumes, radiating new life beyond its borders into needy England. It asks, through its Secretary, The Pioneer Trust, Ltd., 27 Chancery Lane, London, W.C.2, for help, by the taking up of shares, by constructive criticism from business men, trade unionists, labour enthusiasts, lovers of the land, and all men and women who have a sense of social responsibility and the gift of understanding; and it invites those with a vocation for citizenship to become a living part of the New Town experiment.

W. A. Bone.

Problems of National Education. By Twelve Scottish Educationists; with prefatory note by The Right Hon. Robert Morris, K.C., M.P. Edited by John Clarke. (xxvii + 368 pp.) Macmillan & Co. 12/6 net.

It would have been difficult for the editor to have chosen a stronger team than the one responsible for this interesting volume. Although its title suggests a point of view which might make the book of little value to English readers, most of the chapters are quite general in their outlook. Professor Burnet's contribution has been perhaps too exclusively directed to the evil results which the Intermediate examination has had upon the position of classics in Scotch Schools, but in the essay following Dr. Burnet's, Professor J. A. Thomson discusses the Place and Function of Science in a characteristically fascinating way without a single reference to Scotland. Yet the case against the Intermediate examination and the curriculum connected with it has its lessons for us. Can it be true, as Dr. Burnet suggests, that not a single Professor in the Universities of Scotland sends his children to a State-aided Secondary School.

Sir Leslie Mackenzie brings psychological insight, as well as knowledge of physiology and anatomy, to bear upon the problem of Physical Education, though he leaves out of view the problem of whether or not it is possible to bring traditional school activities into line with our clearer grasps of the conditions favourable to physical well-being. After all a child is not a duality at bottom, and there is surely something wrong in a position which suggests the necessity for one set of experts to undo the mischief which another set of experts may have innocently wrought on the poor victim of their attentions. Space will not allow a detailed discussion of the several papers here brought together. They are all as "meaty" as could be desired, and they cover topics as "live" in England as they are in Scotland. As indicating the scope of the book, we may cite the essays by Dr. Morgan on Social Aspects of Education; Mr. Strong, now Professor of Education in the University of Leeds, on Moral and Religious Elements in the School; Mr. A. P. Laurie on Technical Education; Mr. Malloch on Teaching as a Profession: and two suggestive essays on Girls' Education by Miss Fish and Miss Ainslie, who agree in the view that what is good for boys is not necessarily the best for girls. The Editor, who is Clerk to the Glasgow School Board, writes on Local Administration, and Professor Grierson brings the volume to a close by his very critical survey of the present position and functions of the Universities of Scotland.

Infant and Young Child Welfare. By Harold Scurfield, M.D. (ix + 165 pp.)

The Welfare of the School Child. By Joseph Cates, M.D., D.P.H.) (ix + 154 pp.) Cassell & Co. Each 5/- net.

These are the first two volumes of a series dealing with English Public Health, to be issued under the editorship of Sir Malcolm Morris, K.C.V.O. The volumes announced are for the most part in the hands of Medical Officers of Health. Dr. Scurfield is M.O.H. for Sheffield, and Dr. Cates combines the general health work with the school work at St. Helens. They are both therefore writing from abundant experience. Dr. Scurfield's volume is addressed primarily to parents, but the teacher of young children dare not ignore the home life of her charges, and teachers of older girls in upper standards and in continuation schools are usually required to give instruction on the care of infants. These teachers could not do better than soak themselves in the subject matter and spirit of Dr. Scurfield's book. It is the work of a specialist who has his heart in his job, and who knows how to put his points in terms so simple and clear that any layman can understand him. He is no doctrinaire. The book is such a storehouse of telling facts, of direct testimony and of simple rules for home life, and it is inspire by such sincerity of purpose that we strongly recommend it to teachers and indeed to all who are concerned to make the world a happier place for the young.

Dr. Cates writes an interesting descriptive account of the problems which are the immediate concern of the Schools Medical Officer, but he also has the layman in view. Teachers and doctors should of course work in close harmony, and the schoolmaster will find much to interest him in a volume, which, although it is limited to questions of physical welfare and the physical conditions which promote school-health, presents problems enough to occupy school-staffs and education committees for some time to come. The hygiene of mind is perhaps reserved for a later volume in the series, but that involves subtler problems than a busy M.O.H. is likely to be able to tackle. Unfortunately he does not always recognize the existence of the problem, though it concerns both pupils and teachers most intimately.

Handwriting Reform. By David Thomas, with an introduction by Principal Harris. (xii 80 pp.), Thomas Nelson & Sons Ltd.

THIS readable and eminently practical short monograph consists mainly of judiciously chosen quotations from such authorities as Professor Huey, Dr. Montessori, Miss Thompson, Dr. Kimming and Professor Shelley. Mr. Thomas has done his work well. The quotations are well connected together, and there is very little that is superfluous. The book brings home very forcibly the striking unanimity in the conclusions reached by the leading investigators. Is is to be hoped that it will have a very wide circulation among teachers, for it cannot fail to shake the faith of even the staunchest believer in "copper-plate" writing, and it will rekindle hope in the breasts of those who at present despair of the quality of handwriting in their schools. In future editions of the book we hope that Mr. Thomas will print the specimens in the Appendix in their natural size, that he will bring out the real pleasure and pride that children take in "Print Writing," and that he will consider the advisibility of recommending Professor Shelley's script, which has many points in its favour.

W.V.

The Book of the Long Trail. By Henry Newbolt. (xvi + 312 pp.) Illustrated. Longmans, Green & Co. 7/6 net.

IT would be difficult to find a more interesting and stimulating Christmas present for a boy than this. Sir Henry Newbolt has told the adventurous story of eight modern British explorers, beginning with Franklin and ending with Wollaston, in a spirit one would expect of a writer distinguished as he is for his appreciation of the heroic. The style is simple and direct, just suited to the subject matter and to those for whom it is specially written, though there is a complete absence of that tiresome attempt to write a great topic down to the level of undeveloped minds. Indeed most older folk will find in the volume that precious sort of present which they can enjoy quite as much as the lad they give it to, when he will lend it !

A Story Garden for Little Children. By Maud Lindsay. Illustrated. (vi+91 pp). Harrap. 5/- net.

MISS LINDSAY has written these little stories around familiar things—familiar at least to children who know the country—for very young folk. They are just such stories as an intelligent mother invents for her own nursery, half the joy of which comes from their own spontaneity. When printed they lose something of their charm, but there is nevertheless a place for books of the kind in days when mothers are too busy or too harassed to trust to their own creative powers.

The Story Teller. By Maud Lindsay. Illustrated in Colour. (173 pp.) Harrap & Co. 5/- net.

THE stories are for slightly older children. Several are adaptations of old stories, and one is left wondering whether it is possible ever again to achieve the atmosphere of the traditional fairy tale. Miss Lindsay's stories are acceptable enough; children will listen to and enjoy them; but why substitute these for the real thing? The best is accessible enough in this case.

BOOKS RECEIVED.

Experiments with Plants. A First School-book of Science. By J. B. Philip, M.A. (205 pp.) Clarendon Press.
(An attractive book, well printed and illustrated—admirably suited to its purpose.)

Causal Geography of the British Isles. By J. Martin, B.Sc. (viii + 252 pp.) Longmans, Green & Co. 4s. 6d.

Elements of Physics. By R. A. Houston, M.A., Ph.D., D.Sc. (viii + 221 pp.) 6s. net.

Elements of Vector Algebra. By. L. Silberstein, Ph.D. (42 pp.) 5s. net.

General Methods of Teaching in Elementary Schools. By Samuel Chester Parker. (xx + 332 pp.) Ginn & Co. 7/- net.
(The author, who is Professor of Educational Methods in the University of Chicago, has given us a book very different in character from the "School Method" of old. He is concerned with the application of general principles derived from modern psychology and from social and educational investigation. Tradition as such counts for nothing. It is a thoroughly "live" book, and of course up-to-the-very-latest-date, as it should be.)

Mind and Medicine. By W. H. R. Rivers, M.D., F.R.S. (23 pp.) Longmans, Green & Co. 1s. net.

Vol. 5. No. 4.   *March 5th, 1920.*

THE TRAINING OF THE CITIZEN.

By the MASTER OF BALLIOL.

THE war has presented us with three discoveries in the sphere of education. We have found in the first place that war could be a great education, and this in the most literal sense. That war training and war itself could produce not merely improvement in physique and strengthening of character, but also could, and often did—and this was the surprise—develop the natural powers of the mind. This should not have been a surprise; for, after all, education is only the development of the power of thinking, and, as more than one young soldier has found, " You have to do a lot of thinking in the trenches."

Long ago, in the infancy of democracy, it was said: " Now we must educate our masters." Now that they are very manifestly our masters, the need is still more manifest. " What?—a burning desire for education, true education; that is, a love of knowledge for its own sake or for the still higher sake of fitting the student to serve his country! Can there be such a widespread passion now among the masses? " This question has been so put by a sceptical journalist. He may receive some enlightenment if he consults the evidence in the *Report* just issued by the Committee on Adult Education (Cmd. 321), or if he inquires into the experiment of the Army Camps in the last two years. This has been the second discovery. But (to quote the journalistic critic again), assuming the desire, is there the capability among the masses? Here, again, the answer comes from practical experience—experience summarized in the *Report*. It is true that the thoughtful and studious, who will naturally lead the opinions of their fellows in mine, factory, or shop, can never be more than a few thousands; but these thousands are a leaven; they are more in number than could have been guessed; that number is capable of rapid and immediate expansion; and outside these more select students there is a far greater circle of adult men and women capable of far more than we imagined in the way of intellectual interests. Till this war we under-valued the military value of the rank and file of our people because we did not realize their moral capacity. Do not let us go on undervaluing their intellectual capacity; for the discovery of this has been the third educational discovery of the war.

The Government Committee on Adult Education, which has been sitting for two years and has just produced its *Final Report* (Cmd. 321), found that these three facts were implicit in the experience we already had before us. It found also that Adult Education was not a mere phrase or fad, or even a superfluous luxury, but an absolute necessary of the nation's future social and political life. In this we might also learn from the enemy. The Germans pronounced us a profoundly uneducated people, who knew no foreign languages, worked short hours, substituted " good form " for efficiency, depreciated teachers, had no respect for knowledge, were given over to sport and games, holidays, and " week-ends," not to mention strikes and drink. The Germans used to declare that it was their schoolmasters that won them the wars of 1864, 1866, 1870; and they certainly showed in this war what formidable strength can be produced by a universal scientific systematic instruction resulting in an extraordinary unanimity of national aim and an undeniable capacity of sacrifice for an ideal.

True, the German machine lacked variety, buoyancy, and individual initiative—qualities which only grow in an atmosphere of freedom. What we have to learn is how to combine freedom and individual initiative with a more efficient system and organization. Only so can we face our present problems, which all come back to better education as their basis and postulate. Thus, to illustrate this proposition, world-peace depends in the last resort on the proportion of intelligent citizens, British and American, that appreciate the danger and are willing to meet some corresponding obligation. Or, if we take the Imperial position, it has to be readjusted to two opposing facts—the determination of the Dominions to have a say in the future before going to war, and their equal determination to submit to no diminution of their own autonomy. How can these be reconciled but by a public opinion educated out of its mistrust of the term Empire and educated up to the vast potentialities implied in a World Commonwealth?

Then there are our home problems. Is the State to buy up mines, railways, " the trade "? Can Democracy get its will really represented, or must it have recourse to " direct action "? How is " Labour Unrest " to be turned into industrial harmony without a better understanding on each side? Is the tremendous question of women's standing as industrial competitors against men, with its incalculable results on family life and sexual morality, to be settled by an uneducated generation? Or, to deal honestly yet wisely with the two cankers of our society—drink and prostitution—can we trust to anything but the education of that social conscience which is now so callous? The politicians will not take up these problems till there is a public demand, and that means a more enlightened public—in other words, the extension of a true education into adult life.

The first step is to attack the obstacles which now hamper adult education, such as excessive hours of labour, fatigue—whether due to monotony or to unduly exhausting work—insecurity of employment, lack of holidays. On all these conditions the workers themselves are coming to be acutely conscious. They realize that modern industry tends to become more and more mechanical; that it provides less educational interest in the work itself and offers little opportunity to satisfy intellectual, social, or artistic impulses. They demand " industrial control " on the ground that industrial democracy is as essential to individual freedom as is political democracy. Present social conditions also stand in the way. Inadequate housing (nearly half the population living more than one to a room), squalid surroundings, low wages, especially in rural districts, lack of village halls or public rooms—all these create a vicious circle to which the women are tied down even more than the men. These conditions call for reform on moral and social grounds; while it is obvious that they are vicious also on economic grounds.

Though education in this sense was so vital a need, yet the ordinary Englishman had never realized this. He regarded it as a subject inherently dull and dry, because it was too " bookish," too much absorbed in the technique and mechanics of the art, and regarded as " finishing " about eighteen. Indeed, for the mass of the population, education finished before fourteen, and, naturally, education which finished before fourteen was forgotten before eighteen. The mass of the eighteen-year-old recruits were unable to write a simple letter, unable to do a simple sum, and hardly able to read even the simplest book; but with the new Education Act adult education starts at a new level, and also demands wholly new methods. It must begin with the existing avocations and interests of the youth, to show the reasons that underlie his daily work—the relation of his work to that of others and its place in the economics of the nation and of the world. In the Army camps from February, 1917, recruits of eighteen from the woollen district might be seen learning where the different kinds of wool came from, what has been the history of the industry, what are the qualities which make wool the best clothing, what mechanical means are used on it, and what principles are embodied in the machines in wool factories; and so in other cases we have to begin not with abstractions but with concrete objects, and work back to the rationale of them.

To see all this coming out of the Army was like a modern version of Samson's riddle: " Out of the eater came forth meat "! Mr. Fisher, indeed, has said, with one of his happy audacities, that it is a new departure as epoch-making as was gunpowder in military history. For a whole group of discoveries are involved in it; that a modern army may be the means of training a whole population in that physical efficiency and mental alertness which are now seen to be, more than mechanical drill and discipline, the essential things in modern warfare; that part of this training may be the making the recruit a better man at his own future craft, more of a " handy-man," and a more efficient military unit; that alongside there may be, as there should be, a training in the elements of citizenship, so that the recruit gets at least some idea (a) what his nation is and what it stands for in its past history and literature, and what is its place among the other nations of the modern world; (b) what are his duties to it—from the elementary duties of sharing in its defence and submitting to its laws up to the duty of helping to maintain and even to elevate its standards and ideals; (c) what are the economic, political, and international conditions on which his nation's efficiency and well-being depend; its relation to the other constituent parts of the Commonwealth of British nations called the Empire, and the degree to which it can now or in the future enter into closer relations with other civilized nations for the just treatment of less developed races, for the furtherance of international co-operation in science, medicine, law, commerce, arts, and for the increasing establishment of world-peace.

A future age will surely wonder that modern nations, which had in their conscript armies the whole youth put into their hands during those plastic years eighteen to twenty-one, made no use of this unrivalled educational opportunity, and in consequence made such a miserable use of it even from the narrow militarist point of view.

It is not commonly realized what a great mass of efforts went on through the nineteenth century to build up some system of higher education suitable to the needs of adult men and women. These efforts drew their inspiration from different sources—religion, science, politics, economics; many movements contributed, such as Chartism, Co-operation, Trades Unionism. But all the earlier efforts till after 1870 were hampered by the absence of a general elementary education. Even then there was still the gap of the years from fourteen to eighteen; now that this gap is to be filled up, there will be great expansion. Already the standard of work done, according to the report of the Board of Education Special Inspectors, among the best students compares favourably with the best academical work: " they are fit to read for the Oxford Diploma in Economics, and would obtain it without difficulty." Is it not remarkable to find such results among students who have had no education since fourteen, who at first can only read a book with excessive slowness and can hardly put down their thoughts on paper at all? Is it not an interesting discovery to find that the school of life can do as much for mental training as a definite college course? These most recent efforts have all sprung from the workers themselves, and the Workers' Educational Association, thirteen years old, now comprises 219 branches, 2,525 affiliated societies, and over 17,000 members The highest point reached is in the tutorial classes, in which each student pledges himself for three years; the total number of such students in the year before the war was 3,234. These classes are already showing signs of rapid development. In one industrial district, with an adult population of 400,000, the number of students attending tutorial classes, one-year classes, and extension classes was over 7,000. There are institutions such as the Working Men's College, with its 3,939 students. The total numbers included in some form or other of adult education form an appreciable fraction of the population of the country; and the movement is only in its infancy.

There are important lessons to be learnt from these facts. The first is that real education can often be begun again in adult life. The next is that such education should start from the facts which are already part of the learner's familiar experience. The third lesson is that this method, by its freshness and actuality, supplies a new inspiration to the teachers themselves. The fourth lesson is that manual work itself may be so treated as to be a vehicle both of culture and of mental training. Of course, there are defects. The defects in adult education as it stands at present are that too often it is discontinuous; there is apt to be undue reliance on lectures, and not enough class work and personal effort, not enough personal criticism and individual tuition; the teachers are too few, and hence get overworked; and there is not an adequate supply of books. But these defects are all curable, and that not at great cost; and adult education, like other forms of higher education, can never be completely self-supporting. It must always depend largely on voluntary effort and spontaneous enthusiasm, particularly in these, its pioneer, days; but it ought not to be asked to live on this, its precious, capital. The Trade Unions and the Co-operators ought to help more than they do, but so, too, should the Universities, and, above all, the State.

And, finally, about education. We have been exceptionally favoured in this war by having had time enough to bring the lesson of citizenship and patriotism to all our people. But do we really think we shall always have two years of freedom, of liberty to try experiments, and slowly to work up the spirit of the country? Was it not a series of extraordinary accidents, or Providence, which gave us that breathing-time? It took a year for the mass of people in the country to realize the seriousness of the war; and it took one and a half years after that to realize that it could not be won without the effort of everybody in the country, and that conscription was neither here nor there in a thing like this. When this *was* realized. it did not matter whether you called it conscription or not, for, as a man said to me: " How can conscription be called com-pulsory if the community chooses it? " Here was a distinct stage in the nation's education, and that education progressed through the war, but by slow stages. But in future we cannot do that by slow stages. We must have a real citizen community, not the sort of people whom we met at the opening of the war, who said: " How should we be worse off under Germany? " or people who, in some of the great munition works in the North-East and North-West, held the current doctrine there that they would rather see the Fleet go down and Germany rule over England. Of course, they did not know what they were talking about. They had not lived there. I have had that privilege, and know what it would mean. That question is not asked now; but we cannot wait two years for people to find out the answer to such questions. We must have, both for economic survival and for national survival, an educated citizen community in the future.

Can Patriotism be taught? The first impulse of most Englishmen would be to answer this question with an emphatic negative, or even to answer it by asking another—Can religion be " taught "? For, in our examination-ridden world, a subject that can be taught seems to mean one that can be assessed in marks. The ancient world did not have to " teach " patriotism; on the other hand, the Germans have done so; it was the schoolmaster who won for them the war of 1870, they tell us; but, also, we in turn feel it is the schoolmaster, from professor down to usher, that has made the war of 1914 and its peculiar war code. There is also a great body of sentiment in England that has a horror of militarism and jingoism, and is apt to espy these tendencies in any reference to the Union Jack, or any encouragement of Cadet Corps. There is, above all, an English dread of effusiveness or " gush," a dread of even seeming to wear the heart upon the sleeve or to. " make a fool of oneself " by any exhibition of feeling. But anyone who has been in contact with the wage-earners, who form the mass of our population, must have been struck with their growth in conscious patriotism in this later stage of the war. In the first months they were bewildered by the magnitude of the event, by the break-up of their familiar world, by the conflict of voices about the causes of the war, by the instinct to find scapegoats; foreign policy, historical causa-tion, the forces of nationality and absolutism, were to them dim, incom-prehensible; they asked what it was all about, why we could not have kept out of it; one often heard the suggestion that the whole thing was engineered by armament rings, that it was an international capitalist conspiracy, or a plot to bring in industrial conscription; that the workers had no stake in the country, that they would be no worse off under Germans, that British and German workingmen had no quarrel. Then their minds were cleared and purged by many things; the rally of Australians and Canadians, the horrors of Belgium, the experiences of the men back from the front, the torpedoing of the *Lusitania*, the use of poison gas. Now the great majority of them have become the most resolute class in the country, the most prepared for thorough measures. Patriotism has, in this case, been taught, but it was there, latent, all the time. So that, after all, it seems that we had been teaching it; only in our English way, indirectly, fortuitously; it was like character, a sort of by-product of our educational institutions, or, rather, of our social life, our history, and our literature. But we cannot trust to by-products or fortunate accidents in the world that has suddenly opened like an abyss before us; a world challenged by a new and terrific force discovered in nationality, by the realization of what war now means, and by the tremendous call that reconstruction will make upon us.

The very unconsciousness of our patriotism, shown in the slowness with which it came to realize even the primary need of enlistment, is a danger; we were only saved by the sea, which made us an island; and henceforth the sea is replaced by the air, which knows no islands and no frontiers.

It is certain that there are many things that our youth will have to be taught henceforth. One such thing is citizenship; the sense of what it means to belong to a great community with such a history and literature behind it. This sense must be built up out of local patriotism; the history, traditions, characteristics of one's native race and shire and borough afford a fine material for teachers to work on. It must be built up out of corporate life, which is so fine a thing in our colleges and public schools, in our Army and Navy, and which should now be fostered in our elementary and secondary schools. That it is only waiting to be developed is proved by many boys' clubs; and already the instinct of comradeship, the habit of co-operation, is deeply rooted in clubs and societies, trade unions, guilds, and churches. Englishmen receive willingly an appeal to continuity; they recognize their duty to set their teeth and see a war through, as their grandsires did against Napoleon, and that they may hand on a heritage undiminished to their own children.

Young people, too, begin to feel something of the obligations that will follow upon the generation now growing up, to take up the tasks of those who have fallen, to help with the wounded and crippled, the widows and orphans, and to contribute their share to the work of reparation and reconstruction. It would be a great mistake to make no call upon them; they love to be trusted, to be summoned to responsibilities, to feel that they are of use. We see this now in France. War, indeed, if we apply its lessons aright, is a mighty teacher. Even before, there were many signs of the dawn of a new era in education; and now, more than at any time in our past, men's minds are open to a new and more generous conception of what is real education. As a Labour leader said, there is a good deal of new thinking going to come out of the millions who come back from the war; and we at home are having a slow, but sure, awakening. Some idealists used to deprecate national patriotism as inimical to a wider international solidarity; but we see more clearly now that this must be built upon that. They are not incompatible, for are not the rank and file in the trenches almost too ready to respect the best qualities of an enemy—courage, discipline, efficiency? Left to themselves, they would have little hate, and no cruelty. English patriotism would be in little danger of becoming the German type—machine-made, submissive to authority, servile to a formula; we cannot imagine it convincing itself that its Kultur must stamp out other forms, or that the sinking of the *Lusitania*, the treatment of Belgium, or the singing of a *Hymn of Hate* were duties. We outgrew that phase of national arrogance with the defeat of the

Armada. Our English defect is rather a complacent neglect and under-valuing of the foreigner; if our patriotism were made more self-conscious, it would become more open-minded, more teachable. It would steer between that of the United States, which is effusive, almost flamboyant, and that of Germany, with its curious narrow idealism, which is at bottom so materialist, for it accepts a military yoke as the only means to greatness, and argued that our Empire was a "fraud" because it was not based on force. It is impossible to imagine England submitting to "Prussianism" of this sort, as a small section in the Labour World profess to fear. Cromwell said: "Men must know what they are fighting for, and must love what they know"; this need not degenerate into idolatry of the State, or into the State "mobilizing" education, conscience, and religion, as in Prussia. There is some mean between this extreme and the other extreme which had been allowed to prevail in our country under the anarchical Spencerian doctrine of "Man *versus* the State," and the "gospel of individual self-interest," just as there must be some mean between their Potsdam uniformity and our three hundred and eighty-four independent Education Committees. Hitherto, we have all been shy of the word "patriotism," just as the masses were shy of the word "Empire."

Some relevant facts may be put as notes. We should not talk of "creating" interest or imagination, the spirit of co-operation, or of patriotic pride; they are there already, eager to be fed and to be set to work. There is much still we have to learn from the German education, its methodical thoroughness, its instruction in languages, its belief in knowledge, its exaltation of the teaching profession. German defects—the over-long hours, the overloading of the memory, the repression of independence, the lack of humour, the encouragement of national megalomania, the divorce of intellect from morality—these are not dangers which England will easily fall into. We have ceased to believe for the economic world in a harmony which was to evolve itself out of chaos automatically; the same assumption has now to be eliminated from the other spheres of national life. It was a schoolmaster who, when asked what reforms he would propose first, said "he would begin by reforming the British parent." But even this is not so Utopian now as it seemed two years ago. It is notable that from our reformatories 877 boys and from our industrial schools 1,721—amounting to the whole output of three years—volunteered for service, and many of them have won distinctions. We need never despair of our material; it is responsive enough to the right methods.

After all that can be said about boys, the training of girls remains *the* important thing. Nations depend on the mothers of the race; the fundamental duties of improving the physique, saving infant life, acquiring practical arts, appeal at once to girls; the teaching of temperance, thrift, patriotism, is to them the obvious thing to do. It is truly said: "This war has discovered woman."

Practical Conclusions.

School lessons might include a Nelson Day, a Wellington Day, an Empire Day, like the St. David's Day initiated in Welsh schools; other lessons could be on the lives of great pioneers, the best work of great men of letters, the services of great statesmen and reformers. History should begin in biographies. The books we need must be written by flesh-and-blood men, not officials as such; no booksellers' hacks. It is a task worthy of our greatest writers. More use might be made of maps, models, exhibits (we are too bookish in our teaching). Scholars should be taken on educational tours (it is done in Spain!) to historic sites, places of beauty, industrial centres. The modern reforms of medical inspection, proper feeding, manual training, development of brain by hand and eye—these should be treated as the training necessary for citizens of an Empire which covers a quarter of the world, and which must stand or fall by its citizens' character and conduct. Surely, even outlines of the needed social reforms in sanitation, housing, agricultural production, the application of science, &c., might be put before the young in a way to stimulate them without being unduly " subversive " or " revolutionary."

Is it too bold to suggest two other points? (1) More might be done by " practical " methods. Botany, land measures, and, indeed, much of the needed geometry and arithmetic can be better grasped in school gardens than on blackboards; in rural areas, rural economy and practice are not only useful subjects, but can be made the vehicle of much accurate observation and clear thinking; in industrial areas, the teaching can be related to the mine, the forge, and the loom. This would remove the reproach that " school life, which begins at three and ends at thirteen, is to the child a positive evil." The child would learn things by doing them, and he would be doing the very things which are most real to him. This is incipient citizenship. Is not a new Irish patriotism being built up by their agricultural co-operation? (2) Patriotism stands on the home and on the school. The home, however imperfectly, teaches co-operation, sacrifice. The school has hitherto mainly relied on competition, the appeal to self-advancement. But the modern world is becoming more and more inter-dependent— geographically, politically, and in economics, as in medical and other science, in law and other branches of learning, in religious and other thought. Despite this war, and all the more after it, the future must lie in this direction. How can schools teach co-operation and the spirit of mutuality? The answer must be again—*solvitur ambulando.* Service is taught by serving; the sense of membership by the activities of membership. The self-governing school republics here and in the U.S.A. are full of suggestion and encouragement. Already the chief influences of Eton and Winchester, Rugby and Harrow are from their being pocket commonwealths. The principle should be extended to all secondary schools; even in the elementary schools, the meaning and working of a borough or county, of a nation and an empire, might be exhibited by a sort of living models or dramatic representation.

All this, it may be said, implies a school age continued far beyond thirteen and an elevation of teachers to the standard now reached by one in a hundred. This is true, and not the least of the benefits that will come from facing this question is that it forces us to face the education problem and the whole problem of social reform. Our future citizens must " know what they are to fight for, and must have reason to love what they know."

For no one can doubt that we are at a turning-point in our national history. A new era has come upon us. We cannot stand still. We cannot return to the old ways, the old abuses, the old stupidities. As with our international relations, so with the relations of classes and individuals inside our own nation; if they do not henceforth get better, they must needs get worse, and that means moving towards an abyss. It is in our power to make the new era one of such progress as to repay us even for the immeasurable cost, the price in lives lost, in manhood crippled, and in homes desolated.

Only by rising to the height of our enlarged vision of social duty can we do justice to the spirit generated in our people by the long effort of common aspiration and common suffering. To allow this spirit to die away unused would be a waste compared to which the material waste of the war would be a little thing; it would be a national sin, unpardonable in the eyes of our posterity. We stand at the bar of history for judgment, and we shall be judged by the use we make of this unique opportunity. It is unique in many ways, most of all in the fact that the public not only has its conscience aroused and its heart stirred, but also has its mind open and receptive of new ideas to an unprecedented degree.

It is not the lack of good will that is to be feared. But good will without mental effort, without intelligent prevision, is worse than ineffectual; it is a moral opiate. The real lack in our national history has been the lack of bold and clear thinking. We have been well-meaning, we have had good principles; where we have failed is in the courage and foresight to carry out our principles into our corporate life.

This corporate life itself has only been made visible and real to us (as on a fiery background) by the glow and illumination of the war. We have been made conscious that we are heirs to a majestic inheritance, and that we have corresponding obligations. We have awakened to the splendid qualities that were latent in our people, the rank and file of the common people, who before this war were often adjudged to be decadent, to have lost their patriotism, their religious faith, and their response to leadership; we were even told they were physically degenerate. Now we see what potentialities lie in these people, and what a charge lies upon us to give to these powers free play. There is stirring through the whole country a sense of the duty we owe to our children and to our grandchildren to save them not only from the repetition of such a world-war and from the burdens of a crushing militarism, but to save them also from the obvious peril of civil dissension at home. We owe it also to our own dead that they shall not have died in vain, but that their sacrifice shall prove to have created a better England for the future generation.

TRAINING COLLEGE ASSOCIATION OF ENGLAND AND WALES.

PRESIDENTIAL ADDRESS, 1920.

"The Problem of Leisure."

By the Rev. Canon STUART BLOFELD, B.A., B.Sc., F.C.S.,
Principal, Saltley Training College, Birmingham.

I will not waste your time in dwelling upon my obvious unfitness to succeed my many distinguished predecessors in this office. Apologies only serve still further to illustrate the weakness of the mind which makes them, and all I will say is that, in my address to you, I am not attempting to deal, as an expert might,· with any of the many technical aspects of teaching or administration, in a way which, at the hands of former Presidents, would have made a real addition to the Temple of Education. I propose, with what cannot be called much depth of criticism, and, I am afraid, with little constructive result, yet decorated by many patches of purloined opinion, to talk *towards* a subject which, I think, deserves much more adequate treatment at the hands of teachers and sociologists than hitherto. That subject is *Leisure—its Problem and its Use.*

It seems to me that possibly by a fuller recognition of the occupation of Leisure, we shall be calling in that new world which is wanted to redress the balance of the old. Schools and colleges and experts have not well pondered the problem, though I believe—speaking quite at second hand—that the Society of Friends has for years recognized that the practical consideration of the use of leisure is a vital aspect of ordinary education.

But, speaking as a whole, we neither educate the great majority to use their leisure with freedom, resource, and self-control, nor do we provide adequate assistance for those by whom their leisure will otherwise be abused. The problem of leisure is as great a problem as that of the provision of instruction or of employment; and *the problem is a teacher's problem.*

The very progress of the past creates the problems of the future. One tragedy of the nineteenth century, and a resulting problem of the twentieth, lie in the fact that the country has learnt how to acquire wealth, with no clear idea of what to do with it when acquired: and there lies a possible very real tragedy of our immediate future in the enormous acquisition of leisure time soon to be at the disposal of vast masses of people, who at present have no clear idea how to make profitable use of it.

A mind whose vision is inadequately widened by education, the training of whose imagination has been neglected, conceives leisure as something vague, void, and purposeless; and yet the Greek word for leisure —σχολή— is that which has given us *school*—a place where one was to spend one's leisure, for discussions, disputation, or lectures. The equivalence of the two words, school and vacation, seem to support Einstein's Theory of Relativities!

Education to the Greeks was a training for leisure, not for a livelihood. (True, the intellectual pursuits were for the few, while the many
were disciplined in military matters.) The Athenians were restless
people, but they seem to have been conscious of this weakness, and they
claimed leisure, not only for State and Government affairs and to keep
the seasonal festivals, but also for the production and enjoyment of art
and amusement. They seem to have recognized that the only remedy
for restlessness and for being occupied with idealess concerns was to
be occupied with ideas—to find resources in oneself, by being conducted
away from oneself. Aristotle said " The first principle of all action is
leisure."

Now, progress in its intermediate stages inevitably shows lacunæ—
gaps which ultimately must be closed up—and the nineteenth century,
with all its epoch-making, left us with little connexion between art and
industry, work and happiness, economy and humanity, the individual
and society, or between *leisure and education*. And now we are told
that Labour is out for a six hours' working day, at least in certain
classes of industry. This ideal is not new, but when Sir Thomas More
told us that the Utopians appointed and assigned only six hours of the
twenty-four to work, eight hours to sleep, some to feeding, and the rest
to what every man bestoweth " as he liketh best himselfe," he had not
in mind so much the irksomeness of leisureless work as the importance
of learning and handcraft; and the leisure he contemplated· was under
ideal circumstances, varied and ample, and work that was varied,
refreshing, and complete in itself. Whatever the next limitation, we
are face to face with a day, so ordered that we may assume as a basis
for argument the opportunity for eight hours work, eight hours sleep,
and eight hours leisure. This leisure, however unfettered and at the
disposal of the individual, must bear some fruit in the building of
character, and the work and leisure of a man, however widely differing
in content, must be allowed to interact, the one with the other, for the
good of each. A man cannot be happy in his leisure unless he is happy
in his work. I would go further, and declare that no one can be happy
in his work unless he is reminiscent of, or expectant of, a leisure which
gives real happiness. A far more regrettable thing for the community
than its unending demand for higher rates of pay, is the individual's
lack of interest in his work, and it seems very unlikely that in ordinary
industrial circumstances the work to be done can ever easily provide a
satisfaction for its own sake; but something higher is possible than a
soulless round of labour varied by the public-house and the pictures (or
even a mechanical round of office plus club, with other interests no wider
than golf and bridge). There will always be in this dissatisfaction with
work a provocation to social disorganization, until the *purpose* of the
work is seen to be less remote and the general welfare of the community
comes close home as a constantly inspiring purpose, though even then
the link with the life of the real spirit may be practically imperceptible.

Now, leisure rightly used means the refreshment of the body, the
recreation of the mind, and a third thing which, in general, means the
inspiration of the whole being. The first two find their value in a full
recognition of this third—the exercise of free social intercourse.
Personality, which, *bien entendu*, we are out to educate, is not an
isolated phenomenon whose needs may be fully met with adequate
physical exercises or amusements, or even with concentrated or

butterfly-like mental digesting. Personality is the creation of a fellowship; it bears witness to a community; it belongs to others; it is social.

Certain efforts are already being widely made to meet all these great needs; I need do no more than mention them, but I do want to say that we teachers constitute a powerful lever to move central and municipal authorities to increase these efforts, and we must not tire in our exertions.

Parks and playing-fields, play-centres and winter-gardens, libraries, theatrical and musical entertainments return their outlay many times over. The teachers must press for what is wanted in these external needs; for more libraries and clubs, for more opportunities for learning to appreciate the art gallery or the museum, while they make their drawing, painting, and handicraft more resourceful than before. As regards passive entertainment, I know how great the tendency is to be a half-hearted spectator rather than a whole-hearted actor in life; but the soul has to feed as well as energize. I cannot, therefore, forbear to mention the cinema, which has blazed into popularity, unfortunately as a commercial asset, rather than as the outcome of educational motive. I, personally, have no supreme wish that all these moving pictures should be directly educational. There is a wide gap between that and the manifold mischievous exhibitions which are rife. Proper pictures, under proper conditions in proper hours, are the concern of the teacher as well as the parent. But the subject is by itself patient of a separate paper and discussion. Let us remember, however, that a play of Shakespeare, so attractive to the proletariat, and a piece of music (given by the gods, says Aristotle, for the enjoyment of leisure) are both passive entertainments, and we cannot expect that all should act or be active musicians. Music, at least, as some one has said, should be as much a *sine qua non* as sunshine for the parks, or fires for clubs and libraries and schools in winter. At the same time, drama should be an active element in most lives, and we must do more to correct the present regrettable absence of a national tradition of song.

I want to say something here in favour of a right kind of idleness, for, as a *Times* article said recently, there is an idleness which is both sacred and sweet, and such idleness should become possible for a vast majority. Leisure should be a repose from the past as well as a refreshment for the future, punishing the bad man and rewarding the good. It is hard for busy men and women to be idle, and the community in the vast is composed of busy men and women. The busy worker longs for respite, but you cannot watch a crowd of young men and women let loose for a holiday without feeling that in most cases education for leisure has been neglected. Amusement and play there must be, but the beach is scarcely the place to play cards. When the respite comes, unfortunately, in most cases brain and body refuse to answer to the will. A sense of wrong-doing seizes one after a late holiday breakfast, and one is irritated if there is not at hand something to be done. Someone describes it by saying that in a busy life one is always journeying along dusty roads, estimating one's achievements by the milestones one counts, drugging oneself with daily doses of excitement. When these doses are removed, the craving for them sets in. The result is that men either hunt, fish, or knock balls about, or take a 'busman's holiday by attending educational conferences, or, in other cases, seek artificial excitement in cinema or public-house or theatre or the streets or at sports meetings.

To use the picture which the dusty road engenders—the garden of the heart, or the mind, or ,the soul, has been neglected, its walks untended, its flower-beds weedy, its shades sparse, its fountains dry. Lives are empty and interests narrow in proportion as the education is unsatisfying and narrow, leaving half a man's powers undeveloped and his interests untouched, sometimes even giving a distaste for those which it does touch. In a word, the man has nothing internal and at hand to fall back upon ; the child has not been trained to find his highest resources in himself.

> A poor life this, if, full of care,
> One has no time to stand and stare.

The man who can work desperately and idle gracefully gets the best out of life ; but you will not confuse idling with doing nothing. Idling has its innermost mysteries, more truly than conventional activity.

"This one day we'll give to idleness," says Wordsworth ; and he goes even further—

> "Enough of Science and Art ; close up these barren leaves,
> Come forth and bring with you a heart that watches and receives."

It seems, then, clear that education is more really a training for leisure than for a livelihood, and a school or college providing instruction in many branches of knowledge, and giving a very secondary place to those matters which are properly the first support in a man's leisure, is much further from what is right than if its time-table were devoted to the encouragement of hobbies, and the conventional acquisition of knowledge were merely a side-show. A hobby can often teach more effectively, and reveal a bent more fruitfully, than any amount of work in class. Of course, if free-time work is found to take a dominating place in a child's or an adult's interests, this may mean that the curriculum is capable of improvement. After all, we are looking for keenness, and ought to be glad to find it almost anywhere. Free-time interests can, indeed, supply a necessary stimulus to the very routine work itself.

Do not mistake me. I do not suggest that there should be spaces in the time-table labelled "Instruction in Leisure," or "How to be idle." But we have to inspire those who look to us, with a right appreciation of values, sound likes and dislikes, and the power of right choice. And we have to impress Olympus and its lesser gods with these as our primary task, and more and more to persuade them that a series of examination papers, and the inspection of classifications and note-books, and the place on a class-list, founded on these things, are really the side-shows—though still inevitable—of the whole scene. The quicker the better, must the notion be given up that the widening of the range of mental activities, the stimulation of them by discussions, essays, and free talk, can respond to examination tests. Neither the Prime Minister nor the humblest citizen can be ultimately pigeon-holed by examination.

Our predecessors of fifty years ago were concerned with the giving of a mechanical aptitude for reading—the provision of a means on such a large scale that the end was crowded out, and reading became possible for practically all, without a corresponding access to books. More recently we teachers have done much towards creating a right kind of bookloving and reading. We are now confronted with the fact that practically all can read, but that barely four per cent of them use a library.

There is still much to be done to inspire with right ideals of literature, sound standards of hero worship, right appreciation of values. We must still demand that the child who is spending less than thirty hours in school and one hundred and forty hours in what is often a hostile atmosphere (for the indifference of the parent sadly reacts upon the school), shall be able, even in that small quota of time and some of the larger balance, to have access to a room for free silent reading in any school. The love of knowledge wakens early in every sane individual, and the acquisition of it only becomes irksome when counter-attractions are winning. Someone has said that at present, in an elementary school, there is a solemn funeral every day at 12.0 and 4.30 of one personality, and the rebirth of another, so few are the bonds between school and home, parent and teacher. Very well, then, every lesson or lecture in school, evening school, continuation school, and training college must have as its background, as a constant motive of teacher or lecturer, the building-up of a general interest in the scheme of things.

It is commonplace to talk like this; it would be still more commonplace to make detailed suggestions about subjects in particular. But you will forgive my iterating the enormous value of such activities as the making of collections, the keeping of diaries, the editing of some periodical, the running of debating societies (not all of the same type), the preparatory reading for these, the building up and illustrating of note-books, the visits with a purpose to places of interest, the sketching, painting, investigation, and summarizing in every branch of knowledge (as well as—especially in schools—the voluntary contributing of material or historical additions to the institution themselves). Let me leave those.

We have advanced rapidly in our attempts to define education—the more rapid the advance, as we recognize that there is no limiting definition—and we dare not remain content with defining it even as a fitting preparation for skilled work and cultured ease. If its object is the development of the whole human being, his interests, motives, powers, feelings, imagination, as well as his reason and will, then we must find a more honoured place for *free social intercourse*.

We agree that a school no longer consists merely of classrooms and playing fields. We know we must have laboratories, workshops, gymnasia, swimming baths, museums, music rooms, art rooms; even that list does not exhaust the essential. There may quite conceivably be lacking, with all these appointments, something which leaves them little more than bricks, mortar, and fittings. I do not wish to exploit Mme. Montessori or Mr. Edmund Holmes unnecessarily when I speak of the vital necessity of the presence of free social intercourse as an inalienable atmosphere. This is only to recognize a common instinct. The crowds of people who swarm to public-houses on Bank Holidays and other leisure times, or to the ordinary club, are not agitated with an uncontrollable desire to drink beer or even to read newspapers or to play billiards. They are possessed with a mastering wish for free social intercourse—for fellowship; and fellowship is the sharing of experiences and the airing of ideas, and contains elements of restfulness which sometimes solitude cannot give.

Education is a process by which man learns to maintain conversation with the world in which he lives, and it should be also a process in which human beings during a large proportion of normal existence engage in free and easy converse with one another. In saying this, we only declare our acceptance of Thring's definition of education as "life transmitted through the living to the living." I do not think we are sufficiently alive to this. There is not enough opportunity in our colleges for students, or staff and students, quite deliberately to air opinions and ideas of the world's or nature's problems, in which the object is really a free and easy conversation between people who wish to think in company. Study circles—important as they are, and in every college there should be a such a circle concerned with most branches of humanistic knowledge, at least—these are incomplete without the free recognition, encouragement, and organization of gatherings where what is normal as well as what is exceptional may be enjoyed, and a real taste for and habit of mental pleasure acquired, where the thoughts of the best minds may be sifted, where there may be continual controversy as to the values of different idols, subjects, proposals, and achievements, where the volume of thought may keep pace with other universal growths, where it shall be realized that national efficiency is not the same as national extemporizing—or muddling through—where it is recognized that vox populi can never even approach vox Dei, until the democracy knows that it is always on its trial, and that not only knowledge, but a right power of valuation, has to be acquired by the members of an efficient community. And we must not, I think, in such circumstances be afraid of over-encouraging the critical faculty. Swelled head tires of itself soon, and either becomes silent or even begins to become positively constructive, in the right atmosphere. Some glib epigrammatist said the other day that the Englishman has " no fear and no ideas." The truth is that the ideas are largely in embryo and must be brought to the birth and baptized and nourished through such free and easy conversation.

From our animal ancestors we find it easy to say that we inherit certain instincts—fear, self-assertion, pugnacity, sex, the parental, and herd instinct. We recognize that in every normal individual there is passion (I use the word in its widest sense). This passion—this refusal to remain satisfied—we possess in common with God Himself. If we would approach the Divine, we must want like the Divine. This lasting desire must have outlets, and the right outlets will be found not by repression or suppression, in the main, so much as by guidance and training. Now, the normal human being takes enough pleasure in work as makes him feel quite happy and find rest in devoting some of his leisure to certain outlets. It may be an outlet towards actual knowledge —most adolescents are anxious to solve the problems that meet them— it may be towards discovery—many are grateful for opportunities of research, many are explorers; it may be towards social service as leader or followers; it may be towards the expression of personal thought.

There is sufficient variety to present many means—attractive to each—by which every one of our students may exercise himself in normal satisfying activities in or out of time-table times. And he will at the same time learn to value instruction not as a necessary evil, or even as an ultimate bread-winner, but as forming a real trinity with larger knowledge and wider experience. So shall we provide a larger measure of thought and action and self-direction than hitherto; so shall we be conducting a man away from himself, by throwing him back upon himself; so shall we convince him that it is not well to be petty, narrow, self-concerned, or self-satisfied; so shall a man learn to lean upon his own soul and find such resources in himself that selfish individualism shall become intolerable; so that one and all shall realize not only that real education cannot merely happen, but that leisure must not merely happen. and the heavy load is on the teacher for this generation.

A far better teacher than myself would hesitate to propose details of the carrying out of these suggestions. The problems have to be solved, and the details more particularly focussed, by experimenting, before which all difficulties in education, except, perhaps, the financial, ultimately disappear.

The teacher himself requires more leisure (I do not mean more holidays, but some adjustment of, or relief in, the present strain) that his deeper responsibilities may be adequately discharged. And the art of teaching the use of leisure as well as the more directly pedagogic art has to be studied in the interests of parents, teachers, pupils, the State, the Church, and God. I make no apology for bringing you at the close to the threshold of the very highest. Differ as we may, we teachers, if worthy of our calling, always accept our work as a means to an end. That end is a purpose, inclusive of, I hope, but infinitely wider than, our own. That is an undying link between us, and when we further think of our various religious schemes not merely as plans for the salvation of the individual strikingly different in theory, but something much greater—methods through which we can be humble but efficient partners of God Himself—we teachers will exhibit a unity in place of a cleavage. And humanity will begin to accept not only its mental powers and opportunities of work, but the very leisure which it demands for repose and recreation, as something with which to further that unity which is part of God's own perfection.

SILENT READING.

By P. B. BALLARD, M.A., D.Lit.

At the age of nine most children have acquired a fair degree of facility in the mechanical art of reading. Henceforth reading is to them either an elocutionary exercise (reading aloud) or a means of getting ideas (silent reading). And of these two the more important is the latter. It is no exaggeration to say that in adult life ninety-nine out of every hundred books are read silently. The essential aim, therefore, in the teaching of reading should be to give the pupil the power to absorb meaning from the printed page. If he is to gain either pleasure or profit he must understand what he reads. And the measure of his progress in understanding is virtually the measure of his progress in reading. But how are we to measure understanding? It is clear that the time element cannot be ignored. What we have to determine is the rate at which the pupil can master the meaning of a given piece of prose or poetry.

There are in use in the United States at least eight different types of silent reading tests. They generally consist in allowing the pupil a fixed time to read a given passage, and then ascertaining how much of the meaning can be reproduced. But here we encounter the difficulty that makes composition so hard to assess. How can we weigh ideas?

How can we measure meaning? Daniel Starch, in his silent reading tests, tries to get over the difficulty by getting the pupil to write out what he remembers of the passage read, and by counting the number of words written which correctly express the thought. This is equivalent to marking a piece of composition by its length. Some of the other systems require a complicated key by which the reproduction may be scored. The scheme, however, which seems to be most widely used in America is the Kansas Silent Reading Scale. It comprises a series of sixteen exercises which carry marks proportional to their difficulty. Exercise 6, for instance, which is valued at 2.3, runs as follows: " In going to school James has to pass John's house, but does not pass Frank's. If Harry goes to school with James, whose house will Harry pass, John's or Frank's? . . ." The examinee has to fill in the blank at the end. This question is typical of the series—a series which admittedly tests reasoning: but does it test reading? The pupil's mind is required not merely to follow the meaning of the sentence, but to go beyond it; and it is quite conceivable that a child may be able to follow a plain narrative with ease and rapidity, and yet be very slow at dealing with puzzles of the Kansas kind. In any case, the exercises differ *in toto* from the kind of matter people generally read. The last book one thinks of reading is a book of conundrums.

Another peculiarity common to the American silent reading tests is that more than one series is used. There is generally one for the lower grades, one for the middle grades, and one for the higher grades. And although the several series are supposed to be so adjusted in the matter of difficulty that the norms for the various school grades increase regularly, the adjustment is in point of fact never perfect. In the Kansas tests, for instance, the norms for Grade V and Grade VI are nearly the same.

There is further the outstanding disadvantage to the Englishman that the tests and results are arranged by grades and not by ages. The scale is never, except by precarious inference, an age scale.

The test I have devised for my own use is as follows:

SILENT READING TEST
(three minutes).

One fine morning in spring a robin flew down to the brink of a stream to quench his thirst. Seeing a trout in the water he began to talk to him. " I have often wondered," said he, " how you manage to keep alive. If I tried to stay under water like you I should be dead in a few minutes. And, even supposing I could remain alive, I should feel miserably cold in the chilly water without either fur or feathers. Please tell me why you are not drowned, and why you do not perish with cold." " You should never ask two questions at once," said the trout. " Quite right! " croaked an old crow who had heard their conversation and had alighted on the bank beside the robin. He was very old and very wise and very inquisitive. Some thought that it was because he was inquisitive that he was so wise; others thought that his wisdom came from age and experience. Certain it was that he was regarded as the most learned of all the birds of his time, and that he used such long words that the little birds, beasts, and fishes could rarely understand what he was talking about. To return to the robin's questions, the trout replied: " Why don't I get drowned? Why, one does not drown in the water: one drowns in the air." "Nonsense!" said the robin. But the crow looked so severely at him that he trembled, and drooped his tail by way of apology. "As for feeling cold," continued the trout, "I don't know what you mean." The robin was about to say "Liar!" when he caught the crow's eye and restrained himself. Then the crow, having held up his right foot to enjoin silence and attention, delivered himself thus: "It was held by Aristotle, and his opinion is confirmed by modern scientific theory, that there is no living creature that can exist in any and every environment: each requires surroundings suitable to its bodily structure and its bodily functions. To secure a supply of oxygen, which is necessary to maintain the purity and temperature of the blood, each animal is provided with organs which are adapted for extracting this element from the atmosphere, where it is present in great abundance. In land animals, lungs serve that purpose; in fishes, gills. Gills are so constructed that they can only take up the oxygen that is dissolved in water. In the air the gills adhere together and the poor fish dies of asphyxiation. Our friend the trout was therefore quite justified in asserting that the atmosphere drowns fishes. As for his avowed ignorance of the distinction between heat and cold, we must not rashly accuse him of falsehood. It is a well-known psychological fact that sensitiveness to heat and cold is dependent on certain specialized nerve endings in the ·skin." He paused here to see the effect of his oration on his audience. While speaking he had been gradually closing his eyes, in order to think better; but at this point he opened them wide, and found to his disgust that the trout had disappeared and that the robin was struggling with a big, fat worm about twenty yards away.

A double sheet, with the story printed inside, is distributed, and the children told that they will be given three minutes to read it, and that they will afterwards be tested to see how much they can remember. On the word of command the children must open the papers and read silently. At the end of three minutes the papers are collected and the following completion test given out to each child, with instructions to supply the missing words except those marked (x).

COMPLETION TEST
(unlimited time).

One fine morning in (1) a (2) flew down to the brink of a (3) to quench his thirst. Seeing a (4) in the water he began to talk to him. "I have often wondered," said he, "how you manage to (5) (6). If I tried to stay under water like you I should be dead in a few minutes. And even supposing I could remain (x) I should feel miserably (7) in the (x) water without either (8) or (9). Please tell me why you are not (10), and why you do not perish with (x)." "You should never ask (11) questions at once," said the (x). "Quite right!" (12) an old (13) who had heard their conversation and had alighted on the bank beside the (x). He was very (14) and very (15) and very (16). Some thought that it was because he was (x) that he was so (x); others thought that his (17) came from (18) and (19). Certain it was that he was regarded as the most (20) of all the birds of his time, and that he used such (21) (22) that the little birds, beasts, and fishes could (23) understand what he was talking about. To return to the (x's) questions, the (x) replied: "Why don't I get drowned? Why, one does not drown in the (24): one drowns in the (25)." " (26) " said the (x). But the (x) looked so (27) at him that he (28), and drooped his tail by way of (29). "As for feeling (x)," continued the (x), " I don't know what you mean." The (x) was about to say " (30)," when he caught the (x's) eye and (31) himself. Then the (x) having held up his right foot to enjoin (32) and (33), delivered himself thus: " It was held by (34), and his opinion is (35) by (36) scientific theory, that there is no living creature that can exist in any and every (37): each requires (38) suitable to its bodily (39) and its bodily (40). To secure a supply of (41), which is necessary to maintain the (42) and (43) of the (44), each animal is provided with (45) which are adapted for extracting this (46) from the (47), where it is present in great (48). In land animals (49) serve that purpose; in fishes, (50). (x) are so constructed that they can only take up the (x) that is (51) in water. In the air the (x) adhere together and the poor fish dies of (52). Our friend the trout was therefore quite (53) in asserting that the atmosphere (54) fishes. As for his avowed (55) of the distinction between (56) and (57), we must not rashly accuse him of (58). It is a well-known (59) fact that (60) to (x) and (x) is dependent on certain (61) nerve endings in the skin." He paused here to see the (62) of his (63) on his (64). While speaking he had been gradually closing his eyes, in order to think better; but at this point he opened them wide, and found to his (65) that the (x) had (66) and that the (x) was struggling with a big, fat worm about (67) yards away.

The most convenient way to administer the completion test is to distribute strips of paper upon which the missing words are to be written. If the lines on the paper are numbered from 1 to 67 it will facilitate marking. One mark is awarded for each word correctly given. As it is a test of substance memory and not rote memory, synonymous words are accepted. General terms, however, must not be regarded as substitutes for particular terms. For example, " brook " will do instead of " stream," but not " bird " instead of " robin."

This test has the merit of being simple and workable, of being applicable to all readers from the ages of nine to ninety, and of being objective in the sense that two independent examiners will almost inevitably give the same mark for the same achievement. The examinee may, if he wishes, examine himself. It will be seen that the narrative is easy to begin with, and gradually increases in difficulty, so that the dullest reader will be able to remember some and the brightest fail to remember all. I have tried as far as possible to select as missing words those which indicate that the meaning of the test has been understood and yet are not such as an intelligent pupil would infer from the context. The first blank, for instance, cannot be filled by reasoning, for there are many possibilities. The missing word may be " summer " or "April " or any other season or month. And the second word may be any one of the numerous species of birds or insects. In fact, the missing words are not inevitable words: they really test whether the pupil has read the piece, has understood it, and has remembered it.

To prevent the examinee from inferring the missing words at the beginning of the piece from what is said later on, I have omitted the words that afford a ground for retrospective inference and substituted (x). If, for instance, I had printed " trout " instead of (x) in the eighth line, a shrewd lad would at once know that the fourth missing word was " trout." In order to ascertain experimentally to what extent inference could supply the place of direct knowledge acquired from actually reading the piece, I submitted the second paper to a number of intelligent children who had not read the first. In no instance were more than three words guessed correctly.

By applying the test to about 5,000 children from nine to fifteen years of age I arrived at the following norms:

Age	...	9yrs.	10yrs.	11yrs.	12yrs.	13yrs.	14yrs.
Score	...	6	10	14	17	19	21

Through the courtesy of Miss Lloyd Evans, the Principal of the Furzedown Training College, I was able to test the students in training. They made an average score of 41.

The mean variations for the various ages from nine to fourteen were successively 3.5, 5.3, 6.1, 6, 6.1, 6.3. For the training college students it was 6.

It has been urged in criticism of the test that it measures not understanding, but memory. My reply is that it measures both; and in measuring both it measures the actual intellectual gain got from the exercise. Indeed, the two factors are both inseparable and indispensable. If a reader forgets the meaning of the earlier sentences he cannot possibly grasp the meaning of the later sentences. Any word he reads may turn out to be the key-word on which the significance of all that follows depends; and if the key-word, or at least its meaning, be forgotten, his reading becomes vain. Sometimes the key-word comes late and modifies the sense of all that precedes it; and if what precedes is forgotten the point and significance of the whole piece is missed. Browning affords many instances of this kind. They key to " My Last Duchess," for example, is to be found a few lines from the end. The hint that the Duke contemplates a second marriage illumines all that he has previously said, giving it point and purpose and turning the poem into an intelligible whole.

Admitting, however, that it is impossible to understand the piece without also to a large extent remembering it, is it not possible to remember it without understanding it? It is possible, but so highly improbable that the possibility need not be seriously considered. It is only necessary to imagine a similar test given in Latin to an intelligent lad who knows no Latin, but can only read the words as though they were English, to see the futility of supposing a mere verbal memory to be of much service in a three minutes test of this kind. For all practical purposes, if the subject understands the narrative he will be able to supply the missing words; and, conversely, if he remembers the missing words it will be due to the fact that he has understood the narrative.

THE ORGANIZATION OF EDUCATIONAL EXPERIMENT.*

By E. ALLISON PEERS, M.A.,

Director of the Modern Language Association's Department of
Educational Experiment.

———

Among the rarer and finer qualities of the brilliant teacher we sometimes notice a gift which we should all like to possess—a certain sensitiveness to the emotional state of a class which to those quite devoid of it seems almost uncanny. To know by intuition that a spirit of restlessness, however slight, is in the atmosphere, before it makes itself manifest, is more often than not to turn a lesson which would have been a miserable failure into a triumphant success. To realize that, though one's own condition is below the normal, the children are eager and expectant, is an unfailing inspiration; and even the moderately sensitive teacher has often saved his class unnecessary punishment by a correct—if an unconscious—diagnosis of the emotional tone pervading it. We all pity our neighbour who is blind to the beauty of the autumn woods or deaf to the music of the waves. But our pity is even better spent upon those who can enter an atmosphere charged with grief and only be made to realize it by the clumsy medium of words, who are never thrilled by the expectancy of a silent, waiting crowd, who cannot instinctively read the condition of an association like our own from the emotional tone of its annual meetings. Fortunately their number is very small.

The atmospheric conditions of the world of education also are subject to fluctuation, and it is occasionally as well—as for that matter it is in the schoolroom—to tap the educational barometer lest one's sensitiveness should be a little duller than one supposes. But in these days few of us need to consult the harmless, necessary "glass." Not long ago a boy said to me of a master who had just returned from the War: "I'm sure to get my scholarship at Oxford now: you see, he's so *alive!*" That simple expression is at once the text of my discourse to-night and the word to which the barometer is pointing in 1920. Whatever it has been before, the educational world to-day is *alive*: the only question is if its energy is equalled by its vision.

I.

Many of us, individually, since 1914, have known what it is to be alive, and that in more senses than one. Not only have our days been fuller and busier than before, not only has each of us learned habits of activity which will never be lost, but we have developed as a nation a spirit of enquiry, an enthusiasm for sound learning, a desire to prove all things, and to be sure of what is good before holding it fast. Not since the days when Bacon wrote his *Advancement of Learning* has been manifested so general a recognition of the value of experiment and research. And for this there are several reasons. Out there in Flanders, as here in the heart of London, deeds have meant more than words, experiments have ousted theories, plausible generalizations have been swept away by the experiences of those who challenged them. Your

* A Lecture given in substance before the Modern Language Association, on January 8th, 1920, to inaugurate the Department of Educational Experiment.

new type of civilian—·the man in the street who was yesterday the man in the trench—will take nothing for granted before putting it to the test or seeing and weighing the proofs of its efficacy. Again, we have had so many examples of the results of research in science—and particularly in medicine—that we are more disposed to welcome it in other fields of activity. Further, it is fair to urge that the discipline of method, always apt to be irksome, sits nevertheless the more easily upon a nation which has willingly submitted to rule and restraint and emerged from the bondage triumphantly. Three months ago, systematic control and organization piloted the nation through an industrial crisis, while the nation itself underwent restrictions which six years before would have aroused the gravest discontent. It is only natural that the thinking man will realize the value of system and organization in matters connected with his profession, and even welcome the restrictions which scientific research demands.

But perhaps the enthusiasm for research which we seem to see and feel around us depends more upon the general spirit of alertness than upon conscious analogies or elaborate reasoning. The placid jog-trot of our schools has been rudely interrupted; new types of men and women have taught in them; seventy and seventeen have sat round the same common-room table. And now that the War is over, the incongruities are greater than ever. Changed men and women are occupying their old places in the classrooms; newly-realized ideals are accompanied by very definite conceptions of how they can be put into practice; the consciousness of vocation, let us hope, is drawing teachers into the schools, and the voice of common sense is enforcing the paramount necessity for training and higher studies. Some of us, realizing the possibilities of all this, can say with the deepest reverence:

" Now God be thanked who hath matched us with His hour."

But an enthusiasm for the activity of educational thought must not blind us to the need for its proper organization and control.

II.

To the teacher who is alert, and who wishes to develop his knowledge, and to add to that of others, by his own investigations, two clearly marked avenues lie open.

First, there is academic research. And let none say that the gate to that is closed when the student leaves college or takes his first degree. Hard it may be for the teacher to find times in the term when the mind is sufficiently at repose to pursue its studies: impossible it certainly is not. By economy of time and organization of the task in hand many a teacher has produced good research work from his study. And then there are the holidays, with the opportunities they bring for quiet library reading, reflection, and writing.[1] I am sure too few of us realize the immense effect which a teacher's investigations in (let us say) the French language or its literature may have upon his classes. Without inflicting upon them long disquisitions (which Heaven forbid!) he will unconsciously make them realize that the book of knowledge is not sealed; he will infuse into his class-work that originality, that broad-mindedness, that freedom from prejudice which are the indispensable qualities of the

[1] Some valuable advice is given in a pamphlet by Professor F. S. Boas recently published by Messrs. Deighton, Bell & Co., Cambridge, entitled "The Promotion of Modern Language Research among Teachers."

researcher; above all, the moral effect of his teaching will be that of a man who is " alive."

But it is not primarily academic research that is in question to-night. To further that has been founded the Modern Humanities Research Association, to which I have the privilege of being Secretary, and which aims as much at helping those who wish to engage in research but have few facilities for it as at creating and fostering an international brotherhood of Modern Language Research students all over the world. [1] In both these aims, let me say in parenthesis, the Association has already achieved considerable success. But our immediate subject to-night is that type of research called (and hideously called) pedagogical, to which let us, for euphony's sake, if misleadingly, give the term "educational." This type of investigation belongs peculiarly to the schools. It may be · foreshadowed in the Lecture Room of the Training College, and prepared in the Psychological Laboratory. But if it is to be of utility the need for it must arise in the classroom, and it is in the classroom that it must be carried out.

There are some, I believe, among the members of this Association who fear lest amid all the new activities which we have set ourselves the educational side of our work, so prominent in the past, may be neglected. It cannot, it must never be neglected: let us say it with the greatest emphasis. Valiantly as the Association has striven for reform in the past, it must even more valiantly, more fearlessly, attack the future. It must lead the Forward Movement in a way that can be misinterpreted by none. It must be in the vanguard of educational thought, activity, and progress. And to-night we are making one definite advance by initiating something which in other circles also is being mooted and discussed—a Department of Educational Experiment and Research.

III.

But first I must make clear to you the need for such a department in our Modern Language Association. I have sometimes enquired of a parent—when he belongs to that tractable *species* of the *genus* parent, the chattily dogmatic·—why he expects me to take advice from him on my profession of teaching when he would not so much as listen to my opinions on how to train a battalion, to write for a newspaper, or to administer a parish. Most of us have opinions on these matters which, in the presence of an expert, we considerately keep to ourselves. Yet any man who has a boy or a girl who is going to school, or has been at school, or is likely to be at school, considers himself thereby to have qualified for a diploma in education. If the number of teachers who generalize from insufficient data is large, far greater is the number of simple *amateurs* who generalize daily, with all the assurance of experts, from no data at all.

The truth presumably is that education is something from which all parents have suffered, for which all have to pay, and which all believe (or affect to believe) important. That being so, it is probable that even were it proved beyond dispute that the *maximum* of effective work is done by a pupil having x weeks of instruction and y weeks of holidays,

[1] The co-operation of all who value its ideals is solicited by the officers of the Association. Prospectuses and further particulars may be obtained from the Hon. Secretary, at 24 Beaufort Road, Kingston-on-Thames. Those not actually engaged in research may join the M.H.R.A. as Associates.

the chattily dogmatic parent would continue periodically to urge the claims of $(x+z)$ weeks for term, and of $y—z$ for holidays, particularly when the latter expression vanishes. But every teacher knows that the only thing easier to arouse this type of parent is to pacify him, and irresponsible criticisms like these would serve only for amusement were it not that they also come from a far more dangerous quarter. For when opposing opinions are put forward dogmatically by teachers themselves we have a condition of chaos amid which the only wonder is that effective teaching is carried on at all!

Look at all the vague disputing, the acrimony and the invective, the false deductions and the consequently inefficient teaching which followed the introduction and have since marked the gradual establishment of the Direct Method in this country! How much bitterness might have been avoided, how much labour saved, if a tribunal had been appointed for conscientious objections, if a body of practical teachers, scientifically trained, had made thorough investigations and published broadcast their results! Look at the haphazard way in which many still teach grammar! The vagueness of our ideas on the particular merits and the relative value of free composition and prose translation! Look at the confusion of the two functions of dictation! The many controversies which rage round the use of phonetics! The contradictory advice given on the prevention and the correction of errors! Why this indecision? Why this lack of certainty? Because we have not been alive within our classrooms.

Is it not extraordinary how many teachers, alive in their reading, alive on the playing fields, alive in the staffroom and in the houses of their friends, are in a state of suspended animation during school hours, and to educational progress are absolutely dead? Is it not surprising that men and women who are interested in natural sciences or English literature, who enjoy reading French reviews and discussing the problems of international politics, are often content to teach these very subjects in an uninspiring way, to follow accepted methods without so much as enquiring as to their value, to go on for thirty years in the profession without attempting to make the smallest addition to the sum of human knowledge? That any thinking person, and above all that any teacher, should be content to hold vague " opinions " on classroom method, with the means of testing them at hand but entirely neglected, and to generalize and dogmatize without proved data, is surely the strongest condemnation possible of his value to the profession.

Yet what percentage of us can claim to have differed materially in the past from that type of educationist? We have not enquired into methods and acted on what we proved to be true. We have built precept upon precept, line upon line, and theory upon theory, but our bottom storey has been insecure and our fine erection has again and again come toppling down like a pack of cards. Not only can experiment alone enquire into questions of method, but the results of experiment alone can command respect. [1]

---

[1] It is an old heresy that the personality of the teacher is the only thing that matters in teaching, and that it is a factor which will upset all experiments All experimentalists know what careful allowance has to be made for the personal element but they know too that the objection as it stands is mere nonsense. Personality is, of course, a most important factor in education, and a gifted teacher without any knowledge of method will often obtain better results than a mediocre teacher who keeps studiously up-to-date. But why not have everywhere the best teaching obtainable, and the personality where we can, in addition, to inspire it? The objection is no better than the defence of bad teaching made by a master in a well-known school: " *We* are concerned with turning out boys who are *gentlemen!*" As though good manners were the only thing that mattered in education, and it was impossible to combine them with efficient scholarship!

Let me take an example of a general kind to illustrate my meaning. In schools of the Dark Ages, when a boy dropped a book, he was ordered as a punishment to write out a line in it fifty times. It was a bad punishment—not severe enough if the book was dropped out of mischief, quite unsuited to the " crime " if it was dropped by accident— but it was simply a punishment and pretended to be nothing more. But one day, when the same, or another pupil made a bad mistake in a piece of composition, the brilliant idea entered his master's head that if the boy wrote out fifty times the rule he had broken, he might, besides being punished for his carelessness, remember the rule! Accordingly the work was done, and possibly the rule was remembered—or possibly not. Nobody knows. In any case, the writing out of broken rules became the custom, though nobody knew if the practice had the slightest effect. They supposed it must, because—I suppose because they thought it ought to. And throughout the Dark Ages the good old custom went on.

One day there came to the school an Enlightened Visitor, who noted the barbarous custom, and spoke of it wonderingly to the head master. He begged him to abolish it : the head master declined. He said it was injurious to the writing : the head master deplored. . . . He said it bred a dislike for the work concerned. The head master said that that was Discipline and Discipline had made England what it is. Then the Enlightened Visitor touched a vulnerable point : he said it was *ineffective !* (The head masters of the Dark Ages believed in results): " Oh, no; it was a certain cure. Could his visitor prove the contrary? He *thought* so, no doubt, but could he *prove* it? . . ." That is where we come to the need for research.

There are certain facts about education which we know by instinct ; there are others which we can learn by observation and introspection. But educational experiment will enlarge our knowledge and in certain details correct it. Best of all, it will judge between two theories, two opinions, and show us which—if either—is right.

It is not contended that that particular head master would have been impressed had proofs been rained down from Heaven : a man of his stamp would have put up an umbrella. But we can at least congratulate ourselves that such men are rare : the majority of modern language teachers may not be experts in method, but they are certainly amenable to reason and anxious to learn. In the next generation we may hope for better material still. Let us never forget that the time to prepare for the next generation is NOW. We need to experiment now. We must risk being dubbed " theorists " by the reactionaries—and if we organize practical experiments they are sure to call us " theorists " ; we must set about our task in earnest : conduct investigations, multiply workers, standardize conditions, collect and examine the results; and when definite conclusions are reached blazon them far and wide till their truth is recognized—or indisputably disproved.

In any day's teaching—far more in a term's organization—subjects demanding investigation lie at hand.[1] Some are common to all branches of education : the question of formal training ; the best arrangement of subjects in the curriculum ; the length of hours ; the most suitable tests

[1] Workers and others may profitably study Miss C. M. Meredith's book on the Bearings of Modern Psychology on Educational Theory and Practice (Constable, 2/-), especially Chapter vi, " Experiment in Education."

of intelligence for the classification of pupils; the subject which the fable just related opens up—the prevention of the recurrence of mistakes. [1] Others more relevant to the particular work of the Modern Language Association will suggest themselves to you without difficulty. Some would demand long periods of investigation and involve work outside the limits of the classroom as well as in it: such are experiments in suggestion, [2] on the use of imagery in learning modern languages [3], on certain associational processes and on the factor of recall in the learning of vocabulary. Others are simpler and more evidently practical: it is with these that we should begin and perhaps for some time be wholly concerned. I instance the comparative value of learning lists of words by heart and of learning the same words in their context; the most effective methods of teaching difficult points of grammar; the intervention of the mother tongue in direct method teaching [4]; certain methods, believed to be faulty, of using pictures in composition work; and the teaching of foreign spelling. [5]

Some of these experiments aim at making our teaching more effective; others have rather the object of enriching it—and who shall say that the second is not as necessary as the first? Some of them have already been attempted, but the results are unpublished, inaccessible, or undetermined for want of sufficient collaboration. It is our business to secure the collaboration, organize the experiments, and publish the results. Our motto might well be Pascal's dictum: " On peut avoir trois principaux objets dans l'étude de la vérité: l'un de la découvrir quand on la cherche; l'autre, de la démontrer quand on la possède; le dernier, de la discerner d'avec le faux quand on l'examine." We shall need to do all three.

IV.

The scheme at which 1 have been hinting for a Department of Experiment in modern language teaching is no mere vision; it is, on the contrary, ready to be carried into execution. The details which follow have been approved in Council, a Committee has been appointed, and the Department is to be inaugurated with this lecture. We hereby appeal to sympathizers for the immediately necessary funds, and most of all for capable, active, and energetic collaborators.

At the inauguration of any movement there is a leap in the dark to be taken, a feeling of hesitation to be overcome. Our limited prevision of developments and our dependence on the future charge the atmosphere with quite a false sense of oppression. But our belief that we are in quest of truth, and our belief in truth, should be sufficient to clear the air and give us confidence and an earnest of success.

We have gone " promptly yet carefully " to work, and the scheme which follows is the outcome of long thought and consultation. The organization of the Department is no easy matter: we shall probably make many mistakes. But the man who looks fixedly ahead eventually

---

1 *Journal of Experimental Pedagogy*, March and June, 1918. I may perhaps also be allowed to refer teachers to my *French Accuracy Note Book* (Dent, 9d.), for the results of experimental work on this subject.

2 cf. Dr. M. W. Keatinge's " Suggestion in Education " (A. & C. Black)

3 *Journal of Experimental Pedagogy*, Dec. 1913, Mar. 1914.

4 *Ibid*, June and December, 1917.

5 *Ibid*, June, 1918.

ploughs a straight furrow. And we have before us all the time the ideal of a great central Institute for Educational Research, subsidized by grants from the State or endowed by individual generosity, of which there have of late been such notable examples. In co-operation with Associations like our own—the Classical, the Historical, and the various bodies representing mathematics and natural science—with Universities, training colleges, and suitably equipped schools of every grade, such an institute would investigate educational problems of every kind, and if suitably administered and wisely controlled it would be in a position to impress its results upon the rank and file of schools throughout the country.

More it would not be relevant, nor advisable, to say; but perhaps the highest aim our Department can have is to be merged into such a broad and comprehensive scheme as this. Yet we can do no service to ourselves nor to our cause by waiting for its formation. It is ours to lead the way, to adventure boldly, to court criticism, and to win success. It is for those who are here to-night or who may read these words in the future to give us the support without which the attempt must perish at its birth.

Certain difficulties meet us at the outset. It will be said that our collaborators will for the most part be untrained in the work on which they are embarking. We hope before long to offer them opportunities of training which will make them more efficient. But even without previous experience our workers, under careful direction, can accomplish much. We hope also to give all who join us some work which will be in the nature of a preliminary course before they embark upon serious experiment.[1]

There are difficulties to be met more formidable than these. Experimentalists in education are handicapped continually by the intrusion of the personal element which in the natural science laboratory is almost entirely absent. A particular experiment may succeed in one classroom largely because the teacher is in sympathy with his class, or with the investigation; in another the want of such sympathy may make it a comparative failure. Hence—and for other reasons—the necessity for rigorous standardization of conditions and for the multiplication of collaborators before any attempt is made to draw conclusions. Again, the differences between grades of school and between the habits of individual schools of the same grade make it doubly necessary that each investigation should be performed by very many workers. Further, the fact that scientific experiments must be based on accurate psychology, and the equally important fact that the results are to be applied in the classroom, make the collaboration of the psychologist and the practical teacher in every investigation essential. The one must bring to bear his expert knowledge of the child and his skill in planning scientific experiments; the other must see that each experiment is suited to the classroom and be responsible for its actual conduct—for the experimenter should know the material upon which he is working. These demands can only be met by a united and an emphatic response to the appeal which is being made by the new Department.

---

1 Workers might well start by reading such books as Dr. C. S. Myers' " Experimental Psychology " (2 vol., Cambridge University Press) or his small volume in the Cambridge Manuals Series ; Schulze's " Experimental Pedagogy "; Rusk's " Experimental Education " (Longmans) or Whipple's " Mental Tests."

The administration of the Department is entrusted to a small Committee which has been given power to add to its number. The Director, or the Director and the Secretary in collaboration, will draw up the fullest details and the closest instructions for each investigation which it is proposed to make: these details will be submitted to expert psychologists and to the Committee before being sent out for information to those who have enrolled themselves as Workers[1] in the Department. Time-limits—and generous ones!—will be set by which the first stages of the several experiments are to be completed, and workers intending to attempt any one (or more) of them will give notice of their intention. [2]

When the time-limit has expired, the Committee will generally meet to discuss the results, co-opting additional members for the purpose if necessary; interim conclusions will be drawn up, circulated to workers taking part in the experiment, and eventually printed in *Modern Languages*. [3] This will give an opportunity to teachers who have not undertaken the experiment in question, or who have not even joined the Department, to follow up the conclusions and apply them in the practical work of their classes, and during the six months succeeding the publication of these it is hoped that many will test them, both by ordinary school practice and by carrying out the experiment in its original form. At the end of this—or of a longer—period the Committee will draw up final results, which will be published (a) in *Modern Languages*; (b)—if funds permit and the importance of the experiment seems to warrant the expense—fully in pamphlet form for general circulation.

Here you have a statement in the most general form of the Department's method of working. There will naturally be modifications. Particular investigations will demand particular treatment. Sometimes the number of workers for an experiment may be insufficient and its operation may have to be suspended. Sometimes a subject will be found unsuitable for classroom experiment and may have to be passed on to the laboratory. Sometimes meetings of as many collaborators as can attend will be convoked for the purpose of discussing the progress of an experiment. A most important question, too, is how we can most profitably make use of the special facilities for research offered by demonstration schools and training colleges. It is hoped that from the beginning we may be able to enlist the valuable help of professors and lecturers in education, in which connexion I hope I may be allowed to express my thanks to the Reader in Education at Oxford University, the Principal of the Cambridge University Training College for Schoolmasters, and the various ladies and gentlemen from different parts of the country who have written in support of our project or who have spent valuable time in discussing it with me. We are also particularly grateful for the kindly assistance afforded us by Professor J. A. Green, of Sheffield University, and the *Journal of Experimental Pedagogy*.

It must not be supposed, however, that the conducting of experiments on a scientific basis will exhaust the Department's activities. The best work is never done in a narrow channel. Though the carrying out of investigations and the co-ordination and recording of the investigations of others will be our principal object, and for some time to come

---

1 We beg all intending to join us to note the name by which they will be known!

2 Or it may be found simpler to send the full details and instructions only to those who have decided to attempt the experiment in question after studying a preliminary notice of it which will be sent to every Worker. This, like certain other small points of detail, depends partly on the number of Workers enrolled, partly on the nature of each experiment.

3 The bi-monthly journal of the Modern Language Association (A. & C. Black).

will certainly absorb our energies, there are at least three other modes of activity which we shall ultimately make our own.

In the first place, we shall hope to examine and record "experiments" of a non-scientific kind which teachers often attempt with success but are unable to hand on to others.[1] At times we may find it possible to carry out such experiments scientifically; at others we shall record them, if they merit it, in their original form. Then we shall try gradually to amass information as to investigations which have been carried on in the past by others in this country or abroad, or which are at present being carried on across the seas. Much good work, for example, has been done in France, Italy, and America, yet the results are little known in this country and but rarely applied. We shall endeavour to establish co-operation between practical educationists of every country, and we hope that all who read these lines and can help towards that end will do so. Lastly, we shall never lose sight of the great comprehensive central Institute: we shall endeavour to arouse public opinion to a sense of the value of experiment, to hold occasional meetings for discussion where workers will describe what they have done, to impress upon head teachers the importance of encouraging competent assistants to carry out investigations, and upon public bodies and individuals the necessity for subsidizing educational research.

Such, in brief, is our scheme. What do we need to make it a reality and a success? Two things at the outset: Workers and funds.

For workers, we ask in the first place to-night; teachers who can meet in London and discuss results are in our early stages essential, though members from all over the country will be equally welcome. We only ask that those who enrol will make a real effort to keep in continual touch with us, remembering that a great part of efficiency consists in replying promptly to letters, and that even negative information (as they tell us in the Army) is of the highest value. We do not expect any workers to pay subscriptions, though we invite them to send subscriptions or donations if they conveniently can.

For funds we ask with confidence. Our expenses will at present be comparatively small, for no building has to be rented and no officers have to be paid. But it must not be forgotten that expenses of copying, typing, travelling, and postage will grow in proportion to our success, and that if we are to circulate the results which we obtain, our printer's bills will be exceedingly heavy.

To every educationist, then, in whatever field he works, we appeal to make some contribution, however minute, either of work or of money. If this can be done, on however small a scale, we shall have no difficulties, of finance or of administration, for a long time to come.

Ladies and Gentlemen, our Department is not a pretext for oratory, but a practical project—and I do not deal in perorations!

Note.—The Committee will be glad to receive from readers of the *Journal* criticisms of this scheme and suggestions for the work of the Department, as well as promises of support, enrolments, and subscriptions. It is believed that all Universities and Training Colleges have now been communicated with; any omissions should be notified to the Director of the Department, 24, Beaufort Road, Kingston-on-Thames, pending the appointment of a Secretary.

[1] Many of these have been recorded from time to time in the pages of *Modern Language Teaching*.

SWEDISH DRILL IN ELEMENTARY SCHOOLS.

By Miss C. C. GRAVESON, B.A., Vice-Principal, Goldsmiths' College.

At the outset of this paper I should like to state that I write with no expert knowledge of the science of physical exercises, and with no brief for any particular system. What I have to say is bound to be critical rather than constructive, for my idea of what we want to achieve is much clearer than my conception of how to achieve it. While confessing to a strong suspicion that we are on the wrong tack in this matter of physical training, I nevertheless realize that the people who can show a system are in a stronger position than those who have none, and have a right to hold the field until a better claimant appears. What I hope is that this paper may provoke someone with the requisite expert knowledge to state fully the claim for Swedish drill holding its present monopolist position in the elementary schools, so that some of us whose business it is to look on may at least do so with a greater sense of satisfaction. With this hope I have deliberately tried to make this article as provocative as I can.

At present the educational authorities are out for the Swedish system of drill. Some few years ago the Board of Education's medical staff came very properly to the conclusion that the physical training given in the elementary schools was worthless. They looked further, and found that the instruction given in the training colleges was also very defective. There was no common standard of excellence and no uniform system. Some colleges used apparatus, dumb-bells and the like, not to speak of ropes and horses; some introduced music, others spent much time on country dances; different command-words were employed. The Board rightly determined to raise the standard. The means it took was to codify a system in a text-book and insist that this syllabus of Swedish drill should be adopted by all training colleges for elementary teachers and schools alike. It is a long syllabus, involving a thorough course of exercises, from which no divergencies are allowed. Some games and dancing are recommended, but the colleges have to spend so much time and effort to cover the more formal Swedish exercises that the practical application of these to free movement has perforce to take a subordinate place. A severe system of individual examinations at the annual inspection was then inaugurated. In a subsequent annual report by the Medical Adviser to the Board he spoke optimistically of the beneficial effects likely to accrue from this uniform system in the training colleges to the elementary schools of the country.

Within the last few weeks the Board has put forward a new regulation whereby the failure of any student in a training college to pass in the examination in hygiene and physical training will mean failure in the whole examination for the teachers' certificate. The only other subject carrying this penalty is the practice of teaching.

Before coming to more serious matters, I should like to call attention to the fact that, even granting the conveniences and advantages of having a uniform system throughout the country, there is still the important drawback that all experimental work in the region of physical education is now practically denied to the training colleges. In no other subject is this the case. In *other* subjects it is felt that to impose a

---

This article was written and sent to press before the Board of Education's Revised Syllabus for Physical Training was issued. The writer is happy to acknowledge that some of the criticisms contained in it are thereby rendered out of date.

detailed syllabus is to deprive the teacher of the stimulating effect of reviewing his material and selecting from it.

But this is a minor issue. There are more fundamental educational questions.

In recent years a great deal of attention has been paid by psychologists to the subject of formal training. To study a subject, not because it is intrinsically interesting or valuable, but because it brings some supposed mental discipline, is seen to be a comparative waste of time. It is no longer held that by learning Latin one's reasoning powers are so universally trained that law-making or chess-playing become easy accomplishments, or that by mastering twenty nonsense words and fifteen lines of poetry every day one can the better remember one's business engagements or the apt, but irrecoverable, joke. There seems, indeed, to be little overflow from the Latin exercise to the law-making exercise save in power of concentration, which may be transferred. In the region of mind educationists have substituted interest for formal discipline.

I have before me a series of students' essays on " The Place of Formal Training in the Education of a Child, with Special Reference to School Subjects." The students were asked to think about the subject for themselves. The papers take a strong line against formal training in *all school subjects except one*, and naive and amazing contradictions of previous statements begin at this point.

" In drill, the whole subject is formal, since the main thing is to make the children perform exercises accurately and briskly. . . . There is, beside the physical benefit, a mental discipline derived from drill—the children are trained to think quickly and the child's memory power is exercised."

" Drill seems to be a subject apart." ,

" I think drill is the only form of formal training which is absolutely necessary, for the precision and accuracy required in drill do tend to train the child to become sharp and precise."

" Drill lessons are almost wholly formal; the children have to do exercises because they are told to do so, and do not know the reason. However, in history and literature and similar lessons formal training is not necessary, because such subjects are taught because they are worth knowing, for the pleasure of studying them."

" Formal training in drill consists in giving strength and beauty to the body, mental control, and power of thought."

It may be that the conclusions of the writers of these essays are correct, and that in the physical domain formal training *is* more effective than in the training of the mind. But there seem to be indications that this is not altogether the case.

Drill may be regarded as having the same relationship to natural, spontaneous movement as grammar has to literature. Just as in grammar the substance of the sentence, the particular content it is designed to convey, is irrelevant and negligible, so in drill the particular purpose of the movement is beside the question. You put out your arm, not to reach something or hit somebody, but to pull it back again and so accomplish a movement. The movements mean nothing except that they *are* movements and designed to lead to general physical control. In the same way, the sentences of grammar mean nothing except that they *are* sentences, and their analysis (so it was held) leads to general mental control. The pupil who is required to parse the nouns in " Lloyd George wrote 'A Midsummer Night's Dream ' " can do it no whit less well because the statement is not true, just as the boy can do the movement "Arms forward, stretch," quite as correctly whether it brings him within reach of a gingerbread or a Greek lexicon. The moment you begin to think of the sentence as having particular meaning in a context apart from formal function, that moment you begin literature; and, in similar fashion, the moment you regard the movement as having particular meaning in a series or complex of movement, that moment do you come to spontaneous or rhythmic motion—i.e., to purposeful actions, games, and dancing.

Now, it is interesting in this respect to remember that, after a vogue of centuries, the study of grammar has been voted by educationists unsuitable for children except as an incidental help to composition, and it has taken a subordinate place as a kind of doctor-in-attendance on literature. It remains to be seen whether drill will not also come to take a similar incidental and emergency position to games and rythmic movement.

We recall the days of " spelling drill," " needle drill," " pen drill," " parsing drill," and many other " drills " in the elementary schools. The passing away of the term in these connexions is a sign that the emphasis has shifted on to intelligence and freedom. But " drill " remains on many time-tables, not merely as a method of teaching several subjects, but as a subject by itself.

The indifference and half-heartedness of many of the children in the elementary schools to their daily drill cannot be wholly explained on the ground of malnutrition, fatigue, or bad teaching. In the playground the same boys and girls are often most vigorous and active creatures. I have watched drill classes in all types of elementary schools and been struck again and again with the look of unintelligent, acquiescent obedience on the faces of the pupils—the look one used to meet in a grammar lesson in the lower standards. Give the children a purpose, something near and intelligible to achieve, and they will be alert and vigorous in a moment. Even in the drill lesson itself this is noticeable. " See how many of you can stretch so as to touch your toes." " Let us practise swimming movements." " Supposing you had to jump from an upper window in a fire, how would you alight so as to run the least risk of hurting yourself? Let us practise." Such commands will set a whole class whole-heartedly working. To climb up a rib-stall or rope or vault a horse gives the same sense of concrete achievement. Teachers frequently bribe their classes to go through the drill with some show of vigour by promising a game at the end of it.

The whole difference of attitude between Tommy or Jenny in a drill class and Tommy or Jenny in the playground—i.e., the difference between a free, willing personality and a bound, bidden child—is so striking that it is difficult to believe that the drill exercises, in spite of their superior systematization, can be of the same *physical* value as the free movements. Of course, children like to quit the classroom for the hall or playground, and, moving about, even to command is preferable to sitting longer at desks; but this is a different thing from enjoying the drill.

It is, however, possible that the champion for Swedish exercises may answer that it does not matter whether the children like it or see the use of it. So long as they are doing what they are told, they are getting good from it. She may be right; but the similarity between her assertion and the old, discredited cry of the advocate of formal mental training makes one pause.

But here two objections may be raised—first, that these observations are made on the kind of drill that *is* given in many elementary schools, not that which *should*, and *will*, be given by better trained teachers; and, second, that this organized drill is not intended as a substitute for, but as a supplement to, games and dancing.

The first is a very reasonable objection. We are in the vicious circle of bad teachers, bad pupils; bad pupils, bad teachers. Under the conduct of a skilled teacher, it is urged, the drill lesson is both stimulating and popular. In the secondary schools, where they have expert teachers, the children are more interested. This is true. It was true also of the good grammar teacher. Indeed, any, even the most unpromising subject, may be made to blossom in the hands of a skilful teacher. But let us keep to the practical question: "Assuming that this is the best method of physical training, is there any likelihood of there being a sufficient number of good teachers of Swedish drill to go round the elementary schools?" This is a very important question, because many highly-qualified teachers have assured me that children taught on the more formal and scientific Swedish system may suffer more positive, physical harm at the hands of an ill-trained or half-trained teacher than under the less exacting, old-fashioned music-drill system, or, indeed, under no teaching of any kind. Now "fully-trained," according to the standard of, say, the Dartford Training College, means at least three years entirely devoted to the science and art of Swedish physical training. "Half-trained," we may suppose, therefore, means trained intensively for eighteen months. The student in the ordinary training college receives instruction for a period of time of about three hours a week, with one or more weekly lectures on hygiene. She may be by health or build or years entirely unsuited for giving instruction in this subject, though well qualified to teach a reasonable proportion of the dozen other subjects which make up the curriculum of an elementary school. Can such teachers be regarded as even a tithe trained for this very expert task? Yet to them it is entrusted. Even were a system of specialist teaching in this subject devised for the town schools, can it be extended to the country? It surely becomes gravely important to know whether the necessarily amateur drill-teachers we turn out by the thousand yearly from training colleges *are* doing the vast amount of harm, or good, that the experts, differing among themselves, assert.

Even if the quality of instruction were improved, the conditions under which it is given are often bad. In many schools there is no central hall; in wet weather the drill must be taken in the classroom. The schools are often airless and stuffy, the classes unwieldy in size, the children's foot gear clumsy and uncomfortable. The exercises have to be carried on with noise and shuffling, and the pupils can take little pride in the finish and style of their work. The teacher may be young and slender or elderly and stout. She drills in her ordinary costume, there being neither accommodation nor time for changing.

It may surely be asked, is it a wise policy to introduce an elaborate system, even if good, into the schools while the conditions of teaching and equipment are so inadequate?

To the second objection—that the formal Swedish drill is not intended as a substitute, but as a supplement, and that a subordinate one, to games and dancing—I can only express wonder that the actual emphasis in all practical matters *is* put upon Swedish drill. Why does not the Board insist on the right conditions for games and sports, especially in newly-built schools—more space, roofed and open; better equipment and games apparatus, free shoes for poor districts, more time, and these things for girls as well as boys? Why is it not as obligatory upon all trained teachers to know how to play organized games, such as net-ball and cricket, and dance well, as it is to conduct a Swedish drill class? Why is there no practical instruction in the schools in the ordinary movements of life—how to sit still, walk well, catch (or lose) a tram with grace and equanimity? Deportment in the old-fashioned sense may be rightly discountenanced nowadays; but there surely exist some practical suggestions for these things. Truth to tell, in the physical as in the mental world, there seems little necessary overflow from one set of activities to another, and highly capable and expert teachers of physical exercises may lack grace in the movements and postures of ordinary life. Indeed, the artificiality of the drill-class, its very systematization and technicality, seem to make any application to the ordinary activities of life very remote.

That the Board do not actually put the same emphasis on drill and games may be seen from the attitude of the acting teachers, who regard the organizing of games as voluntary and extra work, but the teaching of drill as part of the day's routine. Indeed, one fears that the rate-payer may himself come to think of drill as a cheap substitute for larger playgrounds and open spaces, more swimming-baths and games equipment, a sort of potted physical activity, scientifically concocted to suit his pocket.

I once remarked to an enthusiast of Swedish exercises that, considering the normal activity of young children, drill seems a curiously artificial business. Her answer was that an artificial way of life needs artificial remedies. Drill is required as an antidote to the evils of civilization, especially of school life. Young children are not created to sit in desks for five hours a day. If, in the interests of education, we oblige them to do so, some special physical tonic becomes necessary. Swedish exercises are this tonic. Now, if this is true, and Swedish drill a necessary palliative to the defects of an over-sedentary education, need we, at any rate, glory in our shame? Need we even acquiesce? Should we not first consider whether it *is* necessary for children under twelve to spend so much time in sedentary occupation? In open-air schools the pupils are out of doors and engaged in active occupations to a much greater degree than in the normal schools. Need there be this difference? Next, can we discover whether the present provision of playing grounds is sufficient, whether those that exist are in constant use during school hours for classes in net-ball, cricket, football, racing, skipping, and dancing? Indeed, it often seems to me that if the Board would devise some ingenious and sufficient reason for inducing all children to go to school with a school book or other article balanced on their heads, they would do more to produce a good carriage in our pupils than by hundreds of physical exercises; witness the countries where baskets or jars are ordinarily carried in this fashion. With some *definite* purpose in view, children will work hard. To move their limbs about to order, in the hope of being strong some day, is a very different matter.

The Swedish drill champion may feel that up to this point the strongest argument for this system in the elementary schools has not been advanced. I mean the results in health and strength actually achieved by it. I am quite open to conviction here. If it can be shown that the system beats all others in practical results, the case is empirically won. But *have* experiments been tried over large numbers of young children in which pupils who have been submitted to a generous course of open-air games and spontaneous exercises in school time are compared in respect of weight and measurement with those who have undergone the usual Swedish drill—both courses being in the hands of "average" teachers?

Doctors tell us that to eat food with enjoyment brings more health to the body than to eat food from a sense of duty. Is the principle of this true of physical activities? Has it been proved that Swedish drill undertaken without spontaneity or whole-heartedness has more efficacy than less scientifically ordered movements entered into with joy and delight? Even if immediate superior results come from this drill, do not the added zest for life, the esprit de corps, the delight in activity which comes from games and dancing, count *for the future* of the child more than an immediate addition to weight. By all means, have both if we can.

The present insistence on Swedish drill seems to me definitely to discourage the introduction of organized games and rhythmic movements in the schools. Time is limited, the schools are under orders, and orders must be obeyed. That the *full* Swedish system does include dancing and games, I am well aware; but *in practice* the drill comes first, and the others, like Herbert Spencer's literary pursuits, must perforce "occupy the leisure part of life." Where is this leisure part of the life of the elementary school?

We must not forget, too, that physical drill is much more easily organized by head teachers and undertaken by assistants than out-of-door games. One can get the next lesson up from a book and be done with it. To indifferent, unenterprising, or jaded teachers it is a godsend. On the other hand, inefficient teaching of rounders or net-ball is readily detected and resented by the children themselves. Our old analogy of grammar and literature is again to the point. Grammar was a system obtainable from books; its pedagogy was accepted and definite; it could be taught indifferently well without much trouble. The teaching of literature, on the other hand, was unorganized; it required knowledge, selective power, imagination, and initiative. No wonder there were, and are, strong partizans of grammar, as against literature, as a subject on the curriculum. In the case of drill, however, the Board itself puts forward and champions a system which lends itself readily to poor, but easily conducted, instruction.

One more remark before the close. Music is taboo under the Swedish system of drill. To the Swedish expert its introduction into the sacred syllabus of formal exercises is anathema. Yet I am sure that to many pupils brought up in the old-fashioned " musical-drill " days, music alone made intelligible those otherwise inexplicably artificial movements. If most movements did end in a sudden arrest, at least these jerks occurred on the musical beat, which thus provided the reason for the alternation of movements. The objection to all this, I know, is a very important one—viz., that, with rhythm, *automatic* movement sets in, and the pupil loses the discipline of having to respond immediately to an unanticipated stimulus. But Monsieur Dalcroze has shown us in his system of Eurhythmic exercises that music and bodily movement can be so associated that a highly intelligent response may be demanded from the pupil. Indeed, nothing in the results of this system is more striking than the physical control and quick reaction on stimulus gained by the pupils. They serve to show that the old objection to musical exercises is not insuperable. I am not suggesting that M. Dalcroze's system, which is primarily designed as a *musical* training, can be used as a substitute for drill, but it surely raises hopes that with many necessary adaptations and new emphasis on the side of physical development some part of it might prove a valuable help in training the bodies and minds of the children in the schools.

Finally, does it not seem a mistake to introduce under official ægis any labelled system into the schools? For labelled systems have a terrible way of surrounding themselves with a skin impervious to other systems. Exclusiveness, monopoly, professionalism are inevitable to their growth, and creeds and heresies spring up thickly. Disestablishment becomes harder, even from within. In music the Board allows both notations. It has never tied itself to the Ablett system of drawing or the Armstrong method of science teaching, to Froebellianism or Montessori-ism, or to any other of the shifting educational enthusiasms that lighten our darkness from time to time, however final and satisfactory they may seem at the moment. Why this peculiar fall from principle in the case of the Swedish system of physical exercises? Why an enforced orthodoxy on this subject, while the rest of the curriculum is left free?

CHILDREN AND THE CINEMA:

An Inquiry into some Mental Effects, Etc.

By P. L. GRAY.

CHANCE questions on several occasions led me to suspect that attendance at cinemas might be producing some serious mental disturbances among children. To obtain some idea of the magnitude of these disturbances, as well as fresh information on other points, I instituted an inquiry in a number of schools, and, with the hearty co-operation of the teachers, results were obtained which are certainly interesting, and probably alarming.

Full recognition must be made of the psychological difficulties of such an inquiry, and therefore too much weight must not be laid on the exactness of the figures; but these are given as they were obtained, and conclusions must vary as to their value.

The schools in which the inquiries were made are all in Leeds, and are of varied types, ranging from ' very poor " to " well off," and the numbers of the children were :—

1,455 boys in 10 schools
1,532 girls in 15 schools.

These were generally in the higher classes of the schools, so that the ages of the children would probably be from ten to thirteen years; it was felt that answers to the questions would be less trustworthy if given by children under ten years of age. There is strong reason, however, to think that results obtained from the younger ones would be at least as startling as, if not more startling than, those which are described in this paper.

The definite questions related to—

    (1) The number of attendances in a week by a child to a cinema.

    (2). The number of children who remembered—

        (a) " bad dreams," the origin of which could probably be found in the cinema ;

        (b) " calling out " in their sleep, and

        (c) walking in their sleep, from the same probable cause.

Number of Attendances in a Week.

The inquiry was made in the summer, when it is quite certain that the children attend picture-houses much less frequently than in the winter. One teacher states that his figures would have to be *multiplied by three* to be approximately correct for the winter. In a girls' school where thirty-one out of fifty-eight girls go generally once a week, six go twice, and two three times, the head mistress remarks that " the girls do not seem to favour the pictures very much in the summer ; most of them seem to go many times a week during the winter months; but they consider them, to use the girls' own expression, ' too smelly and stuffy in hot weather.' "

If these statements are true—as they most probably are—any evil effects must be greatly magnified, and the results shown by this inquiry represent a minimum.

The actual figures are given below :—

	Boys.	Girls.
Number of children questioned	1,455	1,532
Number attending generally once a week ...	629	718
Number attending generally twice a week ...	140	153
Number attending generally three times or more	33	36

The percentages work out thus :—

Boys.	Girls.	
43 per cent.	46 per cent.	once a week.
10 per cent.	10 per cent.	twice a week.
2 per cent.	2 per cent.	three or more times a week.

Fifteen children asserted that they generally go four times a week, and two that they go six times.

When it is remembered that these children would generally sit in the part of the house nearest the screen, where eye-strain is at a maximum, and would very often be at the later evening show, some idea of the probable physical effects will be obvious.

Dreams.

The testimony of the children to the disturbing mental effects of certain classes of picture, as shown in " bad dreams," is very striking.

Of the 1,532 girls, 571 recall bad, or " frightening," dreams, 248 remember " calling out " in alarm or horror, and 60 remember walking in their sleep—all as direct results of attendance at cinema shows.

The corresponding numbers for the 1,455 boys were 330, 161, 52.

The percentages work out thus :—

			Girls.	Boys.
Bad dreams ...	...	...	37 per cent.	23 per cent.
" Calling out '	...	...	16 per cent.	11 per cent.
Sleep-walking	...	...	4 per cent.	4 per cent.

These figures refer to the number of children questioned; they would, of course, be much higher if they referred to the number who *attend* the picture shows. Thus, the number of girls who have " bad dreams " would be 571 out of 907—about 63 per cent., and similarly with the other figures.

In close connexion with dreaming, and perhaps even worse in effects on health, are the cases of those who lie awake for long periods before being able to sleep, or who cannot get to sleep again after waking in alarm—e.g., in one school five girls volunteered the statement that they did not dream, but that they have lain awake at nights going over incidents; in each case these were " frightening " episodes.

The most offending type of picture may easily be guessed; it is the " thrilling serial." One of these, called " The Hooded Terror " (or perhaps it had another title, and this was the designation of a character in the story), had been running at most of the " houses " in the weeks preceding the inquiry; nearly every teacher mentions this film as one which had evidently produced some of the strongest and most horrible impressions.

One head master makes the following remarks :—

" I have found numerous cases where children have been awakened by dreaming of the pictures, and have been so frightened as to be unable to sleep for the rest of the night, many imagining when quite awake that their dreams have been ' real.' Others I have found could not sleep again unless the parents were present, some going to parents' rooms and sleeping with the older people. One boy, who was sleeping with his brother, dreamt that the ' Clutching Hand ' was about to grasp him, and fought with such effect to escape that he attacked his brother and knocked out one of his teeth. Some boys told me that they were actually afraid to get out of bed in a morning, as the dreams had been so realistic and had frightened them to such an extent—this with boys ten or eleven years of age. The physical effect after such dreams was to leave the children limp and tired in the morning. Many of our late-comers are picture-goers—some of whom have to wait up for parents who have gone to the ' second house ' I had one case of a boy who fainted after seeing ' so many people killed.' One girl, after visiting the pictures, got up unconsciously and walked in her sleep downstairs, lighted the fire from a candle which she had previously lighted, and was in front of the fire when her parents came down and took her back to bed.

"As a direct result of seeing a film showing the robbery of a stage-coach, five boys decided that they ought to rob someone or something. They went to the pillar-box and took out a number of letters, in one of which was a P.O. for 2s. 6d. and in another a cheque for a number of pounds; they cashed the former and shared the cash; the cheque they could not do anything with, so they hid it, and later it was found undamaged. These boys were brought before the magistrates, and one of them (aged twelve) was birched."

A head mistress appends some interesting remarks from which the following is quoted :—

"A girl of eleven, on reporting her absence of half a day from school, told a tale of going away to Kirkstall Abbey with a gentleman, &c., &c., though she could not give a coherent report of what happened after she got to the abbey. Something of what she had seen on the pictures was woven into her story. She could give a vivid description of the man who had abducted her, but not of his actions. I said I would communicate with the police, and she went to her place apparently satisfied. That noon the mother communicated with me—the child's tale was untrue, ' a mass of lies,' the mother said.

" In another case a girl of twelve—most dull and backward—was missing from school one morning. A relative of the child in school said that the missing girl had been told to go to school by her mother, who daily went to work an hour before the child's departure for school. The girl did not turn up at school in the afternoon either, and no one knew where she was. Next morning I spoke to her privately. I could tell she meant to tell me but little, so I worked myself into friendly conversation, and she told me all.

" She had been to the second performance of the pictures the previous evening, and had been trying to put into real life what she had seen there.

" She seemed to have been particularly struck with a filmed, beautiful lady who was sitting on some rocks working some beautiful fancy work from a dainty Dorothy-bag on her wrist. In due time a young gentleman appeared, and I suppose the couple would be ' happy ever after.'

" So this schoolgirl of twelve, whose parents are but poor, took her bank-book to the Post Office, withdrew the solitary shilling she had in it, purchased a yard of cotton-stuff, took scissors, needle, &c., in a little cotton schoolbag (as near as she could get to the fair lady's Dorothy-bag), and went off for the day.

" When I asked her where she had spent the day she said, ' On the cliffs.'

" Further inquiry showed that she had been all day sitting on a boulder in Horsforth Wood, and had made herself a pinafore from the material purchased in the morning—waiting for the fairy prince. As he did not come, the girl, thoroughly chilled (the weather was bitterly cold), made her way at night to the cars. She had no money, and someone took pity on her and paid the tram fare home.

"Another case: A girl disappeared one evening before her mother returned from work; police assistance was sought, and the girl returned home next day. The mother told that the girl had done ' many queer things lately, and always after she had been to the pictures.' "

Another head mistress says: "After questioning some elder girls, I thought I would go to Class III B—a class of low mental calibre; there I found *one* girl who goes twice a week—the largest proportion of children who go to evening performances, and the highest percentage of ' dreamers,' 22.8 per cent. of the class having had ' frightening dreams as a result of seeing exciting films.''

In one school the head mistress says: " I find that the children who dream are those who visit only occasionally. The twenty-seven who visit regularly confess a nervousness, at first, of gruesome characters, such as ' The Hooded Terror,' but they do not mind now, and, I regret to say, describe some terrifying episodes as commonplace events.

" In the case of ' The House of Hate,' I am told that many little ones in the audience screamed with terror at the character known as ' The Hooded Terror,' and had to be quieted by the attendants."

The next quotations—in the words of some of the girls themselves—are very striking :—

"As I watched this part of the picture, I grew more and more excited. I thought of the girl getting nearer and nearer to her death. Those awful spikes made me shudder. At the very last moment, even, the spikes did not stop coming. I clutched my cousin's arm in fright, and closed my eyes to think about it and wonder if she would be saved at the last moment. Then the picture went off. Every time anybody spoke of it I shuddered."

" I was found on the floor by mother, after dreaming about the ' Hooded Terror.' "

The head mistress from whose school the preceding quotations came says, among other remarks :—

" (1) Girls visiting the pictures during the week are usually late for school the next morning ; they are dull and lifeless, and their work in school suffers.

" (2) Teachers have great difficulty in arousing the children's interest in their lessons—the lessons are too commonplace, lack excitement.

" (3) Pictures give contorted views of right and wrong ; finery in dress and luxurious living are shown as the reward of a lapse in virtue.

" (4) Disobedience and naughtiness in children are commended and laughed at."

But it is not my purpose in this paper to dwell on the moral dangers as such ; if it were I could quote some very strong strictures by several teachers in their notes appended to the statistical results which were the main object of the inquiry. Much might also be said about some pictures which are not directly immoral in subject, but which must tend to arouse certain emotional feelings prematurely : the presentation of details of passionate love-making is unsuitable for children, and, I think most people will agree, must encourage the development of a harmful precocity.

Note.—Nothing in this paper must be taken as a denial of the possible educational value of the cinema, or of the possible harmlessness of it as an occasional recreation. The very depth and strength of the harmful impressions may be taken as an indication of potentialities in a beneficial direction. Certain facts have been noted, with very little comment ; they speak for themselves. It would be well if all parents could be made to realize these facts ; their social significance must be very great. Whatever our opinion as to the actual or possible value of the cinema may be, there can be no doubt that certain harmful effects—such as those described in this inquiry—must be enormous in their aggregate, and it is high time that some definite notice should be taken of them, and some definite attempts at reform should be made.

TRAINING COLLEGE ASSOCIATION.

28th Annual Meeting, January 2nd, 1920,

held at

UNIVERSITY COLLEGE, LONDON.

MORNING SESSION.

Miss Mercier (President 1919) in the Chair.

(1) The Minutes of the last Annual Meeting were confirmed.

(2) The Annual Report for 1919, which had been printed and circulated, was adopted.

(3) The Treasurer's Report for 1919, showing a balance in hand of about £25 on the year's working, was adopted.

(4) Report of the Editor of the *Journal of Pedagogy*:

Professor Green stated that, owing to the increased cost of production, there would be a deficit of about £30 on the year when all accounts were settled. He moved :

That the question of the financial position of the *Journal* be referred to the Executive for their consideration and report.

This was seconded by Mr. Salmon (Swansea), and carried.

(5) RULE IV.—On the motion of Major H. E. Griffiths (Treasurer), seconded by Miss Smith (Whitelands), it was carried:

> That the subscriptions of new members joining the Association after September in any year shall cover the subscription for the following year.

(6) Report of Standing Committee on Superannuation:

The Chairman of the Committee (Rev. R. Hudson) presented a Report on the questions which had been before Committee during the year.

(7) Report of Branches:

> (a) Northern—This was read by Miss Buysman (Ripon), Secretary of the Branch.
>
> (b) London—The Report was drawn up by the Branch Secretary, Miss May (Avery Hill) and had been printed and circulated.

(8) Reports from Subject Sections:

The following Reports were presented by the Conveners—
> English—Miss Stephenson (St. Gabriel's).
> History—Miss Davies (Whitelands).
> Geography—Mr. Fairgrieve (London Day).
> Principles of Teaching—Miss Catty (Goldsmiths').

(9) Consideration of Report on Salaries:

The President stated that a Report was presented at the Ordinary Meeting in October, and was referred, with slight amendments, to the annual Meeting.

The Amended Report had been printed and circulated, and was presented at the Annual Meeting. It was moved by Mr. Davis (Bangor Normal College), seconded by Rev. V. W. Pearson (Sheffield):

> That the distinction between Lecturers and Assistant Lecturers made in the Report before the meeting be abolished.

This was put to the vote, but was not carried.

It was agreed, on the motion of Prof. Adams (London Day), seconded by Canon Morley Stevenson (Warrington):

> That the distinction in salary made in the Report between the two grades of Lecturers be adopted.

With regard to the actual figures of the scale, it was moved by Miss Forth (Salisbury), and seconded by Rev. D. J. Thomas (Home and Colonial):

> That no scale be adopted at the moment, on account of the changes still being made in the salaries of secondary school teachers.

Mr. Curzon (Goldsmiths') moved as an amendment:

> That the initial salaries be stated—for Assistant Lecturers not less than £270, and for Lecturers not less than £400.

This was seconded by Rev. Canon Blofeld (Saltley), and carried.

It was moved and seconded:

> That, in preference to the titles Assistant Lecturer and Lecturer, " Lecturer " and " Senior Lecturer " be adopted.

This was carried.

The whole question was further discussed, and it was finally agreed, on the motion of Rev. R. Hudson:

> That the matter be referred back to the Salaries Sub-Committee for further consideration and report at the Ordinary Meeting in March.

(10) A draft of the conclusions on the Student Teacher Year, agreed to by representatives of the Associations of Head Masters and Head Mistresses and of the T.C.A., had been circulated.

The question was discussed at length, and it was finally agreed that the matter be referred to the Executive, and that a resolution embodying a policy for the Association be brought before the March Ordinary Meeting.

(11) The relation of the Training College to Professional Associations—Prof. Raymont (Goldsmiths') referred to the increasing number of applications from Associations to address the students on various questions. The desirability of entertaining these applications was discussed, for and against. On account of pressure of time, it was agreed that the next business be proceeded with.

(12) Dates for the two Ordinary Meetings for 1920 were arranged as follow—
London—March 15th.
Provincial—October 23rd. Place of meeting to be decided later.

(13) Address by the President for 1920. Rev. Canon Blofeld (Saltley) addressed the meeting on " Leisure."

(14) Elections for 1920.
Officers :
Vice-President—Miss Graveson (Goldsmiths').
Editor of *Journal*—Prof. Green (Sheffield University).
Hon. Treasurer—Major H. E. Griffiths (St. John's).
Secretary—Miss Denning, Whitelands College, Chelsea, S.W.3.

Executive Committee :
Group I—Prof. Nunn (London Day).
Prof. Cock (University College, Southampton)
Mr H. Curzon (Goldsmiths').
Dr. Olive Wheeler (Manchester University).
Group IIa—Miss Lloyd Evans (Furzedown).
Dr. Sleight (Graystoke Place).
Group IIb—Miss Cumberbirch (Hull Munic.).
M- T. P. Holgate (Leeds City).
Group IIIa—Dr. Workman (Westminster).
Rev. H. A. Bren (Cheltenham)
Lieut.-Col. Douglas (Saltley).
Mr J. W Jarvis (St. Mark's).
Group IIIb—Miss Owen (Mather).
Canon Morley Stevenson (Warrington).
Dr Geraldine Hodgson (Ripon).
Miss Walker (Darlington).

———

AFTERNOON SESSION.
Rev. Canon Blofeld (President) in the Chair.

(1) Draft Regulations of the Board of Education submitted for the consideration of the T.C.A. These had been circulated, and were discussed in detail. The question of the nomenclature of sciences in the list of courses had been before the Executive, and was referred by them to the Science Section.

Miss Hartle (Homerton) reported, for the Convener of the Section, that they had agreed that it would be desirable to replace the words " Physics, Botany, Chemistry," by
Biological Science, with emphasis on Zoology and/or Botany ;
Physical Science, with emphasis on Chemistry and/or Physics.

On the motion of Rev. R. Hudson, the Regulations were referred to the Executive, with power to act.

(2) Regulations for the Training of Teachers, 1918, par. 49 (e).

Miss Forth (Salisbury) spoke on the inclusion of physical. training as a "failing subject"; and it was agreed that the opinion of the meeting—that this was undesirable—should be conveyed to the Board.

(3) The Master of Balliol addressed the meeting on "The Education of the Citizen."

(4) Votes of thanks were carried unanimously to the Master of Balliol for his address, and to the President and Officers for 1919.

REVIEWS.

A Short History of Education. By John William Adamson, Professor of Education in the University of London. (xi + 371 pp.) Cambridge University Press. 12/6 net.

THOSE interested in education in England largely held aloof from that general recognition of the importance of historical research in all. departments of knowledge and practice which was one of the characteristics of the intellectual life of the last century. Even yet, acquaintance with the origin and growth of English educational institutions, of the development of English thought and the evolution of English practice, is not regarded as an essential qualification either of the administrator or of the teacher. Yet, in education, as in all else, the past lives in the present, and largly determines the conditions of the problems with which administrator and teacher have to deal.

Happily, that indifference seems to be passing away. The last few decades have seen a quickened interest in researches into the educational records of the past, hitherto buried in public and private collections and largely existing only in manuscript. So, detailed material for a history of our education has become fairly abundant. But there has been urgent need for the digestion of that material into a general survey, full enough to be informing, yet brief enough to be mastered in the limited time which can be devoted to it by the administrator, the teacher, and the student in training. All interested in the matter have been glad to know that Professor Adamson was engaged on such a work. The studies he had already published gave earnest of sound scholarship, sane judgment, and impartiality, and these high qualities are abundantly manifest in the work before us.

In so brief a survey of so wide a field, selection, with attendant omission, is the first, and not the least, difficulty the author must face, and probably no two writers would agree throughout as to what should be taken and what left. The essential for a satisfactory result is that the selection be made on a definite and valuable principle, and not decided merely by custom or determined by agreement with the author's own views or prejudices. The principle adopted by Professor Adamson meets these requirements. It is stated clearly in the preface: " His book makes no pretence to be a ' History of Education,' if the term denotes a survey of the evolution of human culture generally and in particular of the schools of all known civilizations. . . . The present work . . . attempts to set forth briefly the progress of English educational institutions, taking account of such domestic and foreign conditions as have had a direct bearing upon English education."

To show how the English present has grown out of the English past is, then, the aim which Professor Adamson has set himself. He is primarily concerned with schools and universities and their work, and generally he deals with theories in so far as they influenced that work. As, after the momentous changes which began in the fifteenth century, education at home as well as abroad became increasingly national and decreasingly determined by a universally accepted Church system, so " beginning with the fifteenth century, the narrative becomes increasingly English in its survey," and this survey it continues till the opening of the present century. This explains why topics which have usually loomed large in the histories of education hitherto available are here omitted or are but incidentally mentioned; why, for example, we read little of the work of the Italians of the Renaissance, of the Jesuits and the Port Royalists, why nothing is said of Rabelais or of Herbart and little of Froebel; while, on the other hand, the work of Bell and Lancaster receives considerable attention.

In accordance with his general plan, Professor Adamson describes in some detail the chief school books of the past, illustrating by typical extracts. Throughout, indeed, passages from contemporary documents vivify the narrative and put the reader in close touch with the actual work done by students in former days. Such quotations serve the further purpose of a guide to deeper study, as do the references in footnotes to authorities which are not directly drawn upon. To deal fully with the typical rather than scrappily with the whole is the plan wisely adopted throughout. For instance, the admirable short chapter on mediæval universities opens with a considerable account of John of Salisbury, and concentrates on Chartres, Oxford, and Paris, the last illustrated by Robert de Courçon's Statutes of 1215.

Another pleasing feature of the book is the attention given throughout to the education of girls. The treatment of this topic is an excellent example of the kind of evidence the historian often has at his disposal, and of the way in which that evidence should be weighed. Other such examples are not wanting, so that Professor Adamson has given the student not merely a survey of the history of education, but also an initiation into the work of the historian.

The book begins with a lucid and well-balanced summary of mediæval school education before the formation of universities; then follows the review of early university education. In the third chapter we have an account of the education of chivalry, of which the principle was " that education should foster all sorts of capacity, not one only " (p. 49). This, in a later chapter, is seen to have been the seed of the courtly education of which the theory was developed by Castiglione and Elyot, and which was put into practice in the Courtly Academies of France and Germany. Abortive projects for the same type of educational institution in England are also described. This recognition that education is not necessarily scholastic is to be welcomed, and, perhaps, one may express regret that some account was not added of the equally vocational training given through the apprenticeship system of the Guilds. But the " popular education " of which the origins are traced in Chapter V is scholastic. In Chapter IV we have the beginnings of the English Public Schools, well illustrated by Winchester, of the origin and work of which there is an interesting account.

The scholastic influence of the classical revival is next traced in two illuminating chapters. That opposition to the new doctrines was not mere obscurantism is frankly acknowledged. " It is possible that some of the opponents . . . recognized that the struggle was, or might easily become, one between two radically different philosophies of life, of which they deliberately rejected one " (p. 116). This is followed by an account of the effect of the ecclesiastical reformation on schools and universities, and the work of Protestant educators illustrated mainly by Sturm. Professor Adamson is charitable to the authors of the Chantry Act of Edward VI, who, " on their own showing " intended to devote the appropriated funds " to good and godly uses, as in erecting of grammar schools, the further augmenting of the universities, and better provision for the poor and needy " (p. 142). True, " on their own showing " in the preamble to the Act. But " window dressing " was not unknown in Tudor times. As Dr. Gairdner has pointed out, " the *Acts of the Privy Council* speak without disguise as to the real object. For . . . four months after this Act was passed, commissions were issued under it for the sale of Chantry lands, the minutes of the Council declaring that they were granted ' specially for the relief of the King's Majesty's charges and expenses, which do daily grow and increase by reason of divers and sundry fortifications, garrisons, levying of men and soldiers,' &c." Certainly the actual destination of the bulk of the money was neither " goodly " nor " godly."

After chapters on eighteenth-century theory and practice, mainly in England, but with reference also to such writers as Rousseau and La Chalotais, whose doctrines had a European influence, the book ends with five chapters—about one-third of the whole—surveying the development of English education in all its branches and grades since the beginning of the nineteenth century. It is seen, then, that it is the present, with its problems, which determines the relative emphasis laid on successive periods and movements. Not in vague and tentative suggestion of modern views and methods does Professor Adamson find in the past guidance for the present, but in a conception of the present as an organism which has its roots in the past, and can be understood only when its development throughout that past is seen in its relations to other aspects of the national life of which it formed a part. And that is the truth of the whole matter.

Space has permitted but an inadequate sketch of the contents of this valuable book, but enough has been said if it convinces the reader that it is emphatically one which should be studied by all who either are, or propose to be, actively engaged in the work of education, whether as teachers or as administrators. Assuredly it has no rival.   J. W.

England under the Yorkists, 1460-1485.   Illustrated from contemporary sources by Isobel D. Thornley, M.A. (University of London Intermediate Source Books of History, No. 2.) Longmans, Green & Co. 9/6 net.

THE merits of Miss Thornley's work and the fact that this period of English history and its sources have been somewhat neglected in the past both by text-book writers and teachers will combine to give a double welcome to her book. The extracts are throughout well selected and arranged, and the compiler avoids the defect, usually found in collections of this sort, of not providing a sufficient amount of material illustrating particular events and subjects.

Professor Pollard, in his introductory preface, rightly attacks the " stereotyped commonplace " that the sources of English history deteriorate with the decline of the Middle Ages. He gives deserved praise to Miss Thornley's " Brief Account of the Sources," which is an able exposition of the material on which she has drawn. The reader will, however, be inclined to wish that in dealing with the Chronicles, for example, a little more indication had been given of their comparative value and trustworthiness. This would have been appreciated by those who have not easy access to the work of Mr. Kingsford and others in this field.

The value of the book is enhanced by its convenient arrangement into sections, under the heads Political, Ecclesiastical, Constitutional, Economic and Social, and Ireland. Some references of particular interest with regard to the state of education in the period have been collected, including an extract from a private Act of Parliament giving an account of the founding of a grammar school at Acaster. A special feature of the book which is worthy of commendation is the use of hitherto unprinted material. Miss Thornley's book is one of those which represent a distinct advance in source book production, and sets a high standard for the series to which it belongs. L. V. D. O.

Elements of Physics. By R. A. Houston, M.A., Ph.D., D.Sc. (viii + 221 pp.) Longmans, Green & Co. 6/- net.

THIS book is intended for use in schools and for beginners generally. "The work covered is approximately that required for the First Professional Examination in Medicine." An ample groundwork in Elementary Physics is treated under the six headings—Dynamics, Hydrostatics, Heat, Sound, Light, and Electricity and Magnetism.

The author attempts to bring a copious amount of material within a short compass, and runs the risk of overloading with consequent inadequate treatment. The position is rescued by lucidity of description and explanation, assisted by a large collection of clear and helpful diagrams.

The whole treatment of wave motion is a good feature. Practical applications are a valuable asset, e.g., electro-plating, the Dewar flask, &c. The idea of approximation in relation to accuracy of measurement forms a useful appendix. It is stated on page 84 that helium was liquefied in 1911 at $-271.3°$ C., whereas our reference states that the boiling point of helium is $-268.8°$ C., and was reached in 1908.

A diagram showing the principle of the compound microscope might have been included. In treating the convex lens, it is undoubtedly safer to proceed to the general formula with the sign convention rather than remain content, as is done here, with the single formula.

A sufficient supply of examples and answers should help a student to make full use of the book. The hope expressed in the preface appears to be fulfilled; as a text-book it should be valuable and successful. J. R. T.

Causal Geography of the British Isles. By J. Martin, B.Sc. (viii + 246 pp.) Longmans, Green & Co. Price 4/6.

MR. MARTIN is to be congratulated on turning out a really stimulating little book. It may be doubted whether the presentation of the subject as a logical system is the best for pupils in the " Middle Forms in Secondary Schools "; but if one accepts this as the best method of presentation, then there is no gainsaying that Mr. Martin's book shows a distinct advance and is very much superior to the majority of geography school text-books published before the war.

The introductory chapter on Maps, the eighth and ninth chapters dealing with Temperature and Rainfall respectively, seem rather out of place. They cover ground which should have been done as practical work or by observation lessons and experiments in the lower forms of the secondary school, or else in the elementary school, e.g., height of the sun and the length of a shadow. There is a tendency for the human aspect to slip into the background. The author's treatment of Agriculture, History, Fishing, and Minerals is quite interesting, and aids considerably in bringing out the causal relations.

There are over a hundred well-chosen illustrations and diagrams, besides an appendix containing some useful statistics. E. B.

Modern Geometry (The Straight Line and Circle). By Clement V. Durell, M.A. (x + 145 pp.) Macmillan & Co. 6/-

THE text-book is a much altered and improved form of an earlier publication entitled "A Course of Plane Geometry for Advanced Students." Part I (1909). It requires an adequate background of mathematical knowledge, and is eminently suitable for an intelligent upper form. The subjects are treated under the headings Concurrency, Harmonic Ranges, Co-axal Circles, &c.

The first three chapters would probably be revisional, but serve the purpose of taking up problems commonly regarded as an end in earlier forms and introducing them as a basis for a deeper inquiry. The later chapters will make full demands on the student, but give in return an interesting revelation of the possibilities of mathematical analysis. Copious and well-planned exercises are a special feature.

The chapter on vector geometry is interesting. The method of approaching multiplication of vectors is simple and convincing. De Moivre's Theorem follows naturally, and gives great satisfaction. The lack of application of the chapter, however, on subsequent work weakens its position.

The book has many good qualities, and, where the right conditions are found for its use, it can be readily commended. J. R. T.

The Heart of a Schoolboy. By Jack Hood, with a Preface by Rev. E. A. Burroughs. (xv + 104 pp.) Longmans, Green & Co. 3/6 net.

THIS little book will reassure many whose faith in our great Public Schools had been rudely shaken by *The Loom of Youth*. It is a schoolboy's reply to Mr. Waugh's indictment, and an astonishingly sane piece of work it is. The author is a senior boy, a prefect, in fact. His detachment of mind, his capacity for analysis, and his general sobriety of judgment would suggest an older hand were it not for certain not unpleasing immaturities of style, which would sufficiently establish the genuineness of the book even without the word of the sponsor. As it stands, it is a little treatise on education from the point of view of an extremely sensible pupil. Is there anything else quite like it in our educational literature? What he has to say about purity, coarse language, athleticism, interest in studies, and especially in the classics, is as interesting as it is admirable. No secondary schoolmaster should fail to read the book.

A Four Years Course of Literature for Schools. By D. M. Hollom. (xii + 164 pp.) Longmans, Green & Co.

A MOST useful and suggestive book. Coming, as it does, straight from the school workshop, it has necessary limitations. The teacher who adopts the course laid down will certainly ruin it. Only Miss Hollom could use it as it stands with full effect, and she surely changes its detail in some measure every year. Yet the book was worth writing, because it reduces a spiritual attitude to a practical and concrete form. Readers must first catch the attitude and then make a practical plan for themselves. Looking at this one in a critical spirit, they may, for example, object to Mrs. Ewing as too sentimental a writer for school use; they may discard the partial correlation of literature and history which Miss Hollom attempts; and they may feel the order of presentation and the work chosen for study unsuited to themselves. Yet there are few teachers of literature who will not find some help in a plan of work drawn up by an enthusiastic and experienced mistress.

An Introduction to Anthropology. By Rev. E. O. James. (ix + 259 pp.) Macmillan & Co. 7/6 net.

MR. JAMES has rendered students a service by writing this book. It is a thoroughly satisfactory introduction to the complexities of a difficult subject. It would be unjust to expect the literary grace and charm of Tylor's classical work in an author whose object is to bring the results of more recent research into a clear, concise, though by no means dull, text-book form. There are abundant references to original authorities. A real gap in the literature of the subject has been very competently filled.

BOOKS RECEIVED.

The Groundwork of Teaching. Edited by Principal A. Mackie. (167 pp.) Teachers' College Press, Sydney, Australia.

Education: its Data and First Principles. By Professor T. Percy Nunn. (viii + 224 pp.) E. Arnold. 6/- net.

The Child under Eight. By E. R. Murray and H. Brown Smith. (viii + 236 pp.) E. Arnold. 6/- net.

Moral and Religious Education. By Sophie Bryans, D.Sc., D.Litt. (viii + 256 pp.) E. Arnold. 6/- net.

Sir Hobbard de Hoy. By Rev. E. F. Braley, M.A., LL.M. (viii + 153 pp.) Macmillan & Co. 4/6 net.
(Designed primarily for Sunday School Teachers, this excellent little book on the Religious Education of the Adolescent is a real contribution to the Continuation School Problem. It is thoroughly informed with the modern spirit, and the author's oroad-minded treatment of his subject makes it a pleasure to commend it to all who are particularly concerned with the education of youth).

"EQUAL ADDITIONS" *versus* "DECOMPOSITION" IN TEACHING SUBTRACTION.

AN EXPERIMENTAL RESEARCH.

By W. H. WINCH.

Part I.

The Problem of the Experiment.

THE time has gone by when the educationist could hope to determine such questions as this by the endeavour to find some psychological principle or principles in a *Psychology for Teachers* from which definitely relevant inferences might be drawn. And perhaps it is as well that such a statement should come from one who has often been accused of regarding education as a sort of applied psychology and of pressing unduly the claims of psychology upon the educationist. For the practical failure of many so-called psychological inferences has done much to discredit among experienced teachers the application of the methods of experimental psychology to pedagogical research; and the psychologist of to-day will be among the first to admit that he is not really ready and, *qua* psychologist, is not likely to be ready to give definite pronouncements upon disputed issues of school method. Even if we had, which we have not, a developed system of the psychology of number, we could hardly hope for practical guidance upon the question I am now raising about the teaching of subtraction. Writing in 1900,[*] I said: "No methods give more trouble or are less satisfactory than those of teaching subtraction. Even the method of ' decomposition,' clear as it is in relation to very small numbers, loses intelligibility to young children when larger numbers are dealt with; whilst the method of ' equal additions ' requires for its full appreciation the apprehension of the proposition, ' If equals are added to any quantities their differences remain unchanged.' I venture to suggest that a continued insistence upon the *rationale* of these processes with young children is not very profitable."

I was obviously ready with no solution; but was tending against a stage in educational method which I clearly saw was then approaching— a stage in which these questions were not going to be settled by the result of experiments with children, but on their apparent rationality to the adult mind. And when I say this, I do not wish to be misunderstood. I do not mean what the adult thought easier for himself: he knew that he himself worked by equal additions, "borrowing and paying back," as the ridiculous phrasing of his youth had it. I mean, rather, what he believed to be easier or more intelligible for children. The question was scarcely raised as to practical efficiency: there was much victorious argument—quite legitimate argument—about the absurdity of "paying back" where you did not "borrow"; and "decomposition" became, so to speak, the officially recommended method of teaching subtraction. The argument of the teachers who said that they got better results, they thought, with an "equal additions" methods was countered by such statements as "once make your

[*] ",Problems in Education," p. 153. London: George Allen, 1900.

arithmetic rational and accuracy is sure to ensue." Speaking for myself, I do not wish to belittle reasoning in school children. I have spent years of my life in inventing and working with reasoning tests among them. But I should want to be sure that it was always necessary that children should completely understand an arithmetical process *before* they worked by means of it: and I should desire to know which methods were practically the more efficacious. As a teacher primarily and fundamentally, what I am concerned with is not argument, however well supported, but actual experimental results with children under the ordinary conditions of school life.

Dr. Ballard has shown us that a decomposition method has failed relatively in practical efficacy.* I do not ordinarily use the method which he has adopted in this investigation, because so many factors other than those of " method " are involved in the results from schools generally, and the relevant differences between school and school are so numerous that it is hard to get a result which is valid. I prefer to work with smaller numbers, to extend the work over a longer period, and to select " equal and parallel groups " of children with whom to test the efficacy of different school methods. A consilience of result, if such should emerge, will seriously strengthen the common conclusion. I may say that I was not aware of Dr. Ballard's results when I undertook this research; nor was he aware that I was working on the problem. I made it as hard for the " equal additions " method to be successful as I could. For I wished to see what would be the effect if, toward the end of their school career—after having been consistently taught throughout their school lives, in both infants' and senior departments, by the method of decomposition—the children were then taught by the " equal additions " method. Was there any unlearning to do? How long would it take before the children taught by the new method would catch up? Would they ever catch up or surpass the others? If they *would* surpass them, by how much? For we cannot spend time in our schools generally on a new method which is only, so to speak, fractionally better than one already known. Materials for some decision on these and other cognate issues will be presented during the description of the experiment.

1. The children who did the work.

This experiment was carried out with the whole of a class of Standard V and VIb girls taught together under one teacher in a municipal girls' school situated in a fairly good neighbourhood in South-West London. The average age of the class was 11 years 11 months on December 31st, 1914. All the testing and teaching were done by the head mistress, who had had years of experience in experimental pedagogy. We commenced with fifty girls; but, owing to attendance at " Domestic Centres" and some absences through illness, the number finally available for tabulation was thirty-eight.

2. The general plan of the experiment.

Preliminary tests in subtraction were set, on the results of which the girls were divided into two equal and parallel groups. Then one group was taught by a method of equal additions, and the other by a method of decomposition, and tests were made at certain stages in the progress of the two groups.

* This Journal, Dec. 5th, 1914, and March 5th, 1915.

3. The preliminary tests.

Six preliminary sets of exercises in subtraction sums were set, the girls being instructed to work them how they liked, but to get as many done as possible consistent with carefulness as to accuracy. The sums of each set consisted of subtraction in ordinary notation, subtraction of money, and subtraction in avoirdupois weight. The sums were arranged, in sets of three, horizontally—one in decimal notation, one in money, and one in avoirdupois weight; and the girls were required to work the first set of three before proceeding to the next set. Exactly eight minutes were allowed for each paper of tests. The first two sets of three, of one of the test papers, which contained nine sets in all, follow (one mark was given for every correct figure in the "answers"):—

		£	s.	d.	tons	cwt.	qr.	lb.	oz.
(1.)	208,149	301	2	4¼	700	14	2	19	13
	3,786	76	19	11½	29	10	3	12	15

		£	s.	d.	tons	cwt.	qr.	lb.	oz.
(2.)	700,100	600	0	0	146	0	1	0	2
	287,102			11½	84	0	2	14	0

et cetera.

4. The "method" by which the children worked the preliminary tests.

The whole training of these girls had been in accordance with the method of decomposition; but did they really work by it? To assure ourselves on this question, after all the preliminary tests had been done, a number of girls were taken individually in a private room, and asked to work some subtraction sums. I cite some cases in illustration (the exact words used by the girls are given in each case):—

Cissy F——, aged 10 years 0 months, worked as follows (the sum is inset):

624,576   (1) 9 from 6 you cannot, take 1 from the 7 next door
139,829   leaves 6, 9 from 10 is 1 and 6 is 7.
———   (2) 2 from 6 leaves 4.
484,747   (3) 8 from 5 you cannot, take 1 next door leaves 3, 8
———   from 10 leaves 2 and 5 are 7.

(4) 9 from 3 you cannot, go next door, take 1 leaves 1, 9 from 10 is 1 and 3 makes 4.
(5) 3 from 1 you cannot, go next door, take 1 from the 6 leaves 5, . 3 from 10 is 7 and 1 makes 8.
(6) 2 from 6 leaves 4.

"Now," said the experimenter, "work the next sum very quickly." Cissy went on:

2,131   (1) 7 from 11 is 4.
987   (2) 8 from 12 is 4.
———   (3) 9 from 10 is 1.
1,144   (4) 0 from 1 is 1.

Lily I——, aged 11 years 6 months, worked as follows:

tons.	cwt.	qr.	lb.	oz.
36	14	1	9	11
13	18	2	12	13

(1) 13 from 11 you cannot, 13 from 16 leaves 3 and 11 leaves 14.

(2) 12 from 8 you cannot, 12 from 28 leaves 16 and 8 leaves 24.

(3) 2 from 0 is 2.

(4) 18 from 14 you cannot, 18 from 20 leaves 2 and 14 leaves 16. (Wrong, for she has forgotten that she has already used one of the 14 cwts.)

(5) 3 from 5 is 2, 1 from 3 leaves 2.

It is, perhaps, worth noting that Lily sometimes uses the word " leaves " when she is really adding, and that, in dealing with the quarters, she abridged the process, and went wrong in the next column.

Kathleen K——, aged 10 years 4 months, worked very rapidly. She said:

624,576
139,829

(1) 9 from 10 leaves 1 and 6 is 7.

(2) 2 from 6 leaves 4.

(3) 8 from 10 leaves 2 and 5 is 7.

(4) 9 from 10 leaves 1 and 3 is 4.

(5) 3 from 10 leaves 7 and 1 is 8.

(6) 1 from 5 leaves 4.

She was asked why she sometimes subtracted from 10 and sometimes from the figure in the " top line." She replied, " I say from 10 only when the figure in the top line is too small; I look at it to see."

Dora B——, aged 10 years 2 months, began by crossing out certain figures in the " top line " and substituting numbers diminished by one. The experimenter asked her if she had done this in her worked papers. " No," she replied; " I crossed them out in my head." She proceeded:

624,576
139,829

(1) 9 from 6 you can't, borrow 1 from the 7, 9 from 10 is 1 and 6 makes 7.

(2) 2 from 6 leaves 3.

(3) 8 from 5 you can't, borrow one from the 4, 8 from 10 is 2 and 4 makes 6 (wrong, she has diminished the 5 in error.)

(4) 9 from 3 you can't, borrow 1 from the 2, 9 from 10 is 1 and 3 is 4.

(5) 3 from 1 you can't, borrow 1 from the 6, 3 from 10 is 7 and 1 is 8.

(6) 1 from 5 is 4.

Millie H——, aged 10 years, 5 months, found it very difficult to work the sum aloud. Before she had completed the process for any two numbers she would mention the answer required, shake her head and go back again to the process, thus:

£	s.	d.
4	2	8¼
1	10	11¾

(1) ¼d. from ¼d., cannot, ¼d. (shook her head)—I mean ¾d. from 1d. is ¼d., and a farthing makes ½d.

(2) 11d. from 7d. cannot, 11d. from 1s., 8d. (shook her head), 11d. from 1s. a penny, a penny and 7d. is 8d.

The experimenter said to her " are you sure you say as much as that for every figure? " She replied, "Yes, only I say it very fast." From the way in which she intruded the answer before completing she probably did not. .Millie was second in the class in the preliminary tests.

Belinda J——, aged 13 years 3 months, worked as follows:

624,576   (1) 9 from 6 won't go, borrow 1 from 7, that is 10, 10 and
139,829   6 are 16, 9 from 16, 7.
——·——   (2) 2 from 6 leaves 4.
        (3) 8 from 5 won't go, borrow 1 from the 4, that is 10, 10
            and 5 are 15, 8 from 15 is 7.
(4) 9 from 3 won't go, borrow 1 from the 2, that is 10, 10 and 3 are 13, 9 from 13 leaves 4. And so on.

Maud B——, aged 11 years 7 months, said:

624,576   (1) 9 from 10 is 1 and 6 is 7.
139,829   (2) 2 from 6 is 4.
———   (3) 8 from 10 is 2 and 4 is 6. And so on.

———

Pamela T——, aged 11 years 8 months, said:

624,576   (1) 9 from 6 won't go, borrow 1 from the 7 makes 6 there,
139,829   and 6 is 16, 9 from 16 leaves 7.
———   (2) 2 from 6 is 4.
        (3) 8 from 5 won't go, borrow 1 from the 4, makes 3 there,
———   and 5 is 15, 8 from 15 is 7. And so on.

Rose G——, aged 11 years 8 months, said:

624,576   (1) 9 from 10, 1, 7.
139,829   (2) 2 from 6, 4.
———   (3) 8 from 4, 10, 2, 6. (The 4 is wrong; nothing had been
           taken from the 5.)
———   (4) 9 from 10, 1, 4.
        (5) 3 from 10, 7, 8.
(6) 1 from 5, 4.
Rose worked very quickly; she was first in the preliminary tests.

Nora K——, aged 11 years 2 months, worked thus:

624,576   (1) 9 from 6, 10, leaves 7.
139,829   (2) 2 from 6 leaves 4.
———   (3) 8 from 15 leaves 7.
        (4) 9 from 13 leaves 4.
———   (5) 3 from 11 leaves 8.
        (6) 1 from 5 leaves 4.
Nora also is one of the abler girls.

Constance M——, aged 13 years 0 months, one of the less proficient, worked thus:

624,576   (1) 9 from 16 leaves 7.
139,829   (2) 2 from 6 leaves 4.
———   (3) 8 from 14 leaves 6. (This is wrong; the 5 has not been
           diminished.)
———   (4) 9 from 13 leaves 3. (Wrong; an error in actual
           subtraction.)
(5) 3 from 11 leaves 8.
(6) 1 from 5 leaves 4.

The experimenter asked Constance how she got the 16 in her first process. She gave the usual answer, "I borrowed 1 from the 7 leaving only 6." She was then asked why, in the third process, she said 8 from 14. She answered, "I took one for the 7." She was bidden to look again, and discovered her error. The same girl worked a "money sum" as follows:

£ s. d.

4 2 8¼   (1) Farthings. ¾d. from ¼d. I cannot, take 1 from 8
1 10 11¾   leaves 7, that is four farthings, ¾d. from 4 farthings ¼d.,
————   and ¼d. makes ½d.
           (2) Pence. 11d. from 7d. I cannot, take 1 shilling from
————   the 2 shillings, leaves 1 shilling, that is 12 pence, 11d.
           from 12 is a penny, and 7d. is 8d.

(3) Shillings. 10 from 2 I cannot, take one from the pounds, leaves 3, that is 20s., 10 from 20 leaves 10, and 1 makes 11s.

(4) Pounds. 1 from 3 leaves 2.

But Constance did not, I think, always work through the whole process overtly in practice, for she sometimes put down the answer before she had finished her account of the process.

Elsie N——, aged 13 years 4 months, worked thus:

624,576   (1) 9 from 6 you cannot, borrow 1 from 7 leaves 6, drop it
139,829   in by the 6 and it's 10, 9 from 10 leaves 1, and 6
———   makes 7.
          (2) 2 from 6, 4.
———   (3) 8 from 5 you cannot, borrow 1 from the 4 leaves 3,
          drop it in by the 5 and it's 10, 8 from 10 is 2 and 5 is 7.

And so on, "dropping in" the borrowed numbers and making it 10 on each occasion.

In precisely the same way, working in money, she dropped a penny in by the farthings, and made it 4; and, working in avoirdupois weight, she dropped a pound in by the ounces and a quarter in by the pounds.

Florence W——, aged 10 years 8 months, one of the less proficient girls, worked thus:

624,576   (1) 9 from 16, 7.
139,829   (2) 2 from 6, 4.
———   (3) 8 from 15, 7.
         (4) 9 from 13, 4.
———   (5) 3 from 11, 8.
         (6) 1 from 5, 4.

£ s. d.   (1) 3 from 5, a ha'penny.
4 2 8¼   (2) 11 from 12, a penny, is 8d.
1 10 11¾   (3) 10 from 20, 11 shillings.
———   (4) 1 from 3, £2.

————

The experimenter said, "How did you get the 8d. in the second process?" She replied, "There was 7d. left." A rejoinder came, "You did not say you took a penny from the 8d." She answered, "I saw it was less"—meaning the ¼d. was less than the ¾d.

Nora K——, aged 11 years 2 months, worked thus:

160,000   (1) 4 from 0 I can't, go to the next I can't, go to the next
2,394   I can't, go to the next I can't, go to the next, take 1
———   it leaves 5, and makes that (pointing to the 0 imme-
———   diately to the right of the 6) 10. 9 from 0 I can't, go
———   to the next I can't, go to the next I can't, go to the
next, take 1 and it leaves 9, it makes that (pointing to
the 0 in the second place on the right from the 6) 10. 9 from 0 I
can't, go to the next I can't, go to the next, take 1 and it makes
that 9 and this one 10. 9 from 0 I cant, take 1 from the 10 and it
leaves 9 and makes this 10, 4 from 10 leaves 6.

(By a strictly reasonable, but somewhat tedious, process, Nora appears
at last to have worked her decomposition from the tens of thousands
down to the units figure of the minuend.) She continued:

(2) 9 from 9 leaves 0.

(3) 3 from 9 leaves 6.

(4) 2 from 9 leaves 7.

(5) 0 from 5 leaves 5.

(6) 0 from 1 leaves 1.

Cissy F——, aged 10 years 0 months, dealt with a sum containing
several noughts in the minuend in a similar manner. She said:

400,000   (1) 9 from 0 I can't, go next door I can't, go next door I
59   I can't, go next door I can't, go next door I can't, go
———   next door, take 1, leaves 3, and that makes that (point-
———   ing to the nought immediately to the right of the 4 in
———   the minuend) 10, 9 from 0 I can't, go next door I can't,
go next door I cant, go next door I can't, go next door,
take 1 from the 10 leaves 9, and makes that one (pointing to the
nought in the second place from the 4) 10. 9 from 0 I can't, go
next door I can't, go next door I can't, go next door, take 1 from
the 10 leaves 9 and makes that (pointing to the third nought) a ten.
9 from 0 I can't, go next door, take 1, leaves that a 9 and makes
this a 10, 9 from 10 leaves 1.

(2) 5 from 9 leaves 4.

(3) 0 from 9 leaves 9.

(4) 0 from 9 leaves 9.

(5) 0 from 9 leaves 9.

(6) 0 from 3 leaves 3.

Cissy arrived finally, although I think she " slipped " one ineffectual
visit next door; and when she had finished she was asked if she always
went through this long process. She said, " I go very fast." " But
do you say it all in your mind every time?" "Yes, I say it very
quickly," she answered. Other girls were also examined individually,
but no new feature emerged. It is quite clear that these children really
worked by a method of decomposition. By this, I do not mean that
they consciously used the whole process in every case of actual practice;
they could not have worked at the pace they did in their written (not
oral) exercises had they done so. But they always justified themselves
by a method of decomposition, and certainly used it intelligently.

The practical essence of the process is, when decomposing, to
diminish the requisite number in the minuend, and not to diminish it
when *not* decomposing. No additions were made to the numbers in the

subtrahend. The method is clear, and the errors and delays are those involved in the method, and are not imported *ab extra*. I wish to press the point, as it is sometimes asserted that children, consistently taught by a decomposition method, " drop into " another and easier one by themselves in the later years of school life. There seems no evidence for this belief so far as these children were concerned. I make no apology for presenting these individual analyses at such length; they are as useful to teachers as statistical results.

5. The division into two equal and parallel groups.

Each child's marks for the preliminary tests were tabulated, and a division into two equal and parallel groups was effected on the basis of the totals of the last *four* preliminary tests. The first two of the six tests were used only as preparatory practice to enable the children to become " steady " and take up their proper places relatively to one another. The division will be shown later on, with other marks, in one table compendiously; it is asked that it may be granted at present that it was satisfactorily effected.

6. The teaching of the groups.

One of the groups, Group A, received eight lessons in the " equal additions " method of working subtraction sums; while the other group, Group B, received eight lessons in the " decomposition " method. The first two lessons of each series occupied fifteen minutes each; the last six occupied twenty minutes each. Each group was taught separately. The children comprising Group A experienced considerable difficulty at first in disregarding the method to which they had so long been accustomed. From time to time they just dropped back into their old way of working the sums. Then there came a time when the two methods were mingled; thus a compensating number would be added to the subtrahend, even when the minuend had been decomposed. Well on in the series of lessons, even after a child had worked quickly and unhesitatingly almost all through a sum by an " equal additions " method, she would sometimes drop back into a " decomposition " method. This feature was more marked after a few days interval.

In the group taught by decomposition a practical improvement was effected. A number of noughts in the minuend had given rise to some strictly reasonable but very cumbrous procedure, as the reader will see by reference to the analysed cases. The teacher now instructed the children to call all the noughts nines till the last nought on the right was reached, to call that ten, and to remember to subtract one from the number preceding the noughts. In a similar way, £300—£49 14s. 2½d. became £299 19s. 11d. 4 farthings—£49 14s. 2½d. There is no doubt that this added to the practical efficiency of the method, which, it will be remembered, we are trying to test fairly at its very best.

7. A brief account of the lessons in the method of equal addition.

In the first lesson the following examples were worked concretely by the teacher with beans:

10 beans—8 beans--2 beans; 10 beans + 5 beans—8 beans + 5 beans--2 beans. 16 beans—9 beans--7 beans; 16 beans + 10 beans—9 beans + 10 beans--7 beans.

Several girls then came to the teacher's table and worked simila_. examples whilst the others watched. Then the teacher worked on the blackboard 264—142--122 and, after adding 365 to both subtrahend and minuend, again subtracted, One or two more examples were worked, and the children were asked what they had noticed. One girl phrased her answer thus: " Whatever you add on, so long as you add on the same to both, you get the same answer." But another girl said this would not be true if the number you added on was very large, and she was asked to work the following example: 15—10--5; 15+999,999—10 +999,999--5. She was convinced; and another girl said, " Of course, what you put on, you take off when you subtract."

In the second lesson the children were again asked to say what they had discovered in the first lesson. Then the teacher told them they could use this rule in working subtraction sums, and that they were now going to be taught this new way. The girls showed the keenest interest, and the teacher worked the following sum on the blackboard:

8,143   (1) 9 cannot be taken from 3, add 10 to the 3, 9 from 10--1,
2,899   add the 3--4.

—   (2) We have added 10 to the top line, so we must 10 to the bottom line, 10 is 1 in the tens column; 9+1--10, 10 from

—   4 we cannot, add 10, 10 from 14--4.

     (3) We just now added 10 to the 4, and 10 in the ten's column is 1 in the hundreds column, so we add 1 to the 8 in the bottom line, 9 from 1 we cannot, add 10, 9 from 11--2.

(4) We have added 10 to the 1 in the top line, so we must add the same to the bottom line, 10 in the hundreds column is 1 in the thousands column, 2+1--3 and 8—3--5.

There was no notational difficulty; the children quite understood what was meant by 10 in one " place " being equal to 1 which was one place further to the left.

A second example was given and worked by the teacher:

5,629   (1) 6 from 9 leaves 3.
3,976   (2) Nothing has been added to the top line, so nothing must

—   be added to the bottom line. 7 from 2 cannot be taken, add 10, 7 from 10--3 and 2 there already makes 5.

—   And so on.

Various girls were now called upon to work examples on the blackboard aloud. They did this with some hesitation, but were helped out by other members of the class. The greatest difficulty was the tendency to add to the bottom line after adding to the top line, and, *at the same time*, to take one off in the top line as in their old method of decomposition.

The third lesson was at first recapitulatory. The girl called upon to work this sum proceeded as follows:—

7,234   (1) 8 from 4 I can't, go to the 3, take 1, that leaves 2, 8 from
3,698   10--2 and 4 there already makes 6.

—   (2) 9 from 2 I can't, go to the 2, take 1, that leaves 1, 9 from 10 is 1 and 2 make 3.

—   (The teacher gave a gasp of despair, and many of the girls began to laugh. One who had laughed the loudest gave her

version.)

(1) 8 from 4 I can't, add 10, 8 from 10 leaves 2 and 4 makes 6.
(2) 9 from 2 I can't, add 10, 9 from 10 leaves 1 and 2 makes 3.

The teacher asked, " Why did you say 9 from 2; it is 3 in the sum? " She said, " Because I took 1 to give to the 4. Oh, no! " Then she stopped, and the class was now eagerly alert to correct the errors. The next child, though adding to the top and also to the bottom line, diminished in addition certain numbers in the top line. But a number of further examples were worked quite successfully after the teacher had once more demonstrated the method. The lesson concluded with examples worked by the teacher in which noughts predominated in the minuend.

The fourth lesson dealt with money sums. The teacher showed, using coins, that 1s. 6d.—8d. leaves 10d., and that (1s. 6d. + 3d.)—(8d. + 3d.) leaves 10d., &c. Then, prefacing the working with the injunction that, for every penny or shilling or pound added to the top line, a penny, shilling, or pound must be added to the bottom line, the teacher demonstrated on the blackboard, step by step, the method of working a " money-sum " in subtraction by means of the method of equal additions. Finally, these sums were worked by girls on the board, and, though some deviations occurred in the direction of decomposition, the teacher thought the children grasped the method more rapidly as applied to money than they had in " simple " subtraction.

In the fifth lesson subtraction sums in avoirdupois weight were worked on the board, various children being called on for the successive processes. The common errors were adding to the " bottom line " when not required for compensatory purposes, and taking from the top line as required in decomposition; and the teacher's judgment was that the girls were slow.

In the sixth lesson the girls were provided with papers on which were set out nine sums in " simple " subtraction. The girls worked the first sum individually and silently, and then the teacher worked it on the " board." Half the children were wrong in one or more figures in the first and second sums; but in the ninth sum only three girls were wrong; they were fairly quick, the teacher thought.

In the seventh lesson a similar procedure was adopted with eight money-sums, and in the eighth lesson the same procedure was adopted with seven subtraction sums in avoirdupois weight.

8. A brief account of the lessons on the method of decomposition.

In the first lesson examples were given to show that 1 in the tens column is equal to 10 units, and then concretely, by means of beans, the following sums were worked, 13—8-5 and 23—15-8. These sums were worked on the board by the method of decomposition. There is no need to amplify; the reader will be aware that this method was already in use, and in what precise form it was carried out by the girls.

In the second lesson the " top line " contained several noughts. I need not repeat how the children went " next door " and " couldn't," and how long the rearrangement of the top line took before the subtraction itself got fairly under way. A few girls said " go to the next figure, make all the noughts nines except the last—that is 10." But these were abler girls who, presumably, had found this out, for it was not the method of the class, nor of any considerable section of them. The teacher applied this procedure, though it must be confessed that in this lesson its success was not very marked. Then, still working with several noughts in the top line, the girls, one by one, worked sums on the board. An example is inset showing how the girls were now working:

801,001   (1) 9 from 1 I cannot, change the 1 (pointing to the
201,009   thousand), the line then becomes 0, 9, 9, 10; 9 from 10
———   leaves 1, and 1 are 2.
          (2) 0 from 9 leaves 9.
———   (3) 0 from 9 leaves 9.
          (4) 1 from 0 I cannot, change 1 from the 8; the line now
is 7, 9, 10; 1 from 10 leaves 9.
(5) 0 from 9 leaves 9.
(6) 2 from 7 leaves 5.

In the fourth lesson sums in subtraction of money were worked on the board, and ease as well as accuracy was shown by the girls until a large number of noughts were dealt with. The child called on worked thus:

£   s.   d.   (1) ¼d. from nothing I cannot, go to the pence I cannot,
60   0   0   go to the shillings I cannot, go to the pounds, take
56   14   8½   one, change it, that makes 20s. ¼d. from 0 I cannot,
———   go to the pence I cannot, go to the shillings, take
           one, that leaves 19s., change the shilling into pennies,
———   that is 12 pennies, ¼d. from nothing I cannot, ¼d.
           from 1d. leaves ¼d.
(2) 8d. from 11d. leaves 3d.
(3) 14s. from 19s. leaves 5s.
(4) There are 59 pounds, 6 from 9 leaves 3 and 5 from 5 leaves 0.

The girls were now asked for their opinions about this way of working, and one answered, " It is long "; and another said, " It is rather muddly." The teacher then told them that when once they understood how to change the money, it was a waste of time to keep on repeating the same words. And she worked the following sum thus:

£   s.   d.   We cannot take a farthing from nothing, take one of the
9   0   0   nearest coins, this is a pound, change it and it becomes
6   9   10¼   19s. 11d. and 4 farthings.
———   1 farthing from 4 farthings leaves 3 farthings.
           10d. from 11d. leaves 1d.
———   9s. from 19s. leaves 10s.
           £6 from £8 leaves £2.

The girls then worked several similar sums on the blackboard. In the fifth lesson subtraction sums in avoirdupois weight were demonstrated, the teacher dealing with the " noughts " in the same way as in the " money " sums.

The sixth, seventh, and eighth lessons corresponded precisely to those given to Group A, except, of course, that both children and teacher worked by " decomposition."

9. **The trial test.**

After the lessons given on the two methods, it was decided to give a trial test. It was doubtful whether the girls of Group A had become sufficiently familiarized with the method of " equal additions " to enable them to hold their own, even partially, against the long-established " decomposition " method of Group B, or whether they would return to their old method, or confuse the two. The marks obtained will be found in the table given later on. Suffice it to say here that the girls of Group A were slightly inferior to those of Group B, and that from individual questioning and by a scrutiny of the papers it appeared that the girls of Group A had worked by the method of equal additions and that the decomposition method had intruded very little. There was, of course, no question as to the method of Group B.

10. The first series of final tests.

The result of the trial test was considered sufficiently satisfactory to justify a series of final tests. These were four in number, and were the same as those set in the last four preliminary tests, namely, numbers 3, 4, 5, and 6. The results are given later; but it may be said at once that Group A now proved to have the advantage, though a slight one.

11. Two further teaching lessons.

In order to gain additional confidence that the children of both groups were quite clear as to their respective methods, two further lessons, wholly occupied by girls working examples on the blackboard, were given to the two groups. Several sums in which " noughts " succeeded each other in the " top line " were dealt with in these lessons.

12. A second series of final tests.

Finally, a second series of four tests was given to both groups, the results showing that Group A was again victorious, and by a larger margin of difference than before. The nature and reliability of this difference will be shown later.

13. The chronology of the experiment.

(1) Preliminary tests worked by all the girls simultaneously on October 13, 14, 15, 16, 20, 21, 1914, each exercise lasting eight minutes.

(2) Teaching lessons.

Group A—Nov. 9 : 11.30 to 11.45	Group A—Nov. 16 : 11.40 to 12.0
B— „ 9 : 11.10 to 11.25	B— „ 16 : 11.10 to 11.30
A— „ 10 : 11.15 to 11.30	A— „ 17 : 11.10 to 11.30
B— „ 10 : 11.35 to 11.50	B— „ 17 : 11.40 to 12.0
A— „ 12 : 11.35 to 11.55	A— „ 19 : 11.40 to 12.0
B— „ 12 : 11.15 to 11.35	B— „ 19 : 11.10 to 11.30
A— „ 13 : 11.10 to 11.30	A— „ 20 : 11.10 to 11.30
B— „ 13 : 11.40 to 12.0	B— „ 20 : 11.40 to 12.0

(3) Trial test worked by all the girls on November 24, lasting eight minutes.

(4) First series of final tests, worked by all the girls, on November 26, 27, December 1, 2, each lasting eight minutes.

(5) Two further teaching lessons, arranged as before, on December 8 and 9 to Group A and Group B separately.

(6) Second series of final tests, worked by all the girls, on December 10, 11, 15, and 16, each lasting eight minutes.

14. Results.

The results of the preliminary tests, the trial test, and the first and second series of final tests are shown in the following tables:

TABLE I.—SHOWING, SECTION BY SECTION, THE RESULTS OF GROUP A AND GROUP B COMPARED IN ALL TESTS. GROUP A WAS 11 YEARS 11·4 MONTHS, GROUP B WAS 11 YEARS 11·5 MONTHS OLD.

MARKS IN 4 PRELIMINARY TESTS.	GROUP A.—EQUAL ADDITIONS.					GROUP B.—DECOMPOSITION.				
	No. of Girls	Av. mark in 4 Prel. Tests	Av. mark in Trial Test	Av. mark in 1st Series of 4 Final Tests	Av. mark in 2nd Series of 4 Final Tests	No. of Girls	Av. mark in 4 Prel. Tests	Av. mark in Trial Test	Av. mark in 1st Series of 4 Final Tests	Av. mark in 2nd Series of 4 Final Tests
		Eight lessons		Two further lessons			Eight lessons		Two further lessons	
Over 450	2	520	103	537	681	2	517	122	563	724
400 to 450	4	429	101	490	650	4	429	108	495	660
350 to 400	4	379	93	454	575	4	380	96	448	598
300 to 350	4	330	87	421	587	4	329	92	425	526
250 to 300	3	276	82	374	545	3	278	70	347	466
200 to 250	2	225	78	356	468	2	224	63	285	431
Averages		361·7	91·1	440·5	588·4		361·7	92·8	432·1	570·8

TABLE II.—SHOWING, TEST BY TEST, THE AVERAGE MARKS OF GROUP A AND GROUP B COMPARED.

	Preliminary Tests.				Trial Test.	First Series of Final Tests.				Second Series of Final Tests.			
	1st	2nd	3rd	4th		1st	2nd	3rd	4th	1st	2nd	3rd	4th
Group A—Equal Additions	85·8	90·1	93·1	92·7	91·1	100·1	110·8	107·7	121·3	134·8	148·9	151·2	152·8
Group B—Decomposition	87·6	89·3	92·4	92·3	92·8	103·5	105·9	107·8	114·9	128·7	143·3	147·4	151·5

Table II shows us that, at the trial test and at the commencement of the first final series, Group A had not caught up; but in the remaining tests, they have not only done so, but, to some extent, have surpassed Group B. Table I shows us that Group A, the group taught by an equal additions method, surpass Group B in the lower sections only in the trial test, in the 3rd, 5th, and 6th sections in the first series of final tests, and in the three lower sections of the second series of final tests. But have they surpassed them on the whole? To settle that issue we must calculate correlation-coefficients and " probable errors."

Group A began with an average per child per test in the four preliminaries of 90.4; Group B also scored 90.4. The correlation-coefficient worked out from the individual cases of the two series is +.99. The groups are evidently well-balanced, as, indeed, may be seen from the sectionized results in Table I. In the trial test the averages are—for Group A 91.1, and for Group B 92.8. In the first series of final tests the averages per child per exercise are—for Group A 110.1, and for Group B 108.1: the correlation-coefficient is +.62 and the probable error equal to the difference between the means. In the second series of final tests the corresponding averages are, for Group A 147.1, and for Group B 142.7: the correlation-coefficient is +.54 and the probable error more than half the difference between the means. Thus, the advantage of Group A is statistically precarious, considered as a general advantage all along the line, and we should be perfectly safe in concluding only that Group A has equalled Group B considered as a whole. A perusal of the tabular details given previously shows us precisely how this comes about. For, whilst the weaker children, namely, the lower sections, have gained by the substitution of the new method, the girls in the upper sections have not.

15. Summarized conclusions.

(1) The method of equal additions in subtraction taught to children late in school life, who have hitherto worked by decomposition, produces results in a few weeks equal on the whole, and superior in the weaker children, to those produced by the method of decomposition.

(2) The amount of the gain involved does not justify a change of method at this late period of a child's school career.

(End of Part I.)

THE EMOTION OF ADMIRATION AND ITS DEVELOPMENT IN CHILDREN.

By R. C. MOORE, M.A., M.Sc.

I.—INTRODUCTION.

The present research was undertaken in order to—

(1) Obtain data concerning admiration, an emotion which has received comparatively small attention from experimental psychologists.

(2) Study the development of the emotion of admiration with age.

(3) Ascertain sex differences (if any) with respect to the emotion.

(4) Investigate the relative importance of various stimuli which arouse admiration.

McDougall's definition and classification of the emotions have been adopted. He[1] considers admiration to be a true but complex emotion made up of the two primary emotions wonder and negative self-feeling. "Wonder," he says, "is revealed by the impulse to approach and to continue to contemplate the admired object. . . . In children one may observe the element of wonder very clearly expressed and dominant. ' Oh, how wonderful! ' or ' Oh, how clever! ' or ' How did you do it? ' are phrases in which a child naturally expresses its admiration and by which the element of wonder and the impulse of curiosity are clearly revealed. . . . But admiration is more than wonder. We do not simply proceed to examine the admired object as we should one that provokes merely our curiosity or wonder. We approach it slowly, with a certain hesitation ; we are humbled by its presence, and, in the case of a person whom we intensely admire, we become shy, like a child in the presence of an adult stranger ; we have the impulse to shrink together, to be still, and to avoid attracting his attention ; that is to say, the instinct of submission, of self-abasement, is excited, with its corresponding emotion of negative self-feeling, by the perception that we are in the presence of a superior power, something greater than ourselves." With respect to inanimate objects, McDougall states that if the " sense of a personal power is not suggested by any object we contemplate, the emotion we experience is merely wonder, or at least is not admiration."

The subjects tested were children attending Council schools in two districts of the Liverpool area, viz. :—Wallasey and Waterloo. Both are to a very large extent residential suburbs. The fathers of the children, in most cases, were artisans, shopkeepers, clerks, dock workers, or sailors.

The numbers and ages of the children tested are shown in Table I.

The questionnaire method combined with introspective work was adopted for obtaining the data. The questions on admiration were carefully sandwiched in between unimportant questions. The papers were given out to the subjects blank side uppermost. The children were told that on the other side of the paper there were a number of questions which they were to answer. The answers were written[2]

---

1 McDougall, W. : " An Introduction to Social Psychology," pp. 128-131. Published by Methuen & Co.
2 The questions were taken orally and individually with the children aged six years on account of their inability to do the written work.

down after the questions. No suggestions were made, the children being left to answer spontaneously. The children were told to write quickly. No time limit was given, owing to answers to all the questions being required and also on account of the variation in the speed of writing due to age differences. On a given signal the children turned the papers over and commenced the test.

In the preliminary experiments considerable difficulty was experienced in the analysis of the emotions aroused in the younger subjects by inanimate objects. In many cases it was very difficult to decide whether the emotion experienced was wonder or admiration. The introspective evidence, obtained from the younger children, as to whether the objects in question aroused a " sense of personal power "[1] was rather vague and indefinite. Under these circumstances, it was felt to be advisable to confine the present research to the study of the emotion of admiration, as aroused by animate objects, and to reserve

TABLE I.—CHILDREN TESTED.

Age	Numbers.		
	Boys	Girls	Total
6 years...	46	49	95
7 „	50	51	101
8 „	58	61	119
9 „	60	58	118
10 „	46	45	91
11 „	53	44	97
12 „	54	57	111
13 „	48	51	99
Total	415	416	831

the analysis of the emotions aroused by inanimate objects for a future research where the matter could be dealt with at length. On this account, the significant questions in the questionnaire were confined to ones in connexion with admiration aroused by dead and living people, historical and fictional characters.

The following were the questions in the questionnaire dealing with the emotion of admiration :—
1. What living person do you admire most?
2. Why do you admire them?
3. What dead person do you admire most?
4. Why do you admire them?
5. Whom, in all the stories which you have read or heard, do you admire most?
6. Why do you admire them?

1 McDougall, W.: " An Introduction to Social Psychology," p. 131.

Introspections were obtained from many of the children. The tests were also carried out orally and individually on several children who were specially good at introspective work. These latter attended the same schools and were of the same social status, but were not members of the large groups tested.

II.—THE EVALUATION OF THE RESULTS OBTAINED FROM THE QUESTIONS DEALING WITH ADMIRATION.

The data connected with the people admired are first considered. Then an analysis is made of the results dealing with admiration for people and characters in stories. Finally, the reasons for admiration are examined.

A. The consideration of the data derived from the replies to the questions with respect to the people most admired.

The replies to questions 1 and 3, besides being considered separately, have been amalgamated together and all the people (living and dead) who were most admired by the children have been classified into three groups:—

(a) Relatives and acquaintances,
(b) Public and Historic persons,
(c) Religious characters.

Table II gives a summary of this classification.

TABLE II.—CLASSIFICATION OF THE PEOPLE ADMIRED MOST.[1]

Classification	Living People admired			Dead People admired			People (dead and alive) admired		
	Boys	Girls	Combined results for boys & girls	Boys	Girls	Combined results for boys & girls	Boys	Girls	Combined result for boys & girls
1. Relatives and acquaintances	38·9	44·2	41·5	43·9	57·1	50·5	41·4	50·7	46·0
2. Public and historic persons...	54·6	51·2	52·9	51·5	34·4	42·9	53·0	42·8	47·9
3. Religious persons	6·5	4·6	5·6	4·6	8·5	6·5	5·6	6·5	6·1
4. Men admired (combined results for rows 1, 2, and 3)...	73·5	51·9	62·7	73·5	43·3	58·4	73·5	47·6	60·5
5. Women admired (combined results for rows 1, 2, and 3)	26·5	48·1	37·3	26·5	56·7	41·6	26·5	52·4	39·5

It will be seen that in the case of the combined group of boys and girls that " Relatives and Acquaintances " supply 46 per cent of the people admired. A greater number of dead relatives and acquaintances are admired than living ones; while in the case of both living and dead the girls admire more people in this category than do the boys.

The father and mother are most admired by 18 per cent of the children; whilst acquaintances other than relatives are admired by less than 9 per cent. of the subjects. The admiration for living parents

1 The figures given in Tables II, III, V, and VII are percentages.

appears to be much greater than for dead ones, but this is because comparatively few of the children had dead parents. If only the children who had either a dead father or mother are considered, then in over 95 per cent of the cases for both the boys and the girls was the dead parent the most admired of all dead relatives and acquaintances. Of living persons, the boys tend to admire their father to a greater extent than do the girls; while the girls tend to admire their mother slightly more than do the boys. In the case of living persons, for both the boys and the girls the mother is admired by a greater number than the father. There is only a small sex difference shown in the admiration for a dead father or mother. The order of admiration of other relatives is as follows: Sister, grandmother, brother, grandfather, aunt, uncle, and cousin.

TABLE III.—THE ANALYSIS OF THE RESULTS FOR RELATIVES AND ACQUAINTANCES.

Classification of Relatives and Acquaintances.	Living People admired			Dead People admired			People (dead and living) admired		
	Boys	Girls	Average results for boys & girls	Boys	Girls	Average results for boys & girls	Boys	Girls	Average results for boys & girls
1. Father...	9·1	7·3	8·2	2·9	3·6	3·2	6·0	5·4	5·7
2. Mother	18·0	21·6	19·8	4·0	5·8	4·9	11·0	13·7	12·3
3. Father or mother	27·1	28·9	28·0	6·9	9·4	8·1	17·0	19·1	18·0
4. Other relatives	3·7	6·0	4·9	30·1	36·9	33·5	16·9	21·5	19·2
5. Other acquaintances... ...	8·0	9·3	8·6	6·9	10·8	8·9	7·5	10·1	8·8
6. Total for rows 3, 4, and 5 ...	38·9	44·2	41·5	43·9	57·1	50·5	41·4	50·7	46·0

From the detailed results given to questions 1 and 3 it appears that the objects of admiration of the child in early years are found in its environment. Relatives and acquaintances are the people (dead and living) whom it admires most.

This is what we should expect. At this age the child knows little or nothing of the world outside the home, or of the world of history. But at the age of eight (at least as regards the children investigated in the present research) history in story form becomes a school subject. The child has also largely mastered the mechanical difficulties of reading and eagerly seeks books of all kinds.[1] The effect of this is shown in an increase in the admiration of historical characters and a decrease in the admiration of relations and acquaintances.

These facts were also noticed by Earl Barnes in his investigations upon London children.[2] He says "It marks the broadening out of the personality and the substituting of the larger political, social, and

[1] The children tested have the use of the Municipal Library from the eighth birthday.
[2] Earl Barnes: "Children's Ideals." *Pedagogical Seminary*, 1900, vol. vii, pp. 3-12.

world dreams for those of the home and neighbourhood." Goddard remarked upon the same thing when conducting his researches on German children, and, with regard to this matter, Hill [2] says that in early life such a choice is desirable, as "a large and earlier choice of public characters might be evidence of anything but normal ' development of soul,' but rather disillusionment, precocity, or, where the influencing personalities are unworthy, the exchanging of one's birthright for a mess of pottage." A similar occurrence is noted by Gilbertson [3] with regard to Swedish children, and by Chambers [4] in his investigations with American children.

It appears that right through the years investigated the girls surpass the boys in the number of acquaintances chosen, whilst in the choice of historical personages the reverse is true.

Table II shows that on the average for the children and ages tested, Relatives and Acquaintances are admired to a slightly less extent than Public and Historic Persons. The boys admired Public and Historic Persons to a greater extent than the girls. The people chiefly mentioned under this category were kings (especially King George V and King Edward VII), noted soldiers, sailors, statesmen, inventors, explorers, authors, poets, artists, members of Parliament, and justices of the peace. The very great majority of the characters mentioned were English. [5]

The following were included under the heading " Religious Characters ": God, Jesus, Biblical characters (Samuel, Moses, Esther, David, &c.); and others considered by the children to be noted especially for their goodness, e.g., General Booth, Florence Nightingale, Wilberforce, General Gordon. The fact that the children admired these people chiefly for their goodness and not for other qualities which some of them possessed was revealed by the answer to the question, " Why do you admire them?" and was confirmed by introspections. The number of replies from boys under the heading " Religious Persons " gradually diminishes from 13 per cent at the age of six years to 1.8 per cent at the age of thirteen. The corresponding replies from the girls also decrease, but in not such a regular manner. Religious Persons are only greatly admired by a relatively small proportion of the children, viz., 6.1 per cent. The boys' and girls' results yield figures which agree closely on this point, viz., boys 5.6 per cent, girls 6.5 per cent, greatly admire Religious Persons. This percentage is very much less than that either for Relatives and Acquaintances or for Public and Historic Persons.

When we consider the combined results of the data tabulated in Table II from the standpoint of the choice of members of the opposite sex as objects of admiration, we find that the boys admire nearly three times as many men as they do women, while the girls admire rather a larger percentage of women than of men. When the combined results of the boys and girls are taken, male characters are admired more than females in a ratio of about three to two. These results show a large

1 Goddard, H. H.: "Ideals of a Group of German Children." *Pedagogical Seminary*, 1906, vol. xiii, pp. 208-220.
2 Hill, D. S.: "Comparative Study of Children's Ideals." *Pedagogical Seminary*, 1911, vol. xviii, pp. 219-231.
3 Gilbertson, A. N.: "A Swedish Study in Children's Ideals." *Pedagogical Seminary*, 1913, vol. xx, pp. 100-106.
4 Chambers, W. G.: "The Evolution of Ideals." *Pedagogical Seminary*, 1903, vol. x, pp. 101-143.
5 The experimental portion of this research was completed before the outbreak of war.

degree of admiration for members of the opposite sex; this amounts to 26.5 per cent for the boys and 47.6 per cent for the girls of all the people admired. This tendency has also been noted by Barnes, Goddard, and Hill. Commenting on the fact that girls choose a large number of males as objects of admiration, Hill says:[1] "It is surmise to state whether this is due to growing dissatisfaction with the limitations traditionally as well as naturally restricting women, or due to there being more male ideals to choose from. Perhaps both factors are operative. It appears to the present writer that we do not stress enough, in story, reading, picture, and song, the noble qualities of available female characters, contemporaneous and in history.

That the male ideal is commonly made more conspicuous in history and in current events, and that the imitativeness of the child is effected through the examples most vividly presented, rather than by some peculiar dissatisfaction with her sex, seem adequate hypotheses to explain this choice of male ideals by the average girl. In order to point to these factors, however, one need not deny that a sense of ill-adaptation to cope with the demands of life is too common in some young girls because of our artificial modern environment."

The twenty objects of admiration with the greatest frequencies are given in Table IV. The boys', girls', and combined groups are given separately. The results from questions 1 and 3 are combined together.

Comparing the boys' frequency list in Table IV with that of the girls', it is found that fourteen out of the twenty most frequent objects of admiration are common to both lists. The order of frequency, however, is not the same. King George V and Mother are the two most frequent objects of admiration for both boys and girls, but King George V stands first with the boys and Mother with the girls. The frequency of the reply King George V for the boys is very nearly identical with that of Mother for the girls. While the frequency of the reply Mother for the boys is the same as that of King George V for the girls. The third place in each list is taken by Father. Nelson, as might be expected, is a much more frequent object of admiration for the boys than for the girls. There are no great authors amongst the boys' first twenty objects of admiration, whilst Shakespeare, Dickens, and Scott are all in the corresponding list for the girls. In the whole series no instances of undesirable ideals are given. The twenty most frequent replies for the boys' group only contain five women, four of whom are relatives, viz.: Mother, sister, grandmother, and aunt; whilst the fifth woman admired is Queen Victoria. The girls' group gives eight women, viz.: Mother, girl friend, Queen Mary, sister, grandmother, lady friend, aunt, and Queen Victoria. The combined groups give eight women, viz.: Mother, sister, grandmother, girl friend, Queen Mary, aunt, lady friend, and Queen Victoria.

A considerable number of people were given as objects of admiration by the boys and not by the girls, and vice versa, e.g.:—

People Mentioned by Boys and not by Girls.—Lord Roberts, Prince of Wales, Gordon, Wolsey, Baden Powell, Beatty, Clive, Rothschild, General Booth, General White, Napoleon, Columbus, Carnegie, Bonar Law, Rockefellow, Burgess, Archbishop of Canterbury, Chancellor of the Exchequer, Graham White, Duke of Portland, Lord Derby, Duke

1 Hill, D. S.: "Comparative Study of Children's Ideals." *Pedagogical Seminary*, 1911, vol. xvii, 219-231.

TABLE IV.—FREQUENCY TABLE FOR PEOPLE ADMIRED.

	BOYS			GIRLS			BOYS AND GIRLS	
Rank	People admired	Frequency	Rank	People admired	Frequency	Rank	People admired	Frequency
1	King George V	154	1	Mother	152	1	King George V	281
2	Mother	127	2	King George V	127	2	Mother	279
3	Father	68	3	Father	61	3	Father	129
4	King Edward VII	66	4	Girl friend	54	4	King Edward VII	97
5	Nelson	50	5	Queen Mary	52	5	Sister	82
6	God	46	6	Sister	43	6	Grandmother	75
7	Sister	39	7	Grandmother	41	7	God	73
8	Brother	35	8	Grandfather	32	8	Nelson	68
9	Grandmother	34	9·5	King Edward VII	31	9	Brother	65
10	Boy friend	31	9·5	Lady friend	31	10	Grandfather	60
11	Grandfather	28	11	Brother	30	11	Girl friend	56
12	Uncle	20	12	God	27	12	Queen Mary	52
13	Lord Roberts	17	13	Aunt	22	13	Boy friend	38
14	Aunt	13	14	Nelson	18	14	Aunt	35
15	Alfred the Great	10	15	Queen Victoria	15	15	Lady friend	32
16	Queen Victoria	9	16	Alfred the Great	13	16	Uncle	30
17	Lloyd George	8	17	Shakespeare	12	17	Queen Victoria	24
18·5	Mr. Price (local brave man)	7	18	Dickens	11	18	Alfred the Great	23
18·5	Teacher	7	19	Uncle	10	19	Lord Roberts	18
20	King Arthur	6	20	Scott	9	20	Shakespeare	12

of Connaught, Rathbone, Samuel, St. George, Thomas à Becket, Havelock, Captain Oates, Boadicea, Henry V, General Buller.

People Mentioned by Girls and not by Boys.—Dickens, Princess Mary, Queen Elizabeth, Prince Olaf, Clara Butt, Lord Avebury, Milton, Moses, Canute, Julius Cæsar, Sir Thomas More, Grey, Lady Jane Grey, Princess Patricia, Marconi, Black Prince, Queen Alexandra, Stephenson, Beaconsfield, Sir W. Scott, Churchill, Paderewski, Roosevelt, Ella Wheeler Wilcox, Mrs. Blundell, Hetty King, Mrs. Asquith.

B. The Persons and Characters most admired in Stories.

The data for this section was obtained from the answers to question 5. The system adopted for classifying the data in Table I has here to be modified, as characters out of fairy tales, myths, and legends are introduced, and relatives and acquaintances do not occur.

Table V contains a classified summary of the data.

TABLE V.—CLASSIFICATION OF THE PERSONS AND CHARACTERS ADMIRED IN STORIES.

Classification of Persons and Characters	Boys	Girls	Boys and Girls
Fairy Characters	7·5	18·7	13·1
Characters occurring in Myths and Legends	20·2	14·4	17·3
Historical Persons and Characters...	48·0	34·0	41·0
Religious Persons and Characters ...	10·1	5·5	7·8
Persons and Characters, other than the above (Literary Characters)	14·2	27·4	20·8
Male Persons and Characters ...	96·0	58·5	76·4
Female Persons and Characters ...	4·0	41·5	23·6

Very few of the story characters chosen were selected from modern light fiction. They were practically all worthy of admiration when viewed from a high standard. Historical Persons and Characters is the category which contains the most frequent objects of admiration for both the girls and the boys. After them come literary characters. The boys and girls both admire more historical characters than literary ones. Fairy characters are somewhat less admired than those occurring in myths and legends. Considerable sex differences are noted in each category. In the section dealing with Religious Persons and Characters both the frequencies are small.

A number of points of interest occur in each of the classes in Table V, and these will now be dealt with.

(1) **Characters in Fairy Tales.**—Here there is a large sex difference noticeable. Between two and three times more girls than boys admire fairy characters. It appears that the girls admire characters in fairy tales more than the boys, especially during the years eight, nine, ten, and eleven. But it must be remembered that the individual characters most admired by the boys are not those most admired by the girls, e.g., Jack the Giant Killer is chosen several times by the boys, but never once by the girls. Red Riding Hood and Cinderella are the characters most admired by the girls.

(2) **Characters occurring in Myths and Legends.**—In this class also we have a large sex difference, but in the opposite direction to that found above. One and a half times the number of boys than girls admire a mythical or legendary character. Robin Hood was admired by the greatest number of girls, and St. George, Hercules, and Robin Hood by the greatest number of boys. In the case of both sexes the admiration for mythical and legendary characters decreases with increasing age. The development curve for the boys' group is not regular in this respect. At the age of six the characters from the myths or legends appear to make a much greater appeal to the girls than to the boys, but from between the seventh and the eighth year there is a sex difference in favour of the boys.

(3) **Historical Persons and Characters.**—Considerably more boys than girls admire historical characters, but the sex difference is not so marked as in the two previous classes. Nelson, Alfred, and Drake are the chief choices of the boys, whilst Nelson, Alfred, and Grace Darling are those selected most frequently by the girls. The two development curves for this class are roughly parallel to each other. The boys show a greater admiration for historical characters than the girls at all ages. The admiration for historical characters is only small at age six, but rapidly increases until it reaches a maximum at age nine. Beyond this age the admiration for historical characters decreases both for the boys and the girls, but shows a tendency to rise at ages twelve and thirteen for the boys and age thirteen for the girls.

(4) **Religious Persons and Characters.**—This includes, as in Table II, God, Jesus, Biblical characters, and people considered by the children to be noted pre-eminently for their goodness. The boys show a greater admiration for religious characters at age six and most of the other ages than do the girls. For the higher ages tested religious characters are only admired to a small extent by both girls and boys.

(5) **Characters and Persons other than those included in the above four classes.**—These are chiefly characters in prose, fiction, and poetry. Here there is a sex difference in favour of the girls as regards numbers. In the case of the boys a much greater range of reading is shown than in the case of the girls. This is partly due to the fact that the majority of the girls tested, owing to assisting their mothers in the housework, had fewer opportunities for reading than the boys. Robinson Crusoe is the character most frequently chosen by the boys, and Alice in Wonderland and Oliver Twist by the girls. The sex difference in favour of the girls as regards characters in fiction and poetry has also been noted by other investigators, e.g., Goddard[1] in his researches on German children found that 4.0 per cent of the boys and 8.0 per cent

---

[1] Goddard, H. H.: "Ideals of a Group of German Children." *Pedagogical Seminary*, 1906, vol. xiii, pp. 208-220.

of the girls chose characters in fiction. Hill[1] also in his investigations on children in Tennessee found that 5.0 per cent of the boys and 11.0 per cent of the girls chose such characters. These percentages are considerably less than those found in the present research. This is largely due to the fact that in this paper the characters included under the present class are given as a percentage of the persons and characters admired in stories only, while both Goddard and Hill give the results as percentages of the total people admired from all sources. With regard to the children investigated, no literary character was an object of admiration to any child aged six years, but above this age there is a rather large sex-difference in favour of the girls. Goddard, Hill, and Gilbertson found the same thing. Chambers gives a table for "Authors, Artists, and Musicians," and there is shown in it a sex difference in favour of the girls.

Table VI gives the twenty characters most frequently admired by the boys, girls, and both groups combined. In each case Nelson is the character most admired, and Alfred the Great occupies second place. A much larger number of boys than girls admire Nelson. No woman occurs in the first twenty characters admired by the boys, whilst seven women characters occur in the corresponding girls' list.

A number of the persons and characters admired in stories were mentioned by one sex only. The most characteristic of these replies are as follows :—

Persons and Characters in Stories mentioned by Girls only.—Little Nell, William Wallace, Miss Trotwood, Cinderella, Pickwick, Juliet, Sleeping Beauty, Wilberforce, Moses, Rosalind, Bunyan, The Pied Piper, Thomas à Becket, Bo-Peep, Snow Queen, Portia, Sir Thomas More, Peter Pan, Mary Queen of Scots, Sir Walter Raleigh, Boadicea, Queen Elizabeth, Lucy Gray, Queen Victoria, Mr. Micawber, Walpole, Jane Eyre, Camile, Griselda.

Persons and Characters in Stories mentioned by Boys only.— Canute, Samson, David, Black Prince, William Tell, Buffalo Bill, Samuel, Horatius, Blake, Isaiah, Hereward the Wake, Masterman Ready, Agricola, Nick the Detective, Billy Bray, Clive, Napoleon, Buller, Richard Lionheart, Wellington, Sir Galahad, Stanley, Halifax, Kitchener, Martin Rattler.

C. Consideration of the reasons for admiring the given Persons and Characters.

In the preceding sections a study and analysis has been made of the people and characters admired. The reasons for admiring these people and characters will now be considered.

In Table VII a classification is given of the reasons for admiration. Some of the reasons are difficult to classify, as there is no sharp line of demarcation between them.

It will be noticed from Table VII that bravery is the attribute most admired. Under this heading are included not only the bravery exhibited in warlike acts, but also that shown by Captain Scott and

---

[1] Hill, D. S.: "Comparative Study of Children's Ideals." *Pedagogical Seminary*, 1911, vol. xviii. pp. 219-231.

TABLE VI.—FREQUENCY TABLE FOR CHARACTERS ADMIRED IN STORIES.

	BOYS			GIRLS			BOYS AND GIRLS	
Rank	Characters admired	Frequency	Rank	Characters admired	Frequency	Rank	Characters admired	Frequency
1	Nelson	116	1	Nelson	38	1	Nelson	154
2	Alfred the Great	37	2	Alfred the Great	35	2	Alfred the Great	72
3	St. George	32	3	Red Riding Hood	32	3	St. George	37
4	Robinson Crusoe	24	4	Robin Hood	17	4	Red Riding Hood	35
5	Drake	21	5·5	Grace Darling	16	5	Robinson Crusoe	32
6	Hercules	15		Cinderella	16	6	Robin Hood	29
7	God	14		Alice in Wonderland	14	7	Drake	27
8	Robin Hood	12		Florence Nightingale	14	8	God	24
9	King Arthur	10	9	Cromwell	14	9	Columbus	21
10	Livingstone	9		Oliver Twist	14	10	King Arthur	20
	David	8		Columbus	12	11·5	King Edward VII	18
12	Jack the Giant Killer	8	12	King Edward VII	12		Grace Darling	18
	Buffalo Bill	8		God	10	13·5	Alice in Wonderland	17
	Wellington	7		King Arthur	10		Cromwell	17
	Columbus	7	15	Portia	10		Hercules	16
16·5	Hiawatha	7		Brutus	10	16	Cinderella	16
	Napoleon	7		Rosalind	10		Livingstone	16
	William of Orange	7	18	Robinson Crusoe	8	18	Florence Nightingale	15
	Charles Dickens	7	19	Livingstone	7	19	Oliver Twist	14
20	King Edward VII	6	20	Drake	6	20	Hiawatha	12

TABLE VII—REASONS FOR ADMIRING THE GIVEN PERSONS AND CHARACTERS.

Reason for Admiration	1 Living People.			2 Dead People.			3 Story Characters.			Columns 1, 2, and 3 combined.		
	Boys	Girls	Boys and Girls	Boys	Girls	Boys and Girls	Boys	Girls	Boys and Girls	Boys	Girls	Boys and Girls
Bravery ...	12·3	7·8	10·0	29·7	14·4	22·0	51·8	30·3	41·0	31·3	17·5	24·4
Cleverness ...	1·6	2·1	1·9	4·7	7·4	6·0	7·0	12·8	9·9	4·5	7·4	6·0
Goodness ...	14·2	19·5	16·9	11·0	15·0	13·0	12·5	16·2	14·4	12·6	16·9	14·8
Prettiness ...	0·9	2·4	1·6	4·3	8·3	6·4	—	6·0	3·0	1·7	5·6	3·6
Kindness...	17·7	23·2	20·4	18·3	19·3	18·8	4·3	5·7	5·0	13·4	16·1	14·7
Maker of Peace...	—	—	—	5·6	1·4	3·5	—	—	—	1·9	0·5	1·2
Power, Greatness	29·5	16·2	22·8	11·3	7·0	9·2	10·0	5·6	7·8	16·9	9·6	13·2
Riches ...	8·3	3·1	5·7	0·8	—	0·4	1·2	0·4	0·8	3·4	1·2	2·3
Goodness to others	10·1	16·8	13·5	11·7	18·3	15·0	3·4	5·5	4·5	8·4	13·5	11·0
Witty, Humorous	0·9	0·1	0·5	0·8	2·1	1·4	2·0	2·5	2·3	1·2	1·6	1·4
Always happy ...	1·1	1·1	1·1	0·2	0·8	0·5	—	1·0	0·5	0·4	1·0	0·7
Niceness...	1·9	4·7	3·3	1·6	5·2	3·4	7·8	14·0	10·9	3·8	7·9	5·8
Good manners ...	1·4	3·0	2·2	—	0·8	0·4	—	—	—	0·5	1·3	0·9

Captain Oates, by men risking their lives to save others from drowning, by men volunteering to go down a coal-pit as a rescue party after an explosion, by men going out in a lifeboat for rescue purposes, and other similar cases. Bravery is the reason given on the average in rather more than 24.0 per cent of the cases, but the importance of this quality in evoking admiration varies considerably with sex and with the class of people admired. In the case of living people 10.0 per cent are admired for this reason, whilst 22.0 per cent and 41.0 per cent of dead people and story characters respectively are admired on this account. The boys admire bravery to a much greater extent than do girls. This is especially so for dead subjects of admiration, although it is also true to a marked degree in the case of living people and story characters admired. With advancing age the boys slightly tend to admire bravery to a less extent in living people, whilst the relative value of this quality in causing admiration diminishes more rapidly in the girls' group. Admiration for bravery shown by people who are now dead and by story characters also diminishes for both the boys' and girls' groups with advancing age. The development curves for bravery show an approximately similar trend.

Goodness is the quality which, next to bravery, most frequently causes admiration. It is admired to approximately the same extent in both living and dead people and story characters. It is rather more than half as important as bravery in causing admiration. It is considered worthy of admiration to a greater extent by the girls than by the boys. Goodness is the cause of admiration in 16.9 per cent of the cases in the girls' group and only of 12.6 per cent of the cases in the boys' group. Under the heading " Goodness," besides undifferentiated goodness are classified such answers as " noble character," " good character," " did right," " upright man." Especially in the younger children, undifferentiated goodness was frequently given as the cause of admiration. With advancing age goodness tends to be more analysed into various special aspects. The relative importance of goodness as a cause of admiration tends to diminish in the boys' group after age nine. This holds good both for persons and characters admired. The diminution tends to be fairly rapid in the case of persons, but not so rapid in that of characters. The same tendency, but not to the same extent, is noticed in the girls' group for living people admired; but in the case of dead people and characters admired this does not hold true. The development curve for goodness, as a cause of admiration for dead people, shows a minimum at age nine for the girls' group, whilst the corresponding curve for story characters shows a tendency to rise with advancing age. On the whole, goodness as a cause of admiration tends to diminish in relative importance for both the boys' and girls' groups with advancing age. With children aged six years it is admired to a greater extent by the girls than the boys. This is also true for the children aged ten to thirteen.

Kindness is very nearly equal to goodness as a cause for admiration. Kindness is admired in 14.7 per cent of the cases whilst goodness is admired in 14.8 per cent. Also kindness, like goodness, is admired to a greater extent by the girls (16.1 per cent) than the boys (13.4 per cent). This holds true for admiration for persons and also for story characters. It is most admired in living people, whilst in story characters it is admired to only a small extent (5 per cent). Kindness tends to be admired to a less extent with advancing age. The development curves, although showing this general tendency, are somewhat irregular. Between ages six and eleven the development curves for the two sexes are very close together, but after age eleven there is a decided sex difference in favour of the girls.

Greatness and power are on the average the cause of admiration in 13.2 per cent of the cases. These attributes are most extensively admired in living people, and in this group are the chief cause of admiration, being the reason given for admiring 22.8 per cent of the people. The admiration for these two attributes increases with advancing years. At age six it is practically non-existent, whilst at age thirteen it is given as the cause of admiration by 33.0 per cent of the boys and by 21.9 per cent of the girls. The boys admire greatness and power to a considerably greater extent than do the girls. This holds true throughout the ages tested. Also this sex difference tends to increase with age.

" Goodness to others " ranks next after greatness and power as a cause of admiration. It is the quality admired in 11.0 per cent of the cases. This attribute is much more admired in persons than in story characters. •It is more powerful in girls than in boys through all the years tested. It also appears to be appreciated at an earlier age by girls than by boys, e.g., 2.8 per cent of girls admire this quality at age six and 5.1 per cent at age seven, whilst at neither of these ages does any boy admire this attribute. This reason for admiration is given by 5.0 per cent of the boys and by 7.2 per cent of the girls at age eight. The boys development curve is more regular than that of the girls.

Besides the above reasons for admiring persons and characters, a number of reasons of much smaller relative value were also given. Cleverness was admired in 6.0 per cent of the cases. This was admired more by the girls than the boys, and was admired more in story characters than in persons. " Niceness " and " prettiness " were admired by 5.8 per cent and 3.6 per cent of the subjects respectively. Each of these two attributes was more admired by the girls than the boys. Riches were only mentioned as a specific cause for admiration by 2.3 per cent of the subjects. Humorous and witty people and characters were admired by 1.4 per cent, and makers of peace by 1.2 per cent of the children. The late King Edward VII is the person referred to as a maker of peace. No living people and no story characters are admired for this reason. " Good manners " and " always happy " are given as reasons for admiration in less than 1.0 per cent of the cases.

III.—CONCLUSION.

1. The admiration for relatives and acquaintances, which is pronounced in early childhood, diminishes with advancing years. Admiration for public and historic characters increases with age. Characters in fairy tales, myths, and legends are less admired as the child grows older. Admiration for literary characters increases with advancing age. Religious persons and characters only excite slight admiration, which is chiefly aroused in young children and diminishes with advancing age.

2. The number of people of the opposite sex admired is considerable, especially for the girls' group. The girls show a greater admiration for relatives and acquaintances than do the boys. Public and historic characters are more admired by boys than girls. In story characters, the number of the opposite sex admired by the boys is much less than in the case of people, whilst more male characters are admired by the girls than male personages. Characters in fairy and literary stories appeal more to the admiration of the girls than the boys, whilst of characters in myths and legends, historical and religious characters, the reverse is true. With respect to admiration for religious persons and characters the boys and girls closely agree.

3. It is often difficult to demarcate clearly between different reasons given for admiration. Bravery is the attribute most admired, especially by the boys, but admiration for this attribute diminishes with advancing age. Next in importance as exciting admiration are ranked goodness and kindness, which are more admired by the girls than the boys. Admiration for these two qualities shows a slight tendency to decline as the child gets older. Greatness (and power) is the quality which ranks fourth in ability to evoke admiration, and is much stronger in the case of boys than of girls and increases with advancing age. Goodness to others ranks fifth, and is admired much more by the girls than the boys. Admiration for this quality increases with age.

MANY of the back numbers of the *Journal of Experimental Pedagogy* are still available for sale, but copies of the following issues are particularly wanted, and the Editor would be grateful to any College having surplus copies if he might have them: Vol. 2 (No. 2), Vol. 3 (No. 5), Vol. 4 (No. 4), Vol. 5 (Nos. 2 and 3). He is looking particularly for copies of Vol. 5 (No. 3). Owing to a mistake, about thirty subscribers did not get their copies of this issue, and their sets are spoiled. The Editor has a few complete sets for sale; prices on application.

EDUCATIONAL IDEAS IN SOME ENGLISH NOVELS.

By ELEANOR W. ROOKE.

(The substance of a Paper read before the Sheffield Branch of the English Association, on February 9th, 1920.)

THE choice of such a subject as mine is rash in the extreme. All wise persons choose subjects on which they are authorities and the rest of us nowhere. I find myself greatly at a disadvantage, for there is nothing occult, esoteric, or forbidden about such a simple subject as the English novel. Here we are all equals and all on common ground. I am bound to display my lamentable ignorance of many authors who could throw a flood of light on my subject. I shall disappoint many by my omission of all but one of the books which they expected to be "the haunt and the main region of my song"; I mean the modern school novel—*Stalkey and Co., The Hill, The Harrovians, The Bending of a Twig, David Blaize, Mr. Perrin and Mr. Traill, Sonia, The Loom of Youth, The Regiment of Women, Prelude*, and, possibly, *The Bonfire*. It seemed to me, first, that these books were too well known to need talking about, and, secondly, that, intensely interesting as they are as pictures of schools, they are, with one exception, less helpful in educational ideas than some older books. I am also bound to offend in the case of many of the novelists whom I have included.

Then too, not only are we all novel readers—we are also authorities on education—everyone is. Everybody seems to hold, in one way or another, that education ought to be a preparation for life. Then sometimes conflicting ideals of self-culture and service to the community are combined when, as Sir Henry Hadow has expressed it, education aims at developing the highest possible type of citizen. Such was the ideal of the great men of the English Renaissance throughout the sixteenth century:—More, Eyot, Ascham, Spenser; such also that of the woman in the street whom I once heard telling three rude little girls: "They didn't learn you manners at *your* school."

And because they so often fail to learn us manners and things deeper than manners at our schools of every type, we find an apparently different view very widely held; namely, that education rather unfits than fits the student for ordinary life. This is held not only by the ladies who look back on the palmy days before the "Board Schools" made the lower classes forget their station, but by Farmer Sandford, in *Sandford and Merton*, who will not have his daughters sent to boarding school to learn "French and music and wriggling about the room." For says he, "when they come back, who must boil the pot or make the puddings or sweep the house or feed the pigs? Did you ever hear of (young ladies) doing such vulgar things?"

In a different way Mrs. Hammond in that glorious comic study of Mr. Shanks's, *The Old Indispensables*, held a similar view. Cyril Hammond is doing no work whatever at the Circumvention Office and his sister suggests that he would be better in a garage. "I'm sure" says the mother. "Cyril ought not to waste his University education being a mechanic." This lady at least respected an academic education even if it unfitted for life. Not so Mr. Neich, in *Sinister Street*, who, when Michael was suddenly pitchforked by the Head Master into his class, remarked: "Twenty-six miserable boys are already having a detestable and stultifying education in this wretched class. And now comes a twenty-seventh. Very well. Very well. I'll stuff him with the abominable jargon and filthy humbug. I'll cram him with the undigested balderdash. Oh, you unhappy boy; you unfortunate imp and atom. Sit down, if you can find a desk. Sit down and drench your mind with the ditchwater I'm paid to teach you."

Still more forcibly does Mr. H. G. Wells write of this same stultifying effect of education in *The Wonderful Visit*:—

"Ever heard of a pithed frog?" said the tramp.

"Pithed frog," said the angel. "No!"

"It's a thing these here vivisectionists do. They takes a frog and they cuts out his brains, and they shoves a bit of pith in the place of 'em. That's a pithed frog. Well—that there village is full of pithed human beings. . . .

"And you see that little red place there?"

"That's called the National School," said the angel.

"Yes—that's where they piths 'em," said the tramp.

There is a third attitude which I find peculiarly fascinating, since it was once my own. It may be summed up in the phrase "learning for learning's sake," and is exemplified equally well in the Blimbers in *Dombey and Son*, and in the old woman who holds up her hands in bewildered admiration of the "book-learning," while she remarks "I'm no scholar." Persons holding the third view see no possible connection between education and life—education is to them a thing as remote as the moon and with considerably less influence on the individual. If it were sound, it would be singularly comforting to the teacher, at present weighed down by manifold responsibilities. But we know only too well it is not sound, though it is often enough true, as when we find Edwin Clayhanger leaving school at sixteen, having received what was called "a thoroughly sound education." "Knowledge," says Mr. Arnold Bennett, "was admittedly the armour and the weapon of one about to try conclusions with the world, and many people for many years had been engaged in providing Edwin with knowledge. The satirical sketch which follows is, I believe, true of the year 1872—Mr. Arnold Bennett is nothing if not accurate—and it is by no means wholly true to-day; but who is to say our withers are altogether unwrung? Edwin has learnt nothing of natural history, physiology, psychology, physical science, of the geography of his own country, political economy, or logic. He knew nothing of earth and air and sun and stars, of art and the arts, nor of literature as an art. He had not learnt to express himself orally in any language. But he could parse and analyse with superb assurance the magnificent sentences of Milton, Virgil, and Racine. In history he had several times approached the nineteenth century, but it seemed to him that for administrative reasons he was always being dragged back again to the Middle Ages. He knew Henry VIII was a "skilful warrior and politician," but "unfortunate in his domestic relations. He could not remember the clauses of Magna Charta, but he knew eternally that it was signed at a place amusingly called Runnymede. And the one fact engraved on his memory about the battle of Waterloo was that it was fought on a Sunday." Some of us born later than Edwin Clayhanger could tell of an education not altogether dissimilar at the hands of the apostles of learning for learning's sake.

These three views, as I have before implied, are really one. Even those who hold the second or third view feel, consciously or unconsciously, that the first view is the true ideal. We shall find this over and over again in the novel. And with it we shall find a striving, sometimes blind as with Mr. Tulliver, sometimes clear-sighted as with Mr. Barlow, and finally prophetic and triumphant in Mr. Huss, towards the great ideal. We shall find the conflict about public schools raging in the eighteenth century as fiercely as it rages now; we shall find a classical education as contemptuously decried by Samuel Richardson, and the early Victorian, Thomas Hughes, as by modern Georgians; we shall find the disciples of Rousseau in England as enthusiastic theorists as to method and detail as the followers of Madame Montessori to-day. We shall find those who think with Mr. Shandy, the personality of the teacher the all-important factor; others, like Thomas Hughes, that the school life apart from the lessons is the great thing (though he did not undervalue the influence of a great head master); others, who believe with Colonel Newcombe when he said '' There is nothing like a knowledge of the Classics to give a man a fine breeding,'' that the ideal can be reached through the school work itself.

I wish I could classify the novelists neatly under these various heads. But they elude classification. So I relapse into chronological order and, I fear, to some extent into chaos. I feel that I owe you an apology for assuming that the English novel began in 1740, when obviously it hails from a much earlier date. But, since nobody seems quite certain when it did begin, and as I must begin somewhere, and I learnt the date 1740 when I was at school, I thought it would do as well as another.

The book I want to start upon is that mine of wisdom, *Joseph Andrews*. We know that there is nothing new under the sun, and we are pleasantly confirmed in this ancient opinion when we read the comments of Parson Adams and of Mr. Wilson, Joseph's unknown father, on Mr. Wilson's story of his own life. It was, as you will remember, a life of exceptional dissipation and degradation, until he '' came to himself '' (so much so that we wonder that Joseph was pleased later on to exchange the excellent parents of Pamela for such a rake, until we remember that he had been asleep almost throughout the narrative).

Mr. Wilson says: '' I stayed a very little while at school after (my father's) death, for, being a forward youth, I was extremely impatient to be in the world. And to this early introduction into life, without a guide, I impute all my future misfortunes.'' What is this but Mr. Fisher's Act and all the modern agitation for the extension of the school-leaving age?

Mr. Adams, on the contrary, says afterwards to Joseph: '' I have discovered the cause of all the misfortunes which befel him—a public school, Joseph, was the cause of all the calamities which he afterwards suffered. Public schools are the nurseries of all vice and immorality. You may thank the Lord that you were not bred at a public school.'' What is this but *The Loom of Youth*?

And when Joseph makes a spirited defence of public schools as a preparation for life, and as superior to private schools in their discipline, Adams makes a reply which even now might be taken to heart in more than one type of school: '' Discipline, indeed! Because *one man* scourges twenty or thirty boys more in one morning than another, is he therefore a better disciplinarian? " And then comes that touch which is as modern and at the same time as universal as anything in this wonderful book: " This good man thought a school master the greatest character in the world, and himself the greatest of all school masters."

When Adams wished to find out the extent of Joseph Andrews' education, it may surprise us that his examination took the form of questioning him concerning the number of books in the New Testament, their names, and the number of chapters in each. But he was far from thinking this an adequate stock of knowledge, and was delighted with Joseph's efforts to improve his mind by reading and re-reading the Bible, *The Whole Duty of Man*, and Thomas à Kempis, as well as by surreptitious peeps into Sir Thomas Booby's copy of *Baker's Chronicle*. Adams " asked him if he did not extremely regret the want of a liberal education," with no suggestion that in Joseph's position his reading was all that was required.

The character of Parson Adams is well known to all of us, and one pauses to consider what was the education which helped to produce so lovable, so simple, so truly venerable a man. And it might be a blow to certain iconoclasts to find that he was " a master of the ancient and modern languages," but above all was Greek dear to his heart, and who could forget his love of Æsychlus. Surely the advocates of Greek have something to be said for them.

Mr. Alworthy, like Adams, had the greatest horror of public schools, and gave Tom Jones and Blifil a private education, with what ghastly results in both cases we know well, or, if we do not, Colonel Newcombe will be only too glad to tell us.

A private education proved much more successful in the case of Sir Charles Grandison. Richardson seems to have disapproved not only of schools, but of universities as well. He despises classical learning, and in the debate between Ancients and Moderns at Fernhurst he would have been on the same side as Ferrers. He holds up the Oxford product to ridicule in the person of Mr. Walden, a pedantic scholar to whom what he called the learned languages constituted the only education recognizable as such. It is Miss Harriet Byron who tells him " that neither a learned, nor what is called a fine, education, has any other value than as each tends to improve the morals of men and to make them wise and good." Mr. Walden maintains " that without the knowledge of the learned languages, a man cannot understand his own." Harriett, before the days of Farmer, had the courage to " oppose Shakespeare to this assertion."

Mr. Reeves reads Bishop Burnet to show that other subjects besides Latin contains much noble knowledge, and goes on, on the authority of Locke, to claim as good an education for a woman as for a man—in order that she may be the more agreeable and suitable companion for a man of sense and learning.

My Uncle Toby, in Sterne's *Tristram Shandy*, did not share the prejudices of Adams and Allworthy against public schools, for he sent Le Fever's son to one. He had the highest opinion of the value of a good education as a preparation for any career. Corporal Trim, he says, was the best scholar in his company, and for that reason very nearly got his sergeant's halberd. Mr. Shandy, Tristram's father, it need hardly be said, was an eminent educational theorist, and wrote a book, the *Tristra-pædia*, on the subject of his son's training. Fortunately, only the smallest part of that book is read aloud by its author, thanks to Sterne's habit of digression. After summarizing the common course of a boy's education:—"Five years with a bib under his chin. Four years in travelling from Christcross to Malachi. A year and a half in learning to write his own name. Seven long years and more tuptoing it at Greek and Latin. Four years at his probations and negations, the fine statue still lying in the middle of the marble block—and nothing done but his tools sharpened to hew it out. 'Tis a piteous delay," says Mr. Shandy—" I am convinced," he went on, " that there is a North-West passage to the intellectual world, and that the soul of man has shorter ways of going to work in furnishing itself with knowledge and instruction than we generally take with it. The whole entirely depends upon the auxiliary verbs, Mr. Yorick. Only Raymond Lullius and the elder Pelegrini understood this, and the last arrived to such perfection in the use of 'em with his topics, that in a few lessons he could teach a young gentleman to discourse with plausibility upon any subject, *pro* and *con*, and to say and write all that could be spoken or written concerning it without blotting a word, to the admiration of all who beheld him." What a truly Shandean ideal! If it is the ideal of anyone else, may I refer him to Chapter XLIII of Book V of *Tristram Shandy*, in the hope that he will understand it better than I do. " The force of this engine," said Mr. Shandy, " is incredible in opening a child's head." " 'Tis enough, Brother Shandy, cried my Uncle Toby, " to burst it into a thousand splinters."

Mr. Shandy's ideal schoolmaster, or rather tutor, is easier to grasp. He demands a man with no peculiarities of gesture, who shall " neither lisp or squint or wink, or talk loud, or look fierce or foolish, or bite his lips or grind his teeth, or speak through his nose. He shall neither walk fast or slow, or fold his arms, for that is laziness; or hang them down, for that is folly; or hide them in his pockets, for that is nonsense. He shall neither strike nor pinch nor tickle . . . or drum with his fingers or feet in company.

" I will have him," continues Mr. Shandy, " cheerful, faceté, jovial, at the same time prudent, attentive to business, vigilant, acute, argute, inventive, quick in resolving doubts and speculative questions; he shall be wise and judicious and learned." "And why not humble and moderate and gentle-tempered and good?" said Yorick. "And why not," cried my Uncle Toby, " free and generous and bountiful and brave?" " He shall, my dear Toby," replied my father. Is it to be wondered at that, in spite of Uncle Toby's recommendation of Le Fever's son, no tutor seems ever to have been found.

One word more and I have done with Sterne. One of the famous sentimental passages is full of significance for our present purpose. Uncle Toby has just released the fly that had been tormenting him, with a " Get thee gone, poor devil; get thee gone. Why should I hurt thee? This world is surely wide enough to hold both thee and me." " I was but ten years old when this happened," continued Tristram . . . " but the lesson of universal good will has never since worn out of my mind. And though I would not depreciate what the study of Literæ Humaniores at the University has done for me in that respect, or discredit the other helps of an expensive education bestowed upon me both at home and abroad since, yet I often think that I owe one-half of philanthropy to that one accidental impression."

And then comes the pointing finger of which Sterne is so fond, and it points to what I would say myself: " This is to serve for parents and guardians instead of a whole volume on the subject.''

We found that Richardson had ·something in common` with Mr. Alec Waugh; so also has Dr. Johnson. Imlac, the sage of *Rasselas*, was filled with wonder that in almost all countries the most ancient poets are considered as the best—and tried to learn from them; but soon found that no man was ever great by imitation. Imlac's education had really taught him something, though Samuel Butler might have jeered at him; for at school, when he found the delight of knowledge, and felt the pleasure of intelligence and the pride of invention, he began silently to despise riches. Few of us can honestly say as much. The most delightful scholar in the book, the great astronomer, had learnt even more. His immense learning had not blinded his eyes to the higher importance of doing good, and he says: " To man is *permitted* the contemplation of the skies, but the practice of virtue is commanded.'' Many readers are disappointed +o find he was mad. The astronomer was a philanthropist, in spite of his learning; the Princess Nekayah hoped to inculcate goodness through learning. She thought that of all sublunary things knowledge was the best; she desired first to learn all sciences, and then proposed to found a college of learned women, in which she would preside, that, by conversing with the old and educating the young, she might divide her time between the acquisition and communication of wisdom, and raise up for the next age models of prudence and patterns of piety. Nekayah occasionally strikes us as a fool, but we should do well to remember one point in her scheme—as the head of a college and one who had learned *all sciences*, she still proposed to continue to acquire wisdom by conversing with the old. Unfortunately her scheme was not carried out.

Rasselas is commonly compared with Voltaire's *Candide*, though the resemblance is not too apparent. We pass next to two novels bearing the impress of Rousseau's influence. Brooke's *Fool of Quality* is the story of Henry Clinton, younger son of the elderly Earl of Moreland, who is put out to nurse at a farm and allowed to run wild. At five years old he is introduced into his father's house, and shows a sublime contempt for fashionable society and any kind of display, and at the same time a passionate loyalty to his foster-mother delightful to meet with. He is touched by the spectacle of an old man weeping, and we soon find him adopted by this old man, an unknown uncle, who at once begins his education. The uncle, Mr. Fenton, as he calls himself, endeavoured to open his mind and cultivate his morals by 1,000 little fables (the story of the bold sparrows and the good robins, the fish ambitious of flying, and so forth). He never proposed any encouragement or reward to the heart of our hero, save that of the love and approbation of others. He is taught to despise fine clothes as Nessus shirts, to wait on the servants, to give away clothes to the deserving, and to relieve distress. In common with other wise men like Mr. Allworthy and Sir Austen Feverel, Mr. Fenton finds his nephew a thoroughly bad tutor—a pompous old humbug who revels in floggings—but, unlike Thwackum and Adrian Harley, he is soon exposed and dismissed, after a severe reprimand from Mr. Fenton, for using fear as his sole instrument with children, since it leads to lying, and even murder, and can never make a good subject, a good citizen, or a good soldier, or, best of all, a good Christian. On the other hand, Mr. Fenton hates a system of rewards—which rouses avarice, vanity, greed, and envy, when the child's aim should be emulation of what is excellent. His idea of the best way of rewarding merit is worth noting, though we could hardly apply it to modern children.

"Were tutors half as solicitous to make men of worth as to make men of letters, there are 100 pretty artifices, very obvious, to be contrived and practised for the purpose. They might institute caps of shame and wreaths of honour in their schools; they might have little medals, expressive of particular virtues, to be fixed on the breast of the achiever till forfeited by default, and on the report of any boy's having performed a signal action of good nature, friendship, gratitude, generosity, or honour, a place of eminence might be appointed for him to sit on while all the rest of the school should bow in deference as they passed. Such acts as these, I say, with that distinguishing affection and approbation which persons ought to show to children of merit, would soon make a new nation of infants, and, consequently, of men. Such tutors as Mr. Vindex make scoundrels—who impudently usurp the name of gentleman."

A new tutor, Clement, is found. Mr. Clement is not to push the boy into "learning of the languages beyond his own pleasure, neither to oppress or perplex his infant mind (the child is eight) with the deep or mysterious parts of our holy religion." The Law is to come first, the Gospel later. The tutor is further advised to give Henry, "by familiar and historical instances, an early impression of the shortness of life and of the nature of the world. Let him learn," says Mr. Fenton, "the difference between natural and imaginary wants, and to prefer manners and things of an intrinsic value to those valued by fashion. Show him also that the same toils and sufferings, the same poverty and pain, from which people now fly as they would from a plague, were once the desire of heroes and the fashion of nations." He is also to be taught the nature of the constitution of his own country, of true liberty, of the necessity of restraint from wrong-doing; and his education is not to be regarded as complete without " a knowledge of the world, of the views, pleasures, manners, bent, employments, and characters of mankind." Side by side with his moral and mental education, his physical training goes on, and he learns dancing, fencing, bruising, wrestling, and tripping.

We must not overlook the interesting fact that with the earl's son is educated, in precisely the same manner, a young vagabond, picked up by him and supposed to have sprung from the dregs of society.

It is difficult to convey the peculiarly exuberant tone of the book—the boisterously happy relations between guardian and child, the generosity and geniality which pervade so many of the episodes. There is no sign here of the repression which seems to have played so large a part in nineteenth-century education. Brooke has an outspoken horror of it, and gives a painful picture of its prominence in the ordinary education of the girl of the period. " The ordinary female infant," he says, " is instructed in more instances of self-denial than, if dictated by Christianity, would have sainted her for eternity. She is taught to suppress her natural feelings and inclinations, and to bridle the impulses of an affectionate and humble heart. She is taught to prize what she dislikes and to praise what she disapproves, to affect coldness and distance to inferiors whom she regarded, and to proportion her appearance of inclination and respect to the station of the party." No educational reformer dared to make a girl the central figure of his book. Her cause as yet was hopeless. But our next author was deeply interested in her development, and even practised experiments on female specimens.

Thomas Day and his ideals are so well known to educationists that I am probably presumptuous in bringing forward some of the ideas of *Sandford and Merton*. But I cannot very well leave out such a truly remarkable book. I should like to call it epoch-making, but I have no evidence that its revolutionary character was at all generally recognized or its methods adopted.

His, or rather Mr. Barlow's, definition of education as applied to animals arrests us first: "Whenever an animal is taught anything that is not natural to him, this is properly receiving an education." After describing the breaking-in of a horse, he says: "This may very properly be called the *education* of an animal, since by these means he is obliged to acquire habits which he would never have learned had he been left to himself." Of the education of human beings he speaks in the following optimistic fashion: "You see how little reason there is to despair of youth, even under the most disadvantageous circumstances. It has been justly observed that few know all they are capable of: the seeds of different qualities frequently lie concealed in the character, and only wait for an opportunity of exerting themselves; and it is the great business of education to apply such motives to the imagination as may stimulate it to laudable exertions. For thus the same activity of mind, the same impetuosity of temper, which by being improperly applied would form only a wild, ungovernable character, may produce the steadiest virtue and prove a blessing both to the individual and his country." This idea, thoroughly worked out, would fill my paper. Let us rather look into Mr. Barlow's methods. What strikes us first is his delightful custom of telling children, or letting them read, stories of an astounding improbability, with a wealth of interesting detail and a moral whose poetical justice rivals that of the Mikado. These are the stories which children really enjoy, and if children like your stories you can generally do what you like with them. Mr. Barlow has no time-table and no set lessons. One of his principal objects is to cure Tommy Merton of his absurd notions of his own importance as a "gentleman," and his method generally is to confute the child by a series of bewildering and rather unfair questions which eventually force him to contradict himself. I have no doubt this process has its modern name.

More interesting is his method of approaching the ordinary school subjects, and here, I believe, Day proves himself a modern of the moderns. Reading is made so thrilling that Tommy wants to learn. He is introduced to arithmetic by being asked to count grains of corn, and the power of calculation becomes at once a romance and a means of avoiding being cheated; the latter appeals considerably more to Tommy than the former, and he is eager to learn the new subject. Astronomy is begun in a similar natural and practical way, and Tommy is made to observe for himself the movements of the constellations. Leverage, magnetism, the growing and grinding of corn are approached equally gradually. The child's interest in a subject is awakened before its study is begun, so that he is always eager to learn. It must not be forgotten that when Mr. Barlow showed the boys a magic lantern it was moving pictures that he displayed, little knowing that he was the herald of education by the cinema.

Always the boys are *doing* things, and doing them for themselves, whether it is digging in the garden, planting fruit trees, or building a hut; and they are allowed to learn by their own mistakes and omissions (somewhat harshly sometimes, as when the hares strip the bark from the trees because they are left unprotected). Mr. Barlow even goes so far as to curb occasionally his natural love of telling stories, and makes Tommy find for himself the story of the siege of Syracuse, in Plutarch. Again, Tommy learns as much from Harry as from Mr. Barlow, not only reading, but such things as splitting huge roots by wedges and a hammer, and building a hut.

Mr. Barlow is not above the idea of vocational education. "Harry" (who is about seven years old) "being a farmer," says Mr. Barlow, "it is his business to study the different methods by which men find subsistence in all the different parts of the earth." We have all been bored by Mr. Barlow, but we might do well to remember the two lessons which above all he strives to inculcate—I mean fortitude, and a horror of cruelty in any form.

It was in girls' education that Day made his practical experiments, and he shows the most hearty contempt for the boarding-school miss of the day, who "plays most divinely on the pianoforte, talks French even better than she does English, and draws in the style of a master." Far otherwise did old Mr. Simmons bring up his niece, who—to prevent the fashionable "sickly delicacy"—"was accustomed from her earliest years to plunge into the cold bath at every season of the year, to rise by candlelight in winter, to ride a dozen miles upon a trotting horse, or to walk as many, even with the hazard of being splashed or of soiling her clothes." Besides this, "she was acquainted with all the best authors in our own language, nor was she ignorant of those in French, although she could not speak a word of the language. Her uncle had besides instructed her in several parts of knowledge which rarely fall to the lot of ladies, such as the established laws of nature and the rudiments of geometry. She was also thoroughly initiated in every sort of household employment, which is now exploded by ladies in every rank and station as mean and vulgar. As to music, though Miss Simmons had a very agreeable voice, she was entirely unacquainted with it. Her uncle used to say that human life is not long enough to throw away so much time upon the science of "*making a noise*." Nor would he permit her to learn French or any foreign language, "since women are not birds of passage." Foreign manners and foreign adventurers he considered equally undesirable, and he very properly said—and many excellent Englishmen have said the same—"When respectable foreigners choose to visit us, I see no reason why they should not take the trouble of learning the language of the country." Few people have been surprised to learn that Day's own experiments with girls' education were less successful than those of Miss Simmons' uncle.

Maria Edgeworth's father was the intimate friend of Day, and, like him, an educationist. In collaboration with her father, Miss Edgeworth wrote a book on "Practical Education." But, if you will grant that *The Parents' Assistant* is a novel, it is rather there that we shall look for her educational ideals. She realizes what an enormous part in education is played by a child's recreative reading, and boldly takes as her mooto for a work of fiction:

" 'Tis education forms the common mind—
Just as the twig is bent the tree's inclined."

In her preface she expounds her aims in some detail. But stories so exquisite as hers need no explanation. They as far surpass those of *Sandford and Merton* as greatest doth least. The charm of *Simple Susan, Lazy Laurence, The Orphans* cannot be conveyed to those who do not know them; but we may note for our instruction that we find, in most of these stories, groups or individuals sharply contrasted; the good are made really delightful, the bad credible (an uncommon thing); and the virtues of the good become really attractive. I believe for myself, as a child, this book wielded a less potent spell than *Sandford and Merton*, but it is infinitely more artistic. One story, *The Bracelets*, with its prize for the most amiable, made me thoroughly uncomfortable, as it might some grown-up readers. Perhaps the story which has had the most direct influence on children is " *Waste not, want not.*" " It would be curious to calculate," says Lady Ritchie, " how much good time has been sacrificed to saving worthless pieces of string in imitation of this thrifty but fascinating hero." This may make teachers despair, typical as it is of so much of the results of their work—the trivial makes a permanent impression, the important vanishes like the baseless fabric of a vision. But if—though no results may be visible—any of us can pretend to create an atmosphere at all resembling Miss Edgeworth's, then we need feel no regrets.

(To be Concluded.)

NORMAL PERFORMANCES OF TEACHERS.

By Professor J. A. GREEN.

WE have had in recent years long and painstaking investigation into the question of normal performances in arithmetic, &c., of school children of various ages, with results which promise to be of great practical value to teachers. Another question has often occurred to me as worth investigation, with particular reference to the whole problem of professional training, viz.: Whether or not it was possible to arrive at standards of teaching efficiency which might have some objective value.

The Board of Education requires its trainees to be classified into five groups at the end of their Training College Course. Obviously until some objective standards of measurement are obtained, these classes must be based upon impressions, and impressions are apt to vary with the individual upon whom they are made. Of course, a certain average of impression is sought in various ways before so important a decision is reached, but the fact remains that a student classed as A in one college might be a C in another, and vice-versa. His Majesty's Inspectors come along and do what they can to set this straight, but their impressions are, at any rate, relatively momentary, though they may bring a wider experience of the actual school world to bear upon the problem. The whole device is concerned with averaging up impressions, and the final decision is left to a person whose disinterestedness and special experience may or may not be an effective counterweight to the slightness of his acquaintance with the particular candidates whose performance determines his judgment.

As affording some clue to the state of our own minds—I write of those concerned with the training of teachers—I ventured, with some trepidation, to put certain questions to those attending a meeting of the Northern Branch of the Training College Association. My colleagues were extremely kind, and wrote answers to the questions quite independently, though some doubts were expressed as to the validity of the whole inquiry. Without further parley, and especially without any apology for the actual questions, which obviously vary greatly in value and importance, I give them as they stood:

(1) Given an ordinary class of seven-year-olds beginning subtraction, what is a reasonable time in which the class may be expected to master the operation—to the normal level of accuracy? Class to have one lesson a day of thirty minutes. Answer in days.

(2) Given two lessons a week of forty minutes duration, within what time should a thirteen-year-old class be reasonably familiar with the content and movement in a play of Shakespeare's? (Say *Julius Cæsar*.)

(3) A Class is beginning Simple Interest, within what time should they be able to tackle these three questions effectively? (One lesson a day of 40 minutes duration.)

What will £50 amount to in three years at 5 per cent interest, being paid half-yearly?

If the interest on £250 for five years is £75, what was the rate per cent?

I put no money in the bank for a year, but on receiving my pass-book I found myself credited with £4 2s. 6d. interest for that year. How much money had been lying there? (Interest at 7½ per cent.)

(4) How many lines (approximately) will a good English teacher have induced his class of fourteen-year-olds to learn by heart in a term?

(5) A teacher gives a lesson on a poem (say to Standard V). What proportion of the class ought, after a month's interval, to be able to recognize quotations from it amongst a mixed group of citations from that and other sources?

(6) A teacher gives a lesson on the Nile, with a given set of illustrations. Three months afterwards the pictures are shown to the children. How many should be recognized, and by what proportion of the pupils?

(7) How many lessons and how much practice is necessary to make a class reach 80 per cent of efficiency in handling Algebraic indices?

(8) After a single lesson on the barometer to Standard VI, what proportion of the pupils may be expected to write a clear answer to the question why the mercury does not reach the top of the tube?

The answers received to the questions are given in the table below. I give also, for what they are worth, the averages and the Mean Deviation (kindly worked out for me by my colleague, Miss E. M. King).

Teachers, of course, vary in their output, as bricklayers do, if one may be allowed to use what is admittedly a very misleading analogy. One man will get a class over Indices in a fortnight; another will take three months. What is reasonable in this regard, and what sort of thing will an A man do as against his less accomplished colleague? But a qualification seems necessary. The A man may get his high mark for qualities of mind and character which more than make amends for the slow rather than rapid movement of his class. The " nigger-driver " whose whole energies are turned to " output " may do actual harm to the finer side of his pupils. This is true enough. Yet there does remain a teaching quality of great importance which has its counterpart in his influence upon his pupils and which in some directions may be measurable.

For purposes of training, it would be a great help if we had a sort of standard performance for our students to work up to in one direction or another. Failing that, we must continue in that welter of opinion which talks of "good," "successful," "interesting," "valuable" lessons, and leaves the thoughtful student still wondering how the line is drawn between what is called a complete success, a partial success, and a failure.

I hope some of my colleagues will contribute to the solution of this problem, which seems to me of considerable practical importance. The above results illustrate very well the complete absence of anything even approaching objectivity in our judgments when faced with these particular problems. That may be due, of course, to the bad choice of the questions or to different interpretations of them, or to a fundamental falsity in the inquiry. On the first point, I may say they were very

	1	2	3	4	5	6		7	8
	Number of lessons				%	%	%		%
1	15	18	10	200	75	75	66	—	—
2	20	16	20	·190	40	80	80	—	2
3	—	8	—	200	60	60	60	—	60
4	15	12	12	120	50	90	60	6	60
5	10	8	15	—	60	100	80	6	10
6	—	20	40	—	—	—	—	20	50
7	15	8	20	60	85	100	100	—	50
8	10	24	5	120	75	95	—	—	60
9	8	8	10	150	35	50	50	—	30
10	50	10	4	200	30	50	80	—	75
11	12	16	20	200	30	50	50	30	3
12	5	12	15	50	25	60	75	—	10
13	—	26	—	250	75	100	100	—	100
14	5	8	7	60	60	100	50	—	—
15	6	—	4	200	50	75	55	2	80
16	—	24	—	100	25	100	90	—	60
17	10	30	20	—	50	75	50	—	60
18	—	16	—	300	10	66	75	—	5
19	5	12	—	—	20	75	80	—	—
20	—	10	—	—	—	80	80	—	—
21	· 6	10	12	100	60	100	50	—	80
22	7	12	15	200	75	100	75	—	—
23	6	24	10	100	10	50	50	—	—
Total	205	332	259	2800	1000	1731	1456	64	795
Average	12	15	14	156	48	79	69	13	47
Mean Deiration to nearest integer.	7	4	6	60	19	16	15	10	26

hastily drawn up rather to illustrate a state of mind than to represent an ordered expression of it. They are, nevertheless, printed as given, in the hope of stimulating critical and constructive thought. On the second point, I should say that I endeavoured to forestall uncertainties of interpretation, by a short preliminary statement which it is not possible here to reproduce. The last point is perhaps the most serious. Is it right ever to look at the teacher as in sort a producer? May we legitimately expect him to deliver his tale of bricks? Can one teacher properly be compared with another from such a point of view without creating a situation of very grave danger? Are we, in fact, reviving a controversy which ended with the inglorious death of payment by results?

In practice, I fancy, the tale of bricks is exacted by head masters from their staffs when they (alone or in consultation) draw up a scheme of work. Possibly a miscellaneous group of head masters would answer these same questions with much greater precision than we did in our meeting, and it is rather from the point of view of finding out what is a fair expectation in normal circumstances that the whole problem interests me.

DEFINITENESS—A SUGGESTION.

By GERALDINE E. HODGSON, Litt.D.

THE following reflections refer only to "two-year" students in Elementary Training Colleges, and to these only in the matter of the Board of Education's Syllabus for the General Course on Principles of Teaching. It will surely be widely admitted that the majority of just eligible candidates, who have passed from the Elementary to Council Secondary Schools, having there scraped through their qualifying examination for a Training College, are very imperfectly equipped as to knowledge, and, which is more important, have very little skill in handling books or in working by themselves.

The year spent as student-teachers before they enter college—the year, i.e., from seventeen to eighteen—as a rule, is *par excellence* the one in which a good secondary school could, were it allowed to do so, train them in those habits and methods of a student without which no one of us can hope to teach excellently. True, there are suggestions for abolishing this student-teachership, but it obtains now; and it is no exaggeration to say that, from the point of view of the future teacher, the majority of two-years entrants are ignorant of matter and clumsy in means.

Every course in the Syllabus—English, History, Science, &c.— provides a nucleus of definite material, round which the lecturer works with his or her students. The General Course on Teaching stands alone in being vague, fluid, indefinite. No doubt, there are current text-books which may serve as a basis for those paragraphs in the syllabus which can be described, in big words for less things, as psychological and ethical; but such books, it may be said respectfully, are not the finest extant works on Education.

A later paragraph of the Syllabus, which runs: "The choice of the curriculum, its contents, suitability, and varieties, the connexion and development of subjects," seems as if it might afford scope for the use of some of the writings of the world's greater Educators. No one can have less regard than the present writer for what is miscalled "History of Education," crammed up out of Compayré, Paul Monro, and the rest: Books about Books are not for the learner, but for the learned, who can treat them as criticism, good or bad, and perhaps get something out of them. The learner should have the original books; there are such, and they are not impossibly hard either to obtain or to read.

Classic works on Education would not only open up to young students a new world of suggestion, stimulus, and idea, but they would supply just that core of definiteness which seems so sadly to seek in the Board's present recommendations as to Principles of Teaching, and, last not least, they would afford the much-needed starting-points of discussion.

It is true that no one can at present hinder any enthusiastic lecturer from presenting such books to the class; but a definite intimation in the

Syllabus that in such and such books precisely what is needed for a reasonable knowledge of human experiment and progress in Education may be found, would be suggestive to some and encouraging to other lecturers. As a minor consideration, it might stimulate the activities of those too numerous students who refuse interest to matters not included in the Syllabus.

As to the philosophical grounds for this proposal, one need not surely labour the argument that the present is the outcome of the past, and that Nature never makes a jump. If we are going to be wise for the future, and effective in the present, we can scarcely afford to disdain all knowledge of past aspiration and achievement.

Every competent Lecturer could, of course, make his own list. I am not proposing that many books should be forced, and all at once, on immature students, but rather that a few, of singular and diverse merit, should be brought to their notice. Only those which have been written in or translated into English would serve the purpose. In order to give point and substance to this suggestion, I append a representative list. Perhaps the most notable omission is Rousseau's *Emile* which, could anyone be induced to make a judiciously compressed selection, might well be added :

TITLE	AUTHOR	DATE
The Republic ... (Ll. Davies and Vaughan)	Plato	420–328 B.C.
Roman Education[1]	Wilkins	C.U.P. 1905
De Ingenuis Moribus... (Woodward)	Peter Paul Vergerius	1392
De Ratione Studii (Woodward)	Erasmus	1511
The Boke of the Governour ... (Everyman)	Sir T. Elyot	1531
De Tradendis Disciplinis (Foster Watson)	Vives	1531
The Positions (Selections) (Quick)	Mulcaster	1581
The Teacher's Montaigne (Hodgson)	Michel de Montaigne	1588
Letter on Education ... (Temple Classics)	Milton	1644
Concerning Education (C.U.P.)	John Locke	1692(3)
Conduct of the Understanding (C.U.P.)	—	pub. posthumously
Letters and Lectures ... (Felkins')	Herbart	1835
Address to Students of S. Andrews...	J. S. Mill	1867

[1] There being no convenient original Text for the Roman Period, Professor Wilkins' Book is included as a makeshift

THE SCHOOL AND THE COMMUNITY SPIRIT. IV.

THE appearance of Dr. Nunn's book[1] offers a welcome text for the fourth of these informal discussions on a topic of steadily growing importance, for although written avowedly as a plea for the fuller recognition of the individual in our educational practice, it is in effect penetrated through and through by the modern community spirit; and the more concrete his chapters become, the more practical the issues which the author discusses or describes, the more clearly does the social character of the ideal educative process stand out. The book's chief message, if we rightly interpret it, presents a severe indictment of current educational practice. But although Professor Nunn has in mind an ideal school in an ideal society, he has happily found signs of the practical striving after new ideals in the actual world of English schools to lead him to think the time was ripe for a systematic exposition of the principles behind the reform of school practice which is so skilfully and attractively adumbrated in this volume.

Whilst accepting what seems to be the real teaching of the book, it is not easy to reconcile oneself completely to some of its fundamental doctrines. They seem at least to call for discussion. To begin with, What is the key-note of the whole volume? " Freedom to conduct life's adventure in one's own way and to make the best one can of it is the one universal idea sanctioned by nature and approved by reason." This is an " indefeasible right " of the individual. The compelling force of the " social bonds woven inextricably into the texture of man's being," and the full significance thereof, are frankly admitted, and Dr. Nunn has made a brilliant, if not completely satisfying, attempt to build upon this concept of freedom under compelling restraints, an arresting theory of education.

Of course, there is nothing inherently absurd in the concept itself. No freedom is absolute, but man's fetters are often so subtle that their existence is unsuspected. Who could *feel* freer than the despot of the ancient world? Yet his freedom was limited by custom, which controlled the movements of his mind in a way no less exacting than the force of gravity controlled the movements of his body. The difficulty does not lie here, however, but in the assertion of a right, belonging to the individual as such, one that is indefeasible, " sanctioned by nature and approved by reason." May we not also wonder whether the individual who is free to make the best of his life is by an " indefeasible right " free to make the worst of it? Is there possibly here a confusion between what is claimed as a " right " on the one hand, and what is regarded as a duty on the other? Furthermore, is there a " right " to decline to pursue the adventure altogether? So clear a thinker as Dr. Nunn cannot be lightly charged with confusion of thought, yet we confess that he has left us in some degree of uncertainty. It is important to be clear about fundamental conceptions, and particularly about great abstract ideas like " rights," "nature," and " reason." As they stand, Dr. Nunn's sentences recall the philosophical methods of the Enlightenment, when " reason " and " nature " were invoked to prove that society originated in a social contract. [2] It was the same convenient abstractions which gave rise to that " nonsense upon stilts," as Bentham savagely called the doctrine of Natural Rights, which we connect especially with the French Revolution—a doctrine which implies that babies come into the world "with little packets of properties called ' Rights,' ", which for that reason are their inalienable and indefeasible possessions. Liberty was one of those rights. Now, whatever we may think about an adult's right to freedom, we shall not be likely to regard it as the " right " of an infant-in-arms. And the adult himself is denied his freedom if he uses it in a fashion whch society condemns.

The use of the word "nature" in such a context is likely to mislead, even though Dr. Nunn, in a succeeding chapter, carefully explains the sense in which he uses the word., In order to establish the indefeasible right of the individual in human society, let us observe the rôle of individuality amongst animals in general. In a characteristically clear and interesting description of recent biological investigations into the behaviour of lowly animal organisms, he emphasizes the rôle of individuality at various vital levels. The general argument reminds one of Aristotle's famous defence of slavery. "There is a slave or slavery by law as well as by nature." "The male is by nature superior, and the female inferior; the former rules and the other is ruled." "Some are, from the hour of their birth, marked out for subjection; others for rule."[1] In practice, of course, some slaves ought to be free men, and vice versa. That, however, is contrary to nature, the truth of whose teachings is nevertheless easy to see if you look at men as they really are and ignore the accidents of circumstance. It is not difficult by means of an array of indisputable facts to fortify any particular concept we hold to be true "by nature." But is not this the old *a priori* road which science has long since given up? Had not Aristotle a better case for his view that the slavery of some was "according to nature," than Professor Nunn, who would apparently establish (or at least fortify the doctrine of) an indefeasible right in man, by finding it, or something like it, in the behaviour of protozoa? "A lively sense of solidarity in nature," if it is to be used as a ground for accepting a man's inalienable right "to pursue life's adventure in his own way;" must also be accepted as a ground of defence for the *laisses-faire* of individualism in its most extreme form.

As we are not convinced by this particular method of establishing "individuality" or individual liberty, as an indefeasible right in man, we may also note that the form of argument seems to carry us further than Professor Nunn would probably go. He finds this freedom to be "the condition, if not the source, of all the higher goods. Apart from it duty has no meaning, self-sacrifice no value, authority no sanction." He shows the important part individuality—that freedom to conduct life in one's own way—plays in the behaviour of the stentor. Why, then, has research not revealed in its case what must be a stentorian sense of duty and capacity for self-sacrifice? Is it not because these qualities have their origin and their condition in a community and in individuals as such at all?

Moreover, if it is a good thing that individuals should pursue life's adventure in their own way, it is so, we venture to think, because it is socially advantageous, and not because of any indefeasible right in the individual as such. Individual and society are, of course, correlative terms. Each determines the other. So far as we can understand the psychology of the honey bee, his social organization is so rigid that

[1] V Aristotle, "Politics," Bk. I, cc. 5 and 6.

" individual freedom " would be a source of weakness, and the physiological framework of the bee makes " freedom " as it is understood in a Western community of men, impossible. Similarly, in many primitive human communities, the freedom desirable and necessary in our own people would be destructive of the society. What would an indefeasible right to pursue life's adventure in his own way mean even now to a high-caste Hindu?

" Every animal," says Dr. Nunn, " so long as it is alive, continues to affirm and assert itself over against the world of which, from another point of view, it is merely a part. Even the least ' assertive ' of us must recognize that this attitude belongs to every moment of our conscious lives. In every act we say to our world, openly or explicitly, ' I am here and to be reckoned with ; I go a way, that is, so far as may be, my own way, and not merely yours.' " To accept this as a statement of fact, however, does not seem to prove the case for an " indefeasible right." The argument surely falls, as it were, by its own weight. It proves too much, for one of two things seems to follow. Either the " indefeasible right " belongs as much to the lower animals as it does to man, and therefore most men live by a brutal disregard of those rights, or the lower animals' assertiveness is an impertinence, an amiable delusion, and man's self-conscious experience is a proof of indefeasible right.

So we are brought to the real crux of the situation. If we claim indefeasible rights to individual men and women, can we refuse them to any sentient being? Or are we to draw distinctions between the slug which we remorselessly doom to destruction when we catch him asserting himself against so unimportant a bit of our world as a seedling lettuce, on the one hand, and our neighbour's cat caught in the act of invading our larder, on the other? Do we refrain from destroying the cat because of its inherent right to pursue life's adventure in its own way—a right we refuse to the slug? Do we base the differences in our behaviour upon a recognition of higher and lower levels of psychical activity? If so, why do we praise pussy as a good mouser and beat her when she kills our pet canary?

It is hardly necessary to remind our readers that we are dealing only with Professor Nunn's fundamental doctrine. We believe that to be mistaken, and, in fact, to be almost, if not altogether, lost sight of by Dr. Nunn himself in the main treatment of his subject. He has given an altogether admirable exposition of what education in a modern society should be and do, and criticism of his fundamentals under these circumstances may well be thought superfluous. Yet the importance and spirit of the book is such that no one is likely to welcome criticism more than its writer. The book is so good that it demands a close, even a vigorous, examination of its bases.

As against the idea of indefeasible right alleged to belong " by nature " to each of us, it seems more reasonable to hold that there are no rights apart from society ; that all rights are socially derived ; that if we have rights it is because we belong to a society, and the nature of those rights must be (and are in fact) determined by the society to which we belong. Rights and duties are, of course, correlative terms. A right is a claim against somebody else whose duty it is to accede to that claim. It implies a society, and can only be claimed by members of a society, who have duties as well as rights. The stentor, the slug, the flea, have no rights as against man, and cruelty to animals is an offence against humanity, not against the rights of the animals concerned.[1] Even the so-called rights of children rest on a fiction which assigns to them what really belongs to the society of which they will presently receive their freedom.

It seems, in fact, sounder to reverse the whole doctrine and to say that primarily a society has rights as against the individual and the individual has duties to the society, and that, in the last resort, the society has no duties to the individual which are not dictated by its own interests, nor has the individual in himself any rights against society. Societies, of course, vary in type, and it is quite possible for an individual born in a particular society to appeal against its claims to a higher social order which he desires or which he may vaguely call humanity. He may even sacrifice his life to his doctrines, but there are few bad causes which cannot claim their martyrs. The devil has many a powerful advocate.

Even the political theory of the anarchist rests upon a belief in the fundamentally social nature of man. The Hegelian doctrine and its Prussian development went woefully wrong because it identified society and the State. The modern Syndicalist who would destroy the State, of course, conceives a new social order, and Mr. G. H. D. Cole, whose attacks upon the modern State command our attention, only makes his attacks because he believes it to be an obstruction in the way of social development. Professor Nunn's book is too short for him to have dealt clearly with this common confusion, and in one passage he seems, quite unintentionally, to give countenance to a view which looks upon the State as only a preciser way of speaking of society. Certain forms of Socialism are based upon this false identification, and they would clearly substitute one tyranny for another. We shall not, if we keep the distinction in mind, confuse education for citizenship with education for society. The " citizen " is apt to take his State for granted, and the State, in its zeal for its own preservation or aggrandisement, is apt to think of men and women as born to its service. In such a circle of thought, we may be excused for looking askance at the State and for seeing it as a Leviathan in the path of progress.

Although Professor Nunn's book is an eloquent plea for the fuller recognition of the individual in the educative process, it is only fair to remind the reader that he recognizes absolutely that the individual can only fulfil himself by accepting and working for his society, yet it seems to us a mistake to base a claim for fuller recognition on the ground of a natural right inherent in that will to live which is common to all sentient beings. The position outlined in the first chapter is, however, so modified by extremely important qualifications that it would have been difficult to avoid a feeling of having attached too much importance to a phrase or two, of having, in fact, wrested them out of a context so weighted with the social idea as to take all serious meaning from them. But we think too highly of the writer to believe that he would use any phrase lightly, and that when he speaks of an indefeasible right as applying to an individual as such, he is consciously challenging an opposite view.

The general position is more fully expounded in Chapters II to V, which deal respectively with The Will to Live (Horme), The Living Past (Mneme), and The Relations between Horme and Mneme. We propose to examine them, in order to get more light upon what is an

---

1 The whole doctrine of Natural Rights has been most exhaustively treated by the late Professor Ritchie, to whose book " Natural Rights " (Allen & Unwin) readers are referred as the chief source of this argument.

important and interesting problem.. It is a great convenience to bring under one concept (Horme) all purposive and purposeful processes, conscious and unconscious, which enter into vital activity. All acts of will, for example, are hormistic processes in which consciousness is at its highest level. All reflex actions, all that goes on in the dark caverns of the unconscious, the operative forces behind our dreams—whatever a sentient being does as the outcome of its will to live—are thus brought into single scheme. Similarly, all the phenomena of memory, whether conscious or unconscious, are covered by the term Mneme. Attitudes of mind unconsciously acquired from parents, dexterities like hand-writing painfully mastered at various times in my life, my habits—everything I have " forgotten " and all I can consciously recall—belong to my Mnemic self. In instinctive and reflex activity there is at once the hormic and the mnemic element—mnemic because the activity is due to racial memory embodied in specialized nervous organization, hormic because the nervous mechanism is as it were set in motion by a vital impulse. This relationship is typical of all levels of behaviour. Only in thought can we separate Horme and Mneme—the struggle to maintain life and even to enlarge its bounds, and the use we make of the stored-up experience of the past.

In the light of these explanations, we may inquire what further light they throw upon the problem of inherent rights.

"A child is in literal truth the heir of all the ages; *he carries his inheritance, living in his organism*, and his individuality is what he ultimately makes of it." Is this quite acceptable as it stands? We refer especially to the sentence here printed in italics. We might perhaps assert it of a newly-hatched bee, though even the bee is born into an " institutional " society which may be, in part, extra-organic. We may reject the organic view of society itself, but we must recognize the great importance of the fact that man has, as it were, unconsciously worked out a means of extra-organic development so perfect in its form as to outweigh in importance, perhaps even entirely to take the place of, further development within the organism itself. Here, surely, we have a " living past " of far greater significance than the recapitulatory tendencies, real or fanciful, which we may observe in the spontaneous activities of children. Does not the projection of his " mneme " into this external form make a great difference between the " mechanism of knowledge " and " action " in the higher animals and in man? We cannot suppose that this " device of man " has not been accompanied by inner hormic tendencies which give a special character to his engram complexes (inherited and acquired) corresponding to the type of universe he has made. This " living-past " is, of course, a co-operative product. Man owes his supreme position to its existence. He is, in other words, " by nature " socially constructed, and, to paraphrase Aristotle, society is prior to the individual. Horme and Mneme alike are in character social, and the education of the individual consists in helping him to give specific form to the fundamental " urge " to achieve himself by serving his kind, in putting at his service the accumulated experience of the past in the co-operative endeavour of the present.

If Dr. Nunn has not, in his first chapters, done full justice to the social horme which is deeply embedded in our common human nature, he more than makes up for that in his subsequent discussion of educational practice. He begins this part of his book by a chapter which in effect concerns the way in which the " social disposition " is awakened and given definite form. Very young children are not conspicuously social in their activities. They are little egocentrics, and if we seek " recapitulatory " explanation, may this not be reminiscent of a far-off ancestry in which the advantages of social life had not yet been '' discovered ''? May we not compare this non-social, even anti-social component which is presently to be overlaid by the unfolding of the more recently acquired social components in the human mind with the distinction between protopathic and epicritic sensitivity which we owe to Dr. Head's researches? In any case, the egocentricity of the little child quickly succumbs to the " routine and ritual " of the social world in which he finds himself. He takes to both much as the duckling takes to water. Even his play comes soon to demand co-operation, and co-operation demands order and rule.

These illuminating chapters on Routine and Ritual, Play, and the Play Way in Education are altogether admirable, and the recognition of the social aim of education could hardly be more emphatic. The fact is, of course, that when we set out to leave a child (or an adult, for that matter) to pursue life's adventure in his own way, we insist upon the adventure being social in kind. An adventure which denies social obligation altogether would land the adventurer into a hermitage, a prison, or a lunatic asylum. We essay to give our pupil command of social routine, of social instruments, and of organized social experience, and we encourage him to make original use of them, so long, and so long only, as he plays the game. We may and should do more than that. An original mind may believe that he could make a " better show " if the rules of the game were altered, and that the changes he calls for would be a common advantage. The burden of proof and persuasion lies with him, but a society which refuses to hear its prophets has lost the principle of growth. False prophets, however, abound, and is it not better that a true prophet or two should be sacrificed than that society itself should be destroyed by an over-readiness to lend a credulous ear to the disgruntled?

Vigorous championship of the individual seems to us to rest its claims more soundly upon the needs of society itself than upon any rights which belong to the individual as such. Indeed, it is not " individualism " which inspires Dr. Nunn, but the ideal of a higher social order, in and through which a higher type of individual may develop, for we may grant at once the position that a society is to be esteemed not by the complexity and completeness of its organization, but by the character of its members. Happily our own State is the most adaptable instrument of government any society has yet devised. The call is for *socii* equal to the varied responsibilities of the peculiar citizenship it confers upon them, and it is the schoolmaster's job to produce them, or at least to co-operate with other agencies in their production.

We can hardly be wrong in believing that this is Professor Nunn's conception of the function of the school, though he will have no truck with doctrines which deprive man of his dignity as master of his own fate and captain of his own soul. Henley's ringing phrase finds an echo in every Western heart, but for the majority of the human race they are either untrue or blasphemous or meaningless. Why? Because they are " members one of another " in a sense altogether foreign to the Western mind. " The society is prior to the individual." It is a commonplace of psychology that the " self " is socially determined. What, then, do we mean by speaking of man as self-determined?

(To be Continued.)

REVIEWS.

Education, its Data and First Principles. By Professor T. P. Nunn. (vii + 244 pp.) E. Arnold. (Modern Educator's Library.)

THE appearance of Prof. Nunn's book is a real event in the history of English educational thought. It is in effect a new synthesis of current philosophical, psychological, and biological conceptions formed to elucidate the nature and problem of education. As such it illustrates at once the difficulty of the subject and the nature of the equipment a man must have who ventures to deal with it in this large way. So far as I know, the book has no parallel, and certainly no equal. The writer's mastery over current philosophical opinion, his penetrating grasp of the significance of the newer psychology, the range of his acquaintance with recent and relevant physiological and biological research, and his capacity for bringing this knowledge to bear upon the exposition of his educational doctrine could hardly be surpassed. Not less important, though perhaps hardly so uncommon, is his intimate acquaintance with modern educational experiment. His services to practical methodology, particularly in the sphere of mathematics, are well known to schoolmasters. It is a notable gain that one who is himself a great practitioner should have found time and energy to lay bare his pedagogical soul in so thorough a fashion. The result is a book which no "advanced" student of education and no well-informed schoolmaster can afford to neglect; a book, moreover, which will give the academic study of educational theory the centre which it has long needed. As such it must in its turn produce a profound effect upon educational practice.

A book of this quality is bound to challenge criticism, particularly, perhaps, in relation to its fundamental doctrine—the indefeasible right of the individual to conduct his own life in his own way and to make the best he can of it. The question is more fully discussed elsewhere in this issue of the Journal (v. Article on "The School and the Community Spirit"). After all, practice may be right, and its nationalization may be wrong. There can hardly be any question as to the practical "reforms" so brilliantly surveyed in this book; whether the individual has any rights in himself even to be educated at all is a question which the curious may follow further in the article already referred to. J. A. G.

The Groundwork of Teaching. Edited by A. Mackie. (167 pp.) Teachers' College Press, Sydney, N.S.W.

THERE is probably no "liver" school of pedagogy in the British Empire than that of Teachers' College, Sydney. During the last ten years it has produced a long series of monographs on theoretical and practical problems which must have been a great source of inspiration to the teachers of Australia, and this volume on the Groundwork of Teaching is a further instance of its determination to do its own professional thinking and no longer to be content for the profession in Australia to rank as mere imitators of the Mother Country and America. The Head of the School, Principal Mackie, is the editor of this collection of ten separate essays, which cover the whole field of school life and organization in its broader aspects, and he is himself responsible for two of them—The Aims of Schooling and The General Nature of Teaching. Other essays deal with the School System, School Occupations, The Teaching Process, Testing Results, Community Life, &c. They are written by various members of the College Staff and designed especially for students in training.

It is impossible to give the volume the notice which it deserves, alike for the clearness and vigour of the writing and for the enterprise it represents. We may, however, offer it a warm welcome as, what it well may be, a forerunner of the time when first-rate educational books from Australia will be at least as numerous as we now receive from the United States. The relative freedom from tradition which belongs to new countries makes them a splendid field for educational experiment, and we hope that bold and fresh experimentation may find clear expression in the coming publications of this admirable School of Pedagogy.

Needlework Teaching in the Elementary School. By Therise La Chard, Lecturer at Stockwell Training College. Published by Heinemann.

THIS is a helpful book, because of its common-sense and idealistic treatment of needlework. Miss la Chard always has the child worker before her, and the first question is not " What is the traditional or technical way of dealing with this needlework problem? " but " What lies within the scope of this little girl and her limited surroundings? "

The fetish whose worship in school still prevents needlework from becoming the joyous, sane craft it should be, is vigorously attacked and demolished, and in its stead we see ideals of common-sense, intelligent work, set in the ordinary busy life of to-day. ." There is no educational value in darning for half an hour what you can stick on in half a minute "; it is folly to spend time in drafting patterns when good ones can be bought at the nearest paper shop; it is bad to make ugly, dull things under the name of " Thrift Garments "; the constructive ideas are, among other matters, concerned with the advantages of sectional work, the recognition of the rhythmic quality of some stitches, the appeal of colour, the delight in making small clothes. When teachers carry out their teaching of needlework on the lines suggested here, we shall have the girls carrying their pleasure and power out of their school life into the larger world outside.

The Child under Eight. By E. R. Murray and H. Brown-Smith. Published by Messrs. Arnold & Son.

THIS book, published under the editorship of Professor A. A. Cock, not only presents principles and methods underlying the modern teaching of young children, but gives some of the reconstructive ideals which have not yet had time to materialize. " The teacher of to-day says ' I must choose furniture and requisition apparatus.' The teacher of to-morrow will say to her children " I will bring the world into the school for you to learn.' The Local Education Authority of to-day says ' We must build a school for instruction.' The Local Education Authority of to-morrow will say ' We must make a miniature world for our children.'" And it is in the making of this miniature world that the joint authors are concerned. We see the playing, talking, busy child in a world in which he gains just those experiences which will help him to grow joyously and freely.

Mr. Clutton Brock sets us trying to formulate the aim which inspires our work with children, and here we find the manifold ones as widely apart as Frederick Froebel to H. G. Wells focussed and unified. All teachers of young children, as well as their parents, should be interested in this comprehensive study on the education of the child under eight.

Elements of Vector Algebra. L. Silberstein. Longmans, Green & Co., 5/- net.

THIS book consists of a short synopsis of the elements of Vector Algebra, and should prove exceedingly useful as an introduction to a subject which has not hitherto received the attention that it deserves. The results given are, for simplicity, based on Euclidean geometry, and the book is intended only to indicate the main lines on which the subject is developed. The author has recognized the importance of making clear to a beginner the new ideas involved in the Scalar and the Vector products, and has given a very lucid exposition of them. A most important paragraph is devoted to the Linear Vector Operator, which has so many applications in geometry and physics.

A sense of incompleteness is given to the book by the inclusion of a paragraph on Differentiation of Vectors. This might have been amplified, although, as the author states, it does not belong properly to the subject of Vector Algebra.

This introduction to the subject is short, but it contains much valuable matter, and will be of advantage only to those who intend to study the subject further.

The Child Vision: Being a Study in Mental Development and Expression. By Dorothy T. Owen, with an Introduction by Professor R. L. Archer.

(xvi + 180 pp.) Longmans, Green & Co. (for the Manchester University Press). 6/6 net.

THIS first-rate original work should be in the hands of every teacher of English. There is no other book quite so informing and suggestive, and that because the author has consistently kept to the notion that all composition worth the name must be self-revealing. Even description should present a personal impression, unless it is meant to be technical and scientific. The problem of submitting one's mind, as it were, to a subject and developing a clear attitude towards it is the central one for good writing at any stage. The author shows us how even young children may be brought to interest themselves in their own imagery and in the art of reproducing it in words. She takes us to the heart of the situation, and under her skilful, inspiring, and understanding treatment the composition lesson—usually a dull, prosy, and purposeless exercise—becomes a living and enjoyable activity. Space does not allow us to say more. The book is as fresh and stimulating as most books of the kind are jejune and doctrinaire.

Moral and Religious Education. By Sophie Bryant, D.Sc., D.Litt. Modern Educator's Library. Edward Arnold. 6/ net.

THIS should make quite a useful addition to the Modern Educator's Library series. The whole book is well arranged and in outlook is modern. We would recommend readers to start at Book II (" The Moral Ideal "), to follow on with Books III and IV and then to finish by reading Book I (" Self-Liberation by Self-Realization "). This (" The Religious Ideal " and " The Reasoned Presentment of Religious Truths "), first part, although giving the key-note to the rest of the book, is different in style, content, and quality.

The last three books are written in a straightforward, fresh style. They come down to actual practice, and contain much very valuable help to parents and teachers. Apart from numerous references and outlines of schemes in the body of the book, there is a well-selected Bibliography which adds to the value of the book from a teacher's or parent's point of view.

An Introduction to Sociology. By Professor J. J. Findlay. (xi + 304 pp.) Manchester University Press and Messrs. Longmans, Green & Co. 6/- net.

THE book is written primarily for Social Workers and General Readers. It thus escapes many of the vices of the text book, which too frequently sacrifices interest and breadth of view to the necessities of logical presentation. Professor Findlay rarely fails to be both interesting and stimulating, and his present survey of social theory is both, chiefly, perhaps, because he is not content to remain in the upper air of philosophy. He has a keen sense of the things that are happening, a lively appreciation of actual tendencies of which he makes enlightening use. In the conflict of opinion which is at present almost overwhelming, those interested will find much sound and clear guidance in a book so valuable that we could wish it read by all teachers, and particularly by those who work in Secondary and Continuation Schools.

The Universities and the Training of Teachers. By F. J. R. Hendy, M.A. (28 pp.) Clarendon Press. 1/6 net.

THIS inaugural lecture is an admirable plea for more generous treatment of the whole problem at the hands of the University of Oxford. It is probably true to say that Oxford has never understood what we mean by the training of teachers. It has not yet been convinced that training of any sort is necessary. We are glad to think the cause is so well represented by Mr. Hendy, whose lecture surveys the whole field of University life and work in relation to the needs of the schools with great skill and insight. Each University must attack the problem in its own way. Each has much to learn from the rest, and we may hope that Oxford, under Mr. Hendy's lead, will play a great part in working out, in partnership with the schools, a satisfactory solution.

Pschyco-Analysis. A brief account of the Freudian Theory. By Barbara Low, B.A. (191 pp.) Allen & Unwin. 5/- net.

THE author, at one time a Training College Lecturer, has done good service by writing this very readable account of Freud's epoch-making work on the psychology of the Unconscious. Dr. Ernest Jones contributes an introduction. We hope in a later issue to discuss the whole problem in relation to this and other elementary books on the subject. In the meantime, Miss Low's work stands as perhaps the best available short expositions of the whole doctrine, though it suffers somewhat from over-generalization.

The Class-Room Republic. By Ernest A. Craddock. (iv + 80 pp.) A. & C. Black. 2/6 net.

THE literature of self-government in the school is growing apace, and Mr. Craddock's little book is a noteworthy addition to it. He has turned his classroom into a little commonwealth, and he describes with enthusiasm both its difficulties and its triumphs. We commend the book very warmly to all who are seeking to humanize the time-honoured routine of the schools. The way in which this middle form in a London Secondary School rose to a sense of corporate responsibility is a powerful witness to the soundness of the underlying doctrine.

A New Geography of Scotland. By M. J. Newbigin. (172 pp.) Herbert Russell, 3/6 net.

MISS NEWBIGIN'S name is in itself presumptive evidence of sound work in Geography, and this new study of Scotland will, we think, add to her reputation. It is well illustrated by clearly-drawn and well-printed maps and diagrams, and may well be accepted as a first-rate specimen of the New Geography as presented by the best teachers in our Secondary and Central Schools.

Stories from Spenser. By Minna Sterle Smith. (xxii + 203 pp.) Cambridge University Press.

QUITE an admirable attempt to tell the Spenser stories to young people not yet mature enough to read the originals. Much of the Spenserian diction has been retained, giving the text that charming old-world flavour which properly belongs to it. It goes without saying that the book owes much to the scholarship and taste of a well-known Fellow of Newnham.

Australian Meteorology. By Griffith Taylor, D.Sc. (xi + 312 pp.) Oxford University Press. 12/6 net.

WE know no weather study so complete and informing as this, and although written for Australian students, it will be found most interesting and valuable by all schoolmasters who are concerned with geography and climatology. It is beautifully illustrated, and presents the romance of a fascinating modern study most attractively.

A Modern Civil Service and Commercial Manual of Spelling. By H. J. Bown. (136 pp.) Herbert Russell. 1/9 net.

Vol. 5, No. 6. *Dec. 6th, 1920.*

"EQUAL ADDITIONS" *versus* "DECOMPOSITION" IN TEACHING SUBTRACTION.
AN EXPERIMENTAL RESEARCH.
By W. H. WINCH.

Part II.

1. How the second experiment arose.

IT may be remembered that in an experiment on "Equal Additions" *versus* "Decomposition" in teaching subtraction, previously carried out, the conclusions arrived at were as follow:

Children who had been taught for years by the Method of Decomposition, after a few lessons on the Method of Equal Additions, were, when tested, slightly superior to children of equal ability, who had worked all the time, and in conditions as favourable, by the decomposition method. But the amount of the gain involved was so small that it was deemed inadvisable to change the method so late in the school course. It will be remembered that these girls had reached Standards V and VIb.

The question arose whether a different answer would be obtained were the experiment to be carried out with children much younger, and it was finally decided to repeat the whole procedure with the girls of Standards II and III, many of whom had been only three months before in the infants' school. A further point of interest was the fact that many of these children, whilst in the senior school, though not in the infants' school, had been taught by the method of equal additions, and not by decomposition, as in the previous case.

2. The children who did the work.

The experiment was carried out with the whole of two classes, Standards II and III, in a municipal girls' school situated in a fairly good neighbourhood in South-West London. The average age of the two classes was 8 years 6 months on June 15th, 1915. All the testing and teaching was done by the head mistress. The experiment was commenced with 65 girls; but, owing to absences, the number finally available for tabulation was 46.

3. The general plan of the experiment.

Preliminary tests in subtraction were set, and on the results of these the girls were divided into two equal and parallel groups. Then one group was taught by a method of "equal additions" and the other by a method of "decomposition," and tests were made at certain stages of the progress of the two groups.

4. The preliminary tests.

Six preliminary sets of exercises in subtraction sums were set, the girls being instructed to work how they liked, but to get as many done rightly as they possibly could. The subtraction sums were set in ordinary notation, and numbers less than ten thousand were used. The sums were arranged in sets of four, horizontally, and the girls were required to work the first line before proceeding to the second. Exactly ten minutes was allowed for each paper. Two lines of one of the test papers follow:

(1)	3,492	9,000	4,244	8,315
	1,748	9	3,249	2,347
	————	————	————	————
	————	————	————	————
(2)	7,042	8,242	8,693	6,000
	1,387	7,243	2,229	1
	————	————	————	————
	————	————	————	————

5. The method by which the children worked the preliminary tests.

Some of these children had been taught subtraction, not in the infants' but in the senior departments, by the "Equal Additions" method. To make quite sure that they actually worked their sums by this method, after all the preliminary tests had been done, a number of girls were taken individually in a private room and asked to work some subtraction sums. Some cases follow in illustration; the exact words used by the children are given in each case:

Florence B———, Standard IIb, aged 7 years 8 months.

6000   (1) 9 from 0 I can't, add a 1, 9 from 10 is 1.
1259   (2) As I added 1 to the top you must add 1 to the bottom, 6 from
———   0 I can't, add a 1, 6 from 10 is 4.
———   (3) As I added 1 to the top I must add 1 to the bottom, 3 from 0 I cannot, add a 1, 3 from 10 is 7.
       (4) As I added 1 to the top you must add 1 to the bottom, 2 from 6 leaves 4.

Edith B———, Standard IIa, aged 8 years 4 months.

6231   (1) 7 from 1 we cannot, add a 1, call it 11, 7 from 11 leaves 4.
4517   (2) I added a 1 there (pointing to the 1 in the minuend), I must
———   add a 1 there (pointing to the 1 in the subtrahend), 2, 2 from 3
———   leaves 1.
       (3) 5 from 2 I cannot, add a 1, call it 12, 5 from 12 leaves 7.
       (4) Because I added a 1 there (pointing to the 2 hundred), I must add 1 there (pointing to the 4 in the subtrahend), 5, 5 from 6 leaves 1.

The following girls worked in a precisely similar way:

     Martha P———, Standard III, aged 9 years 10 months.
     Amy T———, Standard III, aged 8 years 2 months.
     Elsie C———, Standard III, aged 7 years 11 months.
     Doris D———, Standard III, aged 8 years 8 months.
     Alice B-———, Standard II, aged 8 years 4 months.
     Nellie G———, Standard II, aged 7 years 11 months.
     Winnie C———, Standard II, aged 7 years 6 months.

Several of the children in Standard II were quite unable to work subtraction sums; that is to say, they had not progressed sufficiently far with number work to be able to discover what numbers could be taken from others, and what numbers could not. Several children were unable also to discover the answer to the simplest question in subtraction without the use of the concrete. Their marks will be found in the last sections of the table, given later. Some of the backward children were questioned as to how they worked their sums, and cases are quoted:

Winifred Rose C——, Standard IIb, aged 8 years 1 month, said:

6231   (1) 7 from 1 we cannot, 7 from 7, 14 (writes down 4 only).
4517   (2) 1 from 3 we cannot, 3 and 3, 6 (writes down 6).
——   (3) 5 from 2 we cannot, add a 1 and call it 10, 10 from 5, 15
——   (writes down 5).
      (4) 4 from 6 we cannot, add a 6 and call it 10, 10 from 4, 14
      (writes down 14).

The child took ten minutes to work this sum, and when she thought she was subtracting and was really adding she used her fingers. The teacher said to her, "Who taught you to do these sums?" She answered, "No one; I learned meself" (meaning she taught herself). "Sometimes of a Saturday I take a book and a pencil and I go and do a lot." She was asked, "And are they right?" She said, "Yes." "How do you know they are right?" "'Cos I does they all over twice." The teacher, pointing to the sum she had just worked, asked, "Is this one right?" "I dunno." "Well, what do you think?" After a long pause, and with a sweet smile, the child answered, "I think it's wrong."

Minnie M——, Standard IIb, aged 8 years and 3 months, worked thus:

6231   (1) 7 from 1 we cannot, take a 10 and put it there (writes 1 by
4517   the side of the 1 in the minuend), 7 from 11 leaves 2.
——   (2) 7 from 3 we cannot (writes 1 by the side of the 1 ten in the
——   subtrahend), 7 from 11 leaves 2.
    (3) 7 from 2 we cannot (pointing to the 2 hundreds), put a 1,
    7 from 21 leaves 1.
    (4) 7 from 6 we cannot, put a 1 there (pointing to the left of the
    6 in the minuend), 7 from 16 leaves 8.

This child was very pleased to show how she worked the sums, and on being questioned as to who taught her, as she always subtracted the unit's figure in the subtrahend from all the figures in the minuend, she explained, "You always have to take that one because it's the end one."

Lucy T——, Standard IIb, aged 8 years 3 months, said:

4261   (1) 8 from 1 we cannot, add a 1, that makes 11, 8 from 11
1748   leaves 2.
——   (2) 1 from 6 we cannot (this is the 1 unit in the "top line"), add
——   a 1, that makes 16, 8 from 16 leaves 10 (pointing to the 8 units
    in the subtrahend); no it doesn't, it leaves 11 (writes 1).
    (3) 7 from 2 we cannot, add a 1 and that makes 12, 7 from 12
    leaves 5.
    (4) 1 from 4 leaves 5.

The teacher said to her, "Just now you said 8 from 16 leaves 11. Did you mean that?" The child said she did, and added, "Did I ought to have put down 11?" The teacher said, "What do you think about it?" and she answered, with a rapid clearing of countenance, "1 and carry

1." The teacher said, "Who taught you to do these sums?" She answered, "Mother, and she says she learns me nice."

Edith K——, Standard III, aged 8 years 7 months:

6231 (1) 7 from 1 I can't, add a 1 makes 11, 7 from 11 leaves 4.
·4517 (2) Because I added 1 here (pointing to the figure 1 in the
—— minuend), I must add a 1 here (pointing to the 10's figure in the
—— subtrahend), makes 11, 11 from 3 I can't, add a 1, makes that
13, 11 from 13 leaves 2.
(3) Because I added a 1 here, I must add 1 here (pointing to the
5 in the bottom line), makes that 15, 15 from 2 I cannot, add
a 1, makes that 12, 15 from 12, 15 from 12, 15——from——12
(long pause), turns to the teacher and whispers, "Tell me." The
teacher shakes her head. The child (hopelessly, standing on one
leg and swinging the other), "15 from 12" (suddenly), "Why, I
can't. Shall I put another 1?" The teacher told her to do what
she thought was right. "Well, I'll put another 1, and that
makes 202, 15 from 202, is it 100?" The child wrote down 100
under the 5 in the answer space, and continued:
(4) Because I added a 1 here, I must add a 1 here (pointing to
the left of the 4 thousands), makes 14, 14 from 6 I can't, add a
1, makes 16, 14 from 16 leaves 4. "Shall I do another one?"

Elizabeth Mc——, Standard IIb, aged 7 years 7 months, worked thus:

6000 (1) 9 from 0 we can't, put down a 0.
1259 (2) 5 from 0 we can't, put down a 0.
—— (3) 2 from 0 we can't, put down a 0.
—— (4) 1 from 6 leaves 5.

Maud W——, Standard II, 7 years 7 months. This child worked the same sum as Elizabeth, in the same way.

Doris D——, Standard II, aged 7 years 11 months, said:

6000 (1) 9 from 0 leaves 9.
1259 (2) 5 from 0 leaves 5.
—— (3) 2 from 0 leaves 2.
—— (4) 1 from 6 leaves 5.

Elizabeth Mc——, Maud W——, and Doris D—— worked subtraction sums *without* naughts in the minuend correctly by the equal additions method.

In all about thirty girls were taken thus to work individually and privately. The majority of the girls from Standard III were very ready with the "equal additions" method; several of the children of Standard IIa were found to be conversant with the method, and a fair sample has been given of the method, or rather want of method, used by the more backward children. Not a single child was found to work by the method of decomposition. May I suggest to teachers that it is worth while to find out by individual analysis how the children actually work their subtraction sums; some of the above cases were illuminating.

6.   The division into two equal and parallel groups.

Each child's marks were tabulated, and a division into two equal and parallel groups was effected on the basis of the last four preliminary tests.   The first two of the six tests were used only as preparatory practice to enable the children to become "steady" and able to take their proper places relatively to one another.   The division will be shown later on, with other marks, in one table.

7.   The teaching of the two groups.

One of the groups—Group A—received five lessons on the equal additions method of working subtraction sums; whilst the other group —Group B—received five lessons on the decomposition method.   Each lesson occupied exactly 20 minutes.   Both groups were taught separately, but by the same teacher.   The preceding lessons were an oral Scripture lesson and Physical Exercises in the playground.   No subtraction sums of any kind, other than those dealt with in the respective lessons of the experiment, were worked in either class during the whole period.

8.   A brief account of the lessons by the method of equal additions.

In the first lesson the following examples were worked concretely with brown beans on white paper:

5 beans − 2 beans = 3 beans.
9 beans − 4 beans = 5 beans.
8 beans − 6 beans = 2 beans.

(It had been discovered quite early in the experiment that quite a dozen of the children in Standard II were unable to subtract one number from another without, for example, showing 5 fingers or 5 beans, separating 3 and counting the remainder to discover that 5—3 leaves 2.   They were, indeed, quite unversed in the manipulation of number generally mastered in the infants' school.   To teach these children to subtract numbers up to 18, *without concrete aids*, in addition to a definite method of dealing with numbers seemingly greater in the subtrahend than those in the minuend was almost an impossibility in so few lessons.   The presence of these backward children, of whom, of course, there were an equal number in both groups, rather handicapped the teacher; she could not always tell which children failed through ignorance or unfamiliarity with the method, and which through actual inability to subtract, or, indeed, in some cases, to recognize a larger number as the larger in comparison with a lesser one.   These girls were almost entirely confined to the lowest sections of the groups.)

Various children were called to work similar sums with beans, and these sums, with their answers, were written on the blackboard.

The teacher asked "If Jane had 8 beans and she gave Lotty 2, how many would she have then?"   The answer was given and the sum written on the board.   The teacher then said, "Suppose John gave Jane 1 more bean and Jane gave Lotty 1 more as well, how many would Jane have then?"

The sum was demonstrated with the beans and worked on the blackboard.   Several more questions embodying the same principle were asked and the children questioned as to what they noticed about the answers before and after the numbers were added. Some good answers were given, one child saying, "It is funny, but the answers are just the same before you added the numbers as after you added the numbers." The teacher then asked about the added numbers, and was told the *same* number had to be added to the top and to the under line. One sum was worked with a different addition to the minuend from that to the subtrahend, to show the converse case.

In the second lesson the children were asked what particular thing had been found out during the last lesson. The following are two of the answers: "If we add the same number to both lines we get the same answer as we had before." "Whatever we put on the top line we must put the same on the bottom line if we don't want our sum to be wrong."

This step, as may be imagined, was far too difficult for the more backward girls, and as a concession to them, several more examples were worked with the beans upon the table before being worked upon the blackboard.

Ten was the number now added to the various numbers; thus, $7-3=4$ and $(7+10)-(3+10)=4$. For the benefit of the less forward children the beans were arranged in groups of 7 and 10; 3 beans were taken from 7, leaving 4; 10 beans were taken from the 10, leaving 0. Then on the blackboard:

17 (1) 3 from 7 leaves 4.
13 (2) 1 from 1 leaves 0.
—

—

The first few minutes of the third lesson were occupied by rapid questioning in subtraction, as 3 from 10, 7 from 10, 5 from 10, and so on. The following sum was written on the blackboard:

13—9, 13 10 beans were counted into one heap, 3 into another, and a
9 child was called upon to take 9 beans from the pile of 3.
— This, of course, she could not do. Other children were
— invited to take the 9 away, and the class became very interested. The teacher reminded them that the answer remained unchanged if the same amount were added to the number we had and the number we wished to take away; 10 beans were added to the 3 beans, 9 were counted away, leaving 4. "Now," said she, "we have added 10 to the number we have, we must add 10 to the number we are going to take away; we have taken away 9, now we must take away 10 more"; the 10 beans were removed, still leaving 4. On the blackboard it was worked thus: (1) 9 from 3 we cannot, add 10, 9 from 10 leaves 1 and 3 already there, are 4. (2) We have added 10 to the top line, so we must add one 10 to the under line; one 10 from this one 10 leaves nothing. Further examples were worked in the same way.

The fourth lesson again began with rapid questions. The children were not allowed to work on their fingers, although an answer was occasionally demonstrated by means of them. Then the following sum was written on the blackboard and worked by the teacher:

41 (1) 5 from 1 we cannot, add 10, 5 from 10 leaves 5 and 1 there
25 already makes 6.
—   (2) We added one 10 to the top line, so we must add one 10 to the
—   under-line, which is the number we are going to take away; one 10
    and two 10's make 3, 3 from 4 leaves 1; and so on.

The following sums were also worked: $622-339$, $600-287$. The girls
in Standard III understood the notation required, and also some few of
the girls in Standard II.

In the fifth lesson, after the usual questions in simple numbers, a
sum was written on the blackboard and worked by a member of the
class; but the children seemed rather to lack interest, so slips of paper
and pencils were given out and the girls were instructed to copy and
work the following sum: $6101-2015$. Nearly half the class worked it
wrongly, so it was worked figure by figure on the board, each girl
noticing her mistake. (The most common error was 3 from 6 in the
last figure instead of 2 from 6.) Four sums altogether were worked in
this way on the papers, the teacher correcting each sum upon the board
directly after it was finished. Speed and accuracy improved with each
example.

9. A brief account of the lessons on the method of decomposition.

The change from the "equal additions" method to the method of
"decomposition" with the children in Group B who had learnt the
former was not found nearly so embarrassing as had been anticipated;
that the children quickly adopted the new method was proved by the
fact that when a trial paper was given at the conclusion of the five
lessons only two children reverted to the method of equal additions.
The method by which they had worked was easy to ascertain, as they
were allowed in this exercise to cross out the original figures in the
sums and substitute the result of the decomposition. But the actual
working was slow at this stage; five lessons had certainly proved
insufficient to mechanize the process.

In the first lesson given to Group B several subtractions were made
with brown beans on white paper, the children being told to put out
certain numbers of beans, take other numbers from them, and count the
remainders. For example, $7-5=2$, $9-6=3$, $8-2=6$. Then 6 beans
were put in one bag, 10 in another, and a child was invited to count
out 9 beans. She was first given the bag with 6 in it, and when she
had discovered she could not do so, the bag with 10 was given her.
She was asked how many remained—1 and 6 in the other bag makes 7.

Several other similar little problems were worked out by the
children with the beans, the results being recorded on the blackboard
thus:

16	15	18	14
9	6	9	7
——	——	——	——
——	——	——	——

In the second lesson the beans were again used for one or two easy
sums, which were afterwards written on the blackboard, and then the
children were shown how to deal with larger numbers. The sum was
taken: $23-17$. Two heaps of 10 and one of 3 were counted out. The
following questions were asked: "Are there enough beans in any one of

these heads to take away 17?" "No." "What shall we do, then?"
"Take first 7 from one 10, leaves 3, and 3 we have already makes 6."
"How many more have we to subtract?" "Ten." The sum was written
on the blackboard and worked thus:

23 (1) 7 from 3 cannot be taken, take one of the tens, that is 10 single
17 ones, 7 from the 10 single ones leaves 3, and 3 we have already
— makes 6.
— (2) We have already taken one of the tens, so we only have one
left, 1 from 1 leaves 0.

The following sums were then worked on the blackboard; some by the
teacher, some by individual children:

$$60-27, \quad 34-19, \quad 81-27, \quad 50-3.$$

The third lesson commenced with some rapid questioning in subtraction
similar to that taken with Group A. Then the children were asked:
"How many single ones have we in one in this column, in this? And
so on. Sums containing hundreds were afterwards worked on the
blackboard, as follow:

676 (1) 9 from 6 cannot be taken, take one of the tens, 9 from $10=1$
349 and 6 we have makes 7.
——— (2) We have taken one of the tens, so we only have 6 left, 4 from
——— $6=2$.
(3) 3 from $6=3$.

The fourth lesson commenced in the same way as the third, and then
some sums containing hundreds were worked by the children on the
blackboard. The most common error, as may be surmised, was the
adding of 10 to the subtrahend as well as the subtracting of 10 from
the minuend.

This sum with one naught in the minuend was worked thus:
502 (1) 6 from 2 we cannot, there are no figures in the ten's column
146 so we must take one of the hundreds, leaving 4, change the 100
——— into 10 tens, take one of these, leaving 9. 6 from $10=4$ and $2=6$.
——— (2) 4 from $9=5$.
(3) 1 from $4=3$.

Similarly, sums containing thousands were dealt with, and the children
seemed to have little difficulty with the added figure.

It will be remembered that in the fifth lesson given to Group A the
children had worked on slips of paper after the preliminary exercises,
so exactly the same plan was adopted with Group B. Of course, all
corrections and demonstrations were carried out in accordance with the
method of decomposition.

10. The trial test.

After the five lessons given on each of the two methods it was
decided to give a trial test. It was rather doubtful whether the girls
of Group B had become sufficiently familiarized with the method of
decomposition to be able to hold their own against those children in
Group A with whom the method of equal additions was more firmly
established. The marks, which will be given in the table, show a
decided advantage for Group A, although, as has already been stated,
only two cases showed any reversion to the equal additions method on
the part of the children taught by decomposition.

11. **Three further lessons.**

It was decided after an examination of the papers worked at the trial test to give three more lessons to both groups. These lessons were conducted in a similar way to lesson five; they were really lessons in controlled and corrected practice.

12. **The final tests.**

A series of final tests was now given: these tests were four in number and corresponded in every particular with numbers 3, 4, 5, and 6 of the preliminary tests. The results are given later, although it may be said at once that Group A had a decided advantage, which seemed to increase with practice rather than diminish.

13. **The chronology of the experiment.**

1. Preliminary tests worked by all the girls simultaneously:

Tuesday, June 8, 1915 ... 10 to 10.10 a.m.
Wednesday, „ 9, „ ... „
Thursday, „ 10, „ ... „
Friday, „ 11, „ ... „
Tuesday, „ 15, „ ... „
Wednesday, „ 16, „ ... „

2. Five teaching lessons:

Group A—Friday, July 2... 9.50 to 10.10 a.m.
„ B— „ „ 2...10.15 to 10.35 „
„ A—Monday, „ 5...10.15 to 10.35 „
„ B— „ „ 5... 9.50 to 10.10 „
„ A—Tuesday, „ 6...10.0 to 10.20 „
„ B— „ „ 6...10.25 to 10.45 „
„ A—Wednesday,,, 7...10.15 to 10.35 „
„ B— „ „ 7... 9.50 to 10.10 „
„ A—Thursday, „ 8... 9.50 to 10.10 „
„ B— „ „ 8...10.15 to 10.35 „

3. Trial test worked by all the girls simultaneously on Friday, July 9, 10.0 to 10.10.

4. The additional lessons given to both groups:

Group A—Monday, July 12...10.15 to 10.35 a.m.
„ B— „ „ 12... 9.50 to 10.10 „
„ A—Tuesday „ 13... 9.50 to 10.10 „
„ B— „ „ 13...10.15 to 10.35 „
„ A—Wednesday, „ 14...10.15 to 10.35 „
„ B— „ „ 14... 9.50 to 10.10 „

5. Four final tests worked by all the girls simultaneously:

Thursday, July 15...10.0 to 10.10 a.m.
Friday, „ 16... „ „
Tuesday, „ 20... „ „
Wednesday, „ 21... „ „

14. Results.

TABLE I.

Showing, section by section, the results of Group A and Group B in all tests. Group A was 8 years 5·7 months, and Group B 8 years 5·2 months old.

GROUP A (Equal Additions).   GROUP B (Decomposition).

Marks in 4 Preliminary Tests	No. of Girls	Av. Mark in 4 Preliminary Tests		Av. Mark in Trial Test		Av. Mark in 4 Final Tests	No. of Girls	Av. Mark in 4 Preliminary Tests		Av. Mark in Trial Test		Av. Mark in 4 Final Tests
Over 300	1	324		52		426	1	337		51		350
200 to 300	5	241		45		348	5	244		28		227
100 to 200	7	165	.5 Lessons	37	3 more Lessons	251	7	166	5 Lessons	15	3 more Lessons	219
50 to 100	5	69		17		139	5	69		15		115
Under 50	5	14		13		136	5	14		9		100
Averages...		134·9		29·9		230·8		136·1		18·1		178·2

TABLE II.

Showing, test by test, the Average Marks of Group A and Group B, compared.

	Preliminary Tests				Trial Test	Final Tests			
	1st	2nd	3rd	4th		1st	2nd	3rd	4th
Group A...	32·7	34·0	32·7	35·4	29·9	54·2	59·0	54·8	59·9
Group B...	33·1	34·2	33·9	34·9	18·1	47·6	46·9	37·4	46·2

These tables show that at the trial test Group B was far behind Group A, and although three further lessons were given, in the course of which the children of the "decomposition" group became quite familiar with their method, they did not once succeed in equalling the results gained by Group A. This advantage appears all along the line, among both the abler and the inferior arithmeticians. The usual calculations have been made from the individual figures. The correlation-coefficient between the results of the preliminary tests for Group A and Group B is +.99; the difference between the means is 1.2 (in favour of Group B, be it remembered); its probable error is 1.0. In the trial test the correlation-coefficient is +.63, the difference between the means is 11.8, and its P.E. is 1.7. For the final tests r is . +68, the difference between the means 52.6, and its P.E. is 11.1, which is only one-fifth of the difference.

15. Summarized conclusions.

The method of equal additions shows to decided advantage with young children in accuracy and rapidity; and this is true both in the case of the superior children, who already had learnt something of both methods, and also in the case of the inferior children, who, prior to the experiment, really knew nothing of either method.

MAKING A PLAY.

By A. RUCK, WHITELANDS COLLEGE.

OUR play originated in a lesson on the Norse Myths, relating the story of Odin's sacrifice. The tale itself, with its heroic conceptions (giants and gods), its simplicity of action and motive, and its dramatic close, is one that makes a direct appeal to children. As expression work I suggested a dialogue between Odin and Mimir, when the former asks for a drink from the River of Knowledge and makes his great sacrifice to obtain it.

The dialogues were duly written; the class voted for the best and decided to give the part of Odin to Elsie (the author of the favoured piece) and that of Mimir to the girl who had produced the second best dialogue. The scene was acted in the classroom, and then—many and overwhelming were the suggestions. Why not the two Ravens? Why not the Giants? Why not the people of the Earth? Why not, in short, a whole play?

The idea was certainly entrancing, and was immediately adopted. Now began our work of " making." I use the word advisedly, for the writing of the scenes was but one branch of the undertaking.

First and foremost arose the question of allocating the parts. Whether this is the orthodox order of procedure in playwriting, I know not. The class deemed it the most important. In addition to Giants, Ravens, Elves, and People, it was suggested that we should have a number of gods and goddesses, of whom Odin might take an affectionate farewell before he went down to Mimir's cave. I gave them a list of the chief Norse divinities, with brief explanations of their appearance and character, and we soon had six gods and goddesses in addition to Odin.

The allocation of the parts was in itself a revelation. A gentle, rather shy girl pleaded to be allowed to take the part of Thor, that thunder-voiced hero of the North. I had barely finished telling them about Loki's elusive and mischievous nature, when the character was appropriated by another child, who had decided on details of costume before the rest of the cast had been arranged. When most of them had been given parts, " What about Balder? " I asked, " the most beautiful of the gods." Almost every hand was raised. " Well? " " Please, madam, Winnie Johnstone," came in chorus. Winnie was a fascinating little person, not only unquestionably pretty, but quaintly original, and with the most delicious little lisp I have ever heard.

The characters had been more or less decided on, when I almost spoiled things by an awful blunder. I had forgotten that the charm for the children lay in the fact that they were doing something entirely new, and what was more, doing it by themselves. They had chosen their parts, and wanted to live in these newly assumed characters. But I had not conceived the possibility of acting when only one scene had been written, so treated the class to a more or less learned discourse on the difference between the Greek and Elizabethan drama—Messengers and Chorus, Violent action off the stage, &c. I believe I was really growing eloquent, when, happily, I was brought to earth by a question put to me in all innocence by a naughty little girl at the back, who was evidently finishing up some work from a previous geography lesson. " Please, madam, do Indian women take off their nose ornaments when they go to bed?" This—after Aristotle and the Unities!

I immediately subsided and turned my attention to one of the Light Elves who was trying to decide the momentous question of whether pale blue, pink, or light green was the most usual colour for fairy wings. As the hall was empty, we trooped out to have impromptu acting, and I would here urge the importance of frequent rehearsals, even when the play you are writing is in a very embryonic state. It helps to crystallize vague ideas and aids self-expression. By the end of the first rehearsal, scene one was practically complete.

An incident occurred which showed that the children, though impatient of abstract rules and distinctions, were ready to appreciate and discuss the practical difficulties encountered by the playwright. The 1st Raven's speech reported to Odin the attempts of the Giants to mar the happiness of the Earth, while the 2nd Raven, by telling him of Mimir and the wonderful river, pointed out a way of escape. Two or three of the girls objected to the 2nd Raven's speech on the ground that Odin, as All-Father, would already know of the existence of the river. It was pointed out that though Odin knew, the audience did not. Mimir and the river must be mentioned in order to make the story clear to them. The real question was should the lines be spoken by Odin or the Raven? After some discussion it was decided that, for dramatic reasons, the speech was to be delivered by the 2nd Raven.

The making of costumes and classroom rehearsals continued, when I complicated matters by further Norse tales. Thor's adventures among the Giants, and the marriage of Bragi and Idun—of Poetry with Eternal Youth and Springtime—gained such a hold, that they were to be introduced, willy-nilly, into the original play. Loki, with truly heroic self-sacrifice, even offered to abandon her chosen part of Fire-God and play Bragi to her friend's Idun.

I felt something ought to be done, but what? We were all agreed by this time that our imaginary audience must be taken into account. If we complicated the story by a trial of strength between Thor and the Giants and by the courtship of Idun, would it not rather bewilder the poor audience? Of course Thor would play a part, perhaps the Dark Elves might present him with his magic club and belt. This suggestion was joyfully seized on by the Dark Elves, who up to this had had no definite lines assigned to them. Then about Idun—certainly some reference to her as the goddess of Youth and Springtime must be made. But, was it necessary to go through the marriage ceremony? I felt genuinely relieved when it was decided to leave out unnecessary detail, for I was suddenly appalled by my profound ignorance of Norse bridal customs.

After much talk we came to the conclusion that the scene between Mimir and Odin was the centre of interest, the climax of the play, and the object of the other scenes was to lead up to that.

The first scene was not materially altered. The gods and goddesses were to sit together, talking naturally, but at the same time their lines were to explain the situation to the audience. The next two scenes were to draw a contrast between the happiness on earth and the evil power of the Giants seeking to destroy that happiness. Thus did we explain the necessity for Odin's sacrifice.

Now that we had our outline quite clear, the remaining speeches were soon produced. Some of the children seized on the dramatic parts of the story, while others were steeped in fairy lore and found no difficulty in describing ths tasks of Light and Dark Elves, or the joy of the Reapers in the beauty of the Earth.

The verses themselves are, naturally, crude, but some show, I think, decided promise, while all have the merit of clearness and directness. There is no needless vaporizing about them. This was due, I believe, firstly to the fact that the children had plenty of material to work on—they were thoroughly familiar with the subject matter, had begun to identify themselves with the parts they played—and secondly, they were writing with a definite purpose, to explain and amplify the story. Besides, would they not themselves deliver the lines on the stage? Of all methods of torture still applied to work in schools, surely that of setting formal essays on abstract subjects is one of the least justifiable?

For the next few days I believe the children really lived their parts. The Giants revelled in their wickedness and besought Elsie (alias Odin) to introduce gruesome details into the verse-charms they were to mutter over their cauldron. " Put frogs and toads into it, like Macbeth, you know." One little Dark Elf was never called anything but Raven Locks. But the Ravens were the most engrossed by their parts. They adopted a peculiar form of locomotion, and used (unconsciously) to do the most prosaic things—opening the door, or distributing pencils—with a funny little side hop, which constituted a severe strain on one's gravity.

When one scene was being rehearsed on the stage proper, the rest were happily occupied with their own work; there was no need to tell them what to do. The reapers and house-mothers practised dance steps in one corner of the hall, while, in the other, the giants amicably argued the advisability of three or four turns each round the cauldron.

Another point, which was brought out clearly during the making of the play, was the children's love of pageantry of song and movement. The Elizabethans wrote for a child-like audience. The Odin and Mimir scene was considered an abrupt ending, so a tableau scene was added, ostensibly for the purpose of returning thanks to Odin for his sacrifice, really for the scenic effect of grouping all the characters in their varied costumes around him. Then there was a suggestion about the Earth Scene. " If the Reapers and House-Mothers were very happy, would not they dance about or something." So a country dance was fitted in. There was still something lacking; it came from Balder. "As Frigga is so sad after Odin goes away, don't you think it would cheer her up if we all sang a song? " I suggested a Viking Song I had heard them sing in the hall a day or so before. But no, it was to be " Where the Bee Sucks "— I half-heartedly objected that it was not suitable, but was soon overruled. After all, are the grown-up distinctions between Classical and Romantic so important after all? Surely " the play's the thing."

Actors can never divorce their work from the stage itself, and one of our first thoughts was " Where can we act it? " The school hall had no stage, it is true, but possessed distinct possibilities. I insisted on a curtain as a *sine qua non*. It is very embarrassing to have to arrange stage properties under the critical gaze of an audience. The idea evidently met with approval, for scenes were "discovered" by the curtain rather oftener than I, as manipulator of its wobbly mechanism, quite approved. For the rest, ordinary school-room furniture, a treasure trove in the shape of a box of old costumes and lengths of material, and crinkled paper and tinsel opened up a whole world of possibilities. People with complete stage appliances can know nothing of the joys of make-believe and adaptation. Loki's crinkled paper robe of red and flame was entirely her own, both in design and construction. The Ravens each had three complete sets of wings before they were satisfied about their birdlike appearance. Then, when the Giants needed a cauldron, there was the excitement of discussing the rival claims of a fire-bucket and the stewpan from the Cookery Centre.

We were very punctilious about details. On the final day, Idun, one of the arch-offenders in the matter of "Where the Bee Sucks," came up to me with a very worried air. "Did, or did not, the Norse gods use clocks and watches?" No, decidedly they did not. "Then please keep my wrist-watch till the play is over; it would spoil my costume, would it not?"

The *raison d'etre* of the play was the fact that the children wanted to do it; its supreme justification their sheer joy in the making and the acting of it. It seems presumptuous to try to gauge or even to talk of any further influence on them of anything so spontaneous. But it did serve, out of its very spontaneity, to unearth buried talents and to show them the value of team work, of subordinating individual interests to the good of the whole. It also served to show them that this desirable state of affairs was best arrived at by each concentrating on her own part and putting the best of herself into it. Frigga (unconsciously) embodied the truth in her stern rebuke of a poor little Raven, who was suddenly overcome by an uncontrollable fit of the giggles. "Hugin, you are selfish. Cannot you see that if you do not do your own part properly, you'll spoil the *whole* play."

I believe the children did discover for themselves, by actual practice, some of the underlying principles of playmaking. They learnt, through apprenticeship, something of the technicality of the work. Having themselves fashioned a play, they will have a clearer insight into the difficulties and the beauties of dramatic composition. They will return to Shakespeare with a better understanding and a deeper appreciation, for they will have come a little nearer to seeing in him, not only the great poet, but also the great craftsman—the master playwright.

ALL-FATHER'S SACRIFICE.

SCENE I.

The Palace above the clouds.

[Curtain discovers Odin, Frigga, Balder, Thor, Loki, Idun and Freya.]

[Enter Light Elves.]

L. ELVES (*together*):

    We have many tasks to do,
    But none that would not please you.
    We light the stars, and paint the flowers,
    And redden the fruit, and weave new bowers.

We love the flowers, and every night
We hush them still, and kiss the light.
And laugh and play nigh every day,
And make all people light and gay.

Fair ladies, now we are here
We give you good cheer.
We greet you with flowers,
Which we sprinkle in showers.

[Here flowers are thrown.]

FREYA: Thank you, my gentle elves
For helping to light the stars,
And sending the sunlight down
In soft, warm, golden bars.

IDUN: Thank you, my light-hearted elves, who rule
The raindrops and sunbeams.
You send sweet showers to freshen the flowers
And brighten the glittering streams.
By your gentle help, the people on earth
Are taught to spend happy days.
Except for the cruel power of the giants,
There'd be youth and springtime always.

[Exeunt Light Elves.]
[Enter Dark Elves.]

1ST D. ELF: I am a good little elf;
I dig and search and delve.

2ND D. ELF: And so do I, good Thor;
I search for iron and ore.

D. ELVES (together):
We dig deep down.
We live in the ground.
We've made a big club,
A wonderful club;
And it is for Thor,
The one we adore.

[Here they present the magic club and belt to Thor.]

THOR: Thank you, my merry dark elves,
For my wonderful club and belt.
The giants I now can conquer,
Their evil spells I can melt.

[Puts on belt.]
[Exeunt Dark Elves.]

LOKI: I am the God of Fire,
And in the winter time
I warm the people so well,
They feel not the frost and the rime.

FRIGGA (*turning to Odin*):
I have been thinking things that make me feel so strange
and sad;
I hope that something will occur that will help to make
me glad.
I have been dreaming, dear, that you are going far away;
But I must scatter these thoughts——. Come, Odin, let
us be gay.

BALDER:
I hope your sad thoughts have not been of me.
I had a beautiful dream.
In my dream I was far out at sea,
And at last touched the shore of the land of Sunbeam.
Do not you think that a lovely dream?

[Enter Ravens.]

1ST RAVEN:
In our wanderings we have seen
Evildoers, determined and keen
To work bad magic here to-day.
Cannot we stop them, Odin, say?
Over the cleft, sad sights we saw;
Fogs and mists are being sent o'er
The seas where the fishermen work so hard.
Cannot we stop them, Odin, say?
Cannot we stop the evil to-day?

2ND RAVEN:
And we saw, by a river so bright,
An old man, who by name is Mimir;
And we asked why he sat there all night?
And he said " to guard the river."
And he said if the water you drank
(For this is the water of Knowledge)
You would know as much as if
For years you had been at a college.

ODIN:
Surely I will find this wonderful water.
People who do see me will not know that I am King.
I will go and be disguised as a poor old beggar.
Farewell, my gods and goddesses!
Farewell, my beautiful Frigga!

[Here Odin puts on his traveller's cloak.]

[Exit Odin, attended by the two Ravens.]

THOR:
Why has he gone so far,
Down below, where the giants are?

FREYA:
To get a drink from the magic river.

IDUN:
If he is able to get the water,
I know he will be able to slaughter the giants' plans.

FREYA:
He will sacrifice just anything
Except his son who is so dear to him.

LOKI:
He loves the people of the Earth;
He tries his best to make for them mirth.

FRIGGA (*anxiously*):
    Do you think he will be days
    Going down to the old sage?

THOR: Do not worry, Mother-Queen,
    Let us sing a song;
    I'm sure he will not be
    So very long.

        [All sing " Where the bee sucks "]

SCENE II.

The Earth.

[Curtain discovers three reapers (Odin in background).]

1ST REAPER: The corn is fresh and yellow this year,
    The day is warm and bright;
    The birds are singing loud and clear,
    The nightingale last night——

2ND REAPER: O, but it all depends upon the gentle rain.
    It is the gentle rain that does the work.
    If it were not for that, there'd be no grain,
    And deep down in the ground the grain would lurk.

3RD REAPER: You are right, I say,
    It is the rain
    That blesses the earth
    And swells the grain.

[Enter three House-Mothers.]

HOUSE-MOTHERS (*together*):
    Busy little bees are we,
    We have our work to do;
    We dust and clean and sweep,
    And don't get done till two.

[Reapers and House-Mothers join in a country dance, and then exeunt.]

ODIN (*coming forward*):
    The people on earth seem so happy and bright,
    So very gay and so good,
    That to keep them happy and bright always
    I'd give just anything—I should.
    That is, anything except my dear son Balder;
    That is too great a sacrifice to ask of any father.

SCENE III.

The Underworld.

[Curtain discovers three Giants weaving spells over a cauldron, Odin, above, watching through the cleft.]

1ST GIANT: · I will now weave a charm
    For the giants to harm
    All people who try to do good.
    Three hairs of yours and three hairs of mine
    Will make the charm work out quick and fine.

2ND GIANT: I will now weave a charm,
With my strong right arm.
Two frogs and a toad will work out the charm,
Then they will wonder who wished them harm.
Stir round the pot, Gog, and boil up the charm.·

3RD GIANT: The storms are raging so hard, Gog,
And overhanging the sea is a mist and fog;
The waves jump over the ships so high,
And the moon and stars shine not in the sky.
Odin will feel so sad, and sigh,
When he hears of the evil that's drawing nigh.

SCENE IV.
Mimir's Cave.

[Curtain discovers Mimir, seated by the River of Knowledge. Enter Odin, disguised as a traveller.]

MIMIR: Odin, why have you come?
If your want is in my power,
It will be done.

ODIN: A draught of your water I want you to give,
I would ne'er forget you as long as I live;
For if by your kindness the water I got,
Prosperity and happiness would be your lot.

MIMIR: Before you obtain this wonderful water,
The dearest of all things you must give;
But for the present your thoughts you must alter,
Your son I want not—your right eye must you give.

ODIN (hesitating):
You may have my eye. [Plucks it out.]
Give me the horn, and let me drink;
I will then go back to the blue sky.

MIMIR (handing Odin horn):
When this water you've drunk,
You will be very wise;
The giants you will rule,
And also the skies.

ODIN: I thank you for this wonderful water;
Now, perhaps, the giants' ways I can alter.

SCENE V.
The Earth.

[Curtain discovers Odin in centre of stage with the others grouped round him.]

ALL: * Where is thine eye, All-Father;
Does it lie in the depths of the sea?
Nay, clear in the waters of Mimir
Gleams the price which the sage received;
Bathed in crystal, as each morning wakens,
By the hand of the Ancient of Days.

* From the translation by Katherine Boult. The first four scenes were written by the children.

EDUCATIONAL IDEAS IN SOME ENGLISH NOVELS.

By ELEANOR W. ROOKE.

(Concluded).

Of Dickens I must say very little, for he is too well known to bear a lengthy examination. Moreover, so much has been written on Dickens as a reformer, and I would refer the serious student to a book called *Dickens as Educator*, which is full of valuable information and ideas. Here I would only emphasize his horror of cruelty and of unnatural repression. His educational ideas, as shown in the novels, are mostly negative; the one happy school is Dr. Strong's, in *David Copperfield*, and that, be it noted, was due to the character of the head—generous, gentle, and unworldly. There are a few other points, among many, which I should like to bring forward here. In Squeers's school, in spite of its very obvious drawbacks, we must not forget the scrupulous attention to the boys' health shown by the regular administration of brimstone and treacle, and the exceedingly up-to-date and new idealish element in the curriculum of work of practical usefulness, window cleaning, weeding the garden, and grooming the horse.

We all remember the opening words of Mr. Gradgrind, in *Hard Times*: "Now, what I want is facts. Teach these boys and girls nothing but facts. Facts alone are wanted in life. Plant nothing else, and root out everything else. You can only form the minds of reasoning animals upon facts; nothing else will ever be of any service to them." We all recognize the absurdity of this argument and the appalling nature of the facts offered to children by Mr. Choakumchild. But in these days of dialogues between butterflies and flowers we might do well to remember that, after all, even facts have some educational value.

Mrs. General, in *Little Dorrit*, "had no opinions. Her way of forming a mind was to prevent it from forming opinions. She had a little circular set of mental grooves or rails on which she started little trains of other people's opinions, which never overtook one another and never got anywhere. All articles of difficulty she crammed into cupboards, locked them up, and said they had no existence." Mrs. General may seem almost refreshing to us in these days, when everyone has opinions, many people teach opinions as if they were facts, and when there are no locked cupboards. Even her "papa, potato, poultry, prunes and prism" method may have its attractions to those who dread the entrance into a room of the modern child.

Finally, Dr. Blimber's Academy—less of a caricature than many of Dickens' sketches—has for us all a profound significance. Let us never forget that, now as then, it is not the Squeers or the Creakles who reduce their unhappy pupils to a condition of nervous prostration, or worse, by systematic overwork, forcing and cramming; it is the affectionate, benevolent, beaming Blimbers. The worst crammers, at any rate, in my experience, are always the most amiable and kindly persons with an almost parental affection for those under their care.

• Different as are their methods—as different as caricature and artistic photography—Charlotte Brontë had a fire of indignation in her breast against Mr. Brocklehurst as white hot as ever Dickens felt for Squeers. And it gives us still a malicious, or is it a holy, glee to know that, whereas Squeers neither read nor could appreciate *Nicholas Nickleby*, Mr. Brocklehurst read and understood *Jane Eyre*. Mr. Brocklehurst had his ideal—it was to make girls hardy, patient, self-denying; and everyone knows how he endeavoured to achieve it. Helen Burns is as much the victim of a senseless and brutal tyranny as Smike. The teachers suffered under the system only a little less than the children; Miss Temple alone rose above it—Miss Temple, who stands for ever on her pillar of fame as the first head mistress who is known to have had the courage to act according to her convictions, in defiance of bad governors, a beacon light to all the ages.

In *Villette* we have a totally different type of school. "Madame Beck seemed to know that keeping girls in distrustful restraint, in blind ignorance, and under a surveillance that left them no moment and no corner for retirement, was not the best way to make them grow up honest and modest women; but no other method, she said, was possible with Continental children; they were so accustomed to restraint that relaxation, however guarded, would be misunderstood and fatally presumed on. "After all," Lucy Snowe continues, "Madame's system was not bad; let me do her justice. Nothing could be better than all her arrangements for the physical wellbeing of her scholars. No minds were overtasked, the lessons were well distributed and made incomparably easy to the learner; there was a liberty of amusement and a provision for exercise which kept the girls healthy; the food was abundant and good. She never grudged a holiday; she allowed plenty of time for sleeping, dressing, washing, eating; her method in all these matters was easy, liberal, salutary, and rational: many an austere English school mistress would do vastly well to imitate her—and I believe many would be glad to do so if exacting English parents would let them." How English parents have changed since then! What strikes us most about Lucy Snowe as a teacher is her intense vitality and determination; but what we should perhaps take most to heart, though it is a painful lesson for enthusiasts, is that, while it behoves us to make all our pupils work, we cannot inspire all with our own untiring zeal; that, in fact, the work must be made to fit the pupil, and not the pupil the work. I believe that in *Villette* we see the first signs of special curricula for what are called " special " classes.

The heaviness of Lucy Snowe's lethargic pupils would drive some of us to despair, but bad material and right methods are infinitely less tragic than the ghastly waste of good material through wrong methods which is so vividly depicted in *The Mill on the Floss*. Mr. Tulliver is being harangued by the lawyer, Mr. Riley: " There's no greater advantage you can give your boy than a good education. Not," he added with polite significance, " not that a man can't be an excellent miller and farmer, and a shrewd, sensible fellow into the bargain, without much help from the schoolmaster." But Mr. Tulliver did not mean Tom to be a miller or farmer. " Tom is slow with his tongue," says his father, " and reads but poorly, and can't abide the books, and spells all wrong. Now, what I want is to send him to a school where they'll make him a bit nimble with his tongue and his pen and make a smart chap of him. I want my son to be even wi' those fellows as have got the start o' me with having better schooling." Mr. Riley recommends a clergyman who takes pupils, but Mr. Tulliver thinks a parson might be almost too high learnt to bring up a lad to be a man of business.

Mr. Riley, however, declares, "When you get a thoroughly educated man, he's at no loss to take up any branch of instruction. When a workman knows the use of his tools, he can make a door as well as a window." "I should like to know," says Mrs. Glegg, "what good is to come to the boy by bringing him up above his fortin," and, indeed, declares that Tom is "going headlong to ruin." But, in spite of them, Tom is packed off to Mr. Stelling. "Mr. Stelling was a man to whom teaching came naturally, consequently he set about it with that uniformity of method and independence of circumstances which distinguish the actions of animals understood to be under the immediate teaching of nature. With the unerring instinct of the beaver who built a dam in the second-floor room in a London house, Mr. Stelling set to work at his natural method of instilling the Eton grammar and Euclid into the mind of Tom Tulliver. This, he considered, was the only basis of solid instruction; all other means of education were mere charlatanism, and could produce nothing better than smatterers. He was not a great scholar, not an enthusiast; but he believed in his method of education. Mr. Stelling's duty was to teach the lad in the only right way; *indeed, he knew no other*. He thought Tom thoroughly stupid, and suspected obstinacy or, at any rate, indifference. Tom had never found any difficulty in discerning a pointer from a setter, could predict with accuracy what number of horses were cantering behind him; he could throw a stone right into the centre of a given ripple; he could guess to a fraction how many lengths of his stick it would take to reach across the playground, and could draw almost perfect squares on his slate without any measurement. But Mr. Stelling took no note of these things; he only observed that Tom's faculties failed him before the abstractions hideously symbolized to him in the pages of the Eton grammar, and that he was in a state bordering on idiocy with regard to the demonstration that two given triangles must be equal, though he could discern with great promptitude and certainty the fact that they *were* equal. Whence Mr. Stelling concluded that Tom's brain, being peculiarly impervious to etymology and demonstrations, was peculiarly in need of being ploughed and harrowed by these patent implements." If you grant that the brain, as George Eliot suggests, is an intellectual stomach, the fallacy is obvious.

"He was never told how there came to be such a thing as Latin on this earth; he had no idea that there ever existed a people who bought and sold sheep and oxen and transacted the everyday affairs of life through the medium of this language. All he had learnt about the Romans at the academy was that they were 'in the New Testament"; and Mr. Stelling was not the man to enfeeble and emasculate his pupil's mind by simplifying and explaining, or to reduce the tonic effect of etymology by mixing it with smattering extraneous information, such as is given to girls." It was a boy, and not a master, who made Tom see that even in book-learning there was some attraction, that Greek and English history were crammed with heroes; but he found still more satisfaction in Mr. Poulter, the drillmaster, with his tales of warfare in which he himself had taken part. What a hope this gives for the influence of the new schoolmaster. But these were only interludes in a dreary grind. It is Tom's tutor and Tom's sort of education which makes the Uncle Deanes of the world see all education as utterly futile and fatuous, and it certainly gives a handle to the advocates of vocational instruction.

In a paper like this, *Tom Brown's School Days* can hardly be neglected, though its tone of unashamed didacticism is far more repellent to the modern mind than the more artistically veiled purpose of George Eliot and Charlotte Brontë. One striking point which touches on a burning question of to-day is Squire Brown's rooted principle that it " didn't matter a straw whether his son associated with lords' sons or ploughmen's sons, provided they were brave and honest." So he encouraged Tom in his intimacy with boys of the village." Yes, but he got a little governess for his son, and never for one moment did it occur to him to let him go to the village school. He sent him at nine years old to a private school, where " he got more harm from his equals in the first fortnight than in all the years of daily intercourse with his village friends."

Hughes's comments on the private school system are interesting enough: " Now, the theory of private schools is (or was) constant supervision out of school " (and one thinks of one of the latest and most grotesque of school novels, *The Bonfire*, where this same system is one of the few good points the author can find in Jesuit schools). Hughes goes on: " It may be right or wrong; but, if right, this supervision surely ought to be the especial work of the head master. The object of all schools is not to ram Latin and Greek into boys, but to make them good English boys, good future citizens; and by far the most important part of that work must be done, or not done, out of school hours. To leave it, therefore, in the hands of inferior men " (the unfortunate ushers of the old private schools) " is just giving up the highest and hardest part of the work of education. Were I a private schoolmaster I should say, let who will hear the boys their lessons, but let me live with them when they are at play and at rest." Tom's father had very definite reasons for sending him to Rugby—not merely to make him a good scholar, the Squire " didn't care a straw for Greek particles, nor did his mother; but he sent him partly because he wanted so to go, but more in the hope of his turning out a brave, helpful, truth-telling Englishman, and a gentleman and a Christian."

It appears that Tom fully shared his parents' indifference to the Greek particles, and he might not have gone far in the paths which his father wished him to tread if it had not been for Dr. Arnold (that strong, true man, and a wise one, too, as old Brooke called him, and as many call him still, in spite of Mr. Lytton Strachey). The Doctor saw that the only way to save Tom from being a mere drifter was to give him responsibility, and everyone remembers how young George Arthur was entrusted to his care and the marvellous effect wrought in Tom's character. It was from Arthur, and not from the masters, that any light broke in on his troubled brain. Arthur showed him that the people in the Bible were real; but that was but a small ray of light compared with that which shone on Tom when Arthur begged him not to use cribs and vulgus books, which meant really a new light on everything, revealing as it did the fact that Tom's standards may have been all wrong. Such light comes oftener from strangers than relations; the possibility of it is one of the strongest arguments in favour of a big school. It was perhaps some glimmer of this light which made Tom Brown at Oxford teach in an evening school.

It is a very far cry from Thomas Hughes to Thomas Hardy, of whom I shall say very little. But I read *Jude the Obscure* many years ago, before I had learnt the depths of Mr. Hardy's pessimism. I did not realize that the book was bound to end badly, and I entered with enthusiasm into Jude's yearnings for Oxford and what Oxford could give him; my heart swelled in passionate rebellion as it seemed less and less likely that his ideal could ever be realized, and the book left me—as it must leave every reader—with a sense of tragic waste, a waste which must be going on all round us, till that day when, as Lord Crewe said at his installation as Chancellor of this University, a university education shall be as easy of attainment for the son of the English working-man as it always has been for the son of the Scottish peasant.

One other idea, which I am probably dragging in by the ears, but I cannot leave out, I find more forcibly and convincingly presented in *Two on a Tower* than in any book with which I am acquainted, namely, the dangers of a one-sided education. Swithin St. Cleeve had been at Warborne Grammar School—a place where, said Amos Fry, "they draw up young gamesters' brains like rhubard under a ninepenny pan. They hit so much larning into 'en that a could talk like the Day of Pentecost, which is a wonderful thing for a simple boy, and his mother only the plainest ciphering woman in the world." The boy, with his intellect developed at the expense of his humanity, became so enthusiastic an astronomer, so enraptured with his researches, that he was capable of such an act of grievous cruelty that he ruined a devoted woman's life. Unlike Johnson's astronomer, he was no lunatic.

Meredith is more definitely concerned with education than Mr. Hardy. Sir Austin Feverel, like Parson Adams, considered that the schools were corrupt. He had a system, as we all know, and had written a "Proposal for a New System of Education for our British Youth." The basis of his system—and herein lay its prime weakness—was that he was himself to be Providence to his son. Its aim was doubtless sound: "First be virtuous—then serve your country with heart and soul." He held that there was a malleable moment of incalculable importance in a child's education. "Between simple Boyhood and Adolescence," he wrote in his note-book, "The Blossoming Season, there is one unselfish hour, say Spiritual seed-time. . . . Every act, every fostered inclination, almost every thought, in this Blossoming Season, bears its seed for the future." And yet he allowed Richard to give up outdoor sports, till he came to dwell "in a kingdom where Beauty was his handmaid and History his minister, and Time his ancient harper, and sweet Romance his bride, and the whole sweet system moved to music." What a message of hope this is for teachers, and at the same time what a warning! Even sublimation, if it be entirely one-sided, may have its dangers. And then the father forbade his son to write poetry, and there was an end of all true confidence between them. The theorist is bound to fail, especially when, like Sir Austin, he is also a monomaniac. Few will credit what follows—his system with Richard at the Magnetic Age, though its breakdown is so exquisitely conceived that we would fain believe the whole story. But even after the episode with Lady Blandish all might still have gone well if the infatuated baronet had not persisted in his pose of Providence. The story of Richard Feverel may be an exaggeration, may be even absurdly improbable, but it contains a grave warning to parents, and even to teachers, and will be listened to by them more tolerantly than the invectives of my next author, Samuel Butler. Unfortunately, in real life we meet with more Theobald Pontifexes than Sir Austin Feverels.

Of all novelists before the war, as far as I know, Samuel Butler alone has any signs of two of the most modern educational theories, both part of that strange development called Psycho-analysis. One of these, which he expounds elsewhere as well as in *The Way of All Flesh*, is that of the enormous influence of the unconscious, "that other Ernest that dwelt within him and was so much stronger and more real than the Ernest of whch he is conscious." The other, almost as dear to psycho-analysts, he states as follows::"All our lives long, every day and every hour, we are engaged in the process of accommodation; when we fail in it we are stupid, when we fail flagrantly we are mad. . . . A life will be successful or not according as the power of accommodation is equal or unequal to the strain of fusing and adjusting internal and external changes." I have heard the identical thing at an education conference, only that educationists do not talk about success. Butler felt as forcibly as the most ardent educational reformer that schools and universities, as they were, were a poor preparation for life. He called them "back eddies of the world." He said that no culture was comparable to knowing the ways and farings of many men. Then he narrowed down this fine, broad idea by saying that he would have a speculation master attached to every school and the boys encouraged to read all the best financial papers. He would have liked to see professorships of speculation established at Oxford and Cambridge if it were not for the fact that "the only things worth doing which Oxford and Cambridge can do well are cooking, cricket, rowing, and games, of which there is no professorship." In his appreciation of the enormous importance of money, he has much in common with the newest generation of teachers. In his picture of Dr. Skinner and Roughborough, in spite of bitterness and irony, there is much that is helpful. Dr. Skinner is a humbug, a dabbler in many things besides chemistry. As Alethea says, " He had learnt everything and forgotten everything." Theobald commits Ernest to him, although he does not like him, " because he is unquestionably a man of genius, and no one turns out so many pupils who succeed at Oxford and Cambridge." As is to be expected, the boy finds no inspiration either in the master or the school.

The difficulty of developing body and mind simultaneously was never better recognized than by Butler, nor the struggle of the claims of bone and muscle to make themselves heard more vividly portrayed. His inner self told Ernest that Latin and Greek are humbug. Not so was the preparation for the making of the organ, which Alethea, wiser than Skinner or Theobald, put him to. "All boys," says Butler, " like making things. The exercise of sawing, planing, and hammering " proved exactly what he needed; making even stools and drawers was worth living for. And the organ loomed ahead; for he adored music, though none but his aunt thought of helping him to cultivate what he liked. For those were the days when parents thought that if children's wills were " well broken " they would acquire habits of obedience which they would not venture to break through. Butler shows with unequalled energy the ghastly results of the repressive system in the case of Theobald and the young Ernest, " the cruelty and uselessness of repeated corporal punishment, and the possibilities of development if development is allowed.

I cannot help thinking that Butler would have been profoundly interested in *The Loom of Youth*, which he did not live to read. On a first reading one is struck by its glaring crudity, on a second by its passionate sincerity. The author of *Tom Brown's School Days* would have been cut to the heart to see the outcome of the football worship which seemed to him so fine. Mr. Alec Waugh exposes mercilessly the tyrannous obsession which athleticism may easily become. It is as true of girls' schools as of boys'. Second in prominence to football come the masters, and all teachers will profit by a careful study of this "Mirror for schoolmasters," as the book has been called. In *Mr. Perrin and Mr. Trail* the masters have no chance, because of the detestable Head—here the Head is the best man among them—the fault's their own. Mr. Waugh exposes with all the cruelty of youth their grooviness, their utter lack of understanding a boy's totally different moral and intellectual outlook, their insistence on trivialities, their pomposity combined with feebleness, and their abject terror of a new idea. Under their sway a generation was being taught to blind itself to the higher issues of life. The school work interested the boys not at all, and Mr. Waugh attributes this chiefly to the fact that the master's only idea of work was imitation. According to Mr. Ferrers, "the classical education makes you imitate all the time; there is no free thought. We want French, Maths.; that's the stuff, Riders; get them out your own way—not Virgil's way or Sophocles' way." It was neither through French nor mathematics, however, that Ferrers opened the realms of gold to Gordon; but by letting him read Byron and Swinburne, and Rossetti, and as poetry becomes a reality to him a dim light begins to shine upon the boy's mind. Mr. Waugh could not have created Gordon if he had not himself been infinitely greater than he, and to him it is evident there is some vision of an ideal system where even school work may be a preparation for life.

In *The Loom of Youth* we have a fleeting glimpse of a different type of school from Fernhurst; Uphill, the Jesuit School, with its wide gardens and flowery walks, its flaming rhododendrons and golden gorse. Incidentally, there is an appreciative tribute to the school which admirers of *The Bonfire*, if any exist, would do well to read; but what strikes us most is the old monk's reply to Gordon's remark: "A wonderful place, this, sir." "Yes," he said. "It is the right sort of place to train a boy in. Surround him with beautiful things, make a real perception of beauty the beacon light of his life, when he is young, and he will be safe." I hope the monk really did say it, for it is not quite what other novelists—Thackeray, in *Esmond*; Shorthouse, in *John Inglesant*, though they show some understanding of the power and the devotion of the Jesuit as teacher—would have led us to expect.

And now, before I close with Mr. Wells, I must take one backward step from 1917, the year of the publication of *The Loom of Youth*, to Mr. E. M. Forster, whose one great novel, *Howard's End*, was proclaimed in 1910 as the book of the year. Everybody read it and talked about it, and many who disliked the story were attracted by its moral. For Mr. Forster, like Wordsworth, desired to be considered as a teacher or as nothing, and even the *Celestial Omnibus*, which is a collection of short stories, has an obvious design upon us. I am not capable of doing justice to Mr. Forster's philosophy, but I could not possibly omit him altogether.

The Longest Journey contains a bitter attack on a certain public school. The satire is chiefly directed against a pompous master whose idol is organization, and whose zeal in its cause mounts him in a Juggernaut car in which he rides down unmercifully any individual who stands or lies in his path; incidentally, he turned a master who had hoped to be a friend to the boys from a human being to a machine. What is far more interesting—and here I think he throws some light on Mr. Waugh's book—is his horror of the boarding-school system. The question of the relative merits of boarding and day schools has been hotly debated of late years, but I do not know whether Mr. Forster's argument is to be found exactly in the same form outside this book. His hero, Rickie, says: "I approve of our public school, but I do not approve of the boarding-school system. What is the good of throwing boys so much together? Isn't it building their lives on a wrong basis? They don't understand each other. . . . They don't realize that human beings are simply marvellous. When they do, the whole of life changes, and you get the true thing—but don't pretend you've got it before you have." Rickie believed passionately in family life, and in the true fellowship, later on, of a university. He knew that boys could make real and intimate friendships, but felt that they were not fitted for a great community. It oppressed him to feel the boys in their cubicles and dormitories, part of a beneficent machine, instead of each in his own dear home amongst faces and things that he knew. At Cambridge he had been at a college where undergraduates were individuals, and he bitterly resented the difference when he became a schoolmaster. The education at Sawston seemed full of nothing but restriction, and to Rickie the great thing about education was that it gives freedom.

It is in his better-known book, *Howard's End*, which has apparently nothing to do with education, that we find possibly Mr. Forster's ideas most plainly set forth. Leonard Bast fails because his smattering of education, though it has done much for him, was not enough to give him freedom. The Wilcoxes—rich, arrogant, dishonest—are as revolting as they are because they are not educated. And here the great lesson is to *connect*, and, because the Wilcoxes cannot *connect*, they fail altogether. And this idea of *connecting*, impressive as it is in Mr. Forster, becomes tenfold more impressive in the hands of Mr. Wells, with which I shall close this paper.

It was Mr. Wells's *Joan and Peter* which originally suggested to me the idea of this paper. Then I read it, and found it of little use for my purpose. Like *Kipps*—like *The New Machiavelli*—it expresses not so much ideas on education, but despair at its absolute inadequacy. The ideals were yet to come—and I feel I cannot do better than end with them—whether we admit *The Undying Fire* as a novel or not. Here, at least, is a clear message, and for some of us it has rung like a trumpet call: "What," said Mr. Huss—threatened with dismissal from his head mastership, wracked with pain, faced with death—"what is the task of the teacher in the world? It is the greatest of all human tasks. It is to ensure that Man, Man the Divine, grows in the souls of men. For what is a man without instruction? He is born as the beasts are born, a greedy egotism, a clutching desire, a thing of lusts and fears. He can regard nothing except in relation to himself. . . . And it is we teachers alone who can lift him out of that self-preoccupation. We can release him into a wider circle of ideas beyond himself. . . . We can open his eyes to the past and to the future, and to the undying life of Man. So through us, and through us only, he escapes from death and futility. An untaught man is but himself alone, as lonely in his ends and destiny as any beast; a man instructed is a man enlarged from that narrow prison of self into participation in an undying life, that began we know not when, that grows above and beyond the greatness of the stars. . . ." And then, of his school, he goes on: " For five and twenty years I have ruled over Woldingstanton, and for all that time I have been giving sight to the blind. . . . All those routines of teaching that had become dead we made live again. My boys have learnt the history of mankind so that it has become their own adventure; they have learnt geography so that the world is their possession; I have had languages taught to make the past live again in their minds and to be windows upon the souls of alien peoples. Science has played its proper part; it has taken my boys into the secret places of matter and out among the nebulæ. . . . Some of my boys have already made good business men—because they were more than business men. . . . But I have never sought to make business men, and I never will. . . . My boys have gone into the professions, into the services, into the great world, and done well—I have had dull boys and intractable boys, but nearly all have gone into the world gentlemen, broad-minded, good-mannered, understanding and unselfish, masters of self, servants of man, because the whole scheme of their education has been to release them from base and narrow things. . . . What has made my boys all that they are has been the history, the biological science, the philosophy. For these things are wisdom. All the rest is training and mere knowledge."

Then, at the end of the book, when he has met with a lack of understanding and sympathy from all his hearers, and after he has expounded at length his view of the horror of the world as it now is, Mr. Huss goes on to speak of his ideal world of the future: " I want simply this world better taught, so that wherever the flame of God can be lit it has been lit. Everyone I will suppose *educated*. By *educated*, to be explicit, I mean a knowledge and understanding of history. Everyone I will suppose has been taught, not merely to read and write and calculate, but has been given all that can be told simply and plainly of the past history of the earth, of our place in space and time, and the true history of mankind. . . . Moreover, I will suppose that, instead of a myriad of tongues and dialects, all men can read the same books and talk together in the same speech. . . .

" Think what a difference there would be from our conditions in such a world. In a world so lit and opened by education, most of these violent dissensions that trouble mankind would be impossible. Instead of men and communities behaving like fever patients in delirium . . . they would be alive to the facts of their common origin, their common offspring, and their common destiny. In that more open and fresher air, the fire that is God will burn more brightly, for most of us who fail to know God fail through want of knowledge. Many more men and women will be happily devoted to the common work of mankind, and the evil that is in all of us will be more plainly seen and more easily restrained. I doubt if any man is altogether evil, but in this dark world the good in man is handicapped and sacrifice is mocked. Bad example finishes what weak and aimless teaching has begun. This is a world where folly and hate can bawl sanity out of hearing. Only the determination of schoolmasters can change that."

And in this new world, he says, " I do not ask you to imagine any miraculous change in human nature. I ask you only to suppose that each mind has the utmost enlightenment of which it is capable, instead of its being darkened and overcast. Everyone is to have the best chance of being his best self. Everyone is to be living in the light of the acutest self-examination and the clearest mutual criticism. Naturally, we shall be living under infinitely saner and more helpful institutions. Such a state of things will not, indeed, mitigate natural vanity or natural self-love; it will not rob the greedy man of his greed, the fool of his folly, the eccentric of his abnormality, nor the lustful of his lust. But it *will* rob them of excuses and hiding-places; it will light them within and cast a light round about them. That is the world which such of us schoolmasters and teachers among us as have the undying fire of God in our hearts do now labour, generation by generation, against defeat, and sometimes against hope, to bring about: that is the present work God has for us."

THE RESOURCES OF CHILDREN'S IMAGINATION.

By ETHEL M. KING and J. RIDLEY THOMPSON.

Introduction.

In an examination held in Sheffield in April, 1920, for the selection of Elementary School children for admission to Secondary Schools, the following question was one out of seven which constituted a paper in English:

" Write a sentence of about five lines beginning or ending with the words "Jack awoke!" and giving details of time, place, and circumstance, such as would have made a picturesque awakening for Jack had it really happened."

The answers to this question contained many surprises for the examiners, and it was decided that the collection of children's writings presented an opportunity not to be missed for free inquiry into mental content aroused by so simple a situation as the one presented in the question. The conditions seemed exceptionally inviting. No child could possibly have suspected any purpose other than the ordinary aim of a familiar annual examination; the restrictions and the novelty so often accompanying experiment were entirely absent here; even the question itself was framed without any ulterior motive in the nature of educational research. The large number of answers available for inspection—714 girls and 808 boys—sufficiently guaranteed a good sample as far as concerns children living in a large industrial inland city. A range of two years age difference embraced nearly all the candidates, the heaviest age group being that of the eleven-year-old children.

The chief justification for undertaking the work, however, lay in the answers themselves. On the setting of the question, an examiner would no doubt be prepared to anticipate five or six main types of answer, but the startling diversity in type and in minor detail, soon gave strength to the view that, whatever the question means to a class teacher or examiner, it gave most children a free passport to wander at large in any part of the resources of their imagination. When Jack awakes to find himself bound hand and foot in a cold, damp cell, or, having dreamt of his own execution, awakes just in time to arrest the stroke of the axe, the examiner turns with longing appeal to the phrase "picturesque awakening" and wonders why it lurked outside the examination-room door, loath to relieve the dull monotony or dispel the cloud of horrors that hovered within, all invisible to the innocent invigilator. Either this is but a forceful example of the misread question—an event not unknown elsewhere in our elaborate schemes of examination—or else the quiet appeal of those fair words was insufficient to quicken the dull mind of some or turn the rampant imagination of others into smoother paths. Whatever is the real truth, whether the response is due to the world of experience we impose more or less deliberately on the young, or due to his being merely a child of our race, these answers open the portals for us to survey the wide sweep of childish imagination. This being the case, the arid tracts, and those overwhelmed by a wilder growth, are of no little interest to him who would devote himself to the nurture of child life.

Indication of scheme.

In framing a scheme of analysis an effort was made to allow full opportunity for suggestion from the writings themselves. The system here worked out is no preconceived idea of the authors, and does not knowingly contain any of their prejudice; neither does it, to their knowledge, contain the impress of any classification drawn from ordered philosophy. It is simply a list of headings that appeared best to fit the topics in hand, embracing them all as far as seemed possible and yet preserving those inner distinctions which were the chief objects of the search.

Of course, difficulties occurred, but not so many as might have been expected. An answer would occasionally fall under two headings, but seldom was there any doubt which was the dominant note, and the rule was strictly kept that one answer could only appear once in the classification. The headings themselves are not mutually exclusive, e.g. scares and accidents, but again it was generally easy to allow the essential characteristic of each heading to decide.

The mark awarded by the examiners for the purpose stated at the beginning was held strictly irrelevant; the position of an answer in the scheme is no essential guide to the mark awarded. Of course, an answer describing rural scenery was more likely to receive a high mark than any one containing mere domestic routine; but such a question lies quite beyond the scope of this paper. Here we survey mental content only, and are unconcerned with the quality of the answer.

When the twelve general headings are arranged in the order of the table, there emerges a fairly sharp division into three main systems. The first of these is the single group headed "domestic routine," which represents the mind unquickened or unable to rise above every-day events; at any rate, under examination conditions. The second system contains the groups headed "scares," "accidents," "capture and imprisonment," "war;" and "spirited adventure." The common characteristic of these groups is a combination of risk, danger, and fear, whether it appears as the shrinking feeling of a scare, or, in the opposite extreme, the thrill of bold adventure and mastery over circumstance. The other headings in this system can be arranged in appropriate positions between the two extremes. A third system can be constructed almost as readily from the remaining headings of the table. The common element here is human pleasure, the close, self-hugging pleasure of receiving Christmas and birthday presents forming the extreme case; while the other headings suggest in order the widening interests of children.

The conclusions of this paper will be more easily grasped by applying geometrical illustrations to the second and third systems. The second system, for instance, may be envisaged in the form of an ellipse with the "scare" group at one end and "adventure" at the other. The one focus of the ellipse will represent that submergence or surrender of self before the oppressive weight of danger and horror; and the other focus displays the self in the ascendant, full-blooded and victorious. The "accident" group obviously lies nearer the first focus, "capture and imprisonment" holds a fairly even balance between the two, and "war" experiences for the most part approximate to the adventurous end of the figure. The whole may be conceived as bounded by a closed curve, and the various positions within it are decided by the different proportions in which the extreme factors blend.

By a similar mental construction, the "pleasure" system may be represented by a parabolic curve having for its focus those self-centred interests so well typified in child life by the eager possession of cherished gifts. As the series is extended in the direction of nobler and less-selfish pleasures, we may imagine successive positions along the axis of the parabola more and more remote from the focus; but this process is without end as represented by the infinite extension of an ever-widening curve. With children, of course, the series soon ends, the higher conceptions awaiting the dawn of a fuller day. There is always a strong focussing of self even in the descriptive group, while in the fairyland section, failing to merge into a fictional character, the self often crashes boldly in with unrecognized incongruity.

General distribution.

Under the heading "domestic routine" have been entered all the answers which refer definitely to the unimportant happenings of daily life at home—getting up in the morning, being late for work or school, incurring praise or blame (usually the latter). This group accounts for approximately a quarter of the girls' papers and a fifth of the boys'. The following is a typical example: "When Jack awoke he was very tired and sleepy and so he went to sleep again and his mother called him and he then awoke."

In the second system, we may begin with the "scares," which form the morbid extreme of the suggested ellipse. Since this involves over 43 per cent of the boys' answers and 30 per cent of the girls', a rather more detailed treatment is perhaps advisable.

With both boys and girls, shrinking and fear is the dominant note, but the objective side is not without interest. "Strange noises" are evidently one of the terrors of the darkness for city-bred children; sometimes the noise admits of an innocent explanation, more rarely of a mildly humorous one, but the start of fear and the catching breath of the first awakening are painfully manifest. The "burglar scare" claims the first place with the boys and the second with the girls, and this, too, is perhaps part of the heritage of the city.

A curious fact regarding the relations of children with animals also stands out. In only three cases, out of over fifteen hundred, was delight expressed in the appearance or ownership of animals; while roughly 18 per cent of the scares of both boys and girls were occasioned by dogs, lions, tigers, or "ferocious beasts" unspecified.

With both sexes, about 9 per cent of the fears are of the vague panic type; there were a few cases of highway robbery, a negligible number of ghosts, and a small collection of miscellaneous fears and scares insufficient to warrant separate headings. Three examples will serve as illustration for this group:

(1) ". . . he (Jack) drempt that the king ordered him to be stamped to death by wild horses, but as soon as the horses were rushing upon him Jack awoke."

(2) "Jack was sitting in front of the fire reading a paper. It was in a big house and he ought to have been contented but he was not from 8 o'c in the morning till now which was 6 o'c he had been planning to kill his baby brother and at last he got up and drew a knive. . . ."

(3) "nearer and nearer crept the burglar, until he reached the bedside, then, just as he was taking the much coveted jewel box from the hiding-place he caught the sleeping boy's arm, and Jack awoke!"

Next in order, counting from the morbid extreme, come "accidents" of various kinds. Rather over a quarter of the girls' papers in this section, and about a third of the boys', relate slight occurrences such as the breaking of crockery and similar small disasters. The rest of the papers are almost equally divided between " fire," " drowning," " street accidents," and the familiar " falling dream," though the girls' contain very few of this last kind. The following have been selected as examples:

(1) "Jack awoke! he found the (ship?) on fire, the crew gone off in the boat and the ship stranded in the vast Pacific Ocean. What could he do? He rushed to where the cork raft was kept; alas he could not even move it."

(2) ". . . Jack had been playing on a quarry. At night he ate a great supper and went to bed. . . . He drempt he was falling down a cliff and trying to save himself by trying to catch hold of rocks. . . ."

The war comes in as a vague memory in about 3 per cent of the boys' answers and 2 per cent of the girls'. More than half of these allude to trenches, dug-outs, marching, &c. A few recall air raids or the return of a relative.

Under the heading " spirited adventure," which forms the selfassertive extreme of the ellipse, we find 3.2 per cent of the boys' papers and 0.7 per cent of the girls'. These deal, in the main, with the successful facing of fearful odds in the shape of lions and pirates.

Turning now to the parabola-shaped pleasure system, and beginning from the "self" extreme, we find that between 7 and 8 per cent of both boys' and girls' papers deal with what have been termed family rejoicings, i.e. the *receiving* (never the *giving*) of presents at various appropriate seasons of the year. The same percentage of children relate pleasantly-toned experiences during the holidays, either in camp, or in the country, or more rarely at the seaside. The curve is widening here, and the range of pleasure getting further from self. About 30 per cent of the girls and 20 per cent of the boys give more or less free play to the imagination in the description of scenic effects.

Rural scenery heads the list with both sexes, roughly three-quarters of the boys' papers in this section and two-thirds of the girls' being so classified. The description of the interior of houses claims nearly 20 per cent of the boys' and over 30 per cent of the girls' answers, and the rest are divided between sea and winter scenery. A noticeable feature of these descriptions is the apparent lack of colour-visualization. We read of roses, sunshine, and occasionally of the sky or a winding river, but a colour is very seldom mentioned, and there is a complete absence of the riotous joy in colour which is the inheritance of the children of the warmer south. The following may be taken as representing the highest level of descriptive ability reached by the candidates:

(1) "Jack awoke!, all above him the sky was pink, blue and yellow. In the distance he could see the sun setting in it's beautiful colours. He could hear the lowing of the cows and the bleating of sheep, and it seemed to Jack as though he were in fairyland."

(2) "Jack awoke at 2 o'c when the light of the lamp was not yet burnt away and found himself in the Duke's house . . . and saw the beautiful pictures and carvings of his own room once again, and he thought of how much joy was in store for him on the next day when the banquet was to be held, because of his homecoming."

References to organized games are surprisingly infrequent. They can be traced in less than 2 per cent of the boys' papers, and in fewer still of the girls'. The attention now given to physical training and games in the Elementary School should alter very considerably the state of affairs to which these figures would appear to point.

Fairy lore is touched upon by over 13 per cent of the girls and nearly 5 per cent of the boys.

Only 1 per cent of the girls' scripts and 0.2 per cent of the boys' make any definite reference to the supernatural. In the existing conditions, however, it would be unfair to make any particular deductions from the smallness of the number.

Sex Differences.

A comparison of the percentages on the columns of the table of analysis appears to bring to light some differences in the mental outlook of boys and girls which may be of interest and importance to those engaged in education.

To begin, as before, with the "domestic routine" group, the figures are striking both as to number and proportion. The environment of the home might be expected to count for rather more in the lives of the girls than in those of the boys, but one is hardly prepared for approximately a quarter of the girls' papers and nearly a fifth of the boys' being confined so rigidly to daily drudgery. Such a result would appear to suggest that amongst schoolgirls of an industrial town, to quote Mons. Binet's celebrated reports, the "Armandes" tend to outnumber the "Marguerites." At any rate, the imagination of the girls was far more securely caught in the rather sordid trammels of the daily round, than was that of the boys, and one wonders if this must of necessity be so.   When a girl soared, however, she showed that she could soar higher.   Not only do nearly three times as many girls as boys select the Fairyland topic, but the girls often give a wealth of detail that contrasts very favourably with the meagreness of the boys' accounts. One might imagine that the descriptions given by the girls owed their origin to their favourite books; but in a book-list compiled from information derived from the same papers, the names of fairy stories did not occur particularly often among the girls, while 50 per cent of the boys confessed to the fourpenny dreadful of the "Dare Devil Dick" type.

The lurid incidents which form the basis of this particular class of literature must surely bear some responsibility for the horrors related by the boys in the second group; 43 per cent of their papers, as against 30 per cent of the girls', come into this section, but the boys lead in quality as well as in quantity.   They seem to take a morbid delight in describing terrifying experiences, which are fortunately seldom found in the papers of their less-robust-minded sisters.   The same relation is noticeable in the papers included in the section named "capture and imprisonment"; only half as many girls as boys describe incidents of this nature, and the boys elaborate their accounts with details redolent of the cinema and the " Police News."   The number of boys to girls who describe incidents relating to "capture and imprisonment" is in the ratio of 2 to 1.   They are not very numerous in either case; but, being almost all dreams, are interesting in the light of Dr. McCurdy's recent research into the dreams of war neurasthenics. (See " War Neuroses": New York, 1919.)

On the other hand, however, we have to admit that, if the girls are less bloodthirsty than the boys (whether we ascribe it to the nature of their reading or the restrictions of their lives), they are also far less often lured into the paths of real romance.   Less than 1 per cent of the girls described anything that could be classed as adventure for its own sake, though it is worthy of comment that it is a girl who gives us the one Princess rescued by the Knight from the clutches of the Wicked Dragon, for the honour of his Knighthood.

In the "pleasure" system the divergence between the sexes lies in the "fairyland" and "scenery" groups.   In this latter, the girls devote far more attention to the interior of buildings than do their brothers. They often show considerable power of observation in the precision with which they describe the arrangement of the furniture and pictures, or the texture of the bed coverings.   Even tapestries and antiques creep into some of the castle interiors.   As a rule, the boys are content with the bald statement that it was "a large and beautiful" or, alternatively, "a small and dirty" room, and show no special interest in its appurtenances.

Conclusion.

It remains now to express some of the wider conclusions suggested by this paper.   First, the proportion of children who either did not attempt the question or who failed to raise the imagination beyond the commonest domestic happenings is formidably large.   If these are to be moved beyond their dull orbit, effort must be made to introduce into these lives, by the methods at our disposal, a wider experience and more vivid appeal, so as to catch somewhere a vital spark and illumine a path already made clear by purpose.

In the next large group, containing fear and danger, the complaint is not that so many children run riot here, but that the emphasis is all in the wrong direction. The call is definite for a corrective influence that will reverse the distribution of the group; but the wild growth can only be checked by a frank diagnosis and a clear vision of our aim. Without discipline and nurture the human mind is prone to gloat over the horrible and the ugly; but that is not all, for to the ordinary child our city life is almost organized to hasten the debasing process. The cinema is completely given over to commercial enterprise, and its mark is evident in the thought and imagery of children. Other answers in the same paper give evidence that children are attracted towards much undesirable literature. The Press is full of the morbid element. But the Elementary School must have its position recognized. Here, even if not in the home, the corrective influence, carefully planned and interwoven, must be steadily maintained. The school, for instance, can bring the child to learn and love a field of literature written with this very aim. This is no plea for English classics as such, but for books of thrilling adventure, travel, stirring fiction, and noble exploits, well-seasoned to delight the heart of the young reader. We would not withhold the knowledge of danger and dread occurrence; but would depict in its setting the victorious stirrings of bold spirits, with fine endeavour and tender regard. In drama, as well as in literature, life may be depicted with energy and spirit; but for educational purposes the region is almost wholly unexplored. Opportunity for drawing upon the children's sources of imagination should be given its due place in the essay hour, thereby exposing it to observation and correction.

Lastly, the group of headings described as the pleasure group indicates another aspect of educative influence. There is no surprise and no cause for complaint that the self is the supreme interest. It is from this centre that growing interests are started, related first to matters of close concern and expanding so as to embrace an ever-widening universe. Education, rightly viewed, is a development of interests—the essential condition of a growing mind. The vast undertakings of mankind in art, music, science, and commerce indicate the universe in which young life expands, ever reaching out from the narrow self, and yet in another and no less real sense ever finding and knowing a greater self.

Table of Analysis.

(Percentage of answers falling under each group heading.)

		Boys.	Girls.
1.	Domestic	17.6	23.5
2.	Scares	18.2	14.6
3.	Accidents	9.6	6.6
4.	Capture and Imprisonment	5.9	2.7
5.	War	3.1	2.1
6.	Spirited Adventure	3.2	0.7
7.	Amusements	2.1	1.3
8.	Presents	6.6	6.9
9.	Holiday and Occupational	6.1	6.7
10.	Descriptive	13.8	13.6
11.	Fairyland	4.5	13.3
12.	Semi-religious	0.2	1.0
	Unattempted	9.0	7.1

RELIABILITY COEFFICIENTS.

By E. J. G. BRADFORD.

THE impressionist and non-mathematical phase of experimental psychology and experimental education has given place to a phase which is highly mathematical. The change has taken place so rapidly that the supply of immediately available experimental data is not sufficient to test the applicability of the mathematical methods employed.

In common with other biological sciences, psychology and education deal with very variable material. The degree of variability is an almost unknown quantity; it varies with the sample and with the conditions under which the sample is tested. The phenomenon of variability claims the attention equally of the educationist and of the psychologist. It deserves the serious consideration of all those teachers and organizers in educational matters who are responsible for measuring the educational progress and ability of the children in the schools.

How many pupils secure admission to secondary schools by a stroke of luck? How many fail to do so for a similar reason? The former on examination day are on the crest of their wave of ability, the latter are on that day in the trough of their wave. Under the present conditions of very limited facilities for secondary education there must be many candidates whose fate is entirely dependent on chance.

Would two examinations in any one subject, even if they were of approximately the same difficulty, result in the same order of merit among the individuals tested? The evidence[1] so far accumulated shows that the correlation between the two orders is often less than .70, which is far from complete correlation. The evidence gathered from mental tests also leads one to believe that too much importance is attached to the marks obtained in a SINGLE examination. The force of this objection is considerably diminished when the examination papers are spread over a considerable period of time. Marks suggest a definiteness which is comforting, but which is none the less camouflage. For lack of exact knowledge concerning the variability of human beings, the unfortunate educationist, ostrich-like, buries his head in the sand of marks. Until experiments have been made on a large scale there seems to be no really reliable alternative to hand, or even any reliable facts on which to found an alternative method.

At present neither the degree of variability to be expected, nor the significance of the variability obtained, is known. The collection of data put forward in this paper is intended as a partial but representative collection of the data at present available. To this has been added some new data obtained by the writer. The whole should furnish a fairly reliable standard wherewith to test future results.

Reliability coefficients have been collected from the following published papers:—

Webb. " Brit. Journ. Psych. Mon. Supp." Vol. I, pp. 29-30.
25 coefficients. Average .73.

---

[1] cf. Report of Examiners to the City of Sheffield Education Committee, 1920.

Moore.　This Journal.　Vol. IV, p. 230.
        Boys, 19 coefficients.　Average .76.
        Girls, 19 coefficients.　Average .78.

Burt and Moore.　This Journal.　Vol. I, pp. 369, 372, 375, 377.
        48 coefficients.　Average .61.

Burt.　This Journal.　Vol. I, p. 111.
        20 coefficients.　Average .61.

Reaney.　" Brit. Journ. Psych."　Vol. VII, p. 243.
        33 coefficients.　Average .68.

Brown.　" Mental Measurement,"　p. 114, p. 119.
        48 coefficients.　Average .72.

Carey.　" Brit. Journ. Psych."　Vol. VIII, p. 188.
        15 coefficients.　Average .70.

Smith and MacDougall.　" Brit. Journ. Psych."　Vol.
        5 coefficients.　Average .63.

Unfortunately these coefficients have not been obtained by the same method; nevertheless, they give some idea of the variability of the material with which experimental education has to deal. Some coefficients above have been obtained by correlating the results of the first and second applications of the same test; others by correlating the amalgamation of the first and third applications with the second application. The reliability coefficients taken from " Mental Measurement." are the r_a values, i.e. they are the calculated values which should be obtained between the amalgamated scores of the first and second pairs of applications.

The collected coefficients total 233 in all, and are distributed as follows :—

$$\underset{\cdot00-\cdot09}{2} : \underset{\cdot10-\cdot19}{4} : \underset{\cdot20-\cdot29}{4} : \underset{\cdot30-\cdot39}{5} : \underset{\cdot40-\cdot49}{8} : \underset{\cdot50-\cdot59}{32} :$$

$$\underset{\cdot60-\cdot69}{45} : \underset{\cdot70-\cdot79}{59} : \underset{\cdot80-\cdot89}{51} : \underset{\cdot90-\cdot99}{23}$$

The very low coefficients are undoubtedly due to the nature of the tests—the bisection and trisection of lines. Of the 23 coefficients in the highest group, 12 are coefficients given by Brown; they are calculated values, and hence are somewhat higher than the other values. After neglecting the very high and very low values, and also altering the grouping slightly, the following distribution is obtained :—

$$\underset{\cdot41-\cdot50}{13} : \underset{\cdot51-\cdot60}{31} : \underset{\cdot61-\cdot70}{46} : \underset{\cdot71-\cdot80}{60} : \underset{\cdot81-\cdot90}{53}.$$

For this selected group of coefficients :
    Mean value of $r = \cdot74$.　S.D. $= \cdot146$.　P.E. $= \cdot099$.

For the complete collection of coefficients :
    Mean value of $r = \cdot71$.　S.D. $= \cdot186$.　P.E. $= \cdot125$.

The writer applied six different tests ten times to each of six different classes of school children (three boys and three girls), 224 children in all. The results were amalgamated into pairs of applications,

1 and 2, 3 and 4, 5 and 6, &c.; 144 correlation coefficients were thus obtained between PROXIMATE pairs. The distribution of the "reliability" correlation coefficients was as follows:—

1	**0**	**1**	**13**	**40**	**68**	**21**

·30 — ·39: ·40 — ·49: ·50 — ·59: ·60 — ·69: ·70 — ·79: ·80 — ·89: ·90 — ·99.
Neglecting the two lowest values, the mean value of r is .82.

[The dice experiment which is used below to describe the possible meaning of a reliability coefficient should be regarded as an imaginative picture. It may be no nearer the mark than Jules Verne's description of a submarine, though even that may have influenced the lines of its subsequent development.]

The significance of the average reliability coefficients can perhaps be better appreciated if the results obtained from the applications of the tests are likened to a series of dice throws. Let us throw 50 dice and take the total number of each throw to represent the scores obtained at the first application of the test. Then take one other die and throw that independently. Let the total of the 50 and one dice be taken to represent the second application of the same test. The effect of the addition of the score of one die will represent the effect of individual variability in performance.

The correlation between the two series is given by the following formula:—

$$r = \frac{\sqrt{c}\,\dagger}{10}$$

where c is the number of dice common to both series expressed as the percentage of the total number of dice thrown, i.e., $\frac{50 \times 100}{51}$. In this case

$$r = \frac{\sqrt{98}}{10} \text{ or } \cdot 99$$

A sample of series formed in a similar way is given below:—

1st series.		2nd series.		Value of r.
50	....	50+ 1	....	.99
50	....	50+28	....	.80
50	....	50+50	....	.71
50	....	50+69	....	.60

It will be seen from the above that 50 extra dice need to be added to the original 50 in order to bring the correlation coefficient down to .71. The appearance of the average reliability coefficient of .71 expressed in terms of dice throws is rather startling.

By amalgamating pairs of applications of tests we tend to neutralize the effect of individual variability, and as a result we find that the average coefficient rises to a value of .82. The reduction of the number of dice representing variability from 50 to 25 causes the correlation coefficient to be increased to .82. In other words, the amalgamating of two applications of a test has the same effect as reducing the "" variability " dice by one-half.

---

† A special form of the formula $r = \frac{1}{\sqrt{(1+m)(1+c)}}$ where l is the factor common to both series, and m and c are factors specific to each series.

Is the comparison between mental tests and dice throws justified? At present there is little evidence either for or against the assumptions involved. If we admit that the assumptions are justified, what does the comparison lead us to infer from the statement that the average reliability coefficient is .71? It means that the average deviation of individual scores from the mean score in the first application of a test is equal to the average difference of the individual performances between the first and second applications of the same test. In other words, the mean individual variability is equal to the mean difference of initial ability.

To say that individual variability is the cause of the fall in the value of the correlation coefficient is not strictly correct, unless that term is taken to include differential individual improvability as well. The fact, that some individuals improve more rapidly than others, causes a change in their position in the scatter relative to the other members of the sample tested. The term " variability " is here used in the wider sense.

In what manner and to what extent does variability of the individual performance affect the correlation between tests of somewhat different character?

It is more than probable that these correlations will be lowered in the same way as the reliability coefficient. Not only do the correlation coefficients vary from class to class, but they also vary considerably for the same class when tested on different occasions. The P.E. of r is a measure of the variability to be expected among the different classes; it is not a measure of the variability to be expected from the same class on different occasions. The P.E.'s of the distributions given in the table below are, however, little greater than the P.E. of r.

Tests.		Frequency of values of r.			
R.M.—R. ...	0	1	7	17	5
R.M.—S. ...	3	15	10	2	0
R.—S. ...	1	14	10	5	0
B.A.—F.A.	1	2	2	7	18
B.A.—O. ...	1	7	12	9	1
F.A.—O. ...	1	7	10	12	0
Value of r...	$-\cdot10/\cdot10$	$\cdot11/\cdot30$	$\cdot31/\cdot50$	$\cdot51/\cdot70$	$\cdot71/\cdot90$

The tests referred to in the above table are described in this Journal, Vol. II, p. 432. The correlations are between corresponding pairs of applications of the different tests, e.g. R.M. (1 and 2) with R. (1 and 2); R.M. (7 and 8) with R. (7 and 8); B.A. (3 and 4) with F.A. (3 and 4), &c. Five pairs of applications from six classes give 30 coefficients for each pair of tests.

A glance at the table of frequencies is sufficient to show ·that the differences among the coefficients are considerable. The natural question which arises from a consideration of these distributions is as to how far they are influenced by the reliability of the individual tests. Does a high reliability coefficient correspond with a concentrated distribution of frequencies, and conversely does a low reliability correspond with a widely dispersed distribution? Or, stated otherwise, does the P.E. of the distribution vary concomitantly with the reliability of the tests correlated? There is no suggestion of concomitant variation in the table given below. Possibly this is because the mean reliability of each pair of tests is very nearly the same: the means vary between .79 and .845.

Tests.		Mean r	P.E. of r	A.D. of D	P.E. of D.	Reliability Coefficients.	
1	2					1	2
R.M.	R.	·58	·06	·08	·07	·81	·77
R.M.	S.	·26	·08	·10	·08	·81	·88
R.	S.	·33	·08	·10	·08	·77	·88
B.A.	F.A.	·65	·05	·14	·12	·81	·82
F.A.	O.	·44	·07	·10	·08	·82	·82
B.A.	O.	·40	·08	·10	·08	·81	·82

The P.E. of r is calculated as from an average class of 37. It is the value calculated from r; the value of the P.E. of the mean r would be much less.

The P.E. of the actual distributions is calculated from the A.D. of the distribution (D).

The large value of the P.E. of the coefficients between the B.A. and the F.A. tests is due to the results from one class, a very backward one. The effect of omitting the five lowest coefficients is to lower the P.E. from .12 to .05.

CONCLUSIONS.—When candidates are graded on the result of a single examination, the actual position of any candidate is largely dependent on factors other than the ability which is supposed to be tested. If mental factors vary after the manner of dice factors, then this ability and pure chance (or other independent factors) have an equal influence on the actual position of candidates when the reliability of the test is .71 (a quite common value).

The distribution of the correlation coefficients between the same two tests on different occasions gives a P.E. which is approximately the same size as the P.E. of the correlation coefficient.

The distribution of the correlation coefficients does not appear to be affected by the reliability of the two tests correlated.

It remains to be shown whether or not the mean value of the correlation coefficient is affected by the reliability of the tests correlated. This question is of vital importance to the interpretation of the significance of correlation between dissimilar tests, and to the problem of common factors, e.g. General Intelligence and General Educational Ability.

OUR ILOND COMMUNITY.

By W. H. ROBINSON, Huntsman's Gardens Schools, Sheffield.

THE real test of a process of education is the effect it has on the mind of the pupils. In order to find out what our boys really felt about our system, we had the following conversation with the one who had most evidently the gift of editorship.

"Amongst our records we ought to have a volume giving a full account of our methods, written by the Ilonders, so that anyone who does not know us will be able to see exactly how we carry on, and the effect that our system has upon the Ilonders. I want you to act as Editor and get anyone who is suitable to write a chapter, then let me have the complete volume. Draw out a table of contents and give the titles to various Ilonders to write up. Take complete charge of the whole job and get it done in the best way you can."

The following is the result. The only editing of the volume that we have done for this paper is to excise, for the sake of brevity, matter which has appeared in more than one place, and to add one or two similar papers which have been done at the end of the second term to supplement the original volume. The boys had no idea of wider publicity than their own class exhibition.

Introduction by the Editor.

This book is the work of a set of boys chosen by me as Editor. Their work wholly describes the new ways and methods which have been introduced into the class. The whole system is based on a firm foundation, and each boy strives in work or play to establish a record. —H. A.

Our Ilond.

The Ilond is the class itself, and all of us are Ilonders. We imagine ourselves to be living on an Ilond, and recognize our classroom to be our home. We have no king, for we are a Republic; but we are divided into six tribes of ten men each, each having a separate chief. A friendly rivalry has sprung up between the tribes.

We govern ourselves, for we have an Ilond Parliament, which makes laws, abolishes laws, and settles grievances which spring up between the Ilonders. Each tribe has its own elected representatives, two in number, to supply their wants and to see to the welfare of the tribe. Any wrongdoers are brought before the Parliament and punished; but I am glad to say that very few of the Ilonders are wrongdoers, so that you see we may live in perfect happiness on the Ilond. The captain, who has been elected by popular vote, is Chief of the Ilonders, and he is helped by the chiefs whose work it is to see that every tribesman does his bit towards making our Ilond home a better place to live in.

A weekly report is kept by each tribesman of marks gained during the week, which is handed to the chief to convert the ten reports into one general report for the tribe. When the six general reports are complete, they are reproduced into one for the whole class, which not only shows the position of each tribe, but shows how much each individual has helped to make his tribe the best of all.

The best tribe for general work is the "Invincible Tribe," whilst the Athletes top the list for sport. The chief of the games played is

" Gusto," a game suitable for all healthy and practical boys, and the Athletes have the unbeaten record of winning both class league championships and not having a goal scored against them. The only thing I can say about this is that the boys of the latter tribe work together as one and forget personal grievances for the time, trying to make their tribe victorious.

This idea of the Ilond has produced exceedingly good effects on the class, for each tribesman does his uttermost to bring his tribe out on top. The boys go at their work with a will and enter their sport with a better will, bringing them to realize the truth in the class motto, "The best is nearly good enough for us."

Never a word is mentioned about the cane—as a matter of fact, we haven't one. This is partly due to the Ilond ways and partly because everyone recognizes that well-known motto, "He most lives who thinks most, feels the noblest, acts the best," and does his utmost to "do noble things not dream them all day long."—F. S.

The System of having Tribes.

Since first this class began, it has been split up into tribes called, to distinguish them, the Athletes, Invincibles, Spartans, Trojans, Undaunted, Stoics. Our class of sixty boys chose six boys whom we call chiefs, from among them, and under each chief nine boys decided to go.

Ever since then new ideas have sprung up, until now we have our Ilond Parliament, Debating Society, occasional issues of our Ilond Magazine, &c. In each of these each tribe has its representatives. —L. H.

Our Parliament.

The Editor has given me the honour of writing a portion of the Magazine we are compiling. I am glad to be able to describe the Ilonders' Parliament.

The reason we have formed a Parliament is that when a public meeting is being held there are over fifty boys present, and many of them wish to speak at once. This makes it very unhappy for the speaker and the questioners. Any person who is keenly interested in what is being said, does not want people interrupting. Now we have a Parliament, there is only one member, besides the chief from each tribe who has been elected to represent them, and only one member is allowed to speak at once, with the permission of the chairman. If the member for a certain tribe does not represent them in an honourable way, the tribesmen ask him to resign. If he refuses, they make it uncomfortable for him till he wishes he had resigned.

Our Parliament is not yet at its full height, having only recently been formed; but every time they meet it gradually betters itself. Up to now it has made wonderful improvement in the class. The first thing they did was to consider the question of " Games," and they elected a Sports Committee.

Each tribe picked its own member to represent them. The man picked is supposed to be clever at speaking and good at representing them. A member of Parliament need not be a well-educated man—[i.e. a good scholar.—Ed.] . . . The Parliament decided that the common people should have a vote (for Committees); therefore there was a vote by ballot. . . .—A. S.

Our Debating Society.

Our Debating Society was first formed with the idea of extending the oral merits of the class, and also with consideration to the pupils who are not very good at composition.

The proposer and opposer are allowed five minutes, and their seconders three minutes. The subject is then thrown open for discussion, and the Ilonders are invited to ask the proposer and opposer questions concerning their speeches. As this part of the debate is sometimes somewhat noisy, we have appointed Mr. Hibberd as usher, and he has full permission to put anyone out.—A. S.

. . . Mr. Gascoigne is chairman and Mr. Wilkinson secretary. All the boys enjoy this lesson, because it is out of the ordinary. . .—B.H.

Our Class Government.

The duty of the Parliament is to pass laws and try any persons who have been spoiling the good name of the Ilonders. Our Government consists of a Prime Minister and Cabinet which consists of three persons: A Minister of Labour, whose duty it is to arrange an exhibition and concert at the end of term for the boys who are leaving; also to inspect the labour or work of the tribes of the Ilond. He is also responsible for the apparatus and the monitors' work. The Minister of Physical Training is the second person. The duty of this Minister is to look after the physical training of the Ilonders in conjunction with the Sports Committee. The final person is the Minister of Education, whose duty is to do anything to improve the Ilonders' education. I being the Minister of Education intend, with the help of my staff, to publish a newspaper for the benefit of the Ilonders, called the " Ilond Mercury."—A. W.

Our Exhibition.

Parliament sat on the 7th inst. to decide how to improve the reputation and trade conditions of the Ilond. It was decided that there should be an exhibition showing the handwork of the Ilonders and the volumes they have produced. The Chairman and Exhibition Committee decided to have a concert as well, to give a pleasant send-off to the leavers. —H. T.

The models exhibited were mostly of wood or cardboard, illustrating history and geography; pieces of furniture and common objects made in the mathematics and handwork lessons, and objects made at home. Some clay models also were shown illustrating ancient history. While the table was in our room the head master came in and had a look at the models. He then fetched his class to see the exhibition. At playtime he brought all the other fourteen teachers, and I think each of the teachers thought highly of the exhibition. The next day he asked for the exhibition to be repeated in the hall, so that all the classes of the school might visit it.—H. T.

Our Visit to the Works.

On Monday night, just after school, sixteen of us who were leaving school at the end of the week, went to have a look round Messrs. Hadfield's East Hecla Works. When we arrived, some of the chief men were waiting for us. The first thing they did was to entertain us to tea in the staff dining-room. Directly after tea we were piloted round the casting shops. When we went over the Don bridge we stopped to examine a small locomotive which was coming towards us. [Here follows a full description of things seen.] The next day the captain collected some money among the boys who went, and bought some cigars for those who took us round the works.—W. D.

[Amongst our exhibits is a volume consisting of sixteen illustrated reports of the visit, and of another visit to Messrs. Thos. Firth's Norfolk Works.—ED.]

Brief Extracts from the six chapters on " Our Tribe."

. . . We tribesmen do our best to keep the class a good reputation in the school, not only for the present, but for ever after. We "Invincibles" work when it is work, and play when it is play.—E.G. The aim of our tribe is to be top in everything, but when defeated, it accepts like true sportsmen. Our motto is " Play the game," which we all try to do.—E. G. The two worst men in our tribe are H—— and B——. H—— is at times inclined to be sleepy, and what he needs is a good rousing up by the members of our tribe to make him try to make his work good and neat.—E. B. If any man belonging to our tribe has a grievance, he reports it to the chief, and if he can do nothing, it goes before the captain of the class. . . . When we first came up into Standard VIII, we proposed to be different from other classes and to set an example to the whole school by showing how to get the best work done.—J. L. The name of the tribe for which I am a member of our Ilond Parliament is the " Spartans," which is the name of a famous race of men who used to live in Greece. . . . The work is the same as sport to our tribesmen, because they strive to get to the top of the class as they strive to do in games. . . . The result of the "Spartans" trying to get to the top of the class, together with other tribes, has made a reputation for the class in many things and in many ways.—L. H.

Extracts from Reports on the Visit of the " Sixers."

We received a visit from the Standard VI boys, who, having heard about our Ilond, resolved to give us a very stiff hour's questioning. —J.H. One of the many teasing questions was, "What is the religion of your Ilond?" Being asked to answer, I combined the "Golden Rule" and the text "Love your neighbour as yourself" in my answer, which was rather abrupt, as I was taken unawares. . . . Another boy wished to see some of our manufactures. A——, snapping the chance, answered the question by introducing him to our exhibition. . . . Are policemen required to preserve order? queried one Sixer. He was answered by W., who pointed out that by recognizing our religion no serious wrong is committed. . . . I am not ashamed to say I was relieved when the questions ended.—F. S. The last thing they inquired was, "What is your business?" To this question I replied saying, "Our business is to endeavour to make the world a better place to live in." Of course we do this in a very small and simple manner.—L. F. . . . Having written an original play, the "Undaunted" tribe acted it with great success. . . . The Standard VI boys were much impressed, and thanked us for a fine afternoon.—J. H.

How we defended our Ilond. (Extracts from reports.)

This morning Standard VIII classroom was the scene of an interesting debate between Standard VI and Standard VIII boys on the subject "Is the Ilond system of government a better system than the one of Sixers?'' . . . A lot of Ilonders had prepared speeches, but time pressed and only a few spoke, but those few defended their case splendidly.—F. C. The head master was to have presided, but being too busy, he asked one of the other masters to take his place, and he sent in a jury of six boys from another class.—J. L. The jury gave the verdict in favour of the Ilonders, who cheered vociferously; but although the Sixers were defeated, they kept up their reputation by singing their Sixer's song, "In victory or defeat we smile."—A. B.

Report on Debate by the Chairman of the Jury.

The debate which I heard to-day was, I must say, the finest I have ever heard. Standard VIII relied upon S. and A. to first uphold the cause of the Ilonders. A. did not start well, as he seemed fluttered and nervous. However, he recovered, and made the finest schoolboy speech I have ever heard. S. was a worthy successor, and he too was eloquent. Standard VI were handicapped a little at first, as they had not prepared their speeches. When the discussion was opened, several fine short speeches were made by boys out of both classes. In conclusion, may I thank both Mr. W. and Mr. R. for their kindness in allowing us to be jurymen in the case. I must say that I enjoyed the speeches very much, and so did everyone, I think.—H. W.

Volumes prepared by the Ilonders—many illustrated.

The History of our Ilond from the earliest times, based on ancient and English history, 60 chapters, one by each Ilonder. Travel Pictures —letters written home by Ilonders supposed to have emigrated (100 letters). "The Star Magazine." "The Ilond Mercury." Interesting volumes of cuttings prepared by individuals—Records of visits to works —Ilond trade commissioners' reports from various countries (geography). Miscellaneous trade information in graphical form. Portfolio of forty historical sketches. Miscellaneous drawings.

Brief Extracts from Letters of "Leavers" (written as ordinary composition exercises).

On Thursday night I shall have finished my school life—a thing I am very sorry for. I have enjoyed nearly every lesson we had with you, and I do not at all like the idea of leaving my sportsmanlike schoolfellows. . . . I have had a good school-life, and I hope it will continue while I am at work. If it does, life will have been a great pleasure to me.—E. B.

When I first heard the news that we were to come to this school —[a higher elementary top.—ED.]—I was disappointed; but now I am glad I came. In find it very interesting. This is due to the Ilond ways, the debates, exhibitions, Parliament, and various Committees, and almost every lesson.—F. C.

Most boys who came from other schools mention that they came with trepidation, but have been very happy, e.g. I am very much interested in these affairs, because at my old school we never used to have anything like this, so it is out of the ordinary.—J. L.

When we came into this class—[last term,—ED.]—nearly all the boys were strangers to each other. . . . As time went on everybody began to be useful to the class, and it was not long before we developed a Parliament, &c., &c. . . . I am very sorry that some of the Ilonders are leaving.—A. L.

Since my last letter to you (on entering the class) my views regarding the class have changed somewhat. Then I thought that the remainder of my school-life would be one continual drag. My views have now been changed, and I think school-life is a pleasure in this class. What makes it interesting, in my opinion, is the fact that we work together for one common goal—a hundred per cent efficiency in the shortest possible time.—S. G.

Our work in the class is on the whole getting better every day, and the lads who are leaving are doing their utmost in regard to their work. The Exhibition Committee is helping the lads to be interested in their work, especially if it is for exhibition. Besides this, when other boys from other classes see our work, it may influence them, and then they follow in our footsteps to do like we have done.—F. C.

The idea of the Inter-Tribe sports fixtures, by the Sports Committee, was fine, and on the whole, after to-morrow's concert, the boys who are leaving school will remember it for many a day.—E. G.

. . . Sometimes I have felt as though I were in an island, with islanders, debating on things which really depended on the debate. —E. D.

. . . I have now been in your class six months, and everything has deepened my interest in things. The tribe system is absolutely tophole, and when the Ilond method was introduced, I almost felt that I was in an Ilond by ourselves and the lessons were our trades. When the captain (Mr. Gascoigne) sat in the chair and the speakers of the debate were speaking, the boys looked more like men than mere scholars. Mr. Gascoigne is our Prime Minister, and when Parliament is sitting, I could imagine the Parliament sitting with set faces talking to settle the miners' strike. . . I do not profess to be a good scholar, but the marks system urges me to do my utmost. I try to be equal with my tribesmen, and that is my best. . . . To-morrow night I shall have left school, but the things I have done in Standard VIII will make me remember the rest of my life.—A. B.

[This community could only exist with the consent of the head master. It required a "great" man in authority sometimes to turn a blind eye to the signals indicating disaster to the school. He had vision, supplied constructive criticism, exercised a wise restraint in checking ebullient enthusiasm, and by constant and generous encouragement inspired affectionate loyalty to his wishes. This paper is a small tribute to a great primary school head master, Mr. G. R. Vine, B.Sc., of Huntsman's Gardens Senior Mixed School, Sheffield.]

*[It is unfortunate that space and cost prevent our publishing the actual journals and examples of work produced by Mr. Robinson's boys under the inspiration of the "group spirit." That spirit takes many forms, but wherever team work has been made the basis of class-room activities the results have been remarkable, and we are glad to be able to put on record such evidence of its value as this article affords.—*EDITOR.]

THE SCHOOL AND THE COMMUNITY.

An article by Professor T. P. Nunn dealing with some of the points raised in our last issue has unfortunately to be held over until our next issue.

REVIEWS.

The Teaching and Cultivation of the French Language in England during Tudor and Stuart Times with an Introductory Chapter on the Preceding Period. By Kathleen Lambley. Publications of the University of Manchester. London, Longmans, Green & Co., 1920. (pp. xiii + 438, with appendixes and index). Price, 14/- net.

It has become an honour to have work produced among the Publications of the University of Manchester; Miss Lambley has certainly made good her claim, on the grounds of the breadth and completeness of her researches, to have this work included in the series.

The first part contains a variety of information of great interest on the use of French in England during the thirteenth, fourteenth, and fifteenth centuries. A number of letters are quoted from, but Miss Lambley has not drawn upon the "Recueil de Lettres anglo-françaises" (1265-1399), published by Dr. Tanquerey. (Paris: Champion, 1916.) She is mainly concerned in this first section with such books as set out to teach Englishmen how to *speak* French. She has ample quotations from directions to travellers—how to ask their way; how to take a room at an inn and to see that their horse is well cared for. In these days of high hotel charges, it is interesting to find that sixpence was asked for a day's entertainment, and also that some luxurious person spent as much as eightpence. No small part of the interest in Miss Lambley's work is the information concerning the use of French at the Courts of the Tudors; Henry VII and Henry VIII both spoke that language well, and so did Henry's sister, afterwards wife of Louis XII, and his three children, Mary, Elizabeth, and Edward VI. As French had largely supplanted Latin as a means of communication between people of different nationalities, a sound knowledge of the language was necessary for all Court and diplomatic posts; consequently all persons of rank considered French as an indispensable part of their education. The early French humanists had all felt a leaning towards the Reformation, which is, indeed, best regarded as an application to theology of the spirit of free inquiry engendered by the Renaissance; so, when the Catholic reaction began in France, about 1530, considerable numbers of French scholars came to England and sought to gain a living by teaching French, Latin, Greek, and Hebrew. Their numbers increased during the reign of Edward VI, and they were numerous enough under Elizabeth to necessitate a special census. Whereas the first teachers of French had generally been employed by the great, as the numbers of Frenchmen desirous of teaching increased, their instruction became open to "merchauntes and other common people that are not expert in the sayd langage." Most of the grammars were of the nature of dialogues, often with the French and English in parallel columns. One famous teacher, Claude de Sainliens, who anglicized his name into Holyband, gives in his two works—"The French Schoolemaistr" (1st ed. 1565) and "The French Littelton" (1st ed. 1566)—interesting dialogues, and was at much pains to indicate pronunciation, too. Miss Lambley gives a long extract on pp. 137-8. His plan was to print a *x* below the silent letter, but either he or his printers appear a little careless, since the *s* before *t* is rightly noted as silent in *estre* while no sign is shown under the *s* in *hostelerie*. It would certainly be worth while to collate the very numerous editions set out in the bibliography to see whether all agree in these particulars, and also to see whether the final *t* in *appetit* should be provided with a *x* or not (cf. Brunot "Histoire de la langue française," II, p. 269). Holyband, too, grasped a very important principle in the division of French words into syllables, viz. that they begin with consonants, and compares the English *minion* with French *mignon*, which he divides *mi-gnon*. Grammars such as these, besides being drawn upon by the philologist, are of prime importance to a specialized branch of philology—historical phonetics. Miss Lambley quotes Thurot: "De la prononciation française depuis le commencement du xvie siècle" (Paris, 1881); but she does not mention

Professor Rosset's amplification and interpretation of Thurot's work (v. Brunot, o.c. III, 2, p. xi). Some hints at pronunciation in these early grammars are due to genuine observation; thus one anonymous teacher as early as 1528 says of French *é* that it is produced "a lytell higher in the throte there properly where the Englishman soundeth his e"; it is certainly remarkable that the French sound is so early noted as being 'closer' than the English.

One of the most striking figures in Miss Lambley's work is John Eliote; he spent some six years in France (circ. 1583-9) where he seems to have acquired a vast admiration for Rabelais. On his return, and that he "might not be found an idle drone among so many famous teachers," he set to work and "dezinkhornifistlbulated a fantasticall Rapsody of dialoguisme." Eliote's lessons seem to have been well paid; he states that the usual charge was one shilling a week, probably for one hour's lesson per day; he states that he would charge a gentleman £10 and a nobleman £20 per annum. The method employed by the vast majority of teachers in Tudor times was almost exclusively oral, written work being largely the putting on paper of their oral exercises. In the early seventeenth century (1611), however, appeared the first important French-English dictionary. It is the work of an Englishman, Randle Cotgrave. The existence of a reliable dictionary greatly helped the study of good writers, so warmly advocated by Sir Thomas Elyot and Roger Ascham. It was now possible to study the historians and writers of memoirs: Monstrellet, La Noue, Monlac, as well as Belleforest's "Histoire universelle," Amyot's "Plutarch," Marot, and the poets of the Pléiade. The Universities looked with little favour on the study of French, whereas at the Inns of Court it was held in considerable esteem. After keeping terms at a University and after residence at one of the Inns, the young man of good family usually proceded to travel on the continent. The custom was to settle in Paris or in some other important town, and place oneself in the hands of a tutor or attend a college. All kinds of interesting details about such travel are here set out.

The Restoration very naturally brought in its train a delight in things French—not merely an increased desire to speak and read French, but a liking for French cookery, French dress, valets, tailors, dressmakers, hairdressers, all must be French. The Revocation of the Edict of Nantes further increased the numbers of French residents in England; their influence, however, particularly in spreading in France a knowledge of England, is outside the scope of Miss Lambley's work. We hope that some day Miss Lambley will find occasion to read over her material again and show us the light, that it may throw on the life of the times.   A. T. Baker.

The Modern Educator's Library.
The Teaching of Modern Foreign Languages in School and University.
By Henry Gibson Atkins and H. L. Hutton. London, Edward Arnold, 1920. (pp. vii + 246).

The Great War has placed the question of the necessity of a more widespread acquaintance with the languages of our allies and enemies beyond dispute. Professor Atkins and Mr. Hutton have done us a national service by providing a full treatment of the teaching of modern languages; they have given us a book which all teachers and administrators of education should read and digest.

The Editors make a strong plea for the *spoken* language, and prove how much may be missed by those who only read. What this may mean, the following incident will show. A man of great classical learning who read German with great facility but whose knowledge of the spoken idiom was slight, was once quite non-plussed by a compound which brought the name of the river *Po* into combination with *Ufer*. In vain he consulted his dictionary for *Poufer*, and was only saved by a colleague who pronounced it correctly and instantly revealed its meaning.

In the excellent chapter on "the place of modern languages in the time-table" we find a strong plea for history and geography, and a whole chapter is devoted later to this matter. The authors seem to us to insist a little too strongly on the personality aspect of history and to lay too much stress on great historical figures. To us, French history appears rather in the light of great personalities in the grip of an external force. It is needful early to know how the French Crown gradually acquired sway over the whole of France and what relics of local autonomy remained in some cases down to the Revolution. Without a knowledge of this centralizing tendency it would be difficult to grasp the sentiments pervading the French classical period.

The chapters on Methods and Grammar are very fully treated; they give evidence of ripe experience, and should prove of great value to all earnest teachers.

The authors consider the question of staff in the school, and have much judicious advice to give on its recruitment and organization; we should have welcomed some views on hours and on time allowed for teachers to prepare their work. As a good deal of pressure is being put on Universities to allow a holder of a Higher School Certificate to substitute this, subject for subject, for the University Intermediate, the Universities ought to be assured that the teachers responsible for the last two years instruction should be working under conditions not too dissimiliar from those of a University teacher. The authors discuss "Advanced Courses" in their Chapter VII, and put forward many interesting views; they would have increased our debt to them if they had sketched a few ideal courses and given a number of indispensable books of reference such as any school running advanced courses could provide, seeing that a grant is available for the purpose.

Part II deals with the University. One chapter is devoted to the staff; we are entirely in agreement with the remarks made here; that University teachers are themselves fully alive to the subject is clear from the Report signed by some forty University teachers and printed in extenso in the Government Committee's Report. The authors lay much stress on the interdependence of School and University. This fact has been grasped by more than one University in which Secondary Schools Councils, consisting of representatives of University, heads of and assistants in schools, and of education authorities, have been set up. There are many other chapters of vital interest to all concerned in education, and we heartily recommend this work to our colleagues. A. T. BAKER.

Education in England in the Middle Ages. By A. W. Parry, M.A., D.Sc., Principal of the Training College, Carmarthen. pp. viii + 264. W. B. Clive, University Tutorial Press.

WITHIN the last few decades much light has been thrown upon the cultural condition of the Middle Ages, and the conception of them as times of intellectual darkness, moral anarchy, and religious blindness—a conception due to the play of prejudice in the fields of ignorance—has slowly and reluctantly yielded to the evidence found in the records of the contemned ages themselves.

This evidence is voluminous and detailed on many points. For this very reason, and also because it is not all readily available to the ordinary student, there was call for a summary review of the whole field. This is what Dr. Parry has given us in this little book, which should receive a cordial welcome from all who are interested in the conditions of life of our forefathers. Not that Dr. Parry has written a mere synopsis of the work of his predecessors. By no means. His book shows research at first hand, as well as cognisance of the work of others. Nor does he hesitate to differ from the greatest of his fellow-workers in interpreting the records, as, for instance, in holding that "free" school meant one open to pupils from all parts, not one free from external control, as Dr. Kennedy thought, nor one free from fees, as argued by the late Mr. Leach. Nor does he accept Mr. Leach's interpretation of the term "poor" scholars, as applied to Winchester and Eton. Into such points we have not space to enter: we cite them in recognition of the independence of Dr. Parry's judgment.

Dr. Parry's concern is rather with the provision and organization of schools and universities than with their internal working, though he has something to say on the subjects studied in universities, and devotes a chapter to the Curriculum and Method of schools. Here there seems to be some inconsistency. On p. 133 we are told that "the subjects taught in the mediæval schools . . . were the Trivium, and the more advanced Quadrivium"; while on p. 216 we read that "the extent to which these subjects actually formed part of the school curriculum is still a matter of considerable doubt." Probably the former statement is meant to give the general theory of the curriculum, while the chapter on Curriculum and Method furnishes evidence as to the actual practice. But we think the point deserves Dr. Parry's consideration when a second edition of his book is called for.

The main theme of the book is the growth of public interest in education as shown by the ever-widening circles that shared in the provision and maintenance of schools. This is traced through the three periods into which Dr. Parry divides the development of education in mediæval England—pre-Conquest, education wholly under Church control, and education passing out of the direct control of the Church, though by no means antagonistic to it or even separated from it. Throughout, the statements made are supported by references, which will serve as indications to the student who desires to carry further the work of investigation.

In conclusion, we congratulate Dr. Parry on a scholarly piece of work, and we are glad to learn that it was accepted by the University of London as a thesis for the degree of D.Sc.   J. W.

The History of Social Development. By Dr. F. Müller-Lyer. Translated by E. C. and H. A. Lake. (362 pp.) Geo. Allen & Unwin Ltd. 18/- net.

It is not often a book by a German scholar appearing for the first time in an English dress is heralded by introductions from two distinguished English Professors. The fact that Professor Hobhouse and Professor Urwick have separately commended Dr. Müller-Lyer's book to the notice of English translation is noteworthy testimony to its value, and we may especially commend it to all students of education. "Culture epochs" is a phrase well-worn in the education service. Dr. Müller-Lyer does not use the term, nor does he discuss problems of recapitulation; but his book makes it clear what "Stages of Culture" mean, and the relationship of one stage to another. If we are inclined to accept the doctrine that Ontogeny repeats Phylogeny, let us at least learn what the Sociologist has to teach about Phylogeny. In adopting the "Phaseological method" of presenting the History of Social Development, the author has been able to reduce to order a vast accumulation of sociological material. Even the unlearned can now distinguish the wood from the trees, and we have what Professor Urwick admirably calls a base-book for English students of Sociology.

Education itself is rapidly passing out of the stage in which individual acquisition, under conditions which required an almost rigid isolation of effort, was the chief interest of the schoolmaster. Its theory and practice are being brought into line with the social nature of the pupils. The process of socialization will be stimulated and made more intelligent by a clear understanding of social development on the grand scale. Nothing is better calculated to stir school-folk into freer and more imaginative thought than a great and ordered survey of the deeper currents in the grand stream of the past. What we usually call history is at once more dramatic, superficial, picturesque than Sociology. For that reason possibly History affords less guidance in the interpretation of the present and in forecasting the future. It often misses the unconscious forces determining man's destiny, and it is with these forces that the Sociologist is mainly concerned.

Dr. Müller-Lyer's point of view is economic; some would say materialistic. He is in fact concerned chiefly with problems of food and labour and the organization of society as determined by its fundamental needs; he finds "culture-folk" less happy than "primitive-folk"; but he is not therefore a pessimist, for it is in the coming process of socialization that man, now becoming a conscious unit in a self-conscious community, is presently to attain his full humanity and to make culture minister to happiness. "Humanity, which hitherto has worked as a blind nature force, can now see. Dark shadows still lie in the valleys, but the mountain-tops are beginning to grow rosy with the dawn."

The New State. By M. P. Follett. (373 pp.) Longmans, Green & Co. 12/6 net. (Second Impression).

Miss Follett's book might be regarded as an excellent pendant to that of Dr. Müller-Lyer. She deals with the social organism—if we may be allowed to use that much-abused word—as we know it to-day; the spiritual forces at work within it. Her treatment of community life is psychological rather than sociological. She is concerned with the conscious processes involved in true community life, and with the psychical conditions of social progress which she sees in the gradual advance from a competitive to a co-operative democracy. She takes up the story of human development where Müller-Lyer leaves off, and in a lively and most suggestive way lays bare the weak places in modern community life, which is so often the victim of the clever devices of the political manipulator who has little interest in ideas but lives for votes and the maintenance of majorities.

I know no other book which so vividly describes the true basis of group life, the spiritual development of which can only come from a conscious search for a synthesis amongst the contributory thinking put into the common stock by the members of the group. Instead, that is to say, of parties devoting their energies to majority-making, we should find the ideal group actuated by the idea of the common good and eager to make what use it could of any and every idea which threw light upon its problems. The attainment of a group life of that kind may mean the fundamental revision of the organs of our political life. To recognize that these organs are not necessarily the final achievement of human wisdom is in itself a mark of progress. Political changes are not new to history; they have commonly been the result of an effort to find immediate relief from a galling situation rather than the outcome of a political ideal. The New State as Miss Follett sees it will be the product of a new social ideal involving a keen sense of the responsibilities of citizenship.

We schoolmasters are usually ready to agree that education is concerned with citizenship, though our ideas of citizenship are often as limited and static as those we find in current text-books of Civics. To all those who regard citizenship as active and vital, rather than as passively acquiescent, and who believe the school can do much to produce the type of citizenship demanded by a people in the throes of an awakening self-consciousness, Miss Follett's book will give encouragement and guidance. As our conception of citizenship is freshened, deepened, vitalized, so will our schools be saved from the bonds of a merely academic routine which always tend to fasten themselves more tightly about the unobservant schoolmaster.

Miss Follett's book deserves a place in every training college library, the more so as she herself realizes how much the New State must depend upon its schools.

Five Years Old or Thereabouts. By Margaret Drummond, M.A. Published by Arnold & Son. 5/-. 177 pp.

Every lover of little children will rejoice to read and possess this book. It is a fascinating study of the child just beyond the nursery stage, and treats of his adventures in the broad field of language—speaking, writing, spelling—in number-work, play with Montessori material, and other games; in conduct of life, as drawn up by grown-up people for children; indeed, with his experiments in the great adventure of living itself.

"My Unconscious Collaborator," as Miss Drummond calls her little niece, is not too extraordinary a child to be very helpful to all teachers and guardians of children, as she is seen through her aunt's eyes and interpreted by her trained scientific mind. Constantly we find this type of argument: "Valuable suggestions for school practice are, I think, embedded in the facts I have recorded. Margaret's time is too precious for me to give her a number lesson every day, even if I had the opportunity. She has to give most of it to language study, and nature study, and acquiring control over her body. She has to gather buttercups and daisies, to skip, to run, to jump, to educate her dolls, and to do the hundred other things that an energetic child does. What she requires in number, during the early years when foundations are laid, is an occasional short, clear lesson, and then to be let alone till it has soaked in."

An interesting chapter is given on the Unconscious Mind, and another on sick children, sick not in body but in mind. We must search far back into earliest childhood "to find the beginnings of impulses and prejudices which largely determine our conduct to-day."

Miss Drummond, who writes with the greatest charm and simplicity, often gives us arresting ideas. "Suppose a wizard transformed our classes so that each member looked his mental age, and not his physical one." . . . "If every child could be educated on individual lines until he was seven, we should have little or no complaint of the size of classes in the upper school." . . . "If I were an inspector, I should regard no infant class as satisfactory unless the children were joyful." . . . are a few in illustration.   W. A. B.

Children's Dreams. By Dr. C. W. Kimmins. (ix + 126 pp.) Longmans, Green & Co. 5/- net.

DR. KIMMINS's interesting book is based on an examination of the dreams of about 6,000 children, of whom about 4,000 were in elementary schools, 900 in central or in secondary schools, 600 in industrial schools, and 250 in blind and deaf schools. Dreams of children of eight years were recorded by the children themselves. We imagine that the records here quoted have been subject to some sort of editing. There was, in any case, a vast amount of material, and we are much indebted to Dr. Kimmins for his analytical survey.

Children's dreams, says Freud, are not interesting to the psycho-analyst. There is none of that confusing mixture of "manifest" and "latent" content which is characteristic of the adult dream, the separation of which has thrown so much light upon unconscious mental process. "In the child's dream we have the imaginary fulfilment of an ungratified wish." Most of the examples cited in this book would, we think, come into this category. In most children wishes are not secret, and if secretly cherished, they are not repressed. There is no censor making "ducks and drakes" of the dream material by way of secondary elaboration. In normal cases we only need to win the confidence of a child and he will yield his inmost heart to us. Of course, if this is impossible because classes are too big for the children to know his children intimately, recorded dreams may be a useful means of getting at their longings. But would it be fair to suppose that a boy who dreamed of "junketings" was underfed!

There must come a time when the dreams of the child are beginning to assume the subtler characteristics of adult dreams. Research upon children's dreams will, we think, be more fruitful if the mass method is now abandoned. Dr. Kimmins has probably exhausted its possibilities. Workers who have the necessary psychological training and the opportunity of investigating the dreams of children of different ages, and especially of the same child at different ages, may do great service to psychology, and indeed also to Education. Dr. Kimmins clearly has the same view.

The Psychology of Childhood. By Naomi Norsworthy and Maria Theodora Whitley. (xix + 375 pp.) The Macmillan Co., N.Y. 10/- net.

THE book has been written under distressing circumstances. The original draft was made by Miss Norsworthy, at the time Associate Professor of Educational Psychology at Teachers' College. Her illness and subsequent death left the work to be finished by her colleague, Dr. Whitley, who very kindly undertook to carry it through on the original plan. It is written for Training College students who have already been through a general course in Psychology. Competent as the book is, its perusal has left us with the feeling that it wants the one thing needful in such an undertaking—a sympathetic understanding of living children. The book abounds in knowledge, yet the manner of its presentation suggests other books rather than children as its original source. The authors never grow enthusiastic about their subject. Much of this is undoubtedly due to the difficulties under which it was written, but we are sure that a book on the psychology of childhood must bear upon it the impress of a real love for children if it is to be an inspiration and help to teachers. Perhaps, too, the authors have allowed their desire to be of practical assistance to teachers to weigh too much with them. Instead of confining themselves to the subject matter suggested by the title, they give a good deal of space to didactics. In some ways that may give the book practical value which a first-hand study of childhood for its own sake apparently has not got. The exercises at the end of each chapter are excellent, and almost redeem the whole book from the reproach of remoteness from the realities of child life.

The Philosophy of Speech. By George Willis. (256 pp.) G. Allen & Unwin Ltd. 7/6 net.

IT is not always that a publisher's advertisement of a book is a fair indication of the subject matter and its treatment. Mr. Willis's book is described as a "scholarly, ingenious, and entertaining study of the origin and development of speech, and its relation to the growth of thought." This at once whets curiosity and prepares for disappointment—a disappointment which in this case does not come. Scholarship, ingenuity, and entertainment abound in the book. It is not written for the learned specialist, but for all who are intelligently interested in the problems of life and language. Teachers in general, and English teachers especially, will find it a thoroughly stimulating and suggestive book. The old nonsense which would keep the grammar of tradition as a subject in the primary school because of the logical training it gives, could hardly survive Mr. Willis's vigorous analysis. His chapters on Purism and Correct Speech should kill much of the stupid pedantry which still separates language lessons from realities. The practical conclusions which the author discusses in his final chapter on Speech and Education may not commend themselves to all teachers, but none can read them without being stirred into thinking. Lucidity and charm of style, resourcefulness in illustration, and cogency in argument is conspicuous throughout the book, and the Simplified Spelling Society might profitably review its programme in the light of Mr. Willis's criticisms in the chapter on Spelling Reform.

Educational Psychology. By Daniel Starch. 473 pp. The Macmillan Co., N.Y. 14/- net.

IF we accept Professor Starch's view of the content of Educational Psychology, we cannot fail to regard his book as altogether admirable. Within the limits of the subject as he defines it, he has given us an exceedingly clear summary of recent research into educational problems; advanced students of education will find it an excellent text-book. The standpoint is, however, entirely intellectual. The word emotion does not seem to occur in the book. It certainly is not in the index. Nor is there anything about the psychology of likes and dislikes. We have an exceedingly clear account of the psychology of learning, but nothing on the psychology of appreciation—except an odd sentence or two like "the appreciation of music depends in part upon the accuracy of the discrimination of pitch.'' Under these circumstances, ought not Dr. Starch to find another title for his book? He would surely admit that education has suffered dreadfully in the past from the almost exclusively intellectual spirit in which it has been regarded. Our only quarrel with the book is the implication of its title. It leads us to expect more than the author meant to give. But from his own point of view, why does he give us a chapter on the psychological processes in learning History and leave Geography out? We can understand his saying nothing about Literature in the chapter on Language, but why does he omit Science and Handwork? We repeat, however, that the book is valuable as far as it goes, and should find at least a place in all Teachers' Reference Libraries.

International Politics. By C. Delisle Burns. (x + 189 pp.) London, Methuen & Co., 1920. Price, 5/- net.

LIKE Mr. Burns's previous books, '' Political Ideas'' and ''The Morality of Nations,'' this work, though not written specifically for school use, will be warmly welcomed by teachers, especially by those who are seeking to bring the teaching of history into more fruitful contact with the urgent problems of the age. The author had already an assured position as a student of international relations; he shows here the vivid realization of their nature, and the understanding of the problems they present, which are possible, perhaps, only to men who have been ''up against them'' in the public service. His subjects are of the highest interest and importance—the Great Power system and the smaller States, the problems that spring from contacts between races of varying culture and development, international trade, the functions of diplomacy, and the major organizations—official and unofficial—whose activities cut across national boundaries. In discussing these questions, Mr. Burns does not hide his belief ''that the interest of all nations is not to be found by the ancient process of each seeking his own,'' and ''that war is an altogether evil institution and a useless political method.'' But the great merit of his treatment is that it is largely independent of these presuppositions; for his method is to bring the reader face to face with facts and let them speak for themselves. And few books of this kind contain so rich an array of facts, so impartially selected and so skilfully marshalled.   T. P. N,

A Second Book of School Celebrations. By Dr. F. H. Hayward. (133 pp.) P. S. King & Son. 5/- net.

THESE admirably suggestive books of Dr. Hayward are written in the spirit of an earlier work—''The Lesson in Appreciation''—and though the ''Celebrations'' as here outlined might easily degenerate into sheer banality or end in pathetic bathos, the book has a significance and power which entirely transcends the mechanism (if one may be forgiven that word in this context) into which the author has cast his ideas. The conduct of school celebrations of this kind could only be successful if they were the outcome of a deep, almost a religious, feeling on the part of the chief celebrants, and if the chief celebrants had more than common powers of inspiring like feeling in others. A celebration which resolves itself into a sort of play-acting would be a futile absurdity, and we shall not be thought insensible to the great qualities of Dr. Hayward's book if we express the feeling that few men could rise to the height of emotional power essential to a completely successful service of this kind. In spite of that, few schoolmasters could read the book without finding it a source of inspiration. Its warmth of spirit, its wide sympathies, its wealth of illustration, and its dignified sincerity make it a most suggestive and welcome addition to the pedagogic library.

Needlecraft for Older Girls. Margaret Swanson. Longmans, Green & Co. 7/6. 111 pages.

THIS book is intended as a sequel to ''Educational Needlecraft'' and ''Needlecraft in the School,'' in so far as these deal with the teaching of needlework to the immature mind, and it carries on these interests as they develop in the adolescent stages. There is now a quickened sense of power over technique, a growing judgment, a feeling for restraint, and the ability to work for a considerable time at one project. In the later stages the girl often wishes to make beautiful things for her new life as a mother and home-maker.

Miss Swanson deals vigorously with these activities; design is treated exhaustively throughout, and always in relation to the article in making; for delight in decoration is strong and the hunger for colour as keen as in childhood. "I wanted violet above every other colour when I was fourteen, and now I'm sixty . . . and I still like it," says one mother, and she goes on to tell how strenuously she saved pence to gratify this love, through the years. It is from this dominant selection on the girl worker's part that the teacher's guidance should come. Teachers in continuation schools, who are responsible for the handwork of girls, will find this book constantly helpful.

W. A. B.

A Day Continuation School at Work. Papers by Twelve Contributors. Edited by W. J. Wray and R. W. Ferguson. (xii + 212 pp.) Longmans, Green & Co. 8/6 net.

ALTHOUGH a book by so many writers who have been left fairly free to express their own experience in a particular aspect of the problem with which the book is concerned must lack a certain unity, the volume before us is a valuable contribution to the constructive thinking which the Act of 1918 demands. We are given a lively picture of the pioneer work that has been going on for six or seven years at Bournville—work which is, we understand, now being taken over and developed by the Birmingham Education Committee. All the contributors obviously believe in their job, and what they have to say about it is full of wisdom born of high ideals which have been tried in the fire of actual experience. The writers are at their best when they deal with realities—when they describe what they do and how the pupils respond (or fail to respond). The more general topics are necessarily rather slightly treated, and are perhaps more enthusiastically than "informingly" treated. The word "mentality" ought to be rigorously banished from books on education. What does it mean?

Geography by Discovery. J. Jones. Sidgwick & Jackson Ltd. 2/6. With teachers supplement, 3/6.

THE function of the study of geography as a medium of instruction in citizenship— the imparting of knowledge of the present-day conditions of other peoples—is missed by a too-restricted treatment of geography as discovery, hence the author is amply justified in describing his book as an introduction to the subject. A set of these books sufficient for a class, if made to wander round the upper classes of a primary school as the need arose, would do much to infuse vitality into the dry bones of the subject. Of the 160 pages in the book, 30 are devoted to miscellaneous exercises and notes for the teacher. The questions cover the ground so thoroughly that few teachers could afford to dispense with the notes entirely. The questions deal with peoples, health, food, mode of life, winds, climate, and vegetation. Except for 20 pages devoted to Marco Polo, the subject matter is practically restricted to the Americas and the Atlantic. The chapters deal wih Columbus, Magellan, Cartier, Frobisher, Drake, and Raleigh.

E. B.

The Groundwork of Geography. A. Wilmore, D.Sc. Bell & Sons. pp. 398.

AN enthusiastic geography specialist teacher recently complained that, as a school subject, geography lacked a well-defined nucleus of subject matter. The force of this statement is exemplified by this book. Freedom of choice in subject matter allows of greater bias on the part of the teacher. The bias of the writer of this book is most easily expressed in figures—fractions of the book devoted to each section: Geology .51, Biology .28, Climatology .12, Questions and Glossary .08.

As a school text-book its arrangement is unique. The 27 illustrations are remarkably good. The chapter on climate, for clearness and conciseness, could not be bettered. It would be an excellent book for the V or VI Form. The economic aspect of rocks, plants, and animals is well developed. The historical and political aspects of geography are not treated, but, taken in conjunction with a book such as Fairgrieve's "Geography and World Power," it would form an admirable culmination to the ordinary secondary school course. E. B.

Land-Form Map Book. J. Fairgrieve. University of London Press. Hodder and Stoughton. 2/-.

THE interpretation of maps is an art that can only be mastered by practice of two kinds—the mapping of land forms and the picturing of land forms from maps. This exercise-book provides practice of both kinds; it starts from the contoured map of a simple cone, and, in fifty carefully graded exercises, leads the student to the point at which he can sketch a rough contoured map corresponding to the given landscape photograph. The chief value of the book lies in the sixteen well-chosen maps and photographs. In the words of the author, "the book is an attempt to teach map-reading (not map-spelling) of a particular kind as quickly as possible in the classroom." Such a book should prove a real boon to the middle forms of a secondary school. E. B.

An Outline of Physics. By L. Southern, M.A., B.Sc. (xv + 262 pp.) Methuen & Co. Ltd. 6/6.

THIS outline is not intended to take the place of a text-book. It partly fulfils and partly exceeds the functions of a text-book of physics. It is essentially a guide to laboratory work, but is illuminated by a theoretical treatment in Part I; the whole will make a strong appeal to the intelligent student.

The most interesting aspect of the book is its subscription to the study of method in an intermediate or senior school course. The author makes clear his point of view, and gives many valuable suggestions of procedure. The several branches of physics are admirably brought into unison under the common theory of a pure science. The student will also have the satisfaction of gaining in an elementary course the modern aspect of the subject.

Relativity: The Special and General Theory. A popular exposition by A. Einstein. translated by R. W. Lawson, D.Sc. (xiii + 138 pp.) Methuen & Co. Ltd. 5/- net.

MOST readers of this journal will appreciate the opportunity of reading so clear an account of the epoch-making theory as expounded by its famous originator. The translation is indeed a good one, and reads with all the freedom of an original work. The general reader is advised not to neglect Part III, which portrays the far-reaching deductions of the general theory.

The Book of Good Hunting. By Henry Newbolt. (viii + 272 pp.) Longmans, Green & Co. 10/6 net.

WE cannot do more than give a cordial welcome to Sir Henry Newbolt's latest annual. There is not likely to be a more "likeable" Christmas present for a boy, and as such we recommend it warmly to all who are looking out for a book which a lad will enjoy reading and want to keep.

BOOKS RECEIVED.

(Reviews of several books in this list have had to be held over until our next issue.)

Mental Tests in the American Army. By C. S. Yoakum and R. M. Yerkes. (xiii + 276 pp.) Sidgwick & Jackson. 6/- net.

Mental Tests. By P. B. Ballard. (ix + 235 pp.) Hodder & Stoughton. 6/- net.

Psychology of Sub-Normal Children. By L. S. Hollingworth. (xix + 285 pp.) Macmillan & Co., N.Y. 10/- net.

Feeble-mindedness in Children of School Age. By C. P. Lepage, with an appendix on Treatment and Training by May Dendy. 2nd Edition. (xv + 309 pp.) Manchester University Press. 10/6 net.

Instinct and the Unconscious. By W. H. R. Rivers. (viii + 252 pp.) Cambridge University Press. 16/- net.

History as a School of Citizenship. By Helen M. Madeley. (106 pp.) Clarendon Press. 3/6 net.

Hints on School Discipline. By E. F. Row. (59 pp.) Oxford University Press. 2/- net.

Life in Ancient Britain. By Norman Ault. (xiv + 260 pp.) Longmans, Green & Co. 5/- net. (Limp cloth.)

Suggestion and Auto-Suggestion. By Chas. Baudouin, translated by Eden and Cedar Paul. (288 pp.) G. Allen & Unwin. 15/- net.

The Origin of Man and of his Superstitions. By Carveth Read. (xii + 345 pp.) Cambridge University Press. 18/- net.

Concise Historical Atlas. By B. V. Darbishire. (33 pp.) Bell & Sons. 2/- net.

Stories for the Nature Hour. By A. M. and E. L. Skinner. (253 pp.) G. Harrap. 5/- net.

English Grammar and Composition for Younger Forms. By James Bewsher and Rev. H. A. T. Bennetts. (86 pp.) Longmans, Green & Co. 2/6

School Hygiene. By Chas Porter. (xx + 361 pp.) Longmans, Green & Co. 6/6 (Limp cloth.) 5th Edition.

Exercises in Arithmetic. By A. E. Layng. (xii + 230 pp.) Murray. 3/6 (with Answers, 4/-).

Organic Chemistry for Medical, Intermediate Science and Pharmaceutical Students. By A. Killen Macbeth. (xi + 235 pp.) Longmans, Green & Co. 6/6 net.

Imagination and its Place in Education. By E. A. Kirkpatrick. (214 pp.) Ginn & Co.

The Book of the Great Musicians. By P. A. Scholes. Milford. 4/6.

Musical Appreciation in Schools: Why and How. By P. A. Scholes. Milford. 1/6.

Elementary Harmony. Part III. By C. H. Kitson. Clarendon Press. 3/6.

LaVergne, TN USA
07 June 2010
185276LV00009B/35/P